HARVARD ECONOMIC STUDIES

Volume CXXVII

Awarded the David A. Wells Prize for the year 1963–64
and published from the income of the David A. Wells Fund.

AMERICAN RAILROADS
AND THE
TRANSFORMATION OF
THE
ANTE-BELLUM ECONOMY

ALBERT FISHLOW

Harvard University Press

CAMBRIDGE, MASSACHUSETTS

1965

385
F53a

L.L.

Library of Congress Catalog Card Number: 65-22068
Printed in the United States of America

TO HARRIET

TO HARRIET

Foreword

This book began as a Ph.D. dissertation in the Economic History Workshop at Harvard University. The Workshop, affiliated with the Department of Economics, was established in 1959 under a grant from the Ford Foundation, and Albert Fishlow was its first member. The purpose of the Workshop has been to attract able graduate students to the study of economic history and thereby inject into the discipline a number of well-trained economists, willing to apply the tools of economic and quantitative analysis to the exploration of past economic sequences. Had the phrase not become somewhat vague and controversial, one might say that the Workshop has been dedicated to "New Economic History."

Few things are genuinely novel in this world and no one is without predecessors. Still, it is fair to say that until recently the field of economic history was *dominated* not by economists, but by lawyers and historians. While it is true that representatives of either group succeeded in making signal and lasting contributions to the progress of the discipline, it is equally true that many economic problems were inadequately and superficially treated and often not treated at all. As a result, very uncertain hypotheses tended to gain acceptance as well-established propositions, and at the same time large areas of fruitful and exciting research remained entirely untrodden. At all times, greater familiarity of economic historians with the means afforded by traditional economic theory no doubt would have improved the situation. But the irresistible new impulses came when, in the course of the last four decades or so, economics has become much more strongly committed to operational thinking and empirical verification, while the more recent upsurge of interest in problems of economic development has aroused the economists' lively concern with the study of past economic progress.

Professor Fishlow's study is perhaps the ripest fruit so far of this change in general orientation. It needed the hand of a modern economist and statistician to pose the problem of the economic benefits of railroad construction in the United States before the Civil War in conceptual clarity and in terms which make the problem susceptible to serious empirical treatment. The attempt to quantify the social savings of the railroads and their impact through forward and backward linkages on the various branches of the economy required a momentous effort of data gathering and calculation. This is witnessed by the statistical appendixes in which the author offers a full insight into his laboratory and without which no real appreciation of the importance of the study and of the validity of its interpretative results is possible.

No historical study is ever absolutely conclusive. It is very unlikely, however, that after Professor Fishlow's book the facile assertion that the ante-bellum railroads were constructed "ahead of demand" will be repeated by serious scholars. Nor is it probable that further appraisals of the economic effects of the railroads will far transcend the boundaries of the reasonable zone established by the author which avoids both the enthusiast's overestimation and the sceptic's undervaluation. And as far as the historical "lesson" of the American experience is concerned, the author's stress on simultaneity of railroad construction with general economic progress should give pause to those who somewhat mechanically regard the creation of an "infra-structure" as a "necessary prerequisite" of economic development. In this respect, the conclusions of Professor Fishlow's study of American railroads coincide closely with the historical experience of several major countries in Europe.

One final word may be in order. There is a widespread impression among more conventional economic historians that use of theoretical models and elaboration of careful statistical estimates is likely to proceed at the expense of liveliness of historical presentation and attention to details. The brilliant narrative power displayed in the present volume and the skill with which individual facts — big *and* small — are woven around the author's theses should effectively dispel such apprehensions.

Alexander Gerschenkron

Preface

As the most cursory search of any library catalogue will reveal, there is no dearth of books on railroad history. Economists, historians, and laymen alike have yielded to the temptation to embellish the features of that past. Why then another book and a long one at that? My defense is a difference of emphasis, in both focus and method. This is a study of the transformation of the economy of the United States between 1830 and 1860 in response to the innovation of the railroad. As such it more closely resembles an abridged economic history of the period than a conventional chronicle of an industry. And because railroads possess characteristics common to the broader category of activities labeled as social overhead capital, the final chapter seeks to cast this specific study in that larger mold.

Herein lies only part of the novelty. The concern with quantitative analysis provides the rest. The prime deficiency of qualitative economic history is not its attention to description, but rather its susceptibility to implicit measurement. That is, the very act of specifying a direction of influence usually is accompanied by a judgment concerning orders of magnitude, expressed or not. At the very least, numerical methods impose a greater degree of discipline. They also obviate another pitfall: the extrapolation of the particular to the universal. Averages and sums may be less picturesque, as I fear the reader shall discover, but they are apt to be more representative.

With the recent publication of Robert W. Fogel's simultaneous research efforts, I can claim no monopoly either of method or intent. Yet the present volume may have greater interest on that very account. The two books approach the question of the importance of the railroad somewhat differently, and, not surprisingly, yield different answers. Fogel's principal interest is in the necessity of the innovation: could the United States have developed without it? The question I ask, rather, is how much of a stimulus did the railroad afford and by what means? We both may be correct, therefore, when he affirms that the railroad was not "important" and I that it was.

In the writing of this book, I have incurred debts which it is a pleasure to acknowledge. The Economic History Workshop and seminar at Harvard University, under the tutelage of Alexander Gerschenkron, afforded a stimulating environment in which many of these ideas first took form. Among my fellow students, Paul David especially, and later Peter Temin, were valued commentators and critics at that early stage. Subsequently, I derived substantial benefit from Robert W. Fogel's perceptive criticisms of an earlier draft of this manuscript. Our continuous dialogue on this subject reflects itself in this final version, and I am grateful to him for the time and effort he has graciously taken. Paul H. Cootner, Robert E. Gallman, Stanley Lebergott, William N. Parker, and still others, have permitted me to use their own unpublished material, much of which, happily, has finally appeared. The many comments of colleagues too numerous to name have not gone unappreciated.

At the University of California I was fortunate indeed to find so able and dedicated a research assistant as Samuel A. Morley. The extensive calculations that now appear owe much to his participation. Linda Kee and June Cohn also deserve thanks for help with final revisions during my year's leave at the National Bureau of Economic Research.

For financial assistance I am indebted to the Economic History Workshop and to the Institute for Business and Economic Research at the University of California; the former for providing the margin above subsistence during my student years, the latter for supporting my research and for invaluable aid in typing my manuscript.

My family has clearly borne the greatest burden over these five years. Long-time horizons do not come naturally to children, but ours cheerfully assumed them, to my lasting obligation. The dedication expresses my thanks to my wife as eloquently as I can do it.

A. F.

Berkeley, California
June 1, 1965

Contents

Tables

Illustrations

Part I

Introduction

CHAPTER I

The Problem To Be Studied

Background

On July 4, 1828, Charles Carroll of Carrollton, venerated patriot and sole surviving signer of the Declaration of Independence, presided at the cornerstone ceremonies of the Baltimore and Ohio Railroad. Thus, rather incongruously, was the steam railroad formally welcomed to the United States. But if cornerstone laying was inappropriate, the date itself was doubly fitting. Not only was the economic revolution accompanying the railroad to take its place fully beside the political revolution commemorated on that July day, but a scant forty miles away on the same morning another dedication was taking place. John Quincy Adams, President of the United States, turned the first spade of earth for the Chesapeake and Ohio Canal, whose route was to parallel that of the Baltimore and Ohio for a goodly part of their total distance.[1] The new technology boldly signaled its challenge to the old.

Today, of course, we can look back upon the decisive triumph of the railroad with the comfort of hindsight. How daring was it for those Baltimore merchants to project a general purpose railroad more than three hundred miles in length before the locomotive was even proved a feasible source of power, and with only a few short mining roads then in existence. Only desperate straits could have dictated such a decision, one which seems, even with hindsight, somewhat foolhardy. Ironically,

---

[1] Edward Hungerford, *The Story of the Baltimore and Ohio Railroad* (New York, 1928), I, chap. iii, and Walter S. Sanderlin, "The Great National Project: A History of the Chesapeake and Ohio Canal Company," *Johns Hopkins University Studies in History and Political Science*, LXIV (1946), no. 1, 59–60.

it was the canal that created the impetus. New York's successful breach of the Appalachian Barrier by means of the Erie Canal compelled a response by that city's commercial rivals. The western market, in which Philadelphia and Baltimore had had an especial advantage due to their relatively well developed road systems, was at stake. Since the difficulties of terrain facing these rivals, and Boston too, limited the attractiveness of canals, the English innovation of the steam railroad received careful consideration from the first in these cities. Only Baltimore committed itself wholeheartedly with both public and private support. Pennsylvania, racked with indecision but the necessity to act, wound up with the worst of both worlds: a hybrid, technological monstrosity, composed of two sections of railroad and two of canal. Massachusetts delayed until the innovation proved its staying power and then allowed private enterprise, later assisted by a state loan, to do the job.[2]

Spawned in response to interregional commercial competition, the railroad was soon adopted for other less far-reaching objectives. It could hardly have been otherwise. Once given such publicity, in a country where improved transportation was a matter of pre-eminent and continuous concern and where investment for such improvement was always forthcoming — for turnpikes, canals, steamboats — the diffusion of the innovation was assured. Charleston business leaders, for example, reading of the reports from Baltimore and faced with the challenge of Savannah and the inefficacy of a canal solution, completed in 1833 the then longest railroad in the world, 136 miles from Charleston to Hamburg. At the opposite extreme, in the mining districts, feeder roads of only a few miles from mine to canal were built, as often as not with horses supplying the power. Various cities along the fall line were linked, too, largely to meet the demands of a traveling public: the Boston and Providence, the Camden and Amboy, the Richmond and Petersburg were developed, among others.

In the United States the railroad seemed to find its natural

---

[2] For a discussion of the decision-making process and further references to the literature on commercial rivalry see Julius Rubin, "Canal or Railroad?" *Transactions of the American Philosophical Society*, n.s., vol. 51, pt. 7 (1961).

habitat. Mileage increased more rapidly than any place else in the world. Foreign engineers flocked in increasing number to investigate American technique and adaptation. For one of the features of railroad development in the United States was its divorce from slavish imitation. In 1830, the chief engineer of the Baltimore and Ohio explained the basis for his choice of superstructure: "English methods, which would have required about three times as much iron, were excluded on account of the great cost in this country of that material. The stone sills were considered next in cost to the English railway but preferable. The method with wood was *adopted* on account of its still greater cheapness." [3] Accordingly, the prevalent American mode of construction was one in which strap iron of a typical width of $2\frac{1}{2}$ inches and depth of $\frac{5}{8}$ inches was spiked to a wooden rail. Even upon roads imitative of the best of English technique, where stone was used, the wear of the rails under even the light locomotives of that day compelled a transition to a wooden substructure. Roads in the South often used piling instead of embankments and although the method "failed," its low initial cost and hence the opportunity to demonstrate the advantages of railroad transportation made it less foolish than might otherwise appear.

Not only in the realm of construction did Americans introduce innovations. The form of the locomotive was considerably changed, and improved, by the addition of a bogey truck that enabled turns within a smaller radius. The cow catcher was another response to the constraint of capital funds: where fencing was a luxury that often could not be afforded in the first few years of operation, it was wise to minimize the damage from meeting stray livestock along the right of way. In the type of passenger coach, too, America diverged from the continental design — a concession, perhaps, to the more egalitarian nature of American society. Finally, one may point to the original design for the "T" rail, later to become universal, developed by Robert Stevens of the Camden and Amboy.

These are but a few of the qualitative features of American railroads that differentiated them from their European counter-

[3] Quoted in Hungerford, *Baltimore and Ohio*, p. 70.

parts. The quantitative divergence was equally marked. By
the end of 1839 more than 3000 miles of road, some two thirds
with strap iron, were in operation.[4] To Michel Chevalier, "the
spectacle of a young people, executing in the short span of fifteen years [he included the canals], a series of works which the
most powerful States of Europe with a population three or four
times as great would have shrunk from undertaking is in truth
a noble sight." [5] A system of sorts was already emerging. One
obvious function of the railroad was to connect East and West,
as the Baltimore and Ohio had planned from the first. The Western of Massachusetts, later part of the Boston and Albany, as
well as the New York entry, the ill-fated Erie, and the two Pennsylvania auxiliaries fall into this category. Then there were the
lines oriented to passenger traffic running north and south along
the entire coast and projected as far around as New Orleans.
These roads were numerous, small in size individually, but in
terms of completed line, the largest single system. A third set
of roads was interior to the West, principally composed of state-
controlled systems initiated in 1836 or later; they were to link
the area to the great natural water courses serving the region,
the Ohio River on the South, the Great Lakes on the North.
Beyond these there were the many coal roads in Pennsylvania,
and what Chevalier termed the "railroads which, starting from
the great cities as centers, radiate from them in all directions." [6]

The depression lasting from the end of 1839 to 1843 played
havoc with this nascent network, in spite of the 3000 miles attained by the former year. The East-West lines were forced to
halt far short of their goal, the exceptions being the Western
of Massachusetts, which struggled through with state aid, and
the hybrid Pennsylvania system. Not until 1851 did a single
railroad connect the Atlantic Coast with western waters. Like-

[4] According to Franz Anton Ritter von Gerstner, "Railroads in the United
States," *American Railroad Journal*, XI (1840), 279–281, 298–301, 342–344, 365–
368; XII (1841), 82–88; *Journal of the Franklin Institute*, n.s., XXVI (1840), 227–
230.
[5] Michel Chevalier, *Society, Manners, and Politics in the United States* (Garden
City, N.Y., 1961), p. 260.
[6] Chevalier, p. 222. I have followed pretty much Chevalier's schema presented
in chap. xxii, pp. 219–254.

wise, the interior western roads were forced to virtual collapse. States, unable to borrow abroad, could not continue construction; in one instance, the elaborate rail network projected by Illinois, a full 9 roads serving the entire state, was represented by a mere 24-mile track leading nowhere in particular — and a substantial debt. In the South the debris was equally impressive. Some 90 miles of road already completed were left to disuse and eventual scuttling, let alone those caught in process. The stated goal of linking New York and New Orleans by rail was to wait a long time for fruition. Everywhere, the less ambitious the undertaking, the better it emerged after 1839; hence the localized and disoriented system that actually resulted in place of the integrated scheme described above.

Still, the quest for better transportation did not end with this debacle. Only the sources and the pace changed. In the 1840's New England became the major arena of new construction, and the main contours of its ultimate system were quite obvious by 1850. Three states, Massachusetts, Connecticut, and New Hampshire, possessed mileage roughly half of what they would have 100 years later.[7] Boston, reduced to regional rather than national commercial pre-eminence, was naturally the hub, as well as the financier, of the result. One should also comment upon the completion of the string of 10 independent roads from Albany to Buffalo that provided the first interregional connection — limited though it was to passenger travel at the time. In total, despite the rather disastrous start to the decade, mileage still managed to double by its end so that railroads came to something like 7500 miles at the beginning of 1850.

All the same, technological development preceded more rapidly than construction for much of the interval. Almost all superstructure laid during the decade consisted of heavier edge rail of one form or another laid over a wooden foundation. By 1842 the *American Railroad Journal* was speaking of the "ancient order of flat bar," and even the use of subsills beneath ties was disappearing.[8] Locomotives of heavier weight and more efficient design were appearing, and the former resort to inclined

[7] John F. Stover, *American Railroads* (Chicago, 1961), p. 27.
[8] *American Railroad Journal*, XIII (1842), 352.

planes over stretches of steep grades was ended. Outmoded rolling stock was scrapped in favor of larger and more economical
cars. Telegraphy was first employed in 1851 to signal and schedule
trains more efficiently, while the increasing double tracking of
existent roads narrowed the problem of single-track operation
somewhat.

The great surge in mileage in the 1850's is what really catches
attention, however. From a group of unconnected, small, pas-
senger-oriented railroads of the late 1840's, there emerged in
this last decade before the Civil War an articulate national network of 30,000 miles. It was possible to travel from New York
to St. Louis, or Chicago, or Dubuque, Iowa, by an all-rail route.
Hogs could be shipped from the plains of Illinois to slaughter
houses in Boston. Manufacturers could send their goods from
Philadelphia to Holly Springs, Mississippi. Problems, vexing
ones, remained. There were few bridges over major rivers; a
multitude of guages impeded continuous shipment; schedules
were chaotic in the absence of time zones; trains were small,
locomotive power limited.[9] Not to mention occasional nontech-
nical obstacles: the good citizens of Erie, Pennsylvania, dis-
traught at the unification of the Shore Line route from Cleveland to Buffalo, indulged in outbursts of violence in 1853-1854
designed to rend asunder what railroad presidents had finally
joined.[10] Still, a great stride toward, and beyond, the revolu-
tionary promise of that July day in 1828 had been achieved.

The West emerged with almost 10,000 miles of road, some
constructed with Federal subsidy. Chicago, with the merest
suggestion of rail service in 1849, found itself at decade's end
with no fewer than 10 different railroad lines entering the city,
and with 20 branch and extension lines, more than 4,000 miles
altogether. The rail center of America was firmly established at
this early date. Nor was commercial development the only
beneficiary. Farmers rejoiced at their linkage to a great market,
not only national but international. Western manufacturers,

---

[9] For some of the limitations to integration in 1860 see George Rogers Taylor and
Irene D. Neu, *The American Railroad Network, 1861-1890* (Cambridge, Mass.,
1956), chap. i.

[10] *American Railroad Journal*, XXVIII (1855), 753.

too, while subject to the erosion of markets naturally protected by distance, had much to gain. Rerolling mills appeared in Cleveland and Chicago; locomotive enterprises were found in many of the larger cities before 1857. Even those producing commodities unrelated to the needs of the expanding railroad system could benefit from the increasing local incomes brought in its wake.

The South was more tardy than the West in its acceptance of the railroad in the 1850's. As well it might be. Endowed with a natural system of river access that facilitated a commercial agriculture ahead of other regions and conscious still of the unfortunate consequences of the earlier commitment of the 1830's, the South began to participate only toward the end of the ante-bellum period. Then, with state and local aid prominent in finance, mileage grew sufficiently rapidly that by 1860 the region had about as much road per capita as the country as a whole. Southern ports engaged in commercial struggles similar to those that animated the Atlantic coastal cities and the competing western distributing points. New Orleans, Mobile, Memphis, Savannah, Charleston, Norfolk, Wilmington, North Carolina were among the major participants. The result of such a contest, when finally underway, was, as elsewhere, to accelerate construction, perhaps to the point even of diminishing returns.

The West and East had been joined, of course; not once, but at least four times, with still other minor claimants to the exalted position of trunk lines. When the New York and Erie reached Dunkirk on Lake Erie in 1851, it was an event of national significance. Perhaps the best testimony to that is the attendance at the celebration that ensued. President Fillmore was present, and not he alone. The *New York Herald* noted: "One of the most impressive facts which has struck us in reading of the reports was the presence of so many Presidential candidates in the trains, at one time no less than six. . . . There were at least a dozen candidates for Vice-President along." [11] The ceremonies two years later for the Baltimore and Ohio were

[11] Quoted in Edward H. Mott, *Between the Oceans and the Lakes* (New York, 1899), p. 108.

less spectacular, governors being the highest ranking officials in attendance. This lapse was expiated in 1857 when the completion of the Ohio and Mississippi resulted in an all-rail route between Baltimore and St. Louis. On that occasion the festivities were so lavish and so extended that an entire book was devoted to the subject.[12] In less flamboyant but more profitable fashion, the Pennsylvania and the New York Central, the latter emerging in 1853 as a combination of ten independent lines finally freed of restrictions on freight carriage, celebrated by reaping a very substantial proportion of the traffic.

Eighteen sixty was hardly the end. Properly, one might say it was just the beginning. The great transcontinental lines providing continuous transportation across an entire continent came later. So, too, did the bulk of the complete system. By 1900, 200,000 miles of line were being worked, of which more than half was the product of two decades of frenzied construction, the 1870's and 1880's. Virtually as much mileage was completed in the single year 1887 as England had managed to accumulate in half a century. Steel rails replaced the iron edge rails that had previously displaced the strap iron bars. Locomotives with compound boilers and immense tractive effort replaced the familiar American 4-4-0 that represented the acme of ante-bellum development. Gauge differences were resolved; on a single day in 1886, 13,000 miles of southern road converted from a broad gauge of 5 feet to a standard gauge of 4 feet, $8\frac{1}{2}$ inches.[13] All of these changes, and others, were reflected in two interrelated statistics, the charge per ton-mile and the amount of freight carried. The former plummeted from 38.6 cents to ship a bushel of wheat from Chicago to New York in 1858 to 14.3 in 1890, far exceeding the 10 percent decline in general commodity prices over the same interval.[14] Meanwhile ton-mileage rose from less than 3 billion in 1859 to 142 billion in the first year of the twentieth century. Employee compensation

---

[12] William P. Smith, *The Book of the Great Railway Celebrations of 1857* (New York, 1858).

[13] Taylor and Neu, *Railroad Network*, pp. 79–81.

[14] Taylor and Neu, p. 2.

alone in the single year 1900 would have been almost sufficient to construct the entire ante-bellum system.[15]

It was after 1860, too, that railroad influence became most patent in the life of the nation. The great financiers, Vanderbilt, Drew, Gould, and Fisk, among others, captured the public imagination — and wrath — with their rapid accumulation and dissipation of enormous wealth. The Crédit Mobilier scandal exposed corruption extending into the councils of the Federal government. Without resort to open illegality, stock watering, place discrimination, rebates, and the like earned the railroads a hostile public. In turn, agrarian interests united to pass Granger laws to limit such overweening power, an act of reprisal more symbolic than effective. Even after the establishment of the Interstate Commerce Commission in 1887, another score of years would pass until regulation could take hold. The whole gamut of post-Civil War political and social affairs yields evidence of the railroad's imposing presence.

Still, the ante-bellum period of railroad development requires our close attention. For the study of the introduction and diffusion of new technology it is indispensable. Interesting recent work along these lines, focusing upon the initial decisions of the merchant groups in the various coastal cities, has recently been published.[16] More is yet to be done. The development of financial arrangements to service the, for that period, substantial capital requirements is another fruitful line of inquiry. Only part of the job has been completed by Goodrich's study of governmental aid.[17] But even from the standpoint of its effects, the pre-Civil War railroad network is of relevance. As early as 1855 the New York State Engineer reported, "the railway interest has become one of the most important in the country, not only on account of the large pecuniary investments

[15] The data for the post-Civil War period can be found in U.S. Bureau of the Census, *Historical Statistics of the United States* (Washington, 1960), pp. 423–437. The information for the earlier period on ton-mileage and cost of construction comes from Appendixes A and B.

[16] Namely the work by Rubin, "Canal or Railroad?".

[17] Carter Goodrich, *Government Promotion of American Canals and Railroads* (New York, 1960).

which have been made herein, but also on account of the effect
which its development has had in increasing the value and
changing the relationship of property, trade, and commerce,
and modifying the social conditions of our. people." [18] Within
recent years evidence has been accumulating to suggest a substantial transformation indeed of the economy during the prewar period. Agriculture, which had accounted for 72 percent
of the commodity output in 1839, receded in relative importance
to 56 percent in 1859. Manufactures grew especially rapidly,
their share increasing from 17 to 32 percent. Real product per
capita also rose at a rate greater than the long-term trend between 1844 and 1854.[19] Moreover, having pushed back the
statistical frontier to 1839, there is reason to believe that continuous development earlier could not have proceeded at the
later pace, although periods of considerable advance are not
ruled out. Extrapolation backwards at the trend rate would
indicate a standard of living in 1799, say, below one that seems
plausible.[20] From all of these indications, the American version
of entrance into sustained modern growth, breakthrough, take-
off — whatever you will — seems to have occurred almost coin-
cidentally with the introduction and diffusion of the railroad.[21]
With so much interest currently focusing upon the dynamic
process of growth, and particularly upon how it gets underway,
the role of the railroad before 1860 becomes a question as important as its subsequent contributions.

[18] *Annual Report of the State Engineer and Surveyor on the Railroads of the State
of New York for 1854* (Albany, 1855), p. 3.

[19] Robert E. Gallman, "Commodity Output, 1839–1899" in *Trends in the American Economy in the Nineteenth Century*, National Bureau of Economic Research,
Inc., Studies in Income and Wealth, vol. 24 (Princeton, 1960), Tables 1 and 4,
pp. 16, 26; see also his new estimates in "Gross National Product in the United
States, 1834–1909," in *Output, Employment, and Productivity in the United States
after 1800*, National Bureau of Economic Research, Inc., Studies in Income and
Wealth, vol. 30 (New York, 1965).

[20] See the testimony of Raymond W. Goldsmith before the Joint Economic Com-
mittee, Hearings on Employment, Growth and Price Levels, pt. 2, *Historical and
Comparative Rates of Production, Productivity, and Prices*, 86th Congress, 1st Session,
(Washington, 1959), pp. 277–279.

[21] The extent of discontinuity is not to be exaggerated, however, as some have
been wont to do. One impressive feature of nineteenth-century United States economic growth is precisely its apparent continuity in such spheres as technological progress, internal migration, commercial activity, etc.

Not that the interrelationship is totally unexplored. Walt Rostow, in particular, has seized upon this temporal congruence to bestow upon the railroad the central position in the American take-off: "this period of American takeoff centered on the building of a railway net reaching out to the Middle West. This enterprise created a national market and brought to life vigorous modern coal, iron, and heavy engineering industries." [22] He has ample precedent for his emphasis. Max Weber once termed the railroad the greatest innovation in history. Joseph Schumpeter was hardly more restrained when he wrote that it is possible to treat the economic history of the United States in the last half of the nineteenth century solely "in terms of railroad construction and its effects." [23]

Casual empiricism concurs. Everywhere in the world, in Europe, in the United States, in the underdeveloped areas, mileage multiplied from virtually none in 1830 to 500,000 miles of steel roadway in 1900, a distance more than thirty times that along the Equator. Total expenditure aggregated billions of dollars in a period in which millions were still a relevant unit of account. Investment banks arose to satisfy their wants; stock exchanges featured their securities. The Argentine pampas and the American plains were brought into production, their output flowing around the world. Government participation in the modern economic process was often ushered in by the new technology. The ramifications were dramatic and extensive.

Despite the unanimity of opinion and apparent consistency of fact, there are valid reasons for reconsidering such conventional wisdom as applied to the United States before 1860. Most obvious of all, this was still an era of railroad infancy, both in magnitude and technology. It is not unreasonable to suppose that the accomplishments of the innovation were limited by this fact, as well as by the short period to work themselves out. On the other side, moreover, no study has yet delimited, and subjected to careful historical study, the various effects the

---

[22] Joint Economic Committee, *Comparisons of the United States and Soviet Economies*, 86th Congress, 1st Session (Washington, 1960), p. 593.

[23] Max Weber, *General Economic History* (New York: Greenberg, 1927), p. 297. Joseph A. Schumpeter, *Business Cycles* (New York, 1939), I, 341.

ante-bellum railroad system might be expected to have.[24] The amount of empirical detail we possess is surprisingly sparse; no compilations of receipts, employment, profits, or investment exist. It would almost be fair to characterize modern sentiment by reference to the contemporary writer who, more than a century ago, felt careful investigation superfluous, indeed irreverent: "Nor is it our design to expand upon the value of those grand highways of commerce and travel. . . . Every man, woman, and child has hourly experience of it, far more convincing than volumes of written logic. As well labor to prove the importance of breathing . . ." [25] As our subsequent findings will indicate, the task is less obvious than that.

The Contours of the Study

Economic theory suggests three major types of effects that might follow from transportation innovation. First, there is the direct consequence of lower cost carriage of goods and persons. The ability of the railroad to produce transport services at a lower cost has an analogue in lessened resource requirements. Thus overland transport rates of fifteen cents a ton-mile imply the consumption of fifteen cents of labor, capital, and entrepreneurial inputs for the unit output. A railroad rate of three cents, say, means that twelve cents of inputs formerly needed can be applied to other tasks. The difference in costs of transportation due to the introduction of the railroad therefore provides one measure of the increased production it made possible.

Lower costs of transportation entered in another way, too. They increased the size of the market and hence affected the production decisions of manufacturers and farmers. The op-

---

[24] Leland Jenks's essay, "Railroads as an Economic Force in American Development," *Journal of Economic History*, IV (1944), 1–20, summarizes some paths of influence, but is without historical depth; Caroline E. McGill, *et al.*, *History of Transportation in the United States before 1860* (Washington, D.C., 1917), has a wealth of detail but is without organization.

Robert W. Fogel's simultaneous and stimulating effort to rectify this same lacuna has since come to light in "A Quantitative Approach to the Study of Railroads in American Economic Growth: A Report of Some Preliminary Findings," *Journal of Economic History*, XXII (1962), 163–197, and, more extensively, in *Railroads and American Economic Growth: Essays in Econometric History* (Baltimore, 1964).

[25] Smith, *Celebrations*, p. 3.

portunity to ship boots and shoes from Boston to Iowa more cheaply meant a larger effective demand for the product on the part of Iowans. Contrariwise, Iowa corn sold in Boston at the same price meant higher proceeds and income for the farmer. A larger market meant both a more specialized one and one in which expansion might be more profitable. The greater the specialization at a moment of time, the higher the real income of all through their concentration upon activities they perform especially well; this, a terminal calculation of resource saving successfully measures. The greater the incentives for expansion, the greater is the potentiality of capital formation and technological progress, and thus the higher the rate of growth over time; this possibility, such an approach ignores.[26]

This induced response of other activities, what Hirschman refers to as forward linkage effects, depends upon the variety of industries into which transport enters as an input, the substitutability of transport with other inputs, the proportion of total costs it accounts for, and the extent of the cost reduction introduced by cheaper railroad rates. As part of the social overhead, transportation ranks very high in the first two categories. It is an input into virtually all other production currently or potentially part of the industrial matrix. In many instances, too, substitution is not readily feasible. Fixed mineral sites are, or are not, exploited, depending upon costs of transportation. Relocation is impossible. Even in agriculture, with declining fertility of lands closer to market, the relevant decision may involve subsistence farming with less effort in inaccessible regions rather than commercial production for market on poor land. The aggregate counterpart to the specific cases described here is the notion of a social overhead minimum for every level of output. In an agricultural society, like the ante-bellum United States, where transport costs consumed a large part of total receipts, the leverage of their reduction may be substantial.

Because such a priori analysis suggests substantial elasticity of output to transport innovation, this class of effects can be ignored only at great peril. Current growth theory certainly

---

[26] Fogel seems to imply that direct benefits exhaust the effects of an extension of the market. See his "Quantitative Approach," p. 166.

makes much of social overhead capital; as Rosenstein-Rodan puts it, the most important products of the social overhead "are investment opportunities created in other industries." [27] With regard to nineteenth-century railroads, the *American Railroad Journal* expressed it just as well: "The building of an improved highway is a very small affair to the commerce which is to pass over it. The former is the pioneer of the latter. The expenditure of $1,000,000 upon a railroad is the occasion for the expenditure of ten times that sum to develop what the former has rendered available." [28]

The second set of indirect effects, and the third path of influence, arises from the resource demands generated by railroad construction and operation. Two things are important here: the very magnitude of the railroad interest as well as the special character of its input requirements. High levels of expenditure contribute to full utilization of resources and to more rapid development as well. A sectoral allocation of demand that tends to underwrite the rapid growth of capital goods industries is equally valuable, since industrialization does not seem to thrive without such an infrastructure. Rostow has been particularly emphatic in placing great weight upon these backward linkages. While he pays homage to the reduction of internal transport costs, for the take-off itself it is the derived demands that were crucial. [29]

These three considerations structure and shape the historical analysis. [30] Chapter II deals with the direct benefits, some theoretical, fine points of the concept as well as empirical results. Many of the calculations are reserved to an appendix in the

[27] P. N. Rosenstein-Rodan, "Notes on the Theory of the 'Big Push,' " in Howard S. Ellis, ed., *Economic Development for Latin America* (New York, 1961), p. 60.
[28] *American Railroad Journal*, XXIX (1856), 1.
[29] Walt W. Rostow, *The Stages of Economic Growth* (Cambridge, Eng., 1960), p. 55.
[30] The "lateral" effects of Rostow, by which he means the induced "set of changes which tend to reinforce the industrialization process on a wider front," might seem to be another possibility. But these are so general as to constitute the very process of industrialization and are a *consequence* of the other effects rather than an additional route of influence. See Walt W. Rostow, "Leading Sectors and the Take-off," in W. W. Rostow, ed., *The Economics of Take-off into Sustained Growth* (London, 1963), p. 5.

interests of continuity, although the discussions there are also a valuable guide to the structure of ante-bellum transportation in its entirety. Chapter III then focuses upon railroad expenditures. Both of these subjects are more easily handled than the question of indirect forward linkages. Direct benefits are nothing more than the amount of transport cost reduction, and derived demands at least emanate from the railroads themselves. To ferret out the ramifications of better transportation to a variety of users over a substantial period of time is another and much more trying pursuit. The remaining chapters grapple with different phases of this elusive topic. Chapters IV and V treat the relationship between railroad extension into the West in the 1850's and the surge of migration and agricultural expansion that accompanied it. Chapter VI switches to the industrial boom of the 1840's and the influence of New England railroad growth upon its timing and magnitude. Chapter VII takes up the contribution of the railroad to interregional trade and the importance of a national market. The final chapter integrates these partial analyses by examining the implications of the American experience for the theory of social overhead capital. Four statistical appendixes describing the derivation of new data on output, investment, employment, and equipment concentrate the technical detail for the interested reader; once more, however, an abundance of historical materials is to be found there as well.

CHAPTER II

Direct Benefits: Theory, Measurement, and Interpretation

Introduction

Despite the lofty initial dreams of an interregional trade following iron rails, the early orientation of American railroads, like the English, was more prosaic. Passengers rather than freight flocked to the innovation wherever it was adopted. Here, both canals and stagecoaches gave way immediately before their swifter rival. Inns along the post roads between cities like New York and Boston, or Philadelphia and Baltimore, no longer were crowded with weary travelers. The packet lines on the Erie Canal, which had played an important role in the westward migration of the 1830's, dwindled in the 1840's and finally disappeared in the 1850's. In the interior a similar phenomenon ultimately occurred. As Putnam writes of the Illinois and Michigan Canal, "within a few months after the opening of the railroad, practically all the passenger business deserted the canal for the speedier mode of travel." [1]

The ease and decisiveness of this conquest stands in contrast to the more prolonged contest for freight. Only with the rapid increase in mileage and reduction of rates of the 1850's did railroads successfully challenge the leadership of the canals. The final outcome had been hinted at earlier, to be sure. The triumph of the Boston and Lowell over the Middlesex Canal foreshadowed a denouement which was to be repeated many times over before the Civil War; nor did the far from victorious competition of the Schuylkill Navigation with the Reading Railroad

[1] James W. Putnam, *The Illinois and Michigan Canal: A Study in Economic History* (Chicago, 1918), p. 111.

for the coal trade in the early 1840's bode well for the canal interests. Nevertheless, as late as 1852 Israel Andrews estimated that the tonnage carried on canals was virtually double that transported on railroads, even excluding the large tonnage on the anthracite canals, and despite the shorter length of canal mileage.[2] The trustees of the Wabash and Erie Canal could still emphasize in 1853 (with some disquiet to be sure) that "only a small portion of the produce and merchandise hitherto taking the canal as its natural channel has this year been drawn off by newly opened railroads."[3]

A scant six years later, in spite of the rapid growth of the hinterland which it served, the canal carried a volume of tonnage a quarter smaller than the 1850 level.[4] Such instances can readily be multiplied. The Ohio Canal delivered almost two million bushels of wheat to Cleveland in 1850; ten years later the volume was barely two hundred thousand. Coal deliveries were down 60 percent as well, in spite of the natural advantages of water transportation in the carriage of such a bulk commodity. The western branch of the state system serving Toledo held up somewhat better, but there, too, substantial absolute declines persisted in a period of increasing commerce. Receipts tell of the calamity even better than tonnage figures, for in the face of railroad competition tolls were so drastically reduced upon the water route that revenues fell below maintenance expenses. The reduction in receipts in Ohio amounted to 70 percent during the decade.[5]

The faltering of the canal interest was by no means confined to the West. The Pennsylvania state works dwindled to insignificance and were finally sold by the state in 1857, the largest part, ironically, to the Pennsylvania Railroad. The Chesapeake and Ohio Canal stopped far short of its ultimate goal and sur-

[2] Israel Andrews, *Trade and Commerce of the British North American Colonies*, House Exec. Doc. No. 136, 32nd Congress, 1st Session (Washington, 1853), p. 904.
[3] Quoted in Elbert Jay Benton, "The Wabash Trade Route in the Development of the Old Northwest," *Johns Hopkins University Studies in Historical and Political Science*, XXI, nos. 1–2 (1903), 77.
[4] Benton, p. 102.
[5] C. P. McClelland and C. C. Huntington, *History of the Ohio Canals* (Columbus, Ohio, 1905), p. 170.

vived only by virtue of a prosaic coal trade, for which the Baltimore and Ohio remained an effective competitor. Even that monarch of canals, the Erie, was not immune to the pressure. Receipts on the latter peaked in 1851, the last year in which parallel railroads were hindered by canal tolls. Freight continued to increase but at a perceptibly slower rate. Where the decade of the 1840's had seen a doubling, the total tonnage carried in 1859 exceeded that in 1850 by only 7 percent. There is no question, however, about its continued importance in domestic trade. The ton-mileage upon the Erie was always greater before 1860 than upon any other single transportation route, and during the decade a peak tonnage of more than 3,000,000 tons was reached.[6] Yet equally clearly the menace of railroad competition and the deterioration of that canal's position mark the decade.

Overall, the later 1850's thus saw a reversal of earlier water domination in freight service. Henry Varnum Poor reported the situation accurately when he stated in 1860: "One of the most marked features in the internal commerce of the country is the steadily increasing traffic of our railroads and a corresponding diminution on all our water lines."[7] More exact testimony is forthcoming from the statistical records of freight output. The freight service of canals in 1859 is estimated in Table 1 with reasonable accuracy as 1.6 billion ton-miles, including the anthracite canals. In the same year railroad ton-mileage can be placed at substantially more than 2 billion, or about two thirds again as much.[8] Harvey Segal's recent assertion that "it is unlikely that the canals were surpassed by railroads before 1861" does not show sufficient appreciation of the transport revolution the 30 thousand miles of pre-Civil War railroad had wrought.[9]

The magnitude of such a displacement by no means implies commensurate direct benefits to the economy, although this often has been implicitly assumed. Both marginal as well as sub-

---

[6] Henry V. Poor, *History of the Railroads and Canals of the United States of America* (New York, 1860), p. 367.

[7] *American Railroad Journal*, XXXIII (1860), 404.

[8] Or more exactly, 2,600,000,000 ton-miles. See Appendix A.

[9] In Carter Goodrich, *et al.*, *Canals and American Economic Development* (New York, 1961), p. 246.

TABLE 1. Canal ton-mileage, 1859

Canal	Receipts (dollars)	Tonnage (thousands)	Average haul[a] (miles)	Freight charges per ton-mile[b]	Ton-mileage (millions)
New York System	—	—	—	—	544.3
Chesapeake and Ohio	—	—	—	—	58.8
Mainline (Pa.)	197,549	—	—	3 mills	65.8
Lehigh	—	1,307	80	—	104.6
Schuylkill	—	1,699	80	—	169.9
Delaware Div.	—	770	40	—	30.8
Union	—	263	70	—	18.2
Susquehanna	145,276	—	—	5 mills	29.1
Erie (Pa.)	93,817	—	—	3 mills	31.2
Monongahela	89,957	—	—	3 mills	30.0
West Branch	140,997	—	—	3 mills	47.0
Wyoming	101,449	—	—	3 mills	33.8
Chesapeake and Delaware	—	496	14	—	69.4
Delaware and Raritan	—	1,500	50	—	75.0
Morris	—	638	80	—	51.0
Delaware and Hudson	—	979	90	—	88.1
Ohio System	234,679	—	—	3 mills	70.4
Wabash and Erie	65,073[c]	—	—	5 mills	13.0
Illinois and Michigan	—	367	70	—	25.7
Total					1,554.5

Source: Poor, *Railroads and Canals;* McClelland and Huntington, *History of the Ohio Canals;* Putnam, *The Illinois and Michigan Canal;* Benton, "The Wabash Trade Route in the Development of the Old Northwest"; Chester L. Jones, "The Economic History of the Anthracite-Tidewater Canals," University of Pennsylvania Series in Political Economy and Public Law, no. 22 (1908); Goodrich, *et al., Canals and Development; Report of the Pennsylvania Railroad for the Year Ending December 31, 1859* (Philadelphia, 1860).

[a] For the New York State system and the Chesapeake and Ohio, ton-mileage data were available directly in Poor, *Railroads and Canals,* pp. 361, 604. The other figures were estimated either by multiplying tonnage figures by average haul estimates or by dividing receipts by estimated tolls per ton-mile. The average hauls utilized here are equal or greater than Harvey Segal's calculations in Goodrich, *Canals and Development,* p. 242, except in one instance — the Chesapeake and Delaware Canal. The figure used here is the total length of the Canal reported in Poor. These estimates were derived for the specific canals based on the description of traffic in the sources cited.

[b] Freight rate estimates are slightly more arbitrary. The Ohio system rate was set equal to average charge in the New York system. There is evidence of approximate parity here earlier. In spite of the higher average prevailing upon the Schuylkill and Lehigh canals, the same 3-mill rate was used upon all Pennsylvania canals with the exception of the Susquehanna. (Cf. *Hunt's Merchants' Magazine,* XXXI [1854], 123.) A slightly higher rate existed on the Wabash and Erie and this was applied to the Susquehanna. As can easily be seen, using the lower rate would not change matters substantially.   [c] For 1860.

stantial differences in transport cost are capable of evoking dramatic shifts in allegiance, but with quite different effects. When the Erie Canal was first opened from Albany to Buffalo, freights to the latter city from New York were reduced to a tenth of their former level, and all traffic obviously took the canal. The initial conditions in which "the cost of transportation equalled nearly *three* times the market value of wheat in New York; *six* times the value of corn; *twelve* times the value of oats; and far exceeded the value of most kinds of cured provisions" were profoundly altered.[10] By contrast the later substitution of the New York Central for the canal involved marginal cost reductions at best and much smaller change in transport availability.

An assessment of the direct economic effects of the substitution of rail for water transport must therefore take explicit account of the *amount* of cost reduction involved, not only its existence.[11] Aggregated over the entire railroad system this provides a measure of the financial savings shippers enjoyed from the innovation, and from a social viewpoint, some notion of the reduction in resource inputs required for transportation. Nineteenth-century internal improvements enthusiasts were not without cognizance of this method of reasoning, it should be noted. There are numerous references to transport savings in the literature promoting both canals and railroads. Albert Gallatin stated the principle succinctly and clearly early in the century: "It is sufficiently evident that whenever the annual expense of transportation on a certain route in its natural state exceeds the interest on the capital employed in improving the communication, and the annual expense of transportation (exclusive of the tolls) by the improved route, the difference is an annual additional income to the nation." [12] The Ohio Canal Commissioners went further and presented in 1833 an elaborate calculation of the direct benefits which that state system had

---

[10] Andrews, *Trade and Commerce*, p. 278.

[11] Full appreciation of this point awaited its emphasis by Fogel's "A Quantitative Approach."

[12] Segal reprints the passage from the 1808 *Report on Internal Improvements* in Goodrich, *Canals and Development*, p. 217.

provided for Ohio residents.[13] An equally impressive, if not totally correct, calculation of the direct benefits of railroads in the same state was undertaken by the *Railroad Record* some twenty years later.[14] In a less scientific vein, southern railroad promoters were quick to emphasize such possibilities in their hortatory addresses, and proponents of a Pacific railroad were equally awake to the appeal of such an emphasis.

This chapter applies this approach to the ante-bellum railroad system. A first section spells out the method from the theoretical side. The second section, in conjunction with the appendix, develops some estimates and interprets them.

The Concept of Social Saving

As has been suggested, the key to measuring the direct benefits of railroads lies in the identity of the reduction in financial cost with the reduction in real inputs required per unit of transport output. Lower transport charges and greater productive efficiency are the same phenomenon viewed from different aspects. Because the real inputs made "redundant" by lesser unit requirements can be used to increase aggregate output, there is a net gain to the economy. This constitutes the direct benefits or social saving of the innovation.

Before proceeding to consider the method of valuing such benefits, it is important to emphasize that direct charges are not the only costs of transportation which must be considered. Such attributes as greater speed, freedom from seasonality, smaller risk of loss, direct routing, and others, were always prominent in expositions of the advantages of rail transport vis-à-vis other feasible alternatives. That they were of significance is indicated by even the most cursory look at relative transport charges. On the face of it water transportation possessed a significant rate advantage coupled with declining patronage: "The rates on the roads [New York Central and Erie] on an average are still $3\frac{1}{3}$ times greater than on the [New York

---

[13] Quoted as Appendix A of E. L. Bogart, *Internal Improvements in Ohio* (New York, 1924).

[14] *Hunt's Merchants' Magazine*, XXXI (1854), 502, abstracting the original article appearing in the *Railroad Record*, a Cincinnati publication.

State] canals. This fact taken in connection with their increased traffic, as compared with the canal, proves their great superiority, in public estimation, for many kinds of freight." [15] It is the value of the other attributes that dissolves the apparent paradox.

Some of these offsetting qualitative advantages are readily quantified. Thus greater speed and regularity combined to reduce the average amount of inventory required per unit of sales. Retailers did not need to buy in such large quantities to assure a continuous flow to the consumer. With smaller working capital thus tied up, interest costs were correspondingly lowered. These financial savings are savings for the economy as a whole also. The reduction in inventories can be reinvested elsewhere to yield an annual flow determined by the interest rate, a stream identical to the reduction in private cost. Other qualitative advantages like direct haul without transshipment and greater safety have an analogue in smaller commissions, fewer charges for transfer of cargoes, lower insurance rates, and the like. A comparison of the total costs of distribution by alternative transport agencies captures them without difficulty. Still another advantage of rail shipment, more direct routing, also can be rendered by conversion to total rather than ton-mile charges. Although the distance of water alternatives exceeded rail mileage by half again as much and sometimes even more, as in the lake route from Chicago to Buffalo, compensating adjustment of ton-mile rates eliminates any discrepancy.

While it is thus possible to assign rather exact dollar values to many of these attributes of better transportation, *all* cannot be translated equally efficiently. For example, one of the touted advantages of rail shipment was the reduction in the variance of market price since supply could be better regulated. With lesser uncertainty, windfall gains and losses would be smaller, and inputs of entrepreneurial risk reduced. This might imply increased scope for decision-making in another direction and increased output. While a conceptual scheme can be concocted which would allow for storage of sufficient commodities at market to provide the same result, the costs of such an alternative

---

[15] *American Railroad Journal*, XXXIII (1860), 404.

need not be equivalent to the increases in output made possible by reduced entrepreneurial inputs of risk. It is therefore correct that translation of quality into quantity is always feasible — but sometimes at a large price. The effect of the conversion is to bias the calculation of the benefits upward, for it forces the technologically inferior transportation regime to produce hypothetically the exact same bill of services as the newer one actually could. The costs of such an alternative then may exceed the maximum amount that would have been paid for it, and this is where the bias originates.

Even without qualitative effects, however, the same divergence arises. The inefficient transport technology is forced to produce the same quantity as the advanced one does even though consumers would prefer to do with less at the higher prices. Only if demand for transport is perfectly inelastic with respect to its price so that the quantity purchased is always the same, innovation or no, is the problem avoided. But this is hardly likely. First, there is the usual positive substitution effect. This comes to the fore because location is variable. With producers free to move farther from the market to new sources of supply, or to new markets, the demand for transport inputs will increase as a result of lower price. Two other factors also contribute. If commodity supply is a positive function of received price, then higher transport costs mean smaller production and hence less demand for transportation; for lower transport charges the reverse is true. On the demand side, transport-intensive goods will tend to have lower relative prices in the event of transportation innovation, thereby encouraging consumer demand and ultimately the derived demand for transportation. The higher the proportion of transport costs to final price the greater the force of both of these effects.

Once demand is elastic the measure of social saving is neither unequivocal nor exact. This is easily seen in Figure 1. At first some transformation curve DT prevails, reflecting the maximum production possibilities with the given technology and factor supplies. The effect of transport innovation is a shift outward of the transformation curve from the T-axis with the position on the D-axis fixed: if all resources were devoted to trans-

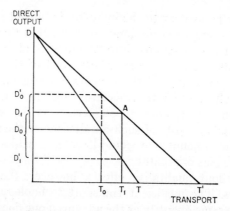

FIGURE 1. The impact of transport innovation

portation, more could now be produced, whereas production of direct output is unaffected by the technological advance. The new equilibrium D, T combination is at A, with T greater than before in response to its lower relative price. Now there are *two* measures of cost reduction, either $(P_0 - P_1)T_0$ or $(P_0 - P_1)T_1$, where the letters and subscripts refer to prices and quantities before and after the innovation.[16] The base weighted measure, in terms of direct product, is equal in Figure 1 to $D_0D'_0$; the current weighted measure, to D'_1D_1, which is obviously greater. This divergence is exactly analogous to the familiar index number problem in the theory of consumers' choice.[17] $D_0D'_0$ is an understatement of the true rise of income which is caused by the innovation since it does not take into account the more favorable transformation opportunities made available, just as

[16] The use of price rather than marginal cost in the subsequent calculations assumes the existence of perfect competition. The additional requirement necessary if $(P_0 - P_1)T$ is to measure social saving is that present factor prices accurately reflect their opportunity cost after displacement. Then the incremental contribution to output will be the same as the reduction in costs. Marginal shifts and perfect competition together imply this condition.

[17] This should not be surprising. Direct benefits of railroads are nothing more than the consumers' surplus of a product (transportation) on which a relatively large proportion of income was spent, and which underwent very rapid price change. Some of the difficulties in its measurement thus correspond to some of the objections which have been levied against the concept of consumers' surplus.

a Laspeyres price index understates the amount of gain subsequent to a price reduction because consumers are not allowed to adjust their market baskets. The final quantity measure contains the upward Paasche bias because the new optimal amount of transportation service is treated as a maximizing solution under the old technology, when in fact it is not.

As long as we are in a world of marginal changes in which price differentials are small and qualitative advantages are not significant, this index number problem is no real handicap. The difference between the Laspeyres and Paasche results is likely to be quite narrow and hence insignificant. Once beyond the confines of the individual project, and with a long interval between introduction of an innovation and measurement of its effect, the distortion becomes considerably more worrisome. Once factor inputs change over time and the transformation curve is shifted outward, the Laspeyres measure no longer is meaningful. Consider Figure 2. There an initial demand curve

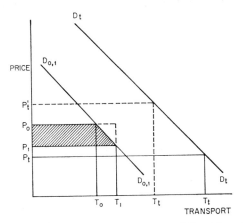

FIGURE 2. The bias in the measure of direct benefits

for transport services in the year *0* is drawn with the equilibrium price and quantity of transport output indicated. The interval from *0* to *1* is sufficiently short that the demand curve can be assumed not to have shifted outward as a consequence of the increased income. Then the biases discussed above are clearly shown by the alternative rectangles which bracket the "true" measure of social saving indicated by the shaded area under the demand curve, $D_{0,1}$. Over time, with increasing income, the demand curve shifts outward to some new position D_tD_t. We observe the output T_t at price P_t which the new transport regime has made possible. The relevant comparison is with some T'_t determined by some higher price P'_t appropriate to the alternative transportation system on the *same* demand curve.[18] Such a point is never observed, of course, and consequently the difference between the Paasche and Laspeyres measures that are available, $(P_0 - P_1)T_1$ and $(P_0 - P_1)T_0$, provides no basis whatsoever for isolating the true amount of social saving. This is to say, unless we can specify the elasticity of demand within the relevant range, we cannot provide even upper and lower limits to the correct direct benefits, let alone measure them perfectly.

Inference of T'_t is not the only difficulty posed by the application of the concept to historical measurement. Another is the very choice of P'_t. The appropriate charge for the alternative transport technology need not equal its quoted price. That existing price reflects observed supply and demand conditions. But the relevant price pertains to a production situation which does not exist, and which can be related to the present price only by assumptions concerning the course of marginal cost over wide ranges of variation. Only if constancy is assumed are actual and potential price identical. Yet with large increases in transport services, constancy is often unlikely. Take just a single contemporary instance: if airplanes were required to transport all existing ton-mileage in the United States, would the appropriate cost be the present charge on air freight? Assumptions of increasing remoteness are necessary the more unrealistic the "feasible" alternative becomes.

The problem is more than theoretical in this case because of the much larger freight capacity of the railroad compared to

---

[18] If costs remain the same with increasing output, that is, when neither economies nor diseconomies of scale prevail, P_t would equal P_1 and P'_t would equal P_0. Only for clarity are different prices used in the diagram.

simple horse and wagon transportation. It has been estimated
that 15,000 ton-miles is the annual maximum per route mile
for the latter (taking account of the practical difficulties of absorbing more than a "reasonable" amount of human and animal
power for such a function). By contrast, the corresponding statistic for railroads is set at more than 3,500,000 ton-miles.[19] Such
estimates need not be perfectly exact for the point to be well
taken. As the demand for transportation by horse and wagon,
say, approaches some critical total, the cost of bidding resources
away from other sectors might well prove to increase rapidly.
Or with expanded canal utilization, there might be a sharp discontinuity due to lack of sufficient capacity. The problem of estimating the aggregate demand curve for transport services
thus has a dual in the specification of the supply curve.

Besides the errors arising from imperfect knowledge of these
functions, two additional sources of measurement bias can be
identified.[20] The first involves violation of the assumption that
the quantity of factor services under the two transportation
alternatives will be constant. If a crude, noncommercial method
of carrying goods to market prevails, individuals may be sacri-
ficing leisure for the essential task of transportation. When a
more efficient distribution network is substituted, instead of
the equivalent input of labor services into other activities, the
result may be increased leisure. Then the calculated social saving overstates the increase in actual product deriving from the
innovation. Low rates on overland transportation reflecting
little alternative productivity would eliminate such bias, but

[19] J. Edwin Holmstrom, *Railways and Roads in Pioneer Development Overseas*
(London, 1934), p. 56.
[20] One possible source of error, divergence of price from marginal cost, is not serious. If monopoly profits prevailed, either in railroads or other forms of transport,
the use of price would overstate real resource use and lead to possible bias in calculation of benefits. For example, if railroads obtained monopoly profits, but other
transport agencies did not, then social savings would be understated because railroads were still cheaper — in a real sense — than prices indicated. At this time,
with severe competition within the industry and without, such a situation was not
common. The possible understatement of benefits because state canal tolls did not
cover capital costs and maintenance is something also relevant then. The generous
margin granted to railroads in the calculations in the appendix to this chapter more
than cancels the small downward effect of these two considerations.

it is doubtful whether available market rates already correct for this possibility.

The case set out above is not without interest in the specific historical context considered here. Phillips describes prerailroad transportation of cotton in the following terms: "The Cotton producers harvested and marketed their cotton in the fall and winter season, when there was little other work demanding attention with men or mules or wagons. . . . It did not matter particularly — since it was the leisure season on the farm — whether the team returned from market in three days or three weeks." [21] If such men and mules and wagons did nothing or very little when the railroad superseded the team, the direct benefits are taken in less toil, an element of real cost, to be sure, but not included in conventional product accounting.

A final and very significant distortion in the calculation of social saving derives from the existence of indirect benefits. Because there are second round effects of the initial reduction in transport cost, namely induced capital formation and expansion in other sectors, the position of the demand schedule for transport services is not independent of movement along it. Since all railroads are taken together as one unit, the magnitude of such a shift may be quite considerable. The net result is that social saving is calculated to include the reduction in required resources upon that portion of increased transport output which is the direct result of induced developmental sequences. Thus the estimate of the direct benefits is dependent upon the strength of the indirect effects, and their total importance is likely to be magnified by such a connection.

Figure 3 describes such a situation graphically. The demand curve for transport services D_0D_0 is drawn as a function of transport prices alone, on the assumption that the level of total activity is given. Its position shifts with variations of the latter. If total activity is unrelated to changes in transport output in any significant way, the argument presented in connection with Figure 2 still pertains, and the gradual outward movement of the curve to some position D_tD_t serves only to eliminate

[21] Ulrich B. Phillips, *A History of Transportation in the Eastern Cotton Belt to 1860* (New York, 1908), p. 12.

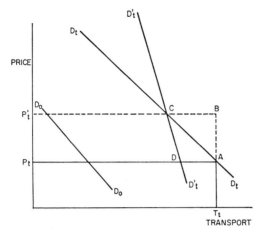

FIGURE 3. The mingling of indirect and direct benefits

any meaningful bounding measure of social saving. Once such a relationship is admitted, some smaller $D'_tD'_t$ is the appropriate curve when indirect effects are netted out. Thus the direct benefit in the absence of any indirect effects will be the area $P_tDCP'_t$, and smaller by a further factor than the calculated area $P_tABP'_t$.

These results make it clear that the necessary use of terminal quantities and imputed costs to reflect the qualitative advantages of railroads will lead to overstatement of the direct benefits, perhaps considerably. So too will the existence of indirect effects, in the sense that our measure implies an overvaluation of transport cost reductions, per se, in a dynamic process. The only significant factor operating in the other direction is neglect of rising marginal costs, but here the impact is minimized — as Figure 4 will show — because the correct T' along the correct demand curve is at a much lower level than the observed output. By and large, therefore, actual measurements of direct benefits will yield upper bounds rather than precise amounts. For certain purposes these may be sufficient. Even when they are not, the previous analysis identifies the principal adjustments that are required to tranform measured benefits closer to the true ones. All of this is still preliminary to the real challenge, which is the derivation of the actual estimates, however approximative they may be.

Some Historical Application

In practice, the accurate measurement of social saving, biases aside, is no easy matter. Strictly speaking, it is necessary to proceed railroad by railroad, specifying exactly the transport services performed by each and reallocating these to the most efficient alternative route. The difference between the total costs incurred under the two regimes then is a measure of the direct benefits. Although mathematical methods provide solutions of such optimization problems quite directly, the bottleneck in this instance is the meager supply of information relating to transportation services in the pre-Civil War decades. Exact methods of calculation are redundant when the quality of the inputs generate far larger margins of error; moreover, if performed for the entire railroad system the computations soon grow beyond reasonable bounds. Instead of such a rigorous approach, therefore, a more aggregative method of analysis is used in the appendix to this chapter to approximate transport cost differences. The effect of such a simplification is still further to exaggerate the computed, as opposed to the "true," benefits.

These calculations are performed for a year at the very end of the pre-Civil War period, namely 1859. In that year more than 2,500,000,000 ton-miles of freight were carried on the nation's railroads, or something like 80,000 per route mile — far short of its modern potential but large for the period. Passenger traffic was likewise not inconsiderable, well exceeding 1,500,000,000 passenger-miles.[22] The magnitude of the railroad interest was thus every bit as impressive as contemporaries claimed. Nonetheless, the social saving was relatively modest. The crux of the paradox lies in the availability of extensive water alternatives, routes with low incremental charges beyond railroad rates and with sufficient capacity to absorb railroad business.[23]

[22] Appendix A contains the calculations of ante-bellum railroad output.

[23] Even apart from waterways, the magnitude of American road construction has been grossly understated. Between 1810 and 1835 the length of post roads increased from 36,406 to 142,774 miles. By 1860 almost 200,000 miles were in operation, de-

In Table 2 are presented the receipts of those railroads in close competition with the major waterways in operation in 1859 (see Map). This first approximation explicitly omits virtually all railroads for which a water route was feasible in the large, that is, could be utilized by a complete rerouting. For example, through shipments over the Memphis and Charleston Railroad could have moved from either terminus to the other via a river and ocean voyage. A water route along the Mississippi to the mouth of the Illinois River and thence to Chicago is one logical means of competition for shipments actually sent over the Galena and Chicago; river trade to New Orleans is another. None of these possibilities is admitted. Nor are all the navigable waterways of the period considered. In sum, the extent of water competition is illustrated only by the most obvious and direct examples. Yet despite such a limitation, almost half of total rail receipts in the year 1859 were earned by railroads in proximate competition with water routes.

The obvious implication of such a result is that far from being an impossible burden, the transportation services provided by the railroads could be shifted at relatively little incremental expense, provided only that excess capacity existed. This seems likely. Consider the largest tonnage to be transferred, that of the trunk lines. The New York State canals in each of the years 1862 and 1863 moved more than one billion ton-miles, and although there were often delays, and hence considerable agitation for widening the canal, the fact remains that the actual movement was double the freight of 1859.[24] This level would absorb almost the complete 1859 ton-mileage transported by the four trunk lines, quite independent of the capacities of the

spite the substitution of railroads for many earlier post roads. (For these data see the various reports of the Postmaster General.) To be sure, many of the roads were poor and could not be used for transportation of freight or persons efficiently; on the other hand, many were widely used for both purposes — after all, it was still necessary to reach the railroad, river, or canal terminal. With water routes so abundant east of the Mississippi, in the absence of railroads the road system could have served a vital and necessary feeder function.

[24] *American Railroad Journal*, XXXVI (1863), 218, and XXXVII (1864), 244, for ton-mileage data for 1862 and 1863; for 1859, see Poor, *Railroads and Canals*, p. 361. These ton-mileage figures are for all the canals in the New York State system, but the Erie Canal was by far the predominant factor in the totals.

TABLE 2.   Receipts of railroads in competition with water routes, 1859 (thousands of dollars)

Railroad groups	Passenger	Freight	Total
Trunk lines[a]	6,951.9	14,029.8	21,746.1
Midwestern through extensions			
Lakes[b]	3,648.5	3,957.3	8,076.3
River[c]	709.2	586.9	1,389.7
Midwestern canal counties[d]	2,500.0	3,100.0	5,900.0
Southern river roads[e]	1,614.3	3,021.1	4,855.3
Coastal line[f]	4,798.8	2,335.1	7,516.3
Anthracite coal[g]	882.5	5,470.0	6,460.6
Total	21,105.2	32,500.2	55,944.3
All railroads	45,792.4	66,477.2	118,845.7

Source: Appendix A, data underlying Table 44.

[a] New York Central; Hudson River (at this time still separate); New York and Erie; Pennsylvania; Baltimore and Ohio.

[b] Buffalo and State Line; Cleveland, Painesville, and Ashtabula; Cleveland and Toledo; Michigan Southern; Michigan Central; Pittsburgh, Fort Wayne, and Chicago.

[c] Marietta and Cincinnati; Ohio and Mississippi.

[d] Estimated as freight originating rather than as the sum of individual roads. See text.

[e] Alabama and Florida; Mobile and Ohio (southern division); Mississippi and Tennessee; Mississippi Central; New Orleans, Great Northern, and Jackson; South Carolina; South Side of Virginia (competitive with Kanawha Canal).

[f] Portland, Saco, and Portsmouth; Eastern; Boston and Providence; New York, Providence, and Boston; New Haven, New London, and Stonington; New York and New Haven; Camden and Amboy; Philadelphia, Wilmington, and Baltimore; Washington Branch of Baltimore and Ohio; Richmond, Fredericksburg, and Potomac; Richmond and Petersburg; Petersburg; Seaboard and Roanoke; Wilmington and Weldon.

[g] Philadelphia and Reading; Lehigh Valley; Delaware, Lackawanna, and Western; Lackawanna and Bloomsburg; New Jersey Central; North Pennsylvania.

Chesapeake and Ohio and Pennsylvania canals for the very extensive way tonnage (primarily coal) of the Baltimore and Ohio and Pennsylvania Railroads, respectively. Lake capacity was obviously up to the task as well, as the Civil War response again indicates.

It will not do, either, to exaggerate the superiority of the interior railroads and to ignore the substantial potential of the western canals. The Ohio canals, which experienced as radical a decline as any, transported more than 1,600,000 tons in 1857; Ohio railroads carried less than three times as much and probably for shorter distances.[25] The Wabash and Erie brought more grain from the hinterland to Toledo in 1858 than any other source, and Toledo was second only to Chicago as a grain forwarder in that year.[26] The Illinois and Michigan Canal, too, was far from dormant, bringing more corn into Chicago in 1859 than its close competitor, the Rock Island, or its more distant rival, the Burlington.[27] Stow's *Capitalist's Guide* even attributed the dramatic decline in the receipts of the former road to water competition, noting "wheat, corn, and pork being the chief productions . . . , it has been found, with extreme low prices, that water communication was much the cheapest mode of reaching market . . ."[28]

Not only canals, of course, but the river systems too, remained important avenues of commerce. The Ohio Valley, in spite of increasing trade diversion, continued to ship substantial quantities southward along the Ohio. The Mississippi River enjoyed its greatest year in 1859–1860, the conjunction of a record cotton crop and favorable river rates. Apart from such prominent examples, the Alabama, Tombigbee, Pearl, and many other southern rivers were plied regularly by steamboats whose flexibility and frequent stops were advantages railroads could not surpass. With the East, such formerly consequential rivers as the Connecticut and Susquehanna had diminished in actual importance, but the Hudson River still functioned as a very effective competitor for both freight and passenger traffic. So purposely limited is Table 2 that railroads paralleling the former water courses have not been singled out.

Nor was the ocean unimportant as a commercial route. The coasting trade was the principal means of north-south interchange both before and after the north-south railroad lines had

[25] *Annual Report of the Ohio Commissioner of Statistics, 1857* (Columbus, Ohio, 1858), p. 38.

[26] *Hunt's Merchant's Magazine*, XL (1859), 698–704.

[27] Bessie L. Pierce, *History of Chicago* (New York, 1941), II, 493.

[28] Frederick H. Stow, *Capitalist's Guide and Railway Annual* (New York, 1859), p. 72.

been constructed. Although the magnitude of north-south trade is an uncertain quantity — Chapter VII goes into this — the evidence clearly suggests that much of the through freight was carried by water rather than by rail.

The final important set of waterways reflected in Table 2 are those serving the anthracite fields of Pennsylvania. There can be no question concerning the quality and quantity of water access to the major markets enjoyed by this region. The Schuylkill Navigation, Lehigh Navigation, Delaware Division Canal, Delaware and Hudson Canal, and still others, brought the southern, middle, and northern fields into efficient contact with Philadelphia, New York, and even Baltimore, the latter via the Susquehanna Canal. As late as 1859, in spite of the railroad building of the early 1850's, the coal trade was divided almost equally between water and rail shipment. The former was slightly the smaller of the two: 3,882,000 tons for railroads versus 3,592,000 tons for the canals.[29]

Table 3 presents an estimate of the direct benefits of the railroad system in 1859. The details of the calculation are presented in the appendix to this chapter. In general, for the competitive groups, the additional cost of water shipment was estimated for the specific freight actually carried by railroads where information was available. For both the trunk lines and their continuations to Chicago this was feasible. Local freight without access to water with the same efficiency as the through was segregated, and alternative costs reckoned at a higher rate. Qualitative railroad advantages like lesser risk of loss in transit, all-season service, ability to transport livestock, and more rapid delivery were all taken into account when relevant. For those groups other than the trunk lines and the shore line route, the results are much cruder and reflect, in part, extrapolation of the more careful calculations possible there. The residual group was granted only an expensive overland alternative. It should be noted that the trunks and their extensions, where detail was

[29] Calculated from the annual review of the coal trade published by the *Miners' Journal* and reprinted in the *American Railroad Journal*, XXXIII (1860), 70. By its inclined planes, the Pennsylvania Coal Company shipped 689,000 additional tons to the Delaware and Hudson Canal; these are not classified in either group.

TABLE 3. Direct benefits, 1859 (millions of dollars)

Railroad groups	Freight	Passenger	Total
Trunk lines	17.4	—	—
Midwestern through extensions			
Lake	16.5	—	—
River	2.0	—	—
Midwestern canal counties	9.3	—	—
Southern river roads	6.0	—	—
Coastal route	4.7	—	—
Anthracite roads	5.5	—	—
Subtotal	61.4	20.7	82.0
Residual	93.5	49.4	143.0
Total[a]	155.0	70.0	225.0

Source: Table 9.

[a] Detail may not add to grand total due to rounding.

the most abundant, accounted for almost 30 percent of the freight receipts in 1859, and still more of the ton-mileage.

The social saving accruing from railroad passenger traffic necessarily was reckoned even more crudely. Alternative costs for such service are not readily obtained since railroad superiority completely vanquished other forms of competition, canal and overland alike. Indication is, however, that such alternatives could have met the requirements at considerably less increased cost than was true in the transport of goods.[30] The evidence for this supposition is presented in the appendix. It is for this reason that benefits are smaller per dollar of receipts than in the calculation of the social saving implied by railroad freight business.

[30] In some contemporary calculations of direct benefits, upon the Pacific Railroad in particular, there is explicit consideration of wages lost by virtue of longer travel by nonrailroad means. See, for example, the calculations presented by S. DeWitt Bloodgood in the *American Railroad Journal*, XXXV (1862), 800. Such an addition to railroad saving is appropriate if the opportunity cost of travel is work. Since most journeys were short, this is an unnecessary complication. Its explicit inclusion would hardly affect the broad conclusions derived from Table 3.

The aggregate (and upward biased) direct benefits are thus estimated at $225 million in the year 1859. Given the gross approximation required to arrive at this figure, as well as its uncertain exaggeration, this is admittedly a shaky basis on which to analyze the importance of railroad direct benefits before the Civil War. Fortunately, other and independent evidence not only suggests that this magnitude is in the appropriate range but even allows us some estimate of the implicit upward bias. The totality of this testimony commands greater respect than any part taken individually.

The first part of this evidence consists of contemporary calculations addressed to the same question. Writing in review of the year 1856, Henry Varnum Poor, editor of the *American Railroad Journal*, estimated that railroads "undoubtedly add, in reducing the cost of transportation, three times the amount of their net earnings to the capital of the country . . ." [31] Since net earnings were conventionally regarded as equal to one-half the gross receipts (and were so estimated by Poor in the same article), such an observation implies that equivalent transportation was feasible at rates on the average two and a half times greater than railroad charges. The absolute amount of direct benefits obtained by using Poor's techniques and earnings figures comes to 188 million dollars for 1856; with our 1859 receipts the estimate for the later year is a lesser 179 million dollars, smaller because Poor's 1856 earnings estimate exceeds our 1859 measurement. Committed advocate of railroads that he was, and with a more complete grasp of data relating to American railroad development than any contemporary, Poor's opinion possesses two important properties: expertness and a nondownward subjective bias.

More explicit is a calculation appearing in the *Railroad Record* in the early 1850's. This computation of benefits created by railroads for the citizens of Ohio appeared in the following form:

Market value of railway investments	$ 35,000,000
Increased value of lands	51,000,000

[31] *American Railroad Journal*, XXX (1857), 1.

Annual gain in transportation
$7,000,000 which is interest on   100,000,000
Annual gain in interest
$1,000,000 which is interest on   15,000,000

The aggregate value was $201,000,000. "Deduct the original cost, and we have a clear gain of capital to the extent of 151 millions of dollars." [32]

The crudeness of the attempt does not invalidate it. To be sure, there is no room in such a calculation for the market value of Ohio railway securities — unless it represented capitalized monopoly profits — but its inclusion is at least understandable as a measure of current asset values in individual portfolios. And the double counting in the inclusion of both increased value of lands and savings on transportation is not peculiar to a nineteenth-century amateur at benefit-cost analysis. Otto Eckstein found it necessary to chastise the Corps of Engineers for a similar error just a few years ago: "Indirect benefits from the enhancement of property value represent double counting; the value of sites which have access to more favorable transportation methods is merely a capitalization of the lower charges on . . . transport . . ." [33] Finally, it is relevant to add that the editor of the *Railroad Record* was Edwin Mansfield who subsequently became Ohio Commissioner for Statistics and did an outstanding job in extending the frontiers of early statistical compilation.

Despite its admitted limitations, therefore, the attempt does represent another informed view of the cost saving aspects of railroad transportation. The conclusion is quite conservative, for upon receipts at the date of writing of approximately $6 million, total direct benefits are reckoned as only $8 million. Ohio, of course, had abundant water facilities — canals, Lake Erie, the Ohio River, to mention the most significant — and this undoubtedly contributes to the low estimate. Yet our comparable calculations credit the railroads of the state with far greater benefits. This divergence again bears out the contention

[32] Reprinted in *Hunt's Merchants' Magazine*, XXXI (1854), 502.

[33] Otto Eckstein, *Water Resource Development: The Economics of Project Evaluation* (Cambridge, Mass., 1958), p. 178. The failure of the two alternative methods to yield the same results in this instance may be charged both to inaccuracy and the nonexistence of an equilibrium world.

that the $225 million estimate of benefits for the entire railroad system in 1859 is a rather extreme upper limit.

We can garner further information from the increase in land values during the decade of the 1850's, the first period for which such data are available. Between 1850 and 1860 total land in farms increased from 294 to 407 million acres; valuation of farm lands and buildings showed a more than proportionate rise from $3.1 billion to $6.4 billion.[34] One important cause of this dramatic increase in land values was the transportation revolution of the 1850's. During that decade the railroad brought initial access to market for many areas heretofore without such advantage and also improved communication for regions already engaged in commercial production. To the land initially yielding zero rent, and indeed with negative value, lower transport costs brought returns for the first time; to the land already in cultivation they brought still greater bounties in proportion to the economic distance from market.[35] The difference in rents between the beginning and end of the decade is a measure of the change in the flow of direct benefits to agriculture over the same interval; capitalized, it is the rise in land value attributable to transportation advance.

Not all of the observed $3.3 billion increase in land values emanates from this source. Land prices were also affected by other influences, chief among them investment in land improvement, increased demand for agricultural products, and expectations of future appreciation of land.[36] Unfortunately, we cannot precisely account for the contribution of these other factors at such an aggregative level, nor can we include them all. But

[34] *Historical Statistics*, p. 239.

[35] If the expansion in supply had caused market price to decline it is possible that rents might have diminished on lands close to market while increasing on those farther away. Then the algebraic sum of changed rents would understate transport benefits. For the 1850's this objection does not seem to carry much weight. Increasing supply was met by increasing demand so that prices did not decline, and land values in New England actually rose, albeit at a much lesser rate than in the interior.

[36] Changing factor proportions, while a potential consideration, is not as important as the substantial expansion in land supply suggests. The agricultural labor force grew almost as rapidly, so that the number of improved acres per worker increased only by 10 percent.

we can gain some notion of the maximum contribution of reduced distribution costs by subtracting for two changes that can be reasonably well specified: investment in improvements and commodity price increases. Since we know expectations worked as another positive influence — the ratio of land values to current income was greater in 1859 than at any other nineteenth-century census benchmark — it follows that we get an exaggerated estimate of the contribution of transportation. Even this affords some check on the order of magnitude involved.

The more direct adjustment is the deduction for investment in land improvement. Since something like 50 million acres of land were improved during the decade, or almost a 50 percent increase in the supply of cropland, we are dealing with a potent influence upon aggregate land values. The expense of bringing land into production varied with its character: timbered land required laborious clearing, while simple breaking of the prairie sod was all that was needed there. Despite the first incursions into the prairie during the decade, far the largest part of acreage improved in the 1850's remained woodland, with its accordant expense. Specifically, Primack classifies 39.7 million acres as forest and only 9.1 million as open, and places the labor inputs at 33 man-days per acre for the former against only 1.5 for the latter.[37] This estimate for clearing of woodland undoubtedly is high. A full 13 days for stump pulling is credited — based upon a single Massachusetts observation in 1841 — while for the very common brushland along the timbered edges of the prairie this additional task was unnecessary. Even in more heavily wooded areas it was not unusual to leave the stumps in the ground to decay while the field was worked. The Primack labor input as it stands, in conjunction with going wages for agricultural labor, implies a money cost of some $30 to prepare an acre for farming, or far more than other estimates suggest.[38]

[37] Martin L. Primack, "Land Clearing under Nineteenth-Century Techniques: Some Preliminary Calculations," *Journal of Economic History*, XXII (1962), 484–497.

[38] See the estimates ranging from $5 to $20 an acre in Clarence H. Danhof, "Farm-Making Costs and the 'Safety Valve': 1850–1860," *Journal of Political Economy*, XLIX (1941), 339–341. Gallman's apparent reconciliation of Primack's

On the weight of this evidence, the average input for woodland
appropriate to this decade has been modified to 20 man-days
per acre. At this lower level the total expenditure still reaches
$800 million, or more than the investment in railroads over the
same interval. Nor was this all; fencing and buildings also were
constructed. These costs were kept down, however, by the ready
supply of materials on the timbered acreage that made up the
bulk of the total. Fencing required only $3 of labor input per
acre on forested land against a sum twice as large on the prairie;
enclosures therefore led to the relatively small investment of $0.2
billion. Building added approximately the same amount.[39] Considering additional improvements to land already in cultivation,
one anticipates increased land values during the decade of at
least $1.2 billion, quite apart from other considerations.

A second factor which operated with great effect during this
particular decade was the pronounced increase in agricultural
prices, the result both of general price inflation and of improved
terms of trade vis-à-vis other sectors. From 1849 to 1859 the
total money supply increased from approximately $354 million
to about $767 million on the impulse of the California gold dis-
coveries.[40] It requires no rigid adherence to the quantity theory
of money to anticipate the direction of the effect upon the price
level. In the case of agriculture this was reinforced by relative
price increases due largely to stronger foreign demand. Warren
and Pearson's index of wholesale prices of farm products went
from a value of 62 to one of 82 between 1848 and 1859 while all

labor input with Ezra C. Seaman's figure of $11 is not convincing since Gallman
uses an agricultural wage including board as a measure of the monetary cost,
whereas the value of board ought to be added to the wage. See Gallman's discussion
of Primack's paper, *Journal of Economic History*, XXII (1962), 516.

[39] Fencing costs vary inversely with the size of the inclosure so any average value
per acre is difficult to determine. Danhof, "Farm-Making Costs" (pp. 345–346),
indicates limits in wooded areas from $224 for a 160-acre farm to $224 for a 40-acre
farm. Basis for the $6 charge on the prairie is found in the report of the Iowa Census
of 1862 that $26 million had been spent for fencing fewer than 5 million acres. See
Clarence H. Danhof, "The Fencing Problem in the Eighteen-Fifties," *Agricultural
History*, XVIII (1944), 172. The building estimate is based upon the reports in
Danhof, "Farm-Making Costs," pp. 353–354.

[40] *Historical Statistics*, pp. 625, 647.

commodities advanced only from 82 to 95.[41] In turn, land values reflected the larger money incomes.[42]

It is not an easy task to disentangle these exogenous demand effects from the increased prices due to lower transport costs. Reduction to national constant prices removes too much; if some farmers did not experience higher prices the capitalized transport gain would be nil. What is needed, rather, is a measure of price change in some final market, one that is not confounded with improving regional terms of trade as access to the interior was eased. There are two possibilities here. A general price index has the advantage of wide breadth and consequent accurate measure of inflationary tendencies; its failing is an inadequate weight to the more favorable sectoral terms of trade. An agricultural price index may contain more error of measurement, but it will come closer to capturing the total impact of demand upon agricultural incomes.

Both approaches yield similar results, with the divergence in the predicted direction. Wholesale prices in general increase something more than 15 percent in both Philadelphia and New York between 1849 and 1859.[43] Bezanson's index of agricultural commodities in the Philadelphia market shows an increase of 24 percent, higher than the average rise because of agriculture's relative improvement.[44] By contrast and exactly as one would anticipate, all prices at Cincinnati, an agricultural marketing center, were up 40 percent over the same interval as the transportation differential between West and East narrowed; agricultural prices alone climbed 60 percent.[45]

Such price increases between the two single years 1849 and 1859, while they affected the incomes of those years, need not

[41] *Historical Statistics*, p. 115. 1910–1914 = 100.

[42] At least one contemporary recognized the need to adjust for price changes before claiming the residual increase for transport progress. See the reprint from the *Railroad Record* in the *American Railroad Journal*, XXXII (1859), 91.

[43] The indexes were presented in testimony of George Rogers Taylor and Ethel D. Hoover in Hearings on Employment, Growth and Price Levels before the Joint Economic Committee, 86th Congress, 1st Session, pt. 2, *Historical and Comparative Rates of Production, Productivity, and Prices*, pp. 394–397.

[44] *Historical Statistics*, p. 119.

[45] *Historical Statistics*; Thomas S. Berry, *Western Prices before 1861* (Cambridge, Mass., 1943), p. 564.

have influenced land valuation proportionately. Although the 1849 and 1859 crops were the last ones available by which to judge the net product of land, only if the price changes between the two years were expected to persist into the future would capitalizations have been adjusted accordingly. If they were viewed as merely temporary, land prices would hardly alter; if the rate of change was compounded, the present valuation would take such prospects into account. As a better measure of the price effects alone, therefore, a moving average of prices of the previous five years, ending in 1850 and 1860, is proposed. For the two general wholesale price indices increases of 17 and 18 percent are indicated; for the agricultural price series, 25 percent.

An adjustment of some 20 percent in agricultural land values is suggested by these data. Although larger than the 10 percent allowance made by the editor of the *Railroad Record* in 1858 in his somewhat similar calculation, there seems no justification for the lower figure. Accepting the former, the sizable sum of $1.3 billion represents the contribution of demand to the total observed increase in value of $3.3 billion.

The residual for technological change in transportation is now limited to $800 million. To this we must add $196 million for the increased value of livestock inventories due to better access to market. The resulting total is only $1 billion. To those who boggle at the thought of such a small remainder, especially as a maximum, I need only point to the large increases in land value in the southern states. There, where railroads were less cost saving owing to efficient water alternatives, one third of the national increase in valuation occurred, with but a one-fourth increase in improved acreage. Higher cotton prices, not transportation, were responsible. This is not the only supporting indication, moreover. A further direct test is possible.

Prior to making that, it is best to transform the change in land values to a change in annual flows. At an interest rate of 6 percent, not far from the mortgage rates then current, the increase in the stream of rents between 1850 and 1860 comes to $60 million. Other rates would affect the result proportionally, although rates much above 7 percent or much below 5 percent are difficult to defend. Willford King, however, does argue for a 4 percent rate to allow for expectations of rising land values. It is not surprising, therefore, that his estimate of total increased returns to land over the decade comes to only $99 million.[46] The implied share for transport improvement would then be far smaller than our own $60 million.

This $60 million is an overestimate of the increased size of annual agricultural income due to lesser transport expense. It is also possible to calculate the same increase in income more directly. Changed regional terms of trade over this period largely reflect improved transport conditions: western farmers far from the market received relatively more for their output than eastern farmers closer in. Calculation of the effect upon income of the more favorable later terms of trade then will approximate the change due to better transportation. Absolute changes in the price level do not enter since only relative variation counts.

Table 4 exemplifies this approach for wheat. If 1848 state relative prices are applied to 1860 quantities, the crop value is 10.2 percent smaller than simple use of the 1860 average price yields. Conversely, the use of 1862 relative prices and the 1850 crop quantities provides a hypothetical crop value 15.6 percent larger than when 1850 national average price is the multiplier.[47] Despite only partial coverage in both years, the results are not substantially affected thereby. The largest southern producer was Virginia, a state in which prices were probably close to the average in both years; and prices in California, emerging as a very large producer for the first time in 1860, were above the average due to the substantial local demand, not better location vis-à-vis the eastern market.

The 10 to 15 percent difference in value of this crop before and after the advent of the railroad is largely to be attributed to

[46] Willford I. King, *The Wealth and Income of the People of the United States* (New York, 1915), p. 157. His estimate of agricultural rent is found on p. 262.
[47] That the calculation using earlier year relative prices and later year quantities would show a larger deviation might be anticipated. This would occur if areas where relative prices were low in 1850 showed the more rapid increase in quantity by 1860. Although there are such tendencies, they are not sufficiently strong. Note in Table 4 that Pennsylvania's product decreases instead of increases, Ohio's remains constant, etc.

TABLE 4. Regional wheat price changes, 1848–1862

State[a]	Crop, 1850 (thousands of bushels)	State relative, 1862[b] (percent of national average price, 1862)	Crop, 1860 (thousands of bushels)	State relative, 1848[c] (percent of national average price, 1848)
Me.	296.3	171.3	233.9	158.0
N.H.	185.7	169.1	239.0	158.0
Vt.	536.0	149.2	431.1	158.0
Mass.	31.2	177.9	119.8	171.8
Conn.	41.8	159.1	52.4	171.8
R.I.	0.0	165.7	1.1	171.8
N.Y.	13,121.5	138.1	8,681.1	129.4
N.J.	1,601.2	143.6	1,763.1	135.1
Pa.	15,367.7	134.8	13,045.2	114.5
Del.	482.5	123.8	912.9	114.5
Md.	4,494.7	153.6	6,103.5	114.5
Ohio	14,487.4	106.1	14,532.6	91.6
Ind.	6,214.4	97.2	15,219.1	68.7
Ill.	9,414.6	84.0	24,159.5	80.2
Mich.	4,925.9	110.5	8,313.2	91.6
Wis.	4,286.1	86.2	15,812.6	72.1
Iowa	1,530.6	76.2	8,433.2	72.1
Mo.	2,981.7	85.1	4,227.6	72.1
Total	79,999.3		122,280.9	

Value of 1850 Crop at 1850 average price ($0.80) $ 64.0 million
Value of 1850 Crop at 1862 relative prices:[d] $ 74.0 million

Value of 1860 Crop at 1860 average price ($0.93) $113.7 million
Value of 1860 Crop at 1848 relative prices:[e] $102.1 million

Source: Crops: *Census of Agriculture, 1860.* National Prices: Gallman, "Commodity Output," pp. 46–52; *Report of the Commissioner of Patents, 1848.* Relative Prices: *Report of the Commissioner of Patents, 1848,* House Doc. No. 59, 30th Congress, 2nd Session, pp. 647–655; *Report of the Commissioner of Agriculture, 1862,* House Doc. No. 78, 37th Congress, 3rd Session, pp. 577–587.

[a] Certain states, principally in the South, were excluded because comparable material for the two dates was unavailable. The coverge encompasses about 80 percent in 1850 and 70 percent in 1860.

[b] National average price ($0.91) calculated by summing product of 1862 crops in individual states and state prices and dividing by total crop.

[c] National average price ($0.87) calculated by summing product of 1850 corps in individual states and state prices and dividing by total crop.

[d] 1862 relative prices are equal to 1850 average price times 1862 relatives.

[e] 1848 relative prices are equal to 1860 average price times 1848 relatives.

the innovation. Yet it would be wrong to mark up all agricultural income by such a margin. Wheat is a limiting case; it was the commercial crop par excellence and the acme of regional specialization. Dairy products showed much less regional variation in price, owing to lesser specialization; likewise, livestock prices, both beef and pork, had a smaller range of variation, not to mention cotton.[48] These products account for more than half of the agricultural value added in 1859. In the same way, increased valuation of all output, including the substantial proportion domestically consumed, overstates actual benefits. If goods were never shipped, economies of lower costs were never realized. A crude estimate suggests that perhaps 70 percent of agricultural products, by weight, never moved by waterway or railroad in 1859.[49] Then 30 percent of the lower 11.4 percent increase in income recorded in the wheat calculations is a more accurate extrapolation of these findings to total agricultural income.[50] The estimated increase for 1859 on this basis is ap-

[48] See the discussion of regional prices in the 1848 *Report of the Commissioner of Patents*, House Exec. Doc. No. 59, 30th Congress, 2nd Session (Washington, 1849), pp. 673–685, and for cotton prices, p. 659.

[49] Total agricultural output entering into gross product in 1859 weighed approximately 35.1 million tons (excluding forest products), as computed from Marvin W. Towne and Wayne D. Rasmussen, "Farm Gross Product and Gross Investments in the Nineteenth Century," in *Trends in the American Economy in the Nineteenth Century*, National Bureau of Economic Research, Inc., Studies in Income and Wealth, vol. 24 (Princeton, 1960), pp. 255–315. Ton-mileage in western and southern states and specifically agricultural ton-mileage in the East add to 1.2 billion in 1859 and is an estimate of agricultural freight to the extent that agricultural commodities shipped in the East offset nonagricultural tonnage in the other regions. An average haul of about 80 miles was probably involved versus something closer to 60 miles for all commodities (as estimated from the *Report on Finances, 1855–56*, Exec. Doc. No. 2, 34th Congress, 2nd Session [Washington, 1856], after correction for the erroneous entry of the Buffalo and Corning Railroad; see Appendix A). This implies a total agricultural tonnage of 15,000,000 of which perhaps half represented duplication. (Based on similar ratios reported at the Eleventh Census in 1890 and by the Interstate Commerce Commission later.) To the 7.5 million tons of agricultural freight originating on railroads must be added perhaps another 3.0 million tons originating on canals and rivers; the Erie carried 1.1 million tons of western grain in 1859 (see Table 33) and cotton deliveries of almost as much traveled by water. This 10.5 million tons is 0.30 of the total agricultural production.

[50] To the extent that there is a correlation between the increase in relative prices and the proportion shipped, use of an average price increase and an average shipment ratio will understate the gain. On the other hand the 11.4 percent increase may overstate the average improvement for all commodities.

proximately $50 million. It is striking how close this comes to the previous $60 million estimate, and how it diverges in the right direction. Such agreement is a persuasive testimonial to the accuracy of the order of magnitude involved.

This $50 million, as it stands, is not yet comparable to the direct estimate of benefits of Table 3.[51] In the first place, it measures the gains of all transport cost reductions, railroad and non-railroad. Thus the downward trend in canal rates during the decade yielded more favorable relative prices just as surely as did the introduction of the railroad; and while such a trend was closely related to rail competition, this represents an indirect benefit rather than a direct gain of lower cost rail service. The effect of this reduction in canal charges can be approximated by a calculation of the saving on the New York state system alone, since this was the dominant carrier. Had the 1859 ton-mileage moved at 1849 rates, it would have cost shippers $8.7 million; in fact, the charges were no more than $3.5 million.[52] Corresponding reductions on the Ohio, Illinois and Michigan, and Wabash canals contributed in similar fashion, but their small outputs can safely be neglected. Ignored at greater risk is the lake trade with its significant and growing role in internal commerce. Less exact information on the level of activity and the change in rates over time makes the adjustment more hazardous. Doubling the $5 million figure calculated above for the Erie route will not put us very far off the mark, however.[53] No further allowance for river commerce is necessary

[51] Since there are reasons to believe the previous estimate based on changing land values is overstated due to inclusion of other influences, we will use this lower $50 million value in the subsequent discussion.

[52] Computed by taking the 1859 ton-mileage figure for the New York canals presented in Poor, *Railroads and Canals*, and the 1849 flour rates presented in the Auditor's report for 1858, as reprinted in the *American Railroad Journal*, XXXII (1859), 177. The 1859 costs were estimated as twice the tolls since freight charges were approximately equal to them. Since the 1849 flour rate was possibly lower than the average for that year, there is a slight, but insignificant, downward bias in the imputed gains to water transportation.

[53] Such a doubling has more to recommend it than mere simplicity. The largest part of the ton-mileage on the canals was from out-of-state produce; a 6:1 ratio prevailed in 1859. All the interstate commerce on the canals, and slightly more, was delivered by the lake trade. Hence the volumes are approximately the same. In the second instance, the division of freight charges between canal and lake was almost equal, although with the Hudson River part of the journey included, the

since there was no equivalent downward march of steamboat rates.[54]

The remaining $40 million requires further adjustment. As it stands, it understates the flow of railroad direct benefits in 1859 for two reasons: first, it takes into account reductions only on agricultural shipments;[55] and second, it deals only with incremental benefits between 1849 and 1859. Even after addition for these exclusions it is likely to fall short of the direct estimate developed in Table 3. This alternative method is free from the liberal and positive errors of measurement inherent in the previous figure, and also, because it relies upon actual market responses to lower transport rates, largely avoids the terminal quantity bias of imputed calculation. As such, after alteration, it should provide a better approximation of "true" benefits.

The required adjustments can be effected with fair success. The exclusion of the nonagricultural sector is the more important of the two. Unfortunately, no commodity breakdown of the flow of rail traffic is available until far past our period; even in the 1880 census only a tonnage, not a ton-mileage, classification is presented. The best that we can do is to rely upon a rough sectional distribution of freight services, an obvious distortion since both eastern and western railroads transported the whole gamut of agricultural products, minerals, and manufactures. Of the total of almost two and a half billion ton-miles transported by railroad in 1859 approximately 37 percent were in the West and the South; the addition of the specifically agricultural tonnage of the eastern trunk lines and other New York railroads yields a revised estimate in excess of 45 percent.[56] If the agricultural freight in the eastern states was an approximate

cost of shipping from Buffalo to New York was slightly greater. The only additional assumption is a proportional decline in both lake and canal rates. This one seems justifiable as well: from 1854 to 1858 there was an apparent reduction of charges for long voyages from 5 mills per ton-mile to 3 mills. See George R. Taylor, *The Transportation Revolution, 1815–1860* (New York, 1951), p. 442; *American Railroad Journal*, XXXII (1859), 197.

[54] Berry, *Western Prices*, chapter iii.

[55] This is not totally correct. The change in agricultural land values due to transportation also reflects locational advantages of consumption as well as production. For practical purposes this offset cannot be taken into account, but is not likely to be serious since we use the lower $50 million estimate.

[56] New York State railroad ton-mileage was distributed to agricultural commod-

offset to the nonagricultural freight in the other regions, this implies that 55 percent of the ton-mileage was nonagricultural at the time. Because agricultural tonnage was more universal and also probably had a larger average haul, we may be crediting too much elsewhere. But in the absence of further information there is little that can be done. The benefits upon these remaining 1.4 billion ton-miles therefore must be added to the $40 million estimate for agricultural products so far obtained.

The average rail contribution on this large residual is a matter of obvious importance to the final outcome. Yet again there is little to go on. We can isolate the transportation of coal, however. The ton-miles on the Pennsylvania, the Baltimore and Ohio, and the Philadelphia and Reading railroads together approximate 280 million; other rail carriage from the anthracite region accounts for at least 100 million more.[57] As is argued in detail in the appendix to this chapter the availability of alternative and parallel water transport limited the savings in this trade considerably. Only one additional cent per ton-mile above actual cost is equivalent to a virtual doubling of prevailing rates and represents an adequate adjustment. For the remaining two thirds of output, an average differential of five additional cents is more than adequate. Fully a fifth of the total was carried by the trunk lines at much smaller real advantage, implying a generous allowance for the residual. With railroad rates for merchandise higher in the first instance, the aggregate nonagricultural ton-mileage probably overstated, and the calculations biased upward by use of terminal quantities in any event, this choice is hardly likely to understate railroad benefits.

The net result of these deliberations is to add $54 million to

---

ities in proportion to the tonnage of vegetable foods, products of animals, and other agricultural products. Since a longer average length of carriage of agricultural commodities probably prevailed, this biases the estimate slightly downward. A similar procedure was used to secure the ton-mileage of livestock and flour for the Baltimore and Ohio. The Pennsylvania Railroad ton-mileage was estimated by separating out through and local agricultural shipments and applying the appropriate average haul to each.

[57] Ton-mileage is estimated from company reports for the Pennsylvania and the Reading, but is directly available for the Baltimore and Ohio; for the magnitude of other railroad service from the anthracite region see the annual review of the coal trade reprinted in the *American Railroad Journal*, XXXIII (1860), 70.

the previous assessment. The final addition consists of an estimate of savings on agricultural shipments in 1849 since the
earlier analysis related only to the increment during the 1850's.
This is small simply because it was not until the 1850's that railroads emerged as significant carriers of agricultural produce:
from 1849 to 1859 ton-mileage in the West increased almost
fortyfold while the national total advanced 600 percent. With
all railroad ton-mileage in 1849 only a minor matter, and with
high average charges too, the level of agricultural benefits did
not exceed $10 million in that year.[58]

This second calculation of direct benefits yields a final total
for freight of $104 million, or $51 million less than the previous
estimate. In the first instance, I am inclined to emphasize the
similarity rather than the divergence. What both estimates
independently affirm is a level of benefits clearly less than $200
million and probably closer to $100 million. In the second in-
stance, it is easy to reconcile the two by reference to the potential magnitude of the terminal quantity bias. Suppose that the
demand curve for freight transportation were of unitary elasticity in the range from 15 cents to 2 to 3 cents a ton-mile. Then
the bias implicit in use of the later output is at least $34.3 mil-
lion.[59] This assumption is not unreasonable. With transportation
costs a very large proportion of price for producers of bulk commodities, with the economy oriented to agriculture at that time,

[58] Total railroad output in 1849 was around 400 million ton-miles (Appendix A).
If ⅓ were agricultural and the average savings as much as 7½ cents, the result is a
$10 million saving. With railroad rates as high as 4 and 5 cents a ton-mile for agri-
cultural commodities, the 7½-cent differential is abundant; it implies that only ⅓
of the agricultural commodities shipped by rail could have been shipped by water.
On the other side, alternative assumptions would not reduce the absolute amount
of the saving significantly.

[59] This result is based upon linear demand curves. The observed percentage reduction in price yields the predicted increase in quantity, given the elasticity. The
difference between the area under the hypothetical demand curve and the calculated
benefits measures the bias. In this particular case, the freight receipts of railroads
competitive with the horse and wagon were roughly $34 million. At a rate of 4 cents
per ton-mile the actual output is 850 million. At a price of 15 cents, with unitary
elasticity, shipments would have been 227 million ton-miles. The terminal quantity
method yields an estimate of direct benefits of $93.5 million, the entry in Table 3.
The true benefits are $59.2 million under these assumptions and thus the bias $34.3
million. The relative importance of the bias is smaller for the water-competitive
groups because the reduction in transport cost due to the railroad is also smaller.

and with location a very obvious choice, elasticity of this limited magnitude over such a wide range does not seem extreme. Perhaps a still more powerful argument is the robustness of the results. If the appropriate elasticity is 2, the error increases to more than $41 million; if 0.5 it shrinks to a minimum of $22 million. For any reasonable assumption, between one half and four fifths of the difference between the estimates is eliminated. What holds for freight applies equally well to passenger travel. Proportional exaggeration is involved there as well.[60]

In sum, then, this discussion suggests that true direct benefits in 1859 probably did not exceed $175 million nor fall much below $150 million. Two methods of calculation, as well as contemporary observation, affirm such a level. Given the variety and the independence of the evidence brought to bear upon this subject such coincidence is reassuring if not conclusive. At any rate, for the purposes of interpretation, it is reliability in the large, not the small, that counts.

The Importance of Social Saving

These direct benefits of $175 million, say, are just about 4 percent of 1859 gross national product.[61] For an innovation still in its infancy, this clearly is an impressive contribution. The nature of the comparison exaggerates, however. A single year chosen at the end of the period fails to convey accurately the character of the contribution over the entire thirty-odd years railroad services were available. Nor does such a simple ratio give adequate notice to the investment required to achieve these results; with unlimited inputs of resources any activity might claim a large effect upon total income. Only if all the railroad investment would have flowed into other transport agencies, and these latter were still the inefficient alternatives we have assumed them to be, is this qualification unnecessary. But we have seen that excess capacity was available without such a large effort.

[60] In addition, the potential error of measurement is substantial. If an additional 10 percent of receipts were grouped with those competitive with water routes, the estimate of direct benefits would decline by more than 4 percent.

[61] Based on Robert E. Gallman's estimate of gross national product of $4.17 billion in his "Gross National Product."

Framing the problem in terms of a rate of return calculation satisfies the objections raised above, and is a more useful approach. Table 5 summarizes the relevant data, which now in-

TABLE 5. Social return of direct benefits to railroad investment (millions of 1860 dollars)

Annual averages	Net capital formation	Direct benefits	Net earnings	Gross returns	Gross returns less net capital formation
1828–1835	4.5	0.3	0.2	0.5	− 4.0
1836–1840	14.0	3.9	2.0	5.8	− 8.2
1841–1845	7.0	14.5	7.1	21.6	14.6
1846–1850	27.9	31.4	15.9	46.2	18.3
1851–1855	72.1	78.7	31.2	109.9	37.8
1856–1860	48.1	155.7	48.5	204.2	156.1

Source: Net Capital Formation: Table 54, Appendix B.

Direct benefits: Interpolation by a constant percentage rate of benchmarks of 0.1 in 1830, 6 in 1839, 30 in 1849, 130 in 1855–1856, and 175 in 1859, and extrapolation to 1860. Benchmarks prior to 1859 were estimated by applying slightly smaller benefits per dollar of receipts than were found in 1859, in recognition of the greater concentration of receipts upon water conpetitive routes at the earlier dates. All benefits were converted to 1860 dollars by application of the general Hoover-Taylor price index published in the Joint Economic Committee Hearings on Employment, Growth, and Price Levels, pt. 2, *Historical and Comparative Rates of Production, Productivity and Prices*, 86th Congress, 1st Session, p. 395.

Net earnings: Interpolation by constant percentage rates of the net receipts data of Appendix A, deflated as described above.

Gross returns: Sum of net earnings and direct benefits. (May not add due to rounding.)

clude private earnings as well. Although certainly not precise, what with the uncertain level of benefits at earlier dates and the necessary of extrapolating between benchmarks, the picture it portrays is probably reasonably accurate: negative returns in the earliest years as the rate of growth of investment more than kept pace with transportation services, a period of increasing benefits partially counteracted by the investment surge of the late 1840's and early 1850's and at last, as the system reached completion, a quinquennium of extremely rapid output growth that dominated investment. Despite this long delayed fruition, viewed over the entire ante-bellum era, the railroad still yielded a very satisfactory internal rate of return of 15 percent. Only an alternative investment with a larger return over this span would have led to higher incomes than actually observed with railroads — so far as their direct benefits alone are concerned. Any investment yielding less would have proved inferior, but not as much as the crude comparison of direct benefits indicates. What is relevant is the foregone opportunity. With an investment with a similar time profile, but earning only 7 percent, the contribution to 1859 income would have been $133.6 million instead of the railroad's actual $226.5.[62] The difference is a matter of some $90 million instead of the crude $175 million with which we began.

That railroads did so well must be credited to the last few years of the period. Had the horizon been 1839 instead of 1860, it is obvious a rejection of the innovation is indicated in favor of some alternative with less distant pay-offs. Indeed, virtually up to the mid-1850's the same conclusion is valid. This concentration of returns has another side to it. Because they coincided with an interval of resource redundancy, the potential increase in income they measure is very likely one that was never in fact fully realized. That is, while more inputs would have been required to transport goods and persons in 1859 without railroads, many of these inputs were idle in any event. Had they been utilized, nonrailroad national income in 1859 could have stood exactly at the level it reached without any assistance from higher productivity in the transport sector.

There is little doubt concerning the depressed status of the late 1850's. Gallman's output estimates indicate an annual rate of growth of 6.8 percent from 1849 to 1854, but only 4.0 percent from 1854 to 1859. The per capita data are even more revealing since they determine whether the increase kept pace with the

[62] The $133.6 million estimate is obtained from solution of the equation

$$\Sigma_t \frac{(kGR_t - NI_t)}{(1.07)^t} = 0,$$

where k is the proportionality factor applied to gross returns that reduces the internal rate of return to 7 percent; $133.6 million thus equals $k \cdot$ $226.5 million.

available labor supply. They are striking in their contrast: there was a gain from $107 to $127 between 1849 and 1854, followed by a modest rise to $134 in 1859.[63] Taylor describes the inevitable accompaniment: "Widespread unemployment appeared in eastern cities and, reaching serious proportions in 1858, placed unprecedented burdens on relief agencies and, as in 1839, led to public demonstration of labor unrest."[64]

In such a context the railroad was a mixed blessing. Horace Greeley made the same point when he observed that railroads were simply not needed for transportation under prevailing conditions.[65] All the potential gain need not have been negated for the point to remain a valid one. If benefits actually realized were one-half their potential value only for the *three* years 1857 through 1859, the calculated rate of return over the *entire* period declines by about 1 percent. What this all comes to is a much smaller role for railroad transport advantages during the antebellum decades than first impressions suggested. Because of the extensive railroad investment required to achieve them, they were a relatively expensive product that other investments could come reasonably close to duplicating. Because they were concentrated at the end of the period they posed no threat to development earlier, and when benefits did come forth in substantial amounts, they then were not crucially necessary to maintain the levels of output actually attained. There is an element of irony in this since aggregate demand was weak owing to the slowing down of railroad resource absorption; yet with continued demand by that sector, net benefits would have been correspondingly diminished.

What made railroad carrying services ultimately dispensable was the prior development of two other innovations, the canal and the steamboat. These lowered transport costs far more than the railroad in its turn. The absolute benefits of canals alone compare favorably with the later railroad achievement. One estimate by Segal places the upper bound of resource saving

[63] Gallman, "Gross National Product," product in 1860 constant dollars, and *Historical Statistics*, p. 7, for population.
[64] Taylor, *Transportation Revolution*, p. 350.
[65] Quoted in George W. Van Vleck, *The Panic of 1857* (New York, 1943), p. 107.

in the early 1840's at $66 million;[66] reduced to $40 million, say, to compensate for its upward bias, these still come to around 3 percent of gross national product then. And they were obtained both with a shorter lag and a much smaller investment. Hunter does not quantify direct benefits similarly, but he has no doubt concerning the over-all impact of the steamboat: "the growth of the West and the use of steamboat transportation were inseparable; they were geared together and each was dependent upon the other." [67] The rapid eclipse of both of these agencies by the railroad from the 1850's on should not obscure the magnitude or the timeliness of their contributions.

This note of disparagement should not be misinterpreted. It applies only to the necessity of the innovation. Railroad direct benefits were beginning to make a difference by 1860, and that era laid the foundation for later resource saving of quite substantial proportions. The growth of output in the 1850's, when railroad transport services began to overshadow those of canals and steamboats, foreshadowed even greater future dominance. Far-reaching institutional changes, like uniformity of gauge, interchange of rolling stock, et cetera, and rapid technological advances like the substitution of steel rails, tripling of locomotive power, and still more rapid growth in freight car capacity, naturally multiplied such later benefits far beyond mere extrapolation of the ante-bellum potential. Railroad ton-mileage grew far faster than any measure of output, and by century's end it was more than forty times its 1859 level.[68] All the while, of course, railroads were being built in areas where alternative transport by horse and wagon was prohibitively expensive. David Wells, with his characteristic perception, aptly suggested the significance of railroad direct benefits for late nineteenth-century America:

The railroad freight service of the United States for 1887 was therefore equivalent to carrying a thousand tons one mile for every person, or every ton a thousand miles. The average cost of this service was

---

[66] In Goodrich, *Canals and Development*, p. 243.
[67] Louis C. Hunter, *Steamboats on the Western Rivers: An Economic and Technological History* (Cambridge, Mass., 1949), p. 32.
[68] Railroad ton-mileage stood at 124 million in 1899. *Historical Statistics*, p. 431.

about $10 per annum per person. But if it had been entirely performed by horsepower, even under the most favorable of old-time conditions, its cost would have been about $200 to each inhabitant, which in turn would represent an expenditure greater than the entire value of the then annual product of the country.[69]

Wells's exclusion of water alternatives at that advanced date considerably overstates the benefits, but does not alter the picture of relative expansion. Some part, a large part, of that achievement was the delayed influence of pre-Civil War investment.

This conjecture of substantial later gains is apparently at odds with Robert W. Fogel's research relating to direct benefits in 1890.[70] He suggests a maximum total contribution in the transport of freight in that year of $560 million, implying that, on average, unit costs by water and wagon would have been less than double actual charges. By contrast, these ante-bellum results suggest a margin of railroad superiority more than twice as great. Applied to 1890 freight receipts, the 1859 differential yields an estimate of benefits of $1.5 billion; if passengers be added in — Fogel excludes them — the extrapolation yields a total saving of $1.8 billion. The issue is a considerable one, the difference between a contribution of less than 5 percent of gross national product in 1890 and one of at least 15 percent, since it is likely the railroad advantage actually increased over time.

Fogel reaches his aggregate estimate by extrapolating his results for the agricultural sector alone, after allowance for construction of new inland water routes and improvement of roads. There are reasons to be wary of the procedure.

In the first instance, and most importantly, the subtraction from railroad benefits of the gains accruing from the hypothetical investment in canals and roads subtly alters the analysis. The contribution of the railroad sector no longer is reckoned as the transport savings it provided in historical fact, but as its potential advantage in a very special, and nonexistent, world.

[69] David A. Wells, *Recent Economic Changes* (New York, 1890), pp. 41–42.
[70] A preliminary statement has appeared in his "Quantitative Approach" and a fuller version is contained in his *Railroads*, chaps. ii and iii, especially. The extension of the agricultural results to the aggregate can be found on pp. 219–224.

The difference in conception has large implications. It is sufficient to transform 1890 benefits in the transport of agricultural commodities from $410 to $214 million, with a proportional reduction in the aggregate estimate based on this result.

There is nothing wrong with building such hypothetical worlds as can be imagined as likely without the innovation of the railroad. But their juxtaposition with the actual circumstances of 1890 then measure the unique attributes of the innovation rather than the realized consequences of the investment in railroads that actually occurred. Distinct objectives legitimately give rise to distinct numerical results. Yet, this unobserved history is not without its problems. Where does one stop? At one juncture, Fogel even hints that the presence of the railroad delayed the development of the internal combustion engine, thus even further reducing its contributions. Why not electric power too, or even technological changes in manufacturing and agriculture? At a lower level of generality, there also is the danger of engineering speculations. Although Fogel has carefully studied the feasibility of such hypothetical investment as he advocates, the fact is that such projects were not built despite their large potential social return. It is not obvious that such a result represented widespread misallocation of resources and not wisdom. Recall that so prominent an engineer as Loammi Baldwin assured in 1826 that a canal through the Berkshires was eminently practical.

The inherent difficulties of measuring what never occurred make me skeptical as well of the $410 million Fogel puts forth as the maximum direct benefits actually realized in the rail conveyance of agricultural produce. The implications of his assumed water and wagon rates do not seem always to be borne out empirically. Here is one case in point. With Fogel's rates, it would have proved cheaper for farmers within four miles of a navigable waterway to have shipped by water regardless of the access of railroads. The counties adjacent to the Illinois River produced something like 8,000,000 bushels of wheat for export in 1890. An allocation to the four-mile strip on either side of the river suggests an export of more than 1,000,000 bushels specifically from that zone. Yet the 1890 census records shipments of only

600,000 bushels of wheat on the river, even though one would
have expected a much larger total because additional area beyond the four-mile zone was closer to water than to rail.[71] Moreover, not a single bushel of corn is alleged to have moved on the
river despite the certain existence of considerable surpluses
within the relevant area. These sample results call attention to
Fogel's failure to take full advantage of the available 1890 data
upon water commerce to test his basic assumptions. Contemporaries questioned the same computed superiority of water
rates advanced by those in favor of increased investment in
natural and artificial waterways, it might be added. Inevitably
in a period of almost universal rail movement, the water rates
available, because they refer to the few instances in which such
transport continued, are unrepresentative of the alternative
structure likely to prevail if all agricultural freight were to be
carried.

The matter is a complex one, however, and a specific critique
of Fogel's often ingenious methods is beyond the scope of this
discussion. I prefer instead to comment upon a third point: the
appropriateness of extrapolation of the results obtained in this
single sector. Fogel begins by subtracting some 35 percent of
his agricultural benefits on the grounds that this proportion is
allocable to other categories of commodities. The causes of this
excess are shared capital costs attributed solely to agricultural
transport and an allowance for inflated wagon rates due to failure
to impute part of the charge to return hauls. Granting the validity of the concern, the gesture is rather magnanimous. Fogel
earlier suggested *total* capital costs of $18 million on waterways
employed in interregional trade, and the aggregate could not
be swelled greatly by the addition of the many smaller water
courses used for shorter hauls. Likewise, *total* alternative wagon

[71] Consumption of 5 bushels per capita was assumed in order to calculate the
total surplus produced in the 18 counties adjoining the Illinois River. Since these
counties extend on each side of the river approximately 30 miles, the proportional
export in the 4-mile zone was obtained by multiplying the aggregate by 4/30.
Population and production statistics come from U.S. Bureau of the Census, *Eleventh
Census of the United States, 1890*, I, *Population*, and V, *Agriculture* (Washington,
1895); the statistics on water transport from XIV, pt. 2, *Transportation* (Washington, 1895), p. 439.

charges are not much more than $200 million. Could rates be so badly overstated when one recognizes the highly seasonal concentration of agricultural exports, as well as the substantial weight difference between imports and exports, both of which would have led to empty back hauls in any event? An allowance of closer to $30 million, not Fogel's $74 million, is required at best.

Simple multiplication by four of the now twice diminished total for agriculture suffices to reach the national estimate of $560 million. Here again it is necessary to demur. It is doubtful agricultural ton-mileage made up as much as 25 percent of the total ton-mileage in 1890. Fogel's estimate of agricultural freight originating — 36.8 million tons — multiplied by the 1932 average haul, the only year when average haul is available by commodity, gives a shipment of 19.7 billion ton-miles, or 24.6 percent of the 1890 total.[72] Now this is probably a maximum estimate since the 1932 average haul might be expected to exceed that prevailing earlier. Much of the short haul traffic had been lost to the truck by the later date, offsetting any possible shortening tendency due to increased consumption closer to surplus areas. Indeed, as a consequence of this substitution, the average haul for all products increased by some 50 percent from the end of the nineteenth century to 1932.[73] If it is assumed that the average haul of agricultural produce bore the same relationship to the over-all average in 1890 as in 1932 — not unreasonable since the composition of freight was almost the same at the two dates — the estimated 1890 haul is only 362 miles, and the share in ton-mileage a lesser 16.6 percent.[74] In light of this last result, a multiplicative factor of five rather than four seems to be the more appropriate. Staying within Fogel's context of rail cost differentials in 1890, but measuring *actual* gains

[72] The results of the special 1932 ICC investigation are presented in Harold Barger, *Output in the Transportation Industries* (Princeton, 1951), pp. 195–199. The 1890 ton-mileage estimate may be found in Table 1 of my "Productivity and Technological Change in the Railroad Sector, 1840–1910," in *Output, Employment, and Productivity in the United States after 1800*, National Bureau of Economic Research, Inc., Studies in Income and Wealth, vol. 30 (New York, 1965).

[73] *Historical Statistics*, p. 431.

[74] The 1890 average haul was taken at 240 miles. The ICC series does not start until 1899 when a figure of 247 is recorded, which changes little over the next 10 years.

(with a lesser allowance for excessive wagon and capital charges), this factor of five yields benefits of $1.5 to $1.9 billion. The critical adjustment is the measurement of realized gains: then our separate research efforts are seen to converge more directly. The consequence is a higher level of 1890 resource saving consistent with the 1859 calculations performed here.

A word concerning extrapolation itself also is in order. Fogel argues against its accuracy on the ground that it overstates aggregate benefits; I also am uneasy about the method, but precisely for the opposite reason. The agricultural benefits as they stand reflect the heavy weight of interregional transport in the total, representing two thirds of agricultural ton-mileage at a marginal saving of scarcely more than one-half cent per ton-mile. Despite the large volume of mineral shipments, most of which had reasonable access to water, it seems doubtful that an average weighted so heavily by a type of transport where alternatives were readily available is relevant to all freight. Beyond this, of course, is the extramarginal aspect of considering alternative transport of some 80 million ton-miles of commodities. Careful consideration of capacity limitations, as sketched earlier, might magnify benefits substantially.

The upshot of all this is that realized gains in 1890 due to the greater transport efficiency of the railroad probably go beyond 10 percent of income rather than falling well below 5. Moreover, to place the railroad contribution by that date in its proper perspective, it is useful to revert to the rate of return framework suggested ealier. Even with the lowest possible $850 million of aggregate benefits at that date, the internal rate of return to railroad investment over its lifetime — counting only direct benefits and private earnings — is an attractive 18 percent despite much capital only recently emplaced.[75] The post-Civil War

[75] This calculation is naturally only a crude approximation. Nevertheless, because later decades receive little weight in calculating the rate of return starting from 1828, the result is not very sensitive to errors of estimation for the post-Civil War period. To obtain those data, benefits were interpolated logarithmically between 1860 and 1890 and net earnings taken from *Historical Statistics*, p. 428. All values were converted to 1909 prices to conform with the net investment series taken from Table 6 of my "Productivity and Technological Change." To simplify the calculation, decadal sums centered in the mid-points of each 10-year interval from the 1830's to the 1880's served as the data inputs.

period thus saw a substantial rise above the ante-bellum rate, even on these restrictive assumptions. A more generous saving in 1890 naturally sends the partial return beyond this level. For an innovation so long lived, and so capital intensive, these are magnitudes not to be despised.

Railroads by 1860 thus stood on the threshold of a significant and increasing influence from the side of direct benefits. Their remarkable rate of return up to that year, considering its implication that railroad investment would have been a wise policy even if no further returns were ever earned, clearly testifies to that. But this rate of return equally confirms the lesser actual contribution over the preceding three decades, and its concentration in the late 1850's. Other influences made themselves felt sooner, and to these we must turn to discover the more significant effects of the early railway system.

APPENDIX TO CHAPTER II

Calculation of Direct Benefits

In a narrow sense this appendix is merely a lengthy description of the calculations underlying the estimate of direct benefits summarized in Table 3. But because that estimate is built up from consideration of the nonrailroad costs of transportation for many different groups of railroads separately, the discussion ranges broadly over many characteristics of ante-bellum transportation: the composition of freight on the trunk lines, typical transshipment and insurance charges for water-borne commerce, variations in tariffs among railroads, and so on. Accordingly it has an interest quite apart from its more technical aspects.

The structure of the discussion is dictated by the earlier analysis of the measurement of direct benefits. What is required is the additional cost of transporting the commodities and persons actually conveyed by railroad in 1859 by the least expensive alternative means. In practice, since waterways afforded the most economical alternative, the task narrows down to specifying the incremental expense for the railroads in proximate competition with water routes. Prior to the Civil War, half of total railroad services falls into this category, a fact which leads not only to limited benefits but also to their more accurate calculation. Where water competition was a reality, alternative costs of transportation are much more easily ascertained from actual rate schedules and the like. From the reasonably firm results computed for the trunk lines, where much detail — to the extent of the precise commodities transported — is available, reasonable extrapolations can be made to groups where information is less abundant.

The final result is an upward biased estimate of direct benefits in any event. No allowance is made here for the adjustments the economy would have made to higher transport prices, adjustments inevitably that would have led to smaller quantities of transport being demanded, and hence smaller benefits. In Chapter II we have set out procedures for estimating such bias, as well as other indirect methods of reaching an unbiased total. The importance of these calculations is their delineation of the order of magnitude of benefits without which the necessary subsequent refinements could not proceed.

The Trunk Lines

We begin with the four great interregional roads, accounting for almost 20 percent of total freight receipts, and a sixth of all gross revenues. Corresponding to these lines were three major water routes: the Erie Canal, the Pennsylvania Mainline, and the Chesapeake and Ohio, completed to Cumberland, Maryland. Only the New York and Erie did not possess a proximate water alternative, although, with various branches from the Erie Canal, the southern tier was not entirely isolated.

The principal traffic upon these railroads consisted of through freight, to the extent of 60 percent of their combined ton-mileage. On the two New York roads its proportional influence was even greater, reaching a maximum of 70 percent in the case of the Erie. Through freight was correspondingly of lesser moment on the two more southerly routes, accounting for only slightly more than 40 percent of shipments on the Baltimore and Ohio. The presence or absence of a flourishing trade in coal largely explains these different degrees of specialization in interregional commerce.

Of the almost 400 million ton-miles of through freight, about 250 million were generated by trade from west to east in agricultural products: livestock, provisions, and most important of all, flour. Transport of the latter two commodities by rail yielded only minor benefits. Lake and canal rates for provisions and flour were quite close to prevailing rail charges. Indeed, it was only during rate wars that railroads were directly cheaper. 1859 witnessed such an event; as the Chicago Tribune reported:

From this time [April] to the end of August the rates were low — ranging from 3 @ 3½¢ for wheat to Buffalo and 5½ @ 6¢ to Oswego — the propellers being obliged to take cargoes at about the same rate as vessels. During the greater part of this time the railroads leading to the East took a large proportion of the Rolling Freight at 30 @ 35¢ p 100 lbs for Provisions, and 60 @ 70¢ for Flour to New York — a rate with which neither propellers nor sail vessels could possibly compete. [1]

More commonly, a premium of some twenty to thirty cents per barrel prevailed for all-rail flour shipment versus consignment by lake and canal. A smaller differential existed between rail transport and a river and ocean route from Cincinnati.[2] For provisions the situation was comparable. With the additional qualitative advantages of rail shipment, however, the apparent premium did not measure the actual difference in costs. Insurance charges of approximately 2 percent when shipping by water accounts for ten cents of the quoted water advantage. Transshipment meant another three cents, and the additional commissions occasioned by more elaborate transfer and forwarding amounted to at least an additional five cents.[3] But note that railroads had to offer both low rates — slightly more than one cent a ton-mile — and incremental qualitative benefits in order to become serious competitors in interregional commerce. Had the average charges of some two cents a ton-mile prevailed, the trunk railroads would never have fared as well as they did. The canal adherents never appreciated this fundamental fact in bandying about a supposed margin of water superiority of four to one while canal patronage showed unmistakable decline.[4]

If at such rates railroads captured part of the flour trade and

[1] *Chicago Press and Tribune*, January 2, 1860, p. 3.

[2] This is one reason for the diversion of Ohio Valley trade from South to East; see Chapter VII. Berry, *Western Prices*, pp. 92–93, 561.

[3] For lake insurance rates see the *Report of the Fourth Annual Meeting of the Board of Lake Underwriters* (Buffalo, 1858), p. 25.

[4] Cf. the Report of the Auditor of the New York Canal Department reprinted the *American Railroad Journal*, XXXII (1859), 196. He uses an average of rail charges on all classes of freight to represent costs of flour movement by rail and easily argues for water superiority. One wonders why, if he was so confident, he was worried about declining canal traffic.

much more of the carriage of animal products, the fact remains that each of these commodities could, and did, move by water. The Erie Canal transported more flour than the four interregional lines combined until the very end of the 1850's and continued to remain a potent factor thereafter. Although only a small tonnage of animal products (excluding livestock) was actually carried by the late 1850's, the water route had earlier demonstrated its capacity in these lines, and in 1862 a majority of provisions were shipped eastward from Chicago by lake rather than rail.[5] (The greater diversion of provisions to railroads was probably influenced by the technology of packing; with a winter pack and navigation closed, there were advantages to shippers in moving their products directly on.) The coexistence of these competitors and the annual variations in the degree of patronage each enjoyed together imply a small margin of superiority for either form of transport. Under such circumstances social saving is naturally limited.

A first estimate of its magnitude starts from the additional cost of water deliveries from New York to Philadelphia and Baltimore, on the assumption that the Erie Canal could serve for through shipments to the former port at charges equal to rail rates. The sum involved is then in the neighborhood of $450,-000. This estimate is secured by reducing total eastward through tonnage by rail to the latter two cities by one fourth in order to derive approximate shipments of flour and provisions; a rate of one cent per ton-mile was applied to this new total (198,000 tons) to get direct charges for water delivery. To this $300,000 was added an estimate of transshipment expense, $.29 per ton, as derived from the actual costs of the Baltimore and Ohio for transshipments at Benwood, Ohio, in 1859. $60,000 represents the surcharge for this factor. Insurance charges of one-half percent on a value of $100 per ton accounts for the final $99,000, although this overstates alternative costs to the extent that inland canals rather than an ocean voyage could have been used.[6]

[5] See Table 35 in Chapter VII.

[6] These transshipment costs included ferrying across the Ohio River from the Central Ohio terminus to Wheeling; the 1859 annual report of the Baltimore and

It is necessary to go beyond such a first approximation to take into account, as well, the additional shipments necessitated in the West by such an alternative routing; goods actually shipped from Pittsburgh or Wheeling first would have had to find their way to the lakes before proceeding by the Erie Canal. The further charge imposed by this requirement suggests that the Pennsylvania Mainline is the more efficient nonrail route to Philadelphia and Baltimore, despite its much higher rate of 2.4 cents per ton-mile.[7] Thus, differential costs by the Mainline approximate $1,109,000, and with charges for shipment to Baltimore, the total outlay is $1.3 million.[8] By the alternative route via Ohio Canal, Lake Erie, and Erie Canal, and then on to Philadelphia and Baltimore, the total expense is a larger $1.4 million. Such a result does not contradict the historical evidence that the Erie Canal and the port of New York did triumph in the western competition. Shipments to New York for foreign export were always cheaper, and so too were shipments from the northern parts of the West bordering the lakes, even for distribution domestically. Only for the Ohio Valley traffic to and from Philadelphia was the Pennsylvania canal barely competitive with the New York waterway. This is why the Mainline remained in use after the Erie had opened and before the railroad came, but without winning an extensive western commerce for Philadelphia.

Under either circumstance, the saving is patently small. If to the assumption of exact equality of rail and canal charges from Buffalo to New York we add an allowance for rail superiority (including all qualitative benefits) of one-half cent per ton-mile, i.e., a margin of 50 percent, the total benefits still only modestly exceed two million dollars by this and the Pennsyl-

---

Ohio is the source for the information. For insurance charges on the coasting trade in this period see *Hunt's Merchants' Magazine*, XLIV (1861), 231.

[7] The rate structure presented by the New York State Engineer in 1854 showed costs of 2.4 cents per ton-mile on the Pennsylvania Mainline. Since transport rates declined over the period, this represents a conservative assumption for 1859. For the 1854 report see *Hunt's Merchants' Magazine*, XXXI (1854), 123.

[8] That is, $1,109,000 measures the *additional* cost of shipment by the Pennsylvania canal than by the Erie Canal or interregional railroad. The latter two have been assumed equal in cost thus far, and the Pennsylvania route was 1.4 cents more expensive than the Erie.

vania route.[9] In light of the New York railroads' ability to secure the provision and flour trade so completely, and since our
gross segregation of tonnage into competitive commodities
possibly oversimplifies, this upward adjustment is probably
merited.[10]

The other important segment of the railroad through traffic
consisted of livestock shipments. This trade was a creature of
the railroad era and cannot be treated in precisely the same
fashion as the commerce in flour or provisions. Water transport, due to its lack of speed and its confinement, never figured.[11]
Prior to the completion of the trunk lines cattle had been sent
to market in the East by overland drives, fattening en route,
or at destination, to compensate for weight loss. Swine were
driven less frequently than cattle, and pork products were usually either salted or locally consumed; nevertheless there is
some evidence suggesting that such drives were neither rare
nor insignificant in magnitude.[12] The direct, rapid, and cheaper
route to market afforded by the railroads naturally carried the
day, with impressive effects upon the industry. Cattle and hog
raising migrated west where animals could be fattened at less
expense upon prairie grass rather than corn, and then shipped
east. Even the packing centers were forced to follow.

The alternative conveyance of the large railroad livestock
tonnage, therefore, is not via lake and canal, but overland. The
relevant real cost is the loss in weight associated with such transportation, or, the same thing, the additional cost of fattening
at an eastern market point, plus the limited labor costs of drov-

[9] Note that this further differential must be added to the charges on the Pennsylvania Mainline too, since the standard of comparison were the Erie Canal rates.

[10] Still, canal rates were lower than rail rates and many of the supposed qualitative advantages did not apply socially, even if privately. For example, the railroads' freedom from seasonality affected western shippers favorably, but not the
economy. For agricultural commodities, production was necessarily seasonal, and
inventories had to be held somewhere, East or West.

[11] One should be cautious in judgments of technological inevitability, however.
The October 19, 1963, issue of *Business Week* (pp. 130–132), carries a story of
successful barge shipment of cattle at lower cost than rail transport.

[12] Generalizations concerning the lack of adaptability of hogs to overland drives
often appear. Yet Berry cites the *Cincinnati Daily Gazette* (in *Western Prices*,
p. 225, n. 26), to the effect that 491,212 hogs were driven east out of a total western
crop of 2,922,099 in 1856.

ing. Gates estimates that the total cost of driving cattle from Ohio and Kentucky to the East was $15 a head. Henlein specifies a charge ranging from $14 to $18 for the trip from Lexington, $10 from Ohio.[13] These direct payments are confirmed by the opportunity costs of the weight loss. A journey of this length, from 500 to 800 miles, meant a weight loss of 150 to 250 pounds, varying with the quality of the stock and actual distance traveled. At an eastern price of 8 cents for beef (net weight),[14] the loss would come to $12 and $20, respectively, appropriately slightly higher than the actual costs. Reduced to a ton-mile basis, then, the implied rate for driving is something like 4 or 5 cents.

Competitive rail charges were less than this, although not as low as the rates charged for flour and provisions. Livestock was classified as first-class freight, which meant average charges of at least double the flour rate, or more than two and a half cents per ton-mile. Indeed, there is some evidence that they were still higher, provoking threats from the cattle raisers to revert to driving.[15] If the relevant differential is taken as high as three cents by generous assumption, and one fourth of the traffic estimated to be of this form,[16] the benefits generated by railroad transportation are equal to $1.9 million.[17]

The entire eastward through traffic of flour, provisions, and livestock thus provided direct savings of only $4.1 million in

[13] Paul W. Gates, *The Farmer's Age: Agriculture, 1815–1860* (New York, 1961), p. 210; Paul C. Henlein, *The Cattle Kingdom of the Ohio Valley* (Lexington, Ky., 1959), p. 125.

[14] Beef was quoted in New York at 5½–6 cents live weight in 1859. Percy W. Bidwell and John I. Falconer, *History of Agriculture in the Northern United States, 1620–1860* (Washington, 1925), p. 501.

[15] Gates, *Farmer's Age*, pp. 212–213; Henlein, *Cattle Kingdom*, p. 126.

[16] The basis for this ratio is the reports of the various railroads involved. The ratio on the Pennsylvania was 35,522 tons of livestock to a total of 129,767 eastward through tonnage; on the Baltimore and Ohio, 16,426 tons out of 135,127. The through "animal products" on the New York Central came to a higher 112,210 tons of 234,241, but included provisions as well. The Hudson River and Erie Railroads did not classify their tonnage as way or through, but animal products on the former were 40 percent of the total and on the latter 20 percent; the proportion on the New York Central was about 25 percent.

[17] Although railroad ton-mileage, as used in this calculation, understates the distance on the less direct overland routes, any downward bias is more than offset by the use of the 3-cent per ton-mile differential.

spite of its importance in total tonnage. The corresponding benefits from the much smaller return trade were not far less, as one might anticipate from the virtual railroad monopoly in transport of highly valued commodities. Yet while most westward commerce forsook the canals immediately, the reason is not to be found in an overwhelming direct cost advantage in favor of railroads. Through shipment of New York dry goods cost the Cincinnati merchant only $1.10 per hundred pounds by water in 1849, just about equivalent to the rail charges of the next decade; even adjusted for changes in the price level, railroads did not provide a great breakthrough.[18] The reason for their competitive triumph is to be found in more subtle but equally real advantages: the competitive advantage of early receipts,[19] freedom from seasonality, smaller charges in breaking bulk, and lower insurance rates. Since the worth of these attributes depends less upon weight and distance than the *value* of the product (because they are reflected in *percentage* charges) it is not surprising that the highest valued commodities should have been the first to transfer allegiance. Moreover, with valuable merchandise, fineness of calculation of transport costs is no longer a crucial necessity, and the railroad may have benefited from that. As Taylor puts it, "travelers and shippers alike, becoming habituated to using the rails in the closed season, often found small differences in cost insufficient to tempt them back . . ."[20]

There can be no doubt, then, concerning the fact of almost total diversion. The relevant question is the social loss to the economy if it had not occurred. A good place to begin is the cost advantage of freedom from seasonality. The loss in output from holding inventories during the 5-month period when navigation was closed would have been almost $2 million. This assumes that westward through tonnage was worth on average

---

[18] Berry, *Western Prices*, pp. 83–86.

[19] Here is an instance of divergence between private gain and social saving. If competitive advantage favored railroads over canals, at the new equilibrium, with everyone shipping by rail, the only gain is the increased utility to the consumer from having next season's fashions early. There is a social gain, but not a saving of productive resources.

[20] Taylor, *Transportation Revolution*, p. 71.

$900 a ton, 3 times the Erie Canal valuation, but befitting the more highly valued goods shipped by rail,[21] and that the appropriate interest rate is 7 percent. One other assumption is involved as well: an even flow of consumption over time so that $\frac{5}{12}$ of the annual shipments represents the maximum inventory to compensate for seasonality, with the average stock one half of that.

Increased speed reduced capital costs in similar fashion, since goods could be replenished over a shorter interval. Owing to the absolute shortness of time involved even by canal, this saving comes to only $180,000. Railroad deliveries 6 days sooner reduced average inventories to one-fourth their former level at best; but the requisite inventories are small to begin with since canal shipments took less than ten days. Of course there may be other reasons for holding inventories, like the advantage of few and large transactions, or the uncertainty concerning consumption patterns, and so forth. Quicker transport may affect these as well. As a first approximation, however, the difference in inventories imposed by the greater discreteness of non-railroad shipments gets at the largest part of the cost advantage.

To complete the calculations, allowances for direct cost differentials, and for the lack of as advantageous canal facilities for Philadelphia and Baltimore as for New York, are necessary. (The discussion of insurance costs is best postponed to the analysis of the midwestern through lines since they applied primarily to the lake trip beyond the interior canals.) The less satisfactory location of Philadelphia and Baltimore for western commerce by canal has already been noted in connection with the eastward through traffic. Our treatment here is identical: with the Mainline charging more than the Erie by 1.4 cents per ton-mile, the greater costs on shipments from Philadelphia and Baltimore come to $954,000 on the 170,000 tons involved. Additional

---

[21] The average value of merchandise shipped on the Erie Canal in 1858 was $326 a ton. *American Railroad Journal*, XXXII (1859), 173. This is too low for railroad freight, however, since its specialty was the transport of higher priced goods. The $900 average used is similar to the assumption made in calculations of the value of interregional trade by the later *Statistics of Foreign and Domestic Commerce*, Senate Exec. Doc. No. 55, 38th Congress, 1st Session (Washington, 1864), pp. 122–137.

costs in getting some part of the goods from Baltimore to Phila-delphia bring the amount to $1.1 million. This route is again the relevant one since the greater roundaboutness by the Erie and Ohio canals makes the latter a more expensive alternative.

As to direct costs, the evidence reveals little difference in favor of railroads. Although canal tolls and the shippers' charges, too, where higher for merchandise, railroad tariffs were also higher, thereby largely nullifying the potential advantage. But again, to compensate for actual rail charges lower than quoted (not uncommon, even in the 1850's) and to compensate for the greater length and handling of water shipments, we allow a margin of one-half cent per ton-mile in favor of railroads. This assumption yields benefits of another $665,000.[22]

In total, then, westward through shipment by rail saved the economy $4.0 million; together with the equivalent $4.1 mil-lion of benefits provided by the eastward flow, the aggregate saving due to railroads are barely more than $8.0 million on freight receipts almost as large.

Such a result is to be expected in the context of efficient water competition. Ironically, therefore, although constructed to prose-cute interregional trade, the trunk lines contributed much more from a social viewpoint on their smaller way tonnage. The com-position of this way traffic did not differ significantly from that of the through trade, with one major exception. That is the large volume of coal shipments via the Pennsylvania Railroad and the Baltimore and Ohio. Other than this, one can generalize, as before, that the shipments from west to east were greater in bulk and composed largely of flour and animal products, and that the reciprocal flow was primarily merchandise. The differ-ence in direct benefits thus stems not from a different type of traffic, but from the lack of the same efficient water alternative that presented itself for the interregional trade. This is most obvious in the instance of the Erie Railroad, without a parallel waterway altogether. But the Baltimore and Ohio was in a simi-

---

[22] This margin is not extended to shipments on the Hudson River, a route cheaper even than the canals. The total allowance is more than abundant to compensate for excluded qualitative advantages. Breaking bulk, for example, could not have cost much more than $50,000.

lar situation: the Chesapeake and Ohio Canal did not join the railroad's right of way until Point of Rocks, a junction almost seventy miles distant from Baltimore; over the intervening distance, shipments would have to move overland.[23]

The Erie reports do not give a classification of way freight by shipping and delivery points. This information would be invaluable for the calculation of the actual benefits it provided. A cruder measure will therefore have to do. The place to start is the amount of overland transport required. Since the branches of the Erie Canal, as well as Lake Erie and the Hudson River at the terminals, intersected the railroad right of way, such overland conveyance was considerably shorter than the length of the railroad itself. There is no part of the line much longer than 100 miles which is not bounded by some water route. Thus, the maximum overland delivery could be only 50 miles in length. If local deliveries and shipments were evenly distributed in the segments, each ton would travel on average 25 miles. Taking all way tonnage on the road, 630,000 tons, and attributing to it 25 miles of overland transport at 15 cents per mile, yields a total expenditure of $2.4 million.[24] To this must be added an allowance for water shipment to the points of overland transshipment. Since we know that the average ton of way

[23] The assumption that the Pennsylvania Railroad had a continuous water competitor will not go unchallenged, since the Mainline Canal included two rail links, the Portage Railroad and the Philadelphia and Columbia. Without them, the rates charged would have been higher both for the through traffic and for the local. We are therefore assuming their availability in the absence of all other railroads (although the Union Canal could, and initially did, substitute for the Philadelphia and Columbia). The reason is that we are not out to measure the return to railroads as a conception — for then do we count the primitive gravity roads in the mines as well? — but as an alternative transport system. That a small amount of trackage was associated with a canal system in the early 1830's does not mean that we must exclude it. (A different treatment, while obviously increasing benefits, still would not alter our conclusions: the Erie Canal could have handled interregional commerce at only slightly greater cost, as we have seen, and additional benefits in the local trade would have affected the aggregate national saving to the extent of perhaps 1 percent.)

[24] The 15-cent per ton-mile overland charge is the common rate quoted for the period. See Taylor, *Transportation Revolution*, Appendix B, and sources there quoted. The use of an average overland delivery overstates benefits somewhat, since economic activity, and hence shipments, were probably concentrated at water nodes.

freight was transported less than 70 miles by rail, and since each
ton has been presumed to move 25 miles overland, the average
additional water shipment, even with roundaboutness, could
not exceed 100 miles. With as high a water rate as 2 cents per
ton-mile the required addition comes to only $1.3 million. From
this total of $3.7 million we must subtract the actual revenue
received by the Erie to secure an estimate of the saving afforded
by direct railroad transportation. These receipts from carriage
of way freight probably come to $1.0 million,[25] thus leaving an
estimated $2.7 million in benefits.

For the Baltimore and Ohio a slightly more refined approximation is possible due to the detail of the company's annual
reports. First the coal shipments will be treated. For the alternative transport of these, there was, from Cumberland eastward, the Chesapeake and Ohio Canal, itself quite specialized
in the coal trade. Some part of the coal shipped via the Baltimore
and Ohio originated at points further west, however, particularly
from the mines at Piedmont. For the overland haulage of 175,000
tons of Piedmont coal 25 miles to Cumberland a differential
charge of around $700,000 is implied. Since the canal rates from
that point would have apparently saved $300,000 to tidewater,
the imputed additional overland cost must at least exceed this
minimum, as it does.[26] Of course, this tells us nothing about the
upper limit involved. In light of the very low canal rates from
Cumberland, and the small proportion of railroad shipments
directly from that point, substantial additional benefits seem
unlikely.

Other way shipments requiring explicit attention are those
originating in, or delivered to, the area between Baltimore and
Point of Rocks. The rest could have reached tidewater at no

[25] As estimated by using the way ton-miles on the Erie and the New York Central
way rate. The latter may have been lower than the Erie rate due to canal competition, and this may exaggerate the saving somewhat.
[26] The cost by canal for shipments of coal was .25 cent per ton-mile. (Taylor,
Transportation Revolution, Appendix B.) Railroad rates of 1859 were 4 times as
large, or 1.2 cents per ton-mile (calculated from the Report of the Baltimore and
Ohio Railroad for that year). At such quoted rates the canal had a maximum advantage of $293,000 from Cumberland. In fact, the advantage may have been
smaller, since the railroad did carry tonnage from Cumberland; but this may have
been designed for Baltimore use in particular rather than reshipment elsewhere.

greatly dissimilar cost via the canal. The magnitude of the tonnage in this area is quite great: of a total, both way and through, of 201,190 tons moving east (excluding coal), 60,000 originated in this zone; corresponding westward deliveries were 56,000 tons of a total of 154,000.[27] Still, the benefits were modest. More than half the tonnage originated or was delivered within a 15-mile radius of Baltimore, and the greatest amount of the remainder was concentrated at Frederick, only 8 miles from Point of Rocks and water access. Minimization of the alternative costs of delivery therefore leads to an expenditure of only $311,000.[28] Railroad receipts of about $50,000 in this movement leaves benefits at roughly $300,000.

For the time being, we can bypass similar detail for the Pennsylvania and New York Central due to the proximity of competing, or potentially competitive, canal systems. Instead, let us take up the dollar value of some of the specific usual premia

[27] These absolute figures relating to 1859 have been estimated by using the 1860 proportions. Data for the earlier year are not available in the annual report.

[28] Calculation of the nonrailroad ton-mileage requires specification of the means of conveyance and the distances and weights involved. The data themselves suggest three divisions, the first within 15 miles of Baltimore, the second from Ellicott's Mills to Frederick, the third from the latter city to Point of Rocks. For the first of these areas, since direct wagon movement was feasible, the average mileage per ton from the Baltimore and Ohio records was used; for the third, shipment by water to Point of Rocks and inland movement to Frederick was indicated, so the calculations could be made there as well. For the intermediate zone, it was necessary to solve a cost minimizing equation to determine the appropriate dividing line between direct shipments to or from Baltimore by wagon and indirect shipments to or from Point of Rocks where the canal was accessible. This equation reads: $a(69 - x)y = by + axy$, in which a is cost per ton-mile of overland transport; b, cost per ton by water to Point of Rocks; x, the number of miles from Baltimore; and y, the number of tons transported. In words, the cost of roundabout transport via water is the same as that of direct haulage at the locational margin. Since y can be divided out, the equation becomes a single equation in one unknown x, dependent upon the parameters a and b. Setting the former at 15 cents per ton-mile and the latter at $2.50 (a cost in excess of 1 cent per ton-mile to reflect transshipment, insurance, etc.), the appropriate division is at the 43rd mile from Baltimore. With the additional assumption that tonnage was evenly distributed in the intermediate zone, the relevant ton-mileage from the appropriate points could be calculated. Total overland ton-miles are 1,454,000 for costs of $218,000; water costs for 37,352 tons amount to $93,000; and total outlay, therefore, to $311,000. Although this sum excludes the additional cost of certain small shipments along the line of the Northwestern Virginia Railroad (a Baltimore and Ohio subsidiary) inland from the Ohio River, it is accurate enough to bear out the minor extent of the problems raised by way tonnage carried by the railroad.

placed upon rail carriage of freight: speed, absence of seasonality, and ability to transport livestock. The adjustment for seasonality takes the same form as previously. The average inventory depends upon the value of the westward *and* eastward way freight; no longer can we utilize the assumption that eastward shipments were totally agricultural. This inclusion will overstate benefits somewhat, since some were agricultural commodities, but their low value per unit of weight at least limits the exaggeration. Accordingly, 800,000 tons of westward freight were valued at $400 per ton, and 1,000,000 tons of eastward freight at $200.[29] This total was reduced by a factor of $\frac{5}{12}$ to represent consumption during the period when navigation was closed, and the average inventory is, of course, one-half that sum. At an annual interest rate of 7 percent, the saving is $3.1 million. Speed, since it proved of little advantage in the longer through trade, and is of even less moment with the shorter absolute time span involved here, may be safely neglected. This is the more so in view of our exaggeration of the saving brought about by all-weather delivery: not only is the agricultural tonnage included, but for many of the shorter hauls, wagon transport is the cheaper alternative.

The railroad's ability to transport livestock with minimum weight loss is another matter. This attribute has to be reflected in the benefits upon way tonnage for the reason of its obvious importance: something like 10 percent of eastward way tonnage was livestock.[30] At the same incremental advantage of 3 cents per ton-mile used previously the addition to benefits is $372,000.

The differential between direct water and rail costs is the

---

[29] These valuations are the same used in *Statistics of Foreign and Domestic Commerce*, pp. 123, 135. Livestock is excluded from the tonnage since it has no place there, as are the eastward shipments of coal of the Baltimore and Ohio. Valued at $200 a ton, the latter tonnage would exaggerate the importance of seasonality considerably.

[30] The 10 percent assumption is grounded in company reports. Livestock made up 5 percent of tonnage on the Pennsylvania, and 7 percent (excluding coal) on the Baltimore and Ohio. Since the New York roads were still more active in this trade, livestock probably was close to 7.5 percent of tonnage. The 10 percent of ton-mileage is appropriate owing to the likelihood of longer than average shipments from the western parts of the respective states. (Note that since *all* way tonnage on the Erie was figured to move overland at 15 cents plus a water journey, no further livestock adjustment for that road is needed.)

only other substantial factor influencing direct benefits. Although there is reason to believe that actual charges favor water rather than rail transport, at least at its most efficient, the extent of the desertion to the railroad even in summer, testifies in the negative. Omitted, thus far, too, are the transshipments, additional haulage to and from terminals, and so forth. Moreover, not all of the canal alternatives were equally attractive: while the Erie might give the New York Central some uncomfortable moments, the Mainline and Chesapeake and Ohio did not do the same to the Pennsylvania and the Baltimore and Ohio. Allowances of one-half cent per ton-mile for the New York Central and Hudson River railroads, and of one-and-a-half cents for the Pennsylvania and the Baltimore and Ohio, and thereby additional benefits of $2.1 million, more than compensate.

Table 6 summarizes the results of these deliberations for the trunk lines. Total benefits come to $17.4 million, including $3.7 million for not very well defined rail advantage. This additional margin is such a large proportion of the whole, after other major sources of saving have been specified, that it seems virtually certain direct benefits did not exceed this sum. These results are striking: freight receipts of $14 million generated only slightly larger benefits. In other words, these railroads only lowered total transport costs by about half, whereas the Erie Canal had reduced rates to one-tenth their previous levels. The truly revolutionary change came in the 1820's, not the 1850's.

Midwestern Through Extensions

Such a minor contribution cannot be generalized to all antebellum railroads. Few were challenged with such efficient and extensive water competition. One group which does bear a close resemblance to the trunk lines, however, is that set of railroads which at this time formed the midwestern extensions of the eastern roads and which later were absorbed by them. The Michigan Central, Michigan Southern, Pittsburgh, Fort Wayne, and Chicago, and the Lake Shore combination from Toledo to Buffalo shared many characteristics of their eastern complements: a large through traffic, competition with a low cost water route,

TABLE 6. Direct benefits provided by the trunk lines, 1859 (millions of dollars)

Source		Benefits
Eastward through freight		4.1
Roundaboutness	1.3	
Additional rail advantage in flour, etc.	0.9	
Livestock allowance	1.9	
Westward through freight		4.0
Seasonality	2.0	
Speed	0.2	
Roundaboutness	1.1	
Additional rail advantage	0.7	
Way freight		9.3
Deliveries on Erie Railroad	2.7	
Deliveries on Baltimore and Ohio		
Coal overland to Chesapeake and Ohio Canal	0.7	
Between Baltimore and Point of Rocks	0.3	
Seasonality	3.1	
Livestock allowance	0.4	
Additional railroad advantage	2.1	
Total		17.4

Source: See text.

and specialization in higher valued agricultural commodities eastward and merchandise westward. Thus the Michigan Southern generated one third of its freight earnings in 1860 by through haulage; the Michigan Central, about half.[31] Through freight was a still larger element on the Pittsburgh, Fort Wayne, and Chicago whose average revenue of 1.1 cents per eastbound ton-mile eloquently bespeaks the competition with the lakes (and among the railways).[32]

Although various reports permit documentation of these gross resemblances, they do not allow even the crude detail of the analysis of the trunk lines. Some disaggregation is possible, however. We may begin, as before, by separating the through and way freight receipts. Using the fiscal year proportions of

[31] *American Railroad Journal,* XXXIII (1860), 304; XXXII (1859), 452.
[32] *American Railroad Journal,* XXXII (1859), 481.

the Michigan Southern and Michigan Central for 1860 and 1859, respectively, it is possible to derive accurate measures for their calendar year receipts; for the Pittsburgh, Fort Wayne, and Chicago it was necessary to discard the apparent information on through receipts since they were defined differently from common usage,[33] and the Michigan Central ratio was used instead. The through earnings of the roads from Toledo to Buffalo were calculated as three fourths of the total, a procedure which other information about these roads justifies.[34] The over-all proportion of through to total freight receipts so calculated is almost exactly 50 percent: $1,964,000 for through tonnage, and total freight earnings of $3,957,000.

Upon this important through traffic, benefits were effectively limited by the opportunity for shipment by the lakes, just as the interregional canals constrained the saving provided by the trunk lines. The major exception, as before, is represented by rail shipments of livestock that could only have moved overland. Fortunately, these can be approximately segregated as Table 7 attests. This estimate cannot be used as it stands. Not only does it refer to 1860 — a much better year for western railroads than 1859 — but the distance inputs are partially overstated since Buffalo was not the final terminus in all instances. Pittsburgh, for example, was about 10 percent closer to Chicago than Buffalo. Applied directly to actual 1859 operating results, these livestock shipments account for about a third of total through tonnage and half of eastbound through freight.[35] These

[33] Through freight was described in the 1858 report of the Pittsburgh, Fort Wayne, and Chicago as freight "emanating either from or destined to points off the line of this road." (*American Railroad Journal*, XXXII [1859], 481). A simple check showed that multiplication of "through" tonnage by total length of the road yielded a much higher ton-mileage estimate than was actually reported.

[34] The 1861–1862 report of the Cleveland, Painesville, and Ashtabula indicates that only 7 percent of the freight tonnage was way. In that same year the average haul was 92 miles on a total length of 109 miles for the Cleveland and Toledo. (*American Railroad Journal*, XXXV [1862], 786, 547.) A. L. Kohlmeier's observations concerning the trade on these roads support this picture for the earlier years as well. See his *The Old Northwest as the Keystone of the Arch of the American Federal Union* (Bloomington, Indiana, 1938), p. 197, for example.

[35] With through freight receipts of $1,955,000 and a ton-mile rate of 1.5 cents, the implied total ton-mileage is about 133,000,000. No lower average rate was charged. If $\frac{2}{3}$ of the total were eastbound, the number of ton-miles in that direction would be less than 89,000,000.

TABLE 7.   Livestock ton-mileage, midwestern through extensions, 1860

	Cattle		Swine	
Origin	Tons shipped[a]	Estimated ton-miles[b] (thousands)	Tons shipped[c]	Estimated ton-miles[b] (thousands)
Cleveland	45,000	8,100	17,500	3,150
Chicago	32,500	16,900	12,500	6,500
Toledo	16,250	4,712	7,500	2,175
Detroit	13,750[d]	0	500[d]	0
Total	107,500	29,712	38,000	11,825

Source: Kohlmeier, *Old Northwest*, pp. 248–249.
[a] Number of cattle converted to tons on assumption of live weight of 1000 pounds.
[b] The ton-miles have been calculated with Buffalo as the terminus.
[c] Number of swine converted to tons on assumption of live weight of 200 pounds.
[d] Shipped over Grand Trunk Railway of Canada, and hence excluded from ton-mileage estimate.

are about twice the comparable proportions on the trunk lines, and larger than reasonable. Accordingly, the above estimate was scaled down to 30,000,000 ton-miles, which at a differential of three cents a ton-mile, yields benefits of $900,000.

Another source of substantial railroad saving on the through traffic arises from the insurance charges necessitated by lake transport, charges reflecting the higher average property loss on lake than rail shipments. (It is unnecessary to reckon such other advantages like smaller inventories because these have already been considered in the previous discussion of the through lines. Since most of the same goods were simply moved along to their ultimate destinations by the midwestern through extensions, another allowance would involve double counting.) Insurance rates for the lake trade varied with time of year, distance of trip, cargo carried, and classification of vessel. As an illustration, the rate from Chicago to ports on Lake Erie for grain was $1\frac{1}{2}$ percent from May to August, but rose to 3 percent by the latter part of October; for shipments of flour, provisions and the like, the comparable rates were $1\frac{1}{8}$ percent and $2\frac{1}{2}$ percent. From Cleveland rates were 1 to $1\frac{1}{2}$ percent lower.[36]

The total value of the through tonnage to which these rates must be applied can be gotten at indirectly. The ton-mileage implied by through freight earnings is something like 133,000,-000. At an average haul of 300 miles, this means carriage of 450,000 tons, say 300,000 east and 150,000 west.[37] If 110,000 tons be subtracted from the former for livestock whose alternative transportation has already been figured, there remain 190,-000 eastbound and 150,000 westbound tons. Valuing the former at $200 per ton and the latter at $900 yields a total value of $173,000,000. At insurance rates as high as $1\frac{1}{2}$ percent on average, the additional charges are $2,600,000. On the generous assumption that these tipped the balance to railroads, rather than offset a water advantage in their absence, the equivalent sum is the social saving involved.

Thus far, benefits are at most $3,500,000. But these midwestern roads, like the trunk lines, fare better in the local trade. Neither of the Michigan lines nor the Pittsburgh, Fort Wayne, and Chicago had parallel water competition along their rights of way. Shipments originating or delivered to intermediate points on the road therefore would have required much more expensive rerouting than the through freight. Not that all of it would have to be overland. The 1857 report of the Pittsburgh, Fort Wayne, and Chicago even explains the disappointing results of that year on the basis of *indirect* Ohio River competition.[38] Goods could and did move from intermediate points in Ohio via the north-south canals to alternative east-west water routes, whether river or lake. The information required to determine the relative importance of such indirect competition is not available. Hence the most conservative course is to treat all local shipments as competitive only with overland haulage. Two cents per ton-mile is as low as way freight could be handled

[36] *Report of Board of Lake Underwriters*, p. 25.

[37] The use of such an average mileage to estimate tonnage eliminates the double counting (and worse) that would result by summing the tonnage of the independent railroads.

[38] Kohlmeier, *Old Northwest*, p. 185.

by railroad; compared to 15-cent wagon rates this means railroads saved 6.5 times actual railroad receipts or something like $13,000,000. It is appropriate to point out here that roads were not as bad as commonly assumed, at least in southern Michigan. The statement of the trade and commerce of Detroit for 1861 indicates that 500,000 bushels of wheat were delivered to the city by horse and wagon, or almost one sixth of total deliveries.[39]

These manipulations indicate maximum total benefits of $16.5 million. Even more than before, this is a substantial overestimate. Not only is a water alternative excluded for any of the way freight, but livestock and other commodities are lumped indiscriminately when the former could be driven overland at a much smaller differential expense. Despite this, railroads fall far short of the benefits typically alleged in their behalf. Railroad charges do not come out as one tenth of alternative costs, the standard case illustrated in the Andrews report and often quoted since (without citation to the original source) as representative of actual prewar transport conditions.

Two other railroads, the Ohio and Mississippi, and Marietta and Cincinnati, were southerly extensions of the trunk lines, particularly the Baltimore and Ohio, into the Ohio Valley. Beyond a general expectation that their traffic was similar in kind to that of the group just discussed, but with lesser importance of livestock, we know little else. Accordingly, extrapolation from the previous results is the best we can do. If the two railroads reduced costs just slightly less than their northern counterparts, total benefits are $2.0 million; if exactly in the same degree, $2.5 million. Crude as the method is, there is good reason to rely more on the first of these estimates. Both of these roads were relatively unsuccessful in their attempt to capture the river trade. A measure of this is their financial failure: both passed into the hands of receivers before 1860. It was not conspicuously low rates and heavy but unprofitable traffic that led to their demise. It was the inability to generate sufficient traffic by attractive enough charges relative to rates of river steamers and other railroads. This suggests their benefits per dollar of receipts were smaller than upon the northern roads.

[39] *American Railroad Journal*, XXXV (1862), 225.

Midwestern Canal Competition

The last group of midwestern lines for which separate attention is feasible entered into competition with the state canal systems of Ohio, Indiana, and Illinois. More than a thousand miles of canal penetrated the rich and abundant hinterlands of these three states, setting in motion in certain instances, reinforcing in others, settlement and ultimate exports. Although railroad competition decisively triumphed in the 1850's, leaving the state waterways a liability of public enterprise, the victory was not an easy one. Railroads were forced to competitive extremes; on the Ohio canals, for example, "the boat owners meet at every point active and ever watchful railroad freight agents with full control of the frequent charge and ready to contract . . . at such rates as they find necessary to receive the business." [40] Such a situation mirrors marginal rather than predominant railroad efficiency at best.

These canal systems menaced not single railroads but the western rail network in these states as a whole. To this rule there were certain prominent exceptions like the parallel lines of the Rock Island Railroad and the Illinois and Michigan Canal, but, in general, the north-south axis of the canal system, in contrast to the east-west railroads, meant little direct, but substantial indirect, competition. This relationship is not appropriately rendered by a calculation of the benefits upon certain roads, and is obviously distorted in the other direction by including all of them. Some intermediate, synthetic approach is needed.

This best begins with a measure of the railroad mileage in the canal counties. In aggregate, 1700 miles of railroad (excluding the Pittsburgh, Fort Wayne, and Chicago which has already been counted) were built in these canal counties before 1860. [41] The concentration ranges from slightly less than a third of total mileage in Ohio, to only a sixth in Indiana and Illinois. If freight

---

[40] Quoted from the Report of the Canal Commissioners in William F. Gephart, "Transportation and Industrial Development in the Middle West," *Columbia University Studies in History, Economics, and Public Law*, XXXIV, no. 1 (1909), 124.

[41] Calculated from the mileages of individual roads presented in Frederick L. Paxson, "The Railroads of the 'Old Northwest' before the Civil War," *Transactions of the Wisconsin Academy of Sciences, Arts, and Letters*, XVII, pt. 1, no. 4 (1914), 267–274.

receipts originating in and delivered to these counties were proportional to the concentration of mileage there, the total would
come to $3.1 million. Such an assumption is plausible. Although
the canal counties produced more than average surpluses, this
is countered by their abundant rail facilities. If these two deviations balanced, receipts per mile of road in the canal counties
would be equal to the state average.

The only other information now required to produce an estimate of direct benefits is the extent of railroad superiority. Since
these geographic areas were contiguous to waterways, the relevant margin is undoubtedly small. The preceding analysis has
shown quite clearly that railroads only halved the cost of transportation, including all qualitative factors, except when overland haulage was the only alternative. Still, to compensate for
the additional wagon haulage to the waterways and the roundaboutness imposed by the latter, some larger, but not much larger,
factor is probably more appropriate. In view of our previous
findings, the $9.3 million for benefits implied by rail costs that
are one fourth of alternative charges does not likely understate
railroad saving.

Southern Railroads

The South was more abundantly provided with river drainage
than any other region in the country. The Yazoo, Tombigbee,
Pearl, Alabama, and Savannah rivers, and the Mississippi of
course, were only the foremost of the many navigable routes
to market which cotton took. More than five thousand miles
of internal waterways were designated navigable by the Inland
Waterways Commission in 1908, excluding rivers still used for
rafting.[42] It is not surprising that the South emerged as a commercial producer for export before internal improvements or
transport innovations took firm hold. Such a circumstance also
helps to explain the lukewarm commitment of the region to
railroads until the late 1850's.

Railroad construction in the South, as it finally emerged, ran

[42] *Preliminary Report of the Inland Waterways Commission,* Senate Doc. No. 325,
60th Congress, 1st Session (Washington, 1908).

basically from the ocean or the gulf to the interior. This meant east-west roads like the Memphis and Charleston and the South Carolina, and north-south lines like the New Orleans, Jackson, and Great Northern, and the Mobile and Ohio. Since rivers drained the same areas, the result was widespread water competition, albeit of varying degrees of efficiency. Even the east-west lines, not paralleled by the predominantly north-south inland waterways, were quite aware of their potential competition: there was always the possibility of shipping to the Gulf by water rather than by rail to Charleston, say.

The direct benefits provided by southern railroads were limited not only by the relatively large amount of freight subject to alternative water carriage, but also by the small difference between water and rail rates. Illustrative of the narrow differential are the comments of the President of the Mississippi Central Railroad in the annual report for 1860:

> The quantity of cotton that has been transported on the road since the first train started, has been 400,000 bales. The amount saved to the producers of this cotton, by a reduction of the cost of transporting it to market, together with a reduction in the cost in return freights, during the same period of time, has exceeded one-tenth of the cost of the road and its equipments.[43]

The total cost of road and equipment at the time of writing was $5,722,314. Ten percent of that sum is about twice the freight receipts in that single year, and five sixths of total earnings cumulated from the year of opening, 1856. The implication, therefore, is that the railroad failed to reduce costs even 50 percent, on a route inland 50 miles and more from the Mississippi River.

An approximation to aggregate benefits is difficult because river competition affected all railroads in part, rather than a few of the railroads totally. The method used for midwestern canal counties is unsuitable here, however. Water routes in the South ran a considerable distance through the pine barrens. Although railroads did the same, they often were not proximate to the rivers. With the cotton not originating in all the

[43] *American Railroad Journal*, XXXIII (1860), 670.

river counties in equal proportion, the amount of railroad mileage in the river counties will not yield a satisfactory estimate of the freight subject to water competition.

What has been done, therefore, is to consider only those railroads whose routes tended to parallel waterways for the largest part of their distance. The railroads selected include the South Carolina, Mobile and Ohio (Southern Division), New Orleans, Jackson and Great Northern, Alabama and Florida, Mississippi and Tennessee, Mississippi Central, and the South Side Railroad of Virginia (which paralleled the James River and Kanawha Canal).[44] This group represents freight receipts of $3 million compared to a total of more than $13 million for all southern railroads. The ratio is therefore comparable to the proportion estimated in the midwestern canal counties. Since the length of southern rivers exceeds that of the western canals by a 5 to 1 margin while the area was less than 4 times as great, such an allocation probably represents water competition reasonably accurately. It is unlikely that the differential advantage of southern railroads was as small as the example of the Mississippi Central indicates, or as large as upon the midwestern roads: southern steamboats did not charge much more than western canals while southern railroads charged considerably more than western railroads. If an intermediate position is taken, namely that railroads cut costs by two thirds, the result is $6 million in direct benefits. This, of course, pertains only to the railroads specified above; the others are assumed to have only the alternative of wagon transportation and are treated later. Altogether, therefore, the contribution of the southern railroads is not neglected by this procedure.

The Coastal Route

As the only effective means of communication in the early nineteenth century, the coasting trade was the first economic

---

[44] The one railroad without parallel water competition was the South Carolina. The Savannah River rather than the Santee River provided the more relevant alternative from the cotton region. Over the longer haul from Memphis via the Memphis and Charleston, the north-south rivers provided the alternative.

tie binding the early United States. It remained the most important link between North and South until the Civil War and even thereafter, not to mention its role within each of the regions. Reliance upon water alone was not wholly satisfactory, and one of Gallatin's major recommendations in his report of 1808 was the construction of a turnpike paralleling the coast from Maine to Georgia. Not until the railroad era was a continuous overland route completed, however, and then only by a variety of poorly coordinated independent lines. No national purpose predominated at the later date and each road was chartered separately to service an existing traffic, largely passenger and local in character.

From the earliest, passenger earnings justified their construction, but freight revenues were scant. So it remained for a long time, as the relative efficiency of long water hauls could not be eroded until after the war. The aggregate freight earnings of these more than a dozen roads are sufficiently large and had a ready enough alternative to merit separate treatment, however. Their $2.3 million of freight receipts could have moved in the coasting trade proper or through inland waterways like the Delaware and Raritan and Chesapeake and Delaware canals. This bare statement of the case admittedly understates the importance of the railroads involved. Much of the tonnage carried by the roads was local and water substitution would not prove economical in all instances. For example, the Richmond and Petersburg Railroad, only 27 miles in length, earned but a fifth of total freight revenues from through tonnage.[45] Of course, a good part of the way freight originated or continued on beyond the terminus of the road, but it takes a long haul to make water transport worthwhile when it is not easily accessible. Farther north, as evidence of this, the coastal packets left most of the shorter deliveries to the railroad, but maintained their domination in the longer trades. With better harbors, there was a greater potentiality in New England for shorter voyages: a daily steamer continued to ply from Nahant to Boston in

[45] Howard D. Dozier, *A History of the Atlantic Coast Line Railroad* (Boston, 1920), p. 87.

the late 1850's, and there was an efficient connection to Glouces-
ter, too.[46]

All the freight carried by those roads cannot be supposed to
have a low cost water option, therefore. If one half is taken as
the proportion that could have gone by water, and one half of
the ton-mileage is presumed to go by wagon, the weighted average of rail superiority comes to one third of the alternative
costs. This result is based upon the fact that water rates were
twice as high and overland rates 4 times as great as actual rail
tariffs. Since the freight charges on these roads were typically
quite high, averaging not much less than 4 cents per ton-mile,
these relationships, if anything, overstate the importance of the
railroad.[47] In total, this calculation suggests direct benefits of $4.7
million.

Anthracite Coal Railroads

The last group of railroads with substantial water competition contains some of the largest carriers of freight in the pre-
Civil War period. The tonnage of the Reading Railroad in 1859
far exceeded that of any other single line and was comparable
to the freight moved by the entire New York canal system.
These roads are impressive for still another reason. They succeeded in a traffic composed almost exclusively of coal, a low-
priced commodity in which water transport was supposed to
have a natural advantage. Yet in spite of this, the railroads
demonstrated not only staying power but even won a slightly
increasing share of the market over time.

Such a result was possible only by full and efficient utilization
of railroad capacity that permitted rates of about a cent a ton-
mile. Although canal rates were still lower, the margin was not
decisive in view of certain advantages of the roads: these in-

---

[46] Edward C. Kirkland, *Men, Cities, and Transportation: A Study in New England
History, 1820–1900* (Cambridge, Mass., 1948), II, 118.

[47] The weighted average of the ton-mile rates for 6 of these roads according to
information on ton-miles from the *Report on Finances, 1855–56* (see Appendix A)
and independent information on freight earnings was 4 cents. There is no evidence
of any downward trend to 1859 for these roads nor any reason to believe that the
sample yields an atypical rate. The railroads used are the Portland, Saco, and
Portsmouth; Eastern; Boston and Providence; New York and New Haven; Philadelphia, Wilmington, and Baltimore; and Richmond and Petersburg.

cluded direct delivery and better handling of the coal en route.[48] A previous competitive struggle showed canal managers that railroads would always follow any reductions exceeding such a differential. Accordingly a stable situation prevailed in the late 1850's.

At such competitive rates and with proximate waterways that, in 1859, despite the railroad construction of the 1850's, managed to command about half of the shipments, the saving from railroads was naturally quite circumscribed. It is difficult to imagine alternative costs for the coal transported by these roads at more than twice their actual railroad levels. This is more than generous in view of the demonstrated ability of the canals to hold their own by charging only marginally lower direct rates. This testimony indicates a qualitative inferiority of only one-third cent per ton-mile at the margin. Even taken as a unit, however, the assumed transference of the coal trade to the canals at a total disadvantage of one cent is more than ample to catch what railroad savings there were. The direct benefits, therefore, could hardly exceed $5.5 million.

Other Roads

The total benefits thus far calculated are $61.4 million upon freight earnings of more than $32.0 million. More than half of railroad ton-mileage has fallen into the various categories discussed. For the rest, no such detailed analysis is either possible or necessary. With railroad costs high in areas without water competition,[49] and with the amount of such carriage relatively limited, the benefits upon these residual receipts were too small to distort the picture of railroad benefits which has begun to emerge. That picture is one of resource savings, to be sure, but noticeably more limited in relative terms than the previous innovation of the canal had provided.

[48] The 1859 rate on the Schuylkill Navigation was about $\frac{2}{3}$ cent per ton-mile. Estimated from tonnage and toll data published in Chester L. Jones, "The Economic History of the Anthracite-Tidewater Canals," 156.

[49] See, for example, the rates charged by some of the smaller Wisconsin railroads for shipments of wheat from the interior. (John G. Thompson, "The Rise and Decline of the Wheat Growing Industry in Wisconsin," *Bulletin of the University of Wisconsin*, Economics and Political Science Series, V, no. 3 [1909], 146.)

These higher railroad costs and charges obviously make inappropriate a simple comparison of average railroad and wagon rates. In 1859 all railroads moved each ton one mile at a charge of 2.6 cents, but it seems likely that this residual group charged at least as much as 4 cents on average. This implies a rate of about 2 cents for the water competitive group already studied. Since the trunk lines, the midwestern through extensions and the anthracite roads — accounting for more than 70 percent of the receipts of this group — fully satisfy this condition, the 4-cent rate for the residual is well founded. Treating all of this additional tonnage as though it would have to go by wagon at 15 cents a ton-mile, the contribution is proportionally more than that of the other group, but still only $94 million. The total upward biased saving on freight is thus about $150 million. Before examining more carefully the sensitivity of this result as well as its implications for overland capacity, let us turn briefly to the saving provided by railroad passenger traffic.

Passenger Direct Benefits

Lower railroad costs in the transportation of persons as well as goods redounded to the social advantage. Admittedly scanty evidence suggests, however, that the direct benefits per dollar of passenger receipts were smaller than for freight receipts. First, stated charges were quite similar for passage by rail or water, with the latter more often than not emerging as the lower of the two. Western steamboats in the 1850's were among the least expensive conveyances in the world. In 1850 deck passage between New Orleans and Pittsburgh was quoted at $6.00; in 1855, the trip from Pittsburgh to St. Louis cost but a third of that — implying rates in both instances of less than one-half cent per passenger-mile. Cabin passage at five times the deck rate could secure at least the equivalent of railroad comfort, and indeed much more, at equivalent rates.[50] An 1848 comparison of charges to western cities by railroad and lake, and canal and lake, confirms this impression: three representative trips from New York to Cincinnati, Chicago, and Zanesville cost

[50] Hunter, *Steamboats*, pp. 421–422

$8.25, $9.00 and $7.62, respectively, by the all-water route; $12.00, $12.50, and $9.75, when the railroad from Albany to Buffalo was used.[51] What was true for the various water alternatives held for stagecoaches as well. This is not surprising in view of the greater facility of overland transport for smaller weights. Stagecoach fares on the Boston-Worcester turnpike were reported to average 6.5 cents a mile.[52] Although the excellence of this particular road obviously precludes simple generalization to the rest of the country, other evidence confirms a smaller differential between stagecoach and railroad than between wagon and railroad. Stagecoach rates for various trips as quoted in an 1848 immigrant's guide are reproduced in Table 8 with the corre-

TABLE 8. Ante-bellum stagecoach charges

Route	Mileage	Charge (dollars)	Passenger-mile rate (cents)
Philadelphia to Pittsburgh	300	15.00	5.0
Wheeling to Columbus	140	8.00	5.7
Columbus to Cleveland	177	10.50	6.0
Lexington to Louisville	75	4.20	5.6
Nashville to Memphis	224	15.00	6.7
Mobile to New Orleans	160	12.00	7.5
Richmond to Knoxville	444	28.50	6.4

Source: I. W. Warner, *Immigrant's Guide and Citizen's Manual* (New York, 1848) as reprinted in Dunbar, *History of Travel*, III, 1119.

sponding passenger-mile rates. In no instance did these exceed 7.5 cents. The charges on the great overland stage trips in the 1850's are consistent with these earlier rates. The Overland Mail Company charged $100 for the trip from San Francisco to Forth Smith, Arkansas, a trip of 1600 miles, for a rate of little more than 6 cents per passenger-mile.[53]

[51] Seymour Dunbar, *History of Travel in America* (Indianapolis, 1915), III, 1120.
[52] Taylor, *Transportation Revolution*, p. 142.
[53] Advertisement for Overland Mail Company for 1858 reprinted in Dunbar, *History of Travel*, IV, 1315.

A second consideration that reduces the direct benefits on the passenger traffic is the irrelevance of the qualitative advantages from a resource standpoint. That travelers could go their ways more comfortably by railroad enhanced their satisfaction; their support of the railroad from the beginning indicates that they valued such comfort highly. Still, from the social point of view, the traveler who arrives wearied after a longer journey does not reduce the economy's capacity to produce — except to the extent that longer periods on conveyances meant shorter periods at work, et cetera. These latter offsets do not come to much because the average passenger trip was typically short. The quality improvement of railroad passenger travel, while it justifies the transfer of allegiance of individuals, unfortunately has no place in our material calculus of productive potential.

In light of this discussion, our allocation of benefits in the carriage of passengers is quite generous, even if below the saving per dollar of freight receipts upon comparably situated railroads. For those railroads near water, it is assumed that railroads reduced transport costs 50 percent, for aggregate benefits of $21 million upon an equivalent amount of passenger receipts. (If benefits per dollar of passenger and freight receipts were the same, the sum would be $39 million.) For the other railroads we assume rail carriage at 3 cents per passenger-mile and stage at 9 cents.[54] Hence, we allow for the bias inherent in citing trips made upon the better roads of the period. These $24.7 million of receipts thus yield benefits of $49.4 million.

Concluding Remarks

Table 9 summarizes the preceding calculations. It indicates total benefits of $225 million, an estimate exaggerated both by errors of measurement and terminal weighting. The former deliberately have been assured positive by liberal allowances for railroad superiority; then there can be no question about the direction of bias. In Chapter II proper, we have already

[54] This is the implied rate for passengers, given a rate of slightly more than 2 cents on the water competitive railroads. There is little doubt that the latter is approximately the right level given the low charges on the trunk lines.

TABLE 9. Railroad direct benefits, upper limit, 1859 (millions of dollars)

Railroad groups	Freight	Passenger	Total[a]
Trunk lines	17.4	—	—
Midwest through extensions			
Lake	16.5	—	—
River	2.0	—	—
Midwestern canal counties	9.3	—	—
Southern river roads	6.0	—	—
Coastal route	4.7	—	—
Anthracite roads	5.5	—	—
Subtotal	61.4	20.7	82.0
Other railroads	93.5	49.4	143.0
Total[a]	155.0	70.0	225.0

Source: See text.   [a] Rounded.

discussed the appropriate compensating corrections. Here it is necessary to emphasize two different points: first, that the other means of transportation could have taken up the burden actually borne by the railroad, and second, that while much assumption has been necessary in these pages, the effect on the final outcome of varying particular ones is quite small.

Where it is particularly necessary to justify sufficient non-railroad transport capacity is for the horse and wagon substitute. The earlier discussion has shown that canals, rivers, and lakes could absorb the additional freight likely to move upon them, but at no time has it been indicated that the same was true of the common roads. Since almost a billion ton-miles have been assumed to be shifted to the latter, the question is no minor quibble.

Holmstrom's estimate of "feasible" maximum ton-miles per route mile implies something like 60,000 route miles of road would have been needed to move this quantity of goods.[55] (Passenger miles can be neglected since the additional total *weight* involved is insignificant.) The number of horses, by the same

[55] Holmstrom, *Railways and Roads*, p. 56.

estimate, would be a little less than 300,000.[56] "Feasibility" in this context is to be understood as an economic rather than a technical constraint: what Holmstrom does is scale down the technical maximum by a large factor to represent the maximum of resources that could be devoted to transportation consistent with other sectoral needs. Neither of these requirements offend the mind accustomed to pre-Civil War magnitudes. At the end of the period there were more than 200,000 postal route miles, of which 55,000 were coach routes. In this tally, some former coach routes superesded by the railroad are excluded. The 1860 census tabulated 7,000,000 horses on farms alone, many of which could have been spared for transport duties, particularly after harvest.[57]

No overwhelming railroad advantage of sheer physical capacity presented itself before 1860, therefore. Moreover, these calculations need not be interpreted literally. That is, not all of this ton-mileage need have gone by horse and wagon. Undoubtedly, the various other waterways would have acquired their share. The inefficiency involved in such a transference means that the maximum figure we get by assuming all moved overland is not too far out of line.

Finally, suppose the cost of overland transport would have soared under the pressure of sharply increased demands. Then, of course, we understate alternative cost and, presumably, benefits. Such an eventuality is not as serious as it seems. Figure 4 shows why. The largest share of the additional direct benefits calculated because of rising costs represents the bias of terminal weighting rather than "true" benefits. Their exclusion from

[56] At $\frac{1}{2}$ ton per horse, a speed of $2\frac{1}{2}$ miles per hour, an 8-hour day and a 300-day year, the maximum annual ton-mileage per animal is 3,000 ton-miles. This in turn means that 300,000 horses on a full-time basis would be needed to move 900 million ton-miles. The half-ton assumption is quite conservative. According to Holmstrom (p. 36), heavy draught horses could draw 1600 pounds, and McGowan takes this as minimum capacity for mules freighting in the rugged California terrain in the 1850's. (Joseph A. McGowan, "Freighting to the Mines in California, 1849–1859," unpub. diss. University of California, Berkeley, 1949, p. 347.) A higher tonnage per animal would reduce the number of horses required.

[57] *Report of the Postmaster General for 1860*, Senate Doc. No. 1, pt. 3, 36th Congress, 2nd Session (Washington, 1861), p. 417; U.S. Bureau of the Census, *Eighth Census of the United States, 1860, Agriculture* (Washington, 1864), p. 162.

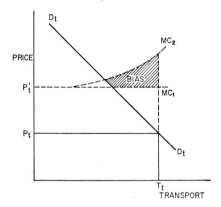

FIGURE 4.   The limited importance of increasing costs

the beginning may assist, rather than preclude, correct interpretation of the results.

Accordingly, I do not believe the objection of inadequate alternative capacity vitiates these results. Nor do I feel the approximation inherent in the calculations destroys all confidence in them. For reasonable changes in assumptions — the explicit recognition of cheap overland transport by sled in the winter, for example, or an allowance for higher overland rates in other places — the total amount of direct benefits will not vary substantially. Social saving of $400 million or $100 million both are far outside such a range. Thus these rough calculations, bolstered by the additional analysis of Chapter II, do provide valuable information about one aspect of the railroad contribution before 1860.

Part II

The Strength of Derived Demands

CHAPTER III

The Magnitude of the Backward Linkages

Introduction

As we saw in the preceding chapter, the resource saving properties of railroad innovation did not play a critical role in antebellum development, in part because they blossomed exactly when excess resource supply pervaded the economy. The divergence of potentiality and actuality in this single instance points up the general relevance of expenditure as well as favorable supply conditions for economic advance. And not only for the short run. One of the attributes common to those long swings of about twenty-year duration that seem to characterize secular American economic development is a significant variation in the intensity of resource utilization. Increasing factor supplies and increasing productivity by themselves are not sufficient to explain variations in the growth rate.[1] The contribution of the railroad sector to aggregate demand, and particularly to fluctuations in it, thus falls within our intended survey of the impact of the railroad upon growth before 1860.

A second path of influence from the side of demand commands our interest as well. That is the specific resource demands of railroads, rather than their generalized effect upon total outlay. In the historical process of successful growth and industrialization, certain sectors have tended to develop domestically at a relatively early stage. These are sectors supplying materials without which sustained rates of capital accumulation were not

[1] See the discussion by Moses Abramovitz in his testimony before the Joint Economic Committee in their Hearings on Employment, Growth, and Price Levels, pt. 2, *Historical and Comparative Rates of Production, Productivity and Prices*, pp. 424–433.

maintained. In particular, iron, engineering, and coal have been recently singled out for emphasis in connection with both industrialization and railroad expansion. As Rostow puts it, ". . . perhaps most important for the take-off itself, the development of railways has led on to the development of modern coal, iron, and engineering industries. In many countries the growth of modern basic industrial sectors can be traced in the most direct way to the requirements for building and, especially, for maintaining substantial railway systems." [2] This is not a new observation. Victor Clark pointed out a long time ago that railroads created "by their own mechanism a new order of industrial demands," [3] and the standard practice of linking the Railroad Age with the Age of Iron and Steel is not terminological happenstance. What Rostow has done, however, is to make the linkage explicit for pre-1860 American development.

Past discussions of both these demand influences have been limited in usefulness owing to the absence of an explicit quantitative reference. Without knowledge of the income, or employment, or demands for coal, generated by the sector it is difficult to assign adjectives implying orders of magnitude. A novel characteristic of the present discussion is reliance upon estimates of investment, employment, and the equipment stock that are presented in three, largely self-contained appendixes. These provide a much more specific context in which to evaluate the effects of railroads from the side of demand.

The Importance of Railroad Expenditure

Railroads, on the eve of the Civil War, stood only second in size to agriculture among American industries. By their own account, somewhat exaggerated as we shall see, they were then the first billion dollar, nonagricultural enterprise in the United States.[4] With farming broken up into such small units — there

---

[2] Rostow, *Stages of Economic Growth*, p. 55.

[3] Victor S. Clark, *History of Manufactures in the United States* (Washington, 1916), I, 351.

[4] The 1860 census reported the cost of construction of American railroads at $1,152,000,000. Capital invested in all manufactures according to the same source was $1,010,000,000. U.S. Bureau of the Census, *Preliminary Report on the Eighth Census* (Washington, 1862), pp. 227–231.

were more than 2,000,000 farms in 1860 — it is easy to see how the many fewer (less than 500) railroads dominated the scene. The Second Bank of the United States with its authorized capital of $35,000,000, a giant corporation in its day, was almost equaled or surpassed in size not once but four times by each of the trunk lines. Even the estimated cost of the whole New York state canal system, almost 900 miles in length, does not compare unfavorably with trunk railroads of half the length.[5]

What these qualitative comparisons imply is a substantial role for railroad expenditure by the end of the pre-Civil War period. Table 10 permits us to be more exact. Railroad invest-

TABLE 10. Components of capital formation before 1860 (millions of dollars)

Year or annual average	Railroad gross investment		New construction		Gross capital formation	
	Current dollars	1860 dollars	Current dollars	1860 dollars	Current dollars	1860 dollars
1839	17.7	17.0	137	140	200	200
1844	8.2	8.5	135	146	187	194
1849	36.7	39.4	206	217	257	258
1854	110.7	103.6	423	431	541	542
1859	60.8	60.4	385	392	532	532
1834–1843	—	12.4	—	120	—	141
1839–1848	—	15.9	—	161	—	216
1844–1853	—	40.7	—	254	—	319
1849–1858	—	70.3	—	379	—	474

Source: Table 54, Appendix B; Gallman, "Gross National Product."

ment over the overlapping decades from 1834 through 1858 never fell much below 10 percent of total capital formation. Over the entire span 1849–1858, railroads accounted for more

[5] The physical assets of the trunk lines at original cost in 1860: New York Central, $30,841,000; New York and Erie, $35,321,000; Pennsylvania, $26,646,000; Baltimore and Ohio, $26,569,000; the cost of the New York State Canal System is given as $55,106,814. *Preliminary Report on the Eighth Census*, pp. 227–231; Poor, *Railroads and Canals*, p. 361.

than 15 percent of investment outlays. In a peak year like 1854 the share was almost a fourth. These results compare favorably with later post-Civil War proportions. Ulmer's estimates of investment over the three decades 1869–1898 decline from 17.4 percent of investment in the first to 6.9 percent in the last.[6] Well before 1860 the railroad had assumed equivalent dimensions.

What is particularly noteworthy is the large role of railroad investment as early as the 1830's. In 1839 it stood almost as important to total construction as in 1859, and only the large forced repayment of capital in the former year causes it to represent a more modest proportion of national investment then. Over the entire span 1834–1843, despite the precipitous reduction in outlays after 1840, railroads absorbed relatively more resources than during the 1890's! This early rise calls attention to the fact that railroads influenced total expenditure long before they were a valuable asset for the transportation of goods. This point emerges still more strongly when we contrast the annual flow of railroad expenditures with those of canals at the very peak of the canal era in the 1830's. In no year after 1831 did canal investment exceed that in railroads.[7] Within less than five years after construction had begun on the first general-purpose American railroad, the Baltimore and Ohio in 1828, the railroad surpassed the canal as a generator of demand, a dominance that was not to be translated to the realm of transport services for more than a score of years. No wonder, then, that a separate journal dealing with railroad interests should begin publication in 1832.

Over time, as railroad transport operations did increase, the payments on current account reinforced those on capital account. Whereas in 1839 investment amounted to $17.7 million

[6] This is a current dollar comparison based on Melville Ulmer's investment estimates (*Capital in Transportation, Communications, and Public Utilities* [Princeton, 1960], Appendix C) and Gallman's new gross capital formation figures. From a 1929 constant dollar comparison with Kuznets' investment aggregates Ulmer gets 20.4 percent in the 1870's, 15.6 percent in the 1880's, and 7.5 percent in the 1890's. As my "Productivity and Technological Change" shows, this constant dollar comparison likely understates the role of railroad investment in the 1880's. The substance of these comparisons remains unchanged, however.

[7] For data on canal investment see Goodrich, *Canals and Development*, pp. 208–209.

and operating expenses to $4.3 million, the ratio was completely reversed in direction by 1859: investment amounting to only $60.8 million, operating expenses to $67.3 million. That, or the year or two previous, dates the transition, a result quite consistent with previous observations concerning the relative lateness of the emergence of the rail system in its transportation services. Still, its phenomenal growth in this capacity — ton-miles increased from less than 60 to 2,600 million in number between 1839 and 1859, passenger-miles from less than 150 to 1,900 million over the same interval — meant a steady reinforcement of the demand generated by actual physical expansion. By 1859, the combined income flow emanating from the railroad sector was perhaps 3 percent of annual product in that year, equivalent to the sum of the value added of the cotton, iron, and machinery industries. Later, of course, the percentage is still greater. By the turn of the century, railroad operating expenses *alone* come to about 6 percent of gross product.[8] Such a result was not unimaginable in 1860, in light of the already accelerating growth of the industry.

The importance of the railroad from the expenditure side is not only a consequence of the increasing share of total investment it represented before 1860. Equally relevant is the volatility of these outlays: large, but stable, expenditures do not promote fluctuation in total demand; large, and variable, expenditures can. Of this volatility there can be little dispute. Chart 1 plots an annual series of estimated gross capital expenditures in constant dollars, as well as a five-year moving average corresponding to it, designed to eliminate movements of lesser duration.[9] Either way, the results are plain. There are two long sweeps of railroad investment in the 1830's and the 1850's. One rises from the period of railroad infancy in the late 1820's to a

[8] For the estimate of gross national product in 1859, see Gallman, "Gross National Product." Pre-Civil War data on railroad operations are from Appendix A, this book. For later data on operating expenses and gross product, see *Historical Statistics*, p. 434 and p. 139.

[9] A period of this length cancels out shorter cyclical fluctuations in much the same way that averages of reference cycles do. See the comparison of both methods in Simon Kuznets, *Capital in the American Economy* (Princeton, 1961), p. 50. The current dollar series behaves similarly and is not plotted for that reason.

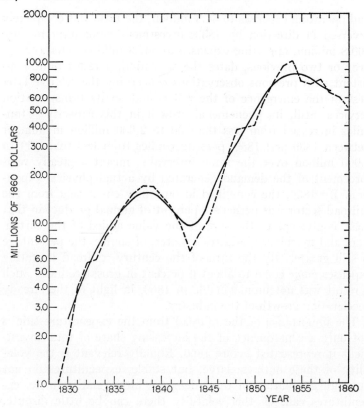

CHART 1.   Railroad gross investment, 1828–1860

peak in the late 1830's and reaches a trough in 1843.[10] The other moves upward from this point to a peak in 1854, with a decline continuing to 1860. There are two additional minor movements that are worthy of mention. These are both the results of pronounced regional variation which, because of the addition of noncorresponding expenditures elsewhere, appear damped in national aggregates. New England investment rose from $2.3 million in 1843 to a peak of $20.4 million in 1848 followed by a relapse to $8.5 million in 1850. This is what accounts for the increased tempo in Chart 1 from 1844 to 1848, followed by a

[10] I am speaking here and later of the annual series unless specified otherwise.

plateau until western investment gets fully underway in the early 1850's. The slight upturn in the later 1850's, on the other hand, is a result of the substantial southern commitment to railroad construction that got fully underway after 1854.[11]

Over this same interval a number of general business cycles were occurring. The National Bureau chronology identifies seven, measured from peak to peak. Their annual dating from peak to trough to peak is as follows:[12]

	1834	1836
1836	1838	1839
1839	1843	1845
1845	1846	1847
1847	1848	1853
1853	1855	1856
1856	1858	1860

Other quantitative investigations, principally that of Cole, have come up with similar timing in indices of prices, volume of trade, land sales, etc., although these, of course, show most pronounced swings in the periods of rapid and extended expansion, and sharp contraction.[13] Such, for example, are the boom of the 1830's, temporarily brought to a halt by the panic of 1837 and to a final collapse in 1839 with the failure of Biddle to sustain the price of cotton; and the boom of the late 1840's and 1850's that saw almost five years of continuous prosperity give rise to a reaction in 1854 finally confirmed by the panic of 1857.

Even the most superficial comparison of this timing in aggregate activity and that shown by railroad investment readily yields two conclusions. First, the pace of railroad expansion was not subject to the frequent reversals shown by total activity, whether the test be actual levels of investment or their rate of change. Second, the major expansions and contractions of the 1830's and 1850's are the ones most intimately associated with

[11] For these regional data in current dollars, see Appendix B, Table 53.

[12] Arthur F. Burns and Wesley C. Mitchell, *Measuring Business Cycles* (New York: National Bureau of Economic Research, Inc., 1946), p. 78.

[13] Cf. Walter B. Smith and Arthur H. Cole, *Fluctuations in American Business, 1790–1860* (Cambridge, Mass., 1935), sects. II and III.

railroad investment, whereas a minor movement like that from 1845 to 1847 is quite independent. These are not new results. Recent research has turned up impressive evidence indicating that there are long swings in construction investment as a whole, not only in railroads, but in housing and commercial building too. Severe contractions, or marked reductions in the rate of growth, occur when such investment peters out. Hence such prolonged and severe declines as those of the late 1830's and the 1850's, as well as those of the 1870's and the 1890's.[14] The railroad experience in the ante-bellum period is not unique.

A full and careful study of the factors responsible for the timing of these various construction swings is still to be performed. One ingredient that explains the length of the process is the long gestation period of construction projects. Typically, railroads required anywhere from three to five years to become fully operative in the 1830's, with a mean closer to the former. As terrain improved and technique advanced, mileage was opened at shorter intervals than this; in the 1850's, sections were opened within a year or two. But the size of individual roads grew, too, and this larger unit of finance was therefore in process for longer periods. Beyond this matter of length, with construction activity generating substantial total demand, the continuation of prosperity served to justify the initial commitment and to encourage further expansion that in turn maintained investment at high levels. Such a cumulative effect reinforced any tendency toward long duration. The contribution of increased productive capacity is another factor to be reckoned. The availability of transport services set in motion induced migration and commercial investment that was not subject to short-term reversal. Chapter IV explores such an inducement mechanism in the 1850's and how it reacted in turn upon railroad investment. Together with the discussion in Chapter V of agricultural response, it provides some indications as to how the boom of the 1850's developed and continued.

Here, however, I wish to concentrate upon a somewhat dif-

[14] See, for example, Abramovitz, *Historical and Comparative Rates*. Other literature is cited in Moses Abramovitz, "The Nature and Significance of Kuznets Cycles," *Economic Development and Cultural Change*, IX (1961), 225–248.

ferent matter, the relationship of railroad investment to the extensive declines of the 1830's and the 1850's. Although the role seems to be quite similar in the two instances, in fact it was quite different. In the earlier period railroad investment was a victim, not a fundamental cause, of the slackening pace of development, whereas in the 1850's the connection ran the other way. In drawing this distinction we hearken back to a previous theme: the substantial delay of the influence of the railroad beyond its earliest introduction.

Railroad expenditures in the 1830's got underway slowly, as Chart 1 attests. After the first impulse for construction provided by commercial rivalry had worn off, it remained for other, and diverse, projects to carry forward the investment. These included the small feeder lines of the anthracite region as well as longer (but still quite short) roads connecting the various fall line cities. Not until the mid-1830's did southern and western construction add any impetus to expenditure. Thereafter railroad investment mounted to substantial sums, principally under the guise of state support and favorable capital markets. Perhaps half the investment of the last part of the 1830's was assisted significantly by governmental action. The expanding boom in railroads and the simultaneous issue of more state bonds between 1836 and 1838 than in the previous half-century is no accident.[15] Englishmen purchased these securities until 1839, with only a temporary check in 1837, owing to the panic and specie suspension in May of that year. Beginning in the spring of 1839 interest rates tightened and although a large volume of bonds still were being sent abroad, merchant banking houses were experiencing considerably more difficulty in disposing of them. By October, with the failure of the Bank of the United States in its scheme to support the price of cotton, the justification for still more drastic curtailment was apparent. State securities were virtually unsalable, and although some small amount of sterling bonds of Massachusetts found a market, the western states were unable to secure further advances. Finally, as states began to repudiate their existing obligations in the

---

[15] Taylor, *Transportation Revolution*, p. 344, quotes B. V. Ratchford on the accumulation of state debt.

RAILROADS AND ANTE-BELLUM ECONOMY

midst of the decline, for they had depended upon additional loans to service prior issues, a complete cessation of capital inflows was inevitable.[16]

Railroad investment did not exactly follow the path traced out by the ease or difficulty of capital availability. During the brief stringency of 1837, for example, outlays continued due to the lag of construction behind financial accommodation. Likewise, in 1839, investment, while strained, did not come to an abrupt halt. For a time there were still the funds or the lines of credit already granted; the latter helps to explain the continued flow of bonds across the Atlantic in the summer of 1839. Then, temporary loans from American banks, particularly the Bank of the United States, helped activity to progress. Lastly, there were such expedients as delayed payments to contractors in land warrants or scrip. As a consequence, total expenditure in 1840 was not much different from that in 1838 and 1839. In some western states it was even greater. In the South, however, the failure in 1839 sounded an almost immediate death knell to internal improvements projects since support for them was so dependent upon successful banking operations and continuing cotton prosperity. Both of the latter interests, themselves quite intertwined, were prostrated by the fall in cotton prices and so too were the railroad projects.[17]

The lag of railroad investment behind conditions in the money market, particularly the London market, endowed it with something of a contracyclical impact both in 1837 and in 1840. Likewise, the recovery in 1838 and 1839 was assisted by the substantial expenditures in each of those years. Canal investment demonstrates a similar tendency, as one might well expect with many of the same states indulging in construction of both sorts of improvements. Current dollar outlays for canals in 1840 are slightly greater than in 1839 and 1838 and continue on in sub-

---

[16] For a discussion of the English capital market in this period, see Leland H. Jenks, *The Migration of British Capital to 1875* (New York, 1927), chap. iii; and R. C. O. Matthews, *A Study in Trade-Cycle History* (Cambridge, Eng., 1954), chap. v.

[17] These observations concerning the disparate regional pattern of investment in the late 1830's and early 1840's are based on the material used in the construction of Tables 46 and 51, as well as Table 53. See Appendix B.

stantial force in 1841. The same sorts of expedients were utilized to make such continuation possible, but just as with the railroads, by mid-1842 there was little chance for keeping construction going on the projects underway.[18]

Do we assert from such nonsynchronous behavior, with previous authorities like Hadley, Cleveland and Powell, and McGrane, that railroad fortunes were relatively unscathed by the depression that set in at the end of the 1830's?[19] The answer is no. Their evidence was the rising crescendo of mileage added from 1836 to 1841: Poor's *Manual* shows the annual construction increasing from 175 miles in the former year to 717 in the latter, with but an insignificant pause in 1838; the census of 1880 series is quite similar in its pattern, if not identical in magnitude.[20] Completed mileage, of course, lags actual construction outlays which peak earlier. This explains part of the error. Equally relevant is the complete inability of the mileage data to indicate how much projected line was ultimately abandoned, or limited to completion in such a poor state that the results were practically worthless. The extent to which railroads *did* feel the depression is forcefully portrayed by a single statistic: more than a tenth of all outlay on railroads during the 1830's fell into the above category. Table 11, which presents the annual distribution of such expenditures, leaves no doubt concerning the disastrous effect of the final collapse of 1839 upon railroad fortunes. While actual investment in 1840 was still not much curtailed, intended expenditure was sharply reduced. Railroads, being a newer technology and also being pressed forward vigorously in the South, were more hampered by failures than canals. What a different picture is this than that painted by McGrane (after Hadley) of the effect of the depression:

[18] Segal discusses canal cycles in Goodrich, *Canals and Development*, pp. 194–201.
[19] Frederick A. Cleveland and Fred W. Powell, *Railroad Promotion and Capitalization in the United States* (New York, 1909), p. 81; Reginald C. McGrane, *The Panic of 1837* (Chicago, 1924), p. 143; Arthur T. Hadley, *Railroad Transportation: Its History and Laws* (New York, 1903), p. 33.
[20] Both of these series are now accessible in E. R. Wicker, "Railroad Investment before the Civil War," in *Trends in the American Economy in the Nineteenth Century*, National Bureau of Economic Research, Inc., Studies in Income and Wealth, vol. 24 (Princeton, 1960), p. 506.

TABLE 11. Expenditures on failed projects[a] (thousands of current dollars)

Year	Outlays
1832	72.0
1833	132.0
1834	171.7
1835	171.1
1836	965.1
1837	1,918.0
1838	3,646.8
1839	3,751.9

Source: See Appendix B, derivation of Table 51.

[a] Failure in this context means investment upon roads whose mileage was abandoned or never completed, as well as upon roads completed but whose use was limited. The drastic write-down of the Northern Cross Railroad of Illinois where outlays exceeded $1,500,000 but which sold at auction in 1847 for only $21,000 is the only significant contribution of the second kind.

. . . the railroads received an added impulse from the crisis. Canals which had been projected on speculation and state aid fell in the crash that came during these years. Naturally a certain degree of odium attached to them as the result of their failure. On the other hand, the railroads which had been planned were so few in number in comparison with the canals that their failure did not attract much attention. Moreover, since the canals were gone, and as some means of communication was necessary, the railroads found themselves in better repute than heretofore. As a result the necessity of new railroads became apparent.[21]

While the railroads thus did not escape wholly unharmed from the major depression of the early 1840's, their fate was largely undeserved. At this time, railroad investment was not the governor of aggregate activity it was subsequently to become. Internal improvements investment was too small a factor in total expenditure to be responsible for the surge in activity from 1834 on to 1837, even though it was moving upward itself at the same time. Segal's contention that canal construction exacerbated the cycle, and hence, presumably railroad investment likewise, since the two follow much the same pattern with

[21] McGrane, *Panic of 1837*, p. 143.

similar magnitudes, will not hold up under closer scrutiny.[22] One linkage, the induced inflation generated by foreign exchange secured from abroad, can be dismissed rather handily. Both railroad and canal borrowing were greater in 1837 through 1839 than before. Yet prices (and the quantity of money) showed the greatest increase from 1834 through 1836.[23] When the internal improvements borrowing and spending developed, it served to shore up an economy coming to the end of a surge of expansion rather than contributing mightily to the initiation of demand. How much it, rather than improved export markets, is responsible for the recovery is also in doubt. Similarly, since land sales, and migration, too, probably, peaked by 1836,[24] and construction expenditures came in large quantity only *after* that date, it is difficult to trace these movements to developments then underway in the transport sphere. Internal improvements schemes in Illinois, Michigan, and Indiana were adopted *after* the population had already become sufficiently numerous in the mid-1830's to worry about markets (though before actual production required them).

More generally, the cycle in railroad investment was a lagged response to general business conditions, and hence to the conditions of finance, which it in turn little influenced. This expresses itself in the inability of the delayed peak of both canal and railroad investment to check the downturn underway in 1840. As a consequence of the lag, many projects were not brought to completion, a classic case of an investment boom constrained by capital availability. Such a pattern inevitably meant a partial synchronization with the pace of the economy as a whole, the upswing and downswing coinciding except in the immediate vicinity of the peak. To speak of the cycle followed by internal improvements expenditure as accentuating total instability is technically correct in that sense. Such a description is potentially

---

[22] Cf. Segal, in Goodrich, *Canals and Development*, p. 207.

[23] *Historical Statistics*, pp. 115, 119, 120, and 121, for prices in different cities. Series E34, p. 625, and E284, p. 647, together provide a measure of the money supply. For the latter see also George Macesich, "Sources of Monetary Disturbances in the United States, 1834–1845," *Journal of Economic History*, XX (1960), 430–431.

[24] Smith and Cole, *Fluctuations*, p. 53.

misleading, however, because it suggests something far different: that such investment was a causal element in determining the contours and duration of the aggregate cycle.

The passive role of railroad investment in the 1830's becomes more evident by contrast to its active effects in the 1850's. By that time, railroad investment was considerably more than 10 percent of total capital formation and a force to be reckoned with. Conjointly, and this is equally, if not more important, expenditures on construction *led* the slowing down of activity in the mid-1850's. Since much precedence is not obvious by reference to the National Bureau turning points presented earlier, it is necessary to reconstruct briefly the cyclical pattern of that decade while at the same time identifying the effects of railroad investment.

Recovery from the severe downturn of the late 1830's was underway by 1843. Led by a remarkable expansion in industry, all measures of economic activity concur in their suggestion of substantial prosperity in the East by the late 1840's. At that time, agriculture in addition received a powerful, favorable impetus from increased foreign demand for foodstuffs incident upon the Irish famine. With something of a lag, as the next chapter elaborates, railroad investment gained force in Ohio and spread farther westward to Indiana and Illinois by the early 1850's. The temporary tightness in eastern money markets in 1848 came as a reflex to the much more serious cyclical decline in England and had little effect upon this continuing expansion in the United States.

Once western expansion was proceeding in strength, the typical manifestations appeared: increasing land sales, high levels of internal and international migration, rising prices, larger capital inflows. Railroad investment rose from $37 million in 1849 to a peak of $111 million in 1854, the hectic pace of construction multiplying the rail network by a factor of about two in less than five years. Tightness in the capital markets constrained continuation of such a pace. As *Hunt's* remarked in mid-1854: "A few of the most desperate class of borrowers for railroad companies are pressing their bonds upon the public; but most of the projected roads, not approaching completion, will be obliged to postpone their operations to a period when the money market will be more compliant." [25] Foreign investment which had increased from a net outflow of $3 million to an inflow of $56 million from 1849 to 1853, declined to $42 million in 1854.[26]

Railroads had still more difficulty in raising funds as the year progressed owing to the Schuyler fraud. Robert Schuyler, trusted president of the New York and New Haven Railroad, announced the failure of his business firm on July 1, simultaneously submitted his resignation from the New Haven, and fled to Europe. It was immediately discovered that Schuyler had been engaged in an illegal overissue of stock for his own use to the amount of two million dollars, or two thirds of the authorized capital stock. "The discovery of the above frauds created a universal panic that for a while threatened to break up the railroad system throughout the country. . . . There is a general retrenchment and taking-in of sail among all classes. . . ." [27] Here we see both the final coup de grâce to increasing railroad investment as well as the altered role of American railroads within the commercial sphere. A railroad scandal now occupied the position formerly reserved to financial derangements.

1854 did not prove the end of the prosperity. Although Thorp characterized the end of the year as a depression, carrying over into 1855, revival began in 1855, and 1856 seemed lively enough.[28] Indeed, in spite of appearances of slackness, as late as August, 1857, *Hunt's* rather overconfidently dismissed concern over the course of business activity, citing underlying strengths of agriculture "to vindicate the hopeful spirit which has characterized this review at the time that many of our contemporaries could see nothing but impending disasters and troubles thickening around us, and to rebuke those whose vocation it appears to be to excite alarm and distrust." [29] In this same August in which the editor ventured his opinion that "the country continues prosperous" the New York branch of the Ohio Life Insurance

[25] *Hunt's Merchants' Magazine*, XXXI (1854), 81.
[26] *Historical Statistics*, p. 565.
[27] *Hunt's Merchants' Magazine*, XXXI (1854), 207, 333.
[28] Willard Thorp, *Business Annals* (New York, 1926), pp. 126–127.
[29] *Hunt's Merchants' Magazine*, XXXVII (1857), 198.

and Trust Company failed, and the panic of 1857 was underway. Two years later the very same *Merchants' Magazine* carried the lament: "The United States can boast of having more idle men and vessels of *all classes*, than any other country in the world of the same population." [30]

It has been customary to treat the panic of 1857 as the end of the prosperity of the 1850's, as well as to emphasize its commercial character and similarity to past reversals.[31] Tradition is in error. The turning point in activity probably occurred much earlier and the panic itself was merely a final overt symptom of an already pervasive weakness. Cole's index of domestic trade peaks quite perceptibly in 1855; land sales likewise reach their maximum in 1854–1855.[32] Migration to the West, as reflected in the censuses of western states taken in 1855 and 1856, seems to have reached its turning point by that date; immigration quite perceptibly peaks in 1854; more than 460,000 persons entered in that year as against only half as many in the one following.[33] Commodity prices continued to rise, it is true, but principally as a result of heightened foreign demand in 1856 and 1857. Both Cole and Berry seem to point to 1856 as the peak in real activity.[34]

Such a correction in timing serves to focus upon domestic

---

[30] *Hunt's Merchants' Magazine*, XLI (1859), 185, cited in Taylor, *Transportation Revolution*, p. 350. Italics in the original.

[31] See the treatment in Taylor, pp. 345–351, as well as that by Van Vleck, *Panic of 1857*, whose very title reveals its emphasis.

[32] Smith and Cole, *Fluctuations*, pp. 104, 114. Loans and discounts of banks likewise peak in 1856 (p. 120).

[33] The Iowa census of 1856 indicates a total population of about 500,000, compared with Federal census totals of 192,000 and 675,000 in 1850 and 1860, respectively. Other returns for 1858 show a population of 634,000. This demonstrates that well over half the population increase of the decade accrued by 1856 and that the peak probably occurred by that date. See Secretary of State, *Census for 1880* (Des Moines, 1883), pp. 200–201; *Historical Statistics*, p. 13; *American Railroad Journal*, XXXII (1859), 678.

The Illinois census of 1855 gives a total population of 1,300,000. In 1850 and 1860 the totals were 851,000 and 1,712,000, respectively. Again the period from 1850 to 1855 witnessed more rapid growth than 1855–1860, which is consistent with a turning point before 1857, although not sufficient to establish it. This census is reproduced in the *American Railroad Journal*, XXXIII (1860), 1129.

Data on immigration are found in *Historical Statistics*, p. 57.

[34] Smith and Cole, *Fluctuations*, p. 107; Berry, *Western Prices*, pp. 520–521.

factors for the decline and to discourage the search for international causes playing upon a weak American financial structure. To Van Vleck, for example, "fundamentally the causes of the panic of 1857 were not localized in the United States. . . . Indeed, anyone who endeavors to explain the panic of 1857 as something divorced and independent of what was transpiring in the Old World will be largely wasting his time." [35] That may be, if one is limited to 1857 as the crucial date and the panic as the central event. From the broader perspective of aggregate activity, the downturn of the 1850's seems to represent the first *industrial* boom in the United States; a cyclical fluctuation primarily associated with the pattern of real nonagricultural investment and independent of the fortunes of cotton. Although banks resumed specie payments almost immediately — in New York on December 14, elsewhere by the beginning of 1858 — and in spite of record-breaking exports of cotton, recovery lagged. Only in the South did prosperity reign: King Cotton was no longer king north of the Mason-Dixon line. In the West, 1859 was still a very poor year, compounded by crop failure, as evidenced by low railroad receipts.[36]

To understand the mid-1850's adequately, then, is neither to emphasize 1857 as the crucial year nor to rely upon international phenomena. Rather, it is to give more weight to the marked cycle in railroad investment that peaked in 1854. From that blow the economy could not manage more than temporary escape; the weakness running through the entire period is sufficient to encourage Abramovitz to label the run of years 1854–1858 as a major depression.[37] We need not go as far as that to establish our own contention that railroad expenditures led and thus helped to generate a significant downturn in the 1850's. This result is in marked contrast to the earlier finding. The following summary comparison makes the difference more evident. There was a double-headed peak in the 1850's (1854 and 1856),

---

[35] Van Vleck, *Panic of 1857*, p. 105.

[36] See Appendix A, Tables 43 and 44. Receipts in 1859, in spite of a substantially larger network, were not much greater than those of mid-1856.

[37] In his testimony before the Joint Economic Committee, *Historical and Comparative Rates*, p. 456.

akin to that of the 1830's (1837 and 1839). In the later decade railroad investment turned down with the first climax and experienced a second decline in 1857 that perhaps helped hasten the ultimate financial crisis; in the 1830's rail investment continued on beyond 1837 strongly and did not decline until 1840.[38]

From the expenditure side, then, railroad investment burst into prominence by the 1850's, more than a score of years after the technical problems of construction and operation had been largely solved both in Britain and in the United States. It was to continue important in this function not only through the rest of the nineteenth century, but even into the beginning of the twentieth.[39] No precise analysis calculating what these expenditures meant to the realized rate of growth is feasible. At one extreme, if we assume the ready availability of other capital-absorbing projects, their influence is nil, since total expenditures are then independent of railroad investment. On the other, if we regard railroad investment as a unique addition to demand, its absence would wipe out a good part of the expansion of the decade.

Neither premise provides a particularly plausible interpretation. The latter is unacceptable for the reason that some degree of substitutability characterizes most dynamic processes; the former ignores two peculiar properties of railroad investment that tended to give it unusual leverage. The first of these are the high capital-output and borrowing-expenditure ratios that characterized the railroad sector. Total capital in manufacturing was perhaps 1.25 times value added (about half as large in comparison with total product); the capital-output ratio for railroads was roughly 5 times as large. Similarly, because the debt-equity ratio in the railroad sector was higher than else-

---

[38] The investment lead of the 1850's also meant a larger role for railroad induced expenditures in other sectors. The investment in construction, land clearing, etc. associated with population redistribution can be traced to the growing rail network.

[39] Ulmer's data in *Capital in Transportation* seriously understate the importance of the railroad expenditures at the beginning of the twentieth century. With about the same increase in track mileage in 1900–1902 as in 1870–1872, his estimated real gross capital investment over the former interval is about half that of the earlier period, even though one would anticipate increased expenditures on stations, other structures, equipment, etc., in the later period. On this see my "Productivity and Technological Change."

where, particularly in the 1850's, the proportion of earnings retained for expansion was necessarily limited.[40] The pressure to pay dividends was stronger on railroads, too, since their ownership was less narrow. Within the context of a multiplier-accelerator model of income determination (that is, demand determined), an excess of planned investment over planned savings results in an increase in income sufficient to generate the necessary savings. Thus anything that increases the gap, such as increased capital requirements or greater resort to borrowing, will increase the rate of growth.[41]

The ability of railroads to create themselves the means for *realizing* their investment plans partially canceled such an inflationary bias. Railroad securities were a financial investment that particularly appealed to foreign lenders. Of a total inflow of foreign capital from 1849 to 1860 of almost $190 million, at least half is accounted for by the export of American railroad securities, principally bonds. In 1856, a partial survey by the Secretary of the Treasury indicated $83 million of railroad securities held abroad, almost all of which were issued during the 1850's. Only state and local bonds competed with railroad securities as an instrument attracting long-term investment, and these were floated during the period primarily to finance subsidies to railroads.[42] The effect of such inflows was to augment the total savings presently available to the community. For both reasons, therefore, whether one accepts a savings constraint or believes in perfect elasticity of supply, railroad investment must be regarded as less than perfectly replaced by other ex-

[40] For the factual basis of these statements, see U.S. Bureau of the Census, *Eighth Census of the United States, 1860, Manufactures* (Washington, 1865), p. 733; Appendixes A and B; Lance E. Davis, "Sources of Industrial Finance: The American Textile Industry, A Case Study," *Explorations in Entrepreneurial History,* IX (1957), 189–203; *Report on Finances for 1855–56,* pp. 422–423.

[41] Alfred H. Conrad makes use of such a model in explaining long-term American economic development in his "Income Growth and Structural Change" in Seymour E. Harris, ed., *American Economic History* (New York: McGraw-Hill, 1961). See pp. 34, 44 for his treatment of the point made here.

[42] For an estimate of the net inflow, as well as discussion of the various estimates of American foreign indebtedness, see Douglass C. North, "The United States Balance of Payments, 1790–1860," *Trends in the American Economy in the Nineteenth Century,* National Bureau of Economic Research, Inc., Studies in Income and Wealth, vol. 24 (Princeton, 1960), pp. 621–627.

penditure, and hence at least partially contributing to the realized rate of growth by the 1850's.

Specific Demands

If generalized railroad expenditures only were involved, they
would hardly command the interest they do. Outlays for residential construction were undoubtedly much larger and perhaps
as volatile, yet no one finds in them the basis for far-reaching
economic change. This difference in treatment corresponds to
a difference in specific demands: houses use brick and mortar,
railroads consume iron and coal. The same distinction could be
drawn between railroads and canals:

> Outlays for canal construction and operating equipment led prima-
> rily to a demand for consumption goods by laborers and by suppliers
> of horses, mules, stone, sand and lumber. . . . But the rails, the loco-
> motives, and to some extent the freight and passenger cars, altogether
> an appreciable part of the total cost of a new railroad, necessitated
> additional large investments in capital equipment which took the form
> of furnaces, rolling and rail mills, foundries, and locomotive works.[43]

How appreciable a part of total railroad costs were charges
for industrial goods? Preparation of the right of way, which
Taylor correctly equates to canal construction in the nature
of its demands, was not a negligible matter. Otherwise, why
the persistence of the tradition that railroad construction work
depended upon large-scale Irish immigration in the late 1840's
and early 1850's. These are not matters about which it is necessary to guess. Table 12 presents the relevant statistics. Their
effect is to furnish a more balanced picture of railroad demands.

Throughout the pre-Civil War period, expenditures for the
preparation of the right of way dominated rail costs. In terms
of the total flow, they came to two fifths; as a proportion of investment, excluding land and most of the charges for discount,
they were even greater, amounting to more than 45 percent in
the earliest period of railroad development and to more than
40 percent in the 1850's in spite of the more favorable terrain
of the western states. These expenditures did not give rise to

---

[43] Taylor, *Transportation Revolution*, p. 347.

TABLE 12. Components of railroad construction cost (percent)

Category	1828–1839	1840–1850	1851–1860
Graduation, masonry and bridging (including fencing)	42	37	37
Superstructure	30	30	28
Equipment	7	9	9
Buildings and machinery	4	5	4
Engineering	4	3	3
Land	7	8	3
Miscellaneous			
Legal expenses, nonrailroad expenditures, etc.	1-2	1-2	1-2
Interest and discount	3-2	7-6	15-14

Source: Table 48, Appendix B.

much more than employment of unskilled labor with picks and shovels. Earth-moving equipment was of the most primitive sort. Men used picks and shovels to loosen and remove the earth, placing it in carts or wheelbarrows which then transported it to the site of an embankment. Railroad contracts placed a premium upon propinquity of excavation to embankment, since the dirt was usually transported free of additional charge for the first 100 feet. A few early steam excavators, and before that pile drivers for certain roads, can be identified, but they are clearly the exception rather than the rule. Moreover, their multiple appearance should not lead us to exaggerate their number: the same excavators used upon the Western Railroad were subsequently sold to the Troy and Schenectady.[44] From their limited use one can conclude that they did not work out very well. What this added up to, as Appendix C demonstrates, was greater labor input per dollar of railway construction than for construc-

[44] H. J. Habakkuk gives the example of steam excavators too much weight in seeking to argue for capital intensive methods of construction in the United States. *British and American Technology in the Nineteenth Century* (Cambridge, Eng., 1962), p. 51, n.1. The fact of a few pile drivers originally on the Syracuse and Utica that reappeared elsewhere does not bolster the case. *American Railroad Journal*, XIV (1842), 177, 225; Frank W. Stevens, *The Beginnings of the New York Central Railroad* (New York, 1926), pp. 152–153.

tion as a whole, and so, sizable employment. In 1859, as many as 140,000 men were at work building railroads, and earlier in the decade, still more.

Nor does the inclusion of bridge construction affect the argument to any significant degree. In the first place, such outlays came to no more than a few percent.[45] Secondly, while the use of iron for this purpose was increasing in the 1850's — witness the construction of the Niagara Suspension Bridge — it was still much in the minority. Pennsylvania in 1859 reported 196 stone arched bridges, 806 wooden structures, and only 76 of iron.[46] The Massachusetts reporting form for this period qualified its inquiry for the amount spent on iron bridges with the phrase "if any" in parentheses. As well it might: in 1856 only 3 railroads, out of a total of more than 40, had iron bridging to the extent of 379 feet with an expenditure of $12,000. The Virginia reports indicate, too, that less than 5 percent of expenditures on bridging were for iron structures. Of 178,423 feet of bridging in New York in 1855, 1,016 were made of iron.[47] As late as 1887, 17 Illinois railroads reported 268 iron and stone bridges, 3,563 wooden ones. The comparable tally for Michigan is 107 and 705, respectively. Even New York had fewer bridges of iron than of wood.[48] While a numerical count understates the amounts of wood and iron used at the later date, it does indicate how wooden structures persisted even with much lower relative prices of iron.

These results can alternatively be phrased in terms of the actual industrial demands. The expenditure for iron rails, and equipment of all kinds, including that in shops, came to only 20 percent of total costs in the first decade, and to perhaps a third in the two later ones. This aggregation takes into account the variable share of iron rails in the superstructure account

---

[45] See Appendix B, Table 47.

[46] *Hunt's Merchants' Magazine*, XLII (1860), 302.

[47] *Annual Reports of the Railroad Corporations in the State of Massachusetts, 1856* (Boston, 1857); *Annual Reports of the Railroads of the State of Virginia to the Board of Public Works, 1860* (Richmond, 1861). *Annual Report of the Board of Railroad Commissioners of the State of New York for 1855* (Albany, 1856), pp. 38–39.

[48] J. L. Ringwalt, *Development of Transportation Systems in the United States* (Philadelphia, 1888), p. 302.

over time; in the earlier period when strap iron was used and large inputs of wood and stone were common, expenditures for iron rails were less than half of superstructure costs, whereas by the 1850's they came to 70 percent.[49] Industrial demands are exaggerated, however, by the total inclusion of freight and passenger cars, which together came to about half of the cost of equipment. Until very late, such rolling stock required skills like carpentry and materials like lumber almost as much as any other. The distribution of expenditure for a freight car built upon the Western and Atlantic at the late date of 1886 bears out this observation: for the body of the car, lumber and labor came to two thirds of the cost; even including the trucks, where iron did come into play, these two components ranged between a fourth and a third of total costs.[50] Passenger cars, with more expensive interiors, required a still less industrially oriented input mix. In 1876, the iron inputs into a passenger car came to a fourth of total costs; plush, together with the hair for the seats, accounted for 10 percent.[51] Only coal cars were made of iron in any significant quantity before 1860, and even then it was far from the dominant mode. The 1867 distribution of coal cars on the Philadelphia and Reading indicates a total of 4081 eight-wheeled coal cars of which 3 were made of iron; of the four-wheeled cars 2834 were iron and 2114 wooden.[52]

The divergence from the British experience is marked in this matter of industrial demands. An extract from the *London Mining Journal* reprinted in the *American Railroad Journal* in the 1840's points up the magnitude of iron demands there;[53] alongside on the right are comparable estimates for American railroads of the same period, on the assumption of equivalent mileage under construction (1,000 miles):[54]

[49] See Appendix B, Table 47.

[50] Ringwalt, *Transport Development*, p. 338.

[51] Ringwalt. Even though the relative price of iron had declined by this later date, it does not seriously affect the argument.

[52] Henry V. Poor, *Manual of the Railroads of the United States for 1867–68* (New York, 1868), p. 261. The rarity of iron cars of any other sort is evident in the discussion of a proposed passenger vehicle of iron in the 1859 *American Railroad Journal*, XXXII, 569.

[53] *American Railroad Journal*, XVIII (1845), 270.

[54] For these estimates of American iron requirements see Table 14.

250 tons per mile for rails	250,000	101 tons per mile for rails	101,000
70 tons per mile for chairs	70,000	7.5 tons per mile for spikes and chairs	7,500
"Iron for wagons, stations, engines, tanks, etc., computed from inspection of railway companies' accounts, that each mile of railway requires 300 tons per mile above the weight of permanent rails and chairs"	300,000	Iron content of rolling stock, etc.	13,000

Admittedly the British estimate of 620,000 tons is high, not so much for rails and chairs as for the other miscellaneous uses. Although the ratio of equipment per mile was much larger — about four times as large for locomotives and freight cars, ten times for passenger cars — this is still not the explanation of the divergence.[55] Nor is there any substantial difference in size of engines or carrying stock that could explain it; indeed the English wagons were typically 4-wheeled and smaller.[56] Even making an allowance for this overstatement, and using the most conservative of contemporary reckoning, which set British demands at 500 tons per mile,[57] the consumption of iron in the United States was one-fourth that abroad. The American practice of building single-track roads with lighter weight rails, and substituting, wherever possible, more abundant use of wood, made a substantial difference.

All of this is not to deny the significant change the railroad

[55] Based on the ratios on the London and Northwestern lines reported by Dionysius Lardner, *Railway Economy* (London, 1850), pp. 77, 89.
[56] Lardner, p. 100.
[57] Estimate made by an American importer of English iron in describing the English iron trade. *American Railroad Journal*, XVIII (1845), 522.

did represent. Certainly when contrasted with the canal, the difference is both large and meaningful. Still, it is necessary to credit the sheer *absolute* size of the railroad interest for the impressiveness of the total industrial demands. One third of the outlay is after all less than everything, and it was the size of the multiplicand that counted quite heavily too.

When we extend the discussion to operations on current account, the same caution is needed. By and large, the major inputs into the daily workings of the railroad system then, or now, were labor services, not materials. This was true in the 1830's when scattered reports of individual roads confirm a ratio of wages and salaries to expenses of two thirds, in the 1850's when the New York state reports permit of more observations, and in 1880 when census data first become available. In 1856, our calculations for 16 railroads indicate that outlays for wages came to 54.2 percent of operating expenses after an adjustment to exclude such extraneous items as taxes, legal expenses, damages awarded, and so on.[58] This probably still leaves too much for materials since salaries are probably excluded from the report. In 1880, when the census data are more explicit as well as complete, $195 million constitutes the railroad payroll out of a total of $300 million in expenses, adjusted as before to exclude nonmaterial purchases.[59] From this last information, it would appear materials made up only one third or less of railroad operating inputs. As output expanded, then, employment grew concomitantly: from 5,000 in 1839 to 85,000 in 1859 according to the estimates of Appendix C.

To be sure, some of this employment did help to disseminate and evoke technical skills. But by no means is this true of the entirety. Track walkers, brakemen, manual laborers, and the like exceeded the engineers and shop workers. In 1856 in New York, 33.4 percent of the nonconstruction employees were en-

[58] Calculated from the reports of 16 railroads with the necessary information from the *Annual Report of the Board of Railroad Commissioners of the state of New York for 1856* (Albany, 1857). Since no totals were tabulated in the Report, an approximation was used. The 1859 ratio of taxes, etc., to operating expenses for all railroads (more readily computed since totals are given in that year) was applied to the 1856 data. The adjustment required was 11.5 percent; any error is probably inconsiderable.

[59] U.S. Bureau of the Census, *Tenth Census of the United States*, IV, *Transportation* (Washington, 1883), pp. 8, 13.

gaged in maintenance of road, only 17.8 percent in repair of machinery. In 1880, again with more detail available, and in spite of increasingly sophisticated repair facilities, only about a fifth of employees were classified as shopmen, of which in turn, carpenters made up more than a fourth. Trackmen outnumbered engineers, 122,489 to 18,977.[60]

Railroad accounts infrequently permit direct determination of material purchases and hence cannot be used to check upon the inference that only about one third of outlay fell into this category. Maintenance of way includes the cost of rails and ties for renewals as well as more prosaic tasks such as removing slides from cuts, opening ditches, raising and widening the embankment, and adjusting the track. In similar fashion, the broad category, repair of equipment, includes car wheels, lumber, and the labor of machinists. Only the fuel account furnishes virtually an exclusive accounting of commodity inputs; yet even there the labor cost of preparation is included. Nevertheless, with a bit of additional information, these accounts do provide useful confirmation. Maintenance of road, for example, ran to about a fourth of total operating expenditures. Of this probably about half went for purchases of iron, ties, other lumber, ballast, and other materials. Repairs of equipment ranged between 15 and 20 percent of expenses. Again, indications are that materials inputs were half of the aggregate. Adding in an additional 10–15 percent for fuel as directly reported in the accounts puts us just about at the one-third mark for total commodity purchases.[61]

[60] *Tenth Census*, IV, *Transportation*, p. 13; New York Commission *Report, 1856.*
[61] The percentages were calculated from a sample of fifty 1858 and 1859 railroad reports appearing in the *American Railroad Journal*. Three roads appear twice. The precise results by region, with standard deviations in parentheses, are:

Account	East	West	South	Total
Maintenance of way	25.8	25.1	30.7	27.2
	(7.5)	(8.3)	(5.6)	(7.5)
Repairs of rolling stock	16.2	17.9	14.5	16.1
	(7.8)	(3.6)	(7.5)	(6.8)
Fuel	15.1	15.0	9.9	13.6
	(6.2)	(5.3)	(4.5)	(5.9)

The New York State summaries indicate similar magnitudes, as do the 1880 national statistics of 24.3, 18.0, and 11.0 percent.
The basis for allocating materials and labor inputs within these accounts is

The difference between this one third of operating expenses and the previous one-third allocation of construction cost is considerable, however. Not only were investment outlays much larger in aggregate during the period than operating expenses, but the materials component of the latter hardly represents derived demand entirely for "industrial" goods. Nowhere does this show up more clearly than in a closer look at fuel requirements. For the major part of pre-Civil War railroad needs were met by cordwood, not coal. It is true experiments with mineral fuel began quite early. The Baltimore and Ohio tried anthracite coal in the 1830's, to the extent of designing their locomotives with vertical boilers. The reason was not economy; the danger of fire had some weight, "but, more than all, the precedent of the English railways then just coming into successful operation, which pointed to a mineral fuel as seemingly the only fuel fit for locomotive engines, were the considerations which induced its use." [62] American flexibility, called into play by the much higher expenses per mile of coal-burning engines, led to almost universal use of wood well into the 1840's. Even in the coal regions, engines continued to burn wood as various efforts to produce a successful coal-burning locomotive had little luck. In 1849, the *Journal of the Franklin Institute* could not make a useful comparison of the results of the few coal-burning engines then coming into use on the Philadelphia and Reading Railroad because it claimed there were none on other roads.[63]

The principal difficulties impeding a satisfactory technical solution were the higher combustion point of coal, which meant less rapid ignition and less lively combustion, and a much more in-

admittedly limited, but the results will stand up, I believe. See *American Railroad Journal*, XXXII (1859), 50–51, 164; Arthur M. Wellington, *The Economic Theory of the Location of Railways* (New York, 1887), pp. 143–155, 161–167. The proportion of cost of iron to total outlay for maintenance of way is generally $\frac{1}{4}$ to $\frac{1}{3}$, which is consistent with this imputation. *American Railroad Journal*, XXXII (1859), 568, 585, gives this information for the Boston and Worcester, the Boston and Providence, and the Reading for a number of years; see also New York State reports at the end of the 1850's.

[62] *Journal of the Franklin Institute*, 3rd ser., XVIII (1849), 82–83.

[63] Actually, at this time, the Baltimore and Ohio was trying to use Ross Winans' "camels," so called because the cab appeared as a hump on the boiler. Still the observation does indicate how rare coal burners were. *Journal of the Franklin Institute*, p. 9.

tense, concentrated heat once the fire was underway. The last served to wear out fireboxes at an appallingly rapid rate. A variety of means were finally used to make coal burning practical by the mid-1850's. Fireboxes were redesigned with side sheets of copper for longer wear; the area of the grate was increased to permit a thinner layer of coal, thereby encouraging a continuing fire but reducing the heat; hollow stay bolts that allowed better circulation of air also helped achieve the former goal, while water grate bars, hollow tubing through which cooling water might flow, replaced simple cast-iron structures. A large number of alternative boilers and fireboxes vied for popularity in those early years of experimentation.[64]

The history of the Baldwin Works cites 1854 as the date when the "use of coal, both bituminous and anthracite, as a fuel for locomotives, had by this time become a practical success." [65] This characterization is undoubtedly influenced by the success of the Baldwin works in filling such orders. More generally, however, there were still skeptics until the beginning of the Civil War who refused to admit of coal's ascendance; and those that did, did not rush to convert their existing equipment or to purchase new coal burners. The pages of the railroad literature at the end of the 1850's are replete with reports of comparative results with the two alternative fuels, and it is only then that a consensus in its favor began to emerge. The *Railway Times* of 1859 testifies to caution at even that date, moreover; the Boston and Maine management concluded from its examination of comparative performances: "Thus it will be perceived, that very little reliance can be placed upon loose statements, frequently published in the periodicals of the day, as to the great economy of coal . . ." [66]

The energies engaged in the search for a technical solution, as well as the economy of coal, varied widely geographically. Those roads in the eastern part of the country, and certain Illinois and Ohio roads as well, facing rising cordwood consumption per

[64] For a discussion of these and other technical details, see Angus Sinclair, *Development of the Locomotive Engine* (New York, 1907).
[65] *History of the Baldwin Locomotive Works, 1831–1923*, p. 56.
[66] *American Railway Times*, August 29, 1859. See, too, the letter by J. H. Boardman in the *American Railroad Journal*, XXXII (1859), 120–121, taking issue with the presumed savings on coal on the New Jersey Railroad.

mile as trains became longer and heavier, and simultaneously beset by increasing wood prices as local supplies gave out, were the leaders in the transition. Coal either lay directly on their lines or was easily accessible at low prices, and this was what made for economies in substitution. One could anticipate perhaps a third more mileage per ton of coal than per cord of wood under equivalent conditions, and sometimes more.[67] With prices of wood as high as $7.40 a cord on the Boston and Providence, say, and with an average of $4.46 for all Massachusetts, coal at $5 a ton and less could mean considerable saving even after allowance for extra repairs due to the ravages of the hotter coal fires. More often than not, however, it was the cheapness and availability of coal rather than the extraordinary cost of wood that led to change. The New England roads, in spite of probably the highest prices for wood, lagged behind, while the Baltimore and Ohio; Pennsylvania; Chicago, Burlington and Quincy; Illinois Central; among others, were in the van. Their costs for wood were typically less than $4 a cord, but coal could be gotten for as little as $1.30 (bituminous) and never more than $3; in addition, it was elastic in supply, while wood was increasing in price.[68] For these roads substitution of coal led to reductions of fuel costs by 50 percent. The delivered cost of coal to less well placed roads in the West was not low enough to make a large difference, especially with wood quoted as cheap as $2.20 a cord in Indiana and other parts of the West. Consequently most lines in that region had nary a coal

[67] Wellington, *Location*, p. 139, uses a conversion ratio of 1.5 cords of good hardwood to 1 long ton of coal. Practical experience even before 1860 seems to bear this out. See, for example, the comparison on the Pennsylvania Railroad cited in *De Bow's Review*, XXVII (1860), 118–119; or the comparison on the New Jersey Railroad in *American Railroad Journal*, XXXIII (1860), 625–626. Other instances are cited in that Journal's "locomotive department" to the effect that as little as 25 pounds of coal was used per mile or that more than 80 miles per ton in contrast to the usual 40 miles a cord obtained. Note, therefore, how bad Illinois coal was, with the Chicago, Burlington, and Quincy, and the Illinois Central getting fewer miles per ton of coal than per cord of wood! (*American Railroad Journal*, XXXII [1859], 629; XXXIII [1860], 589.) Only the very low price of coal made the experiments worthwhile in those instances.

[68] *American Railway Times*, January 29, 1859. *American Railroad Journal*, XXXII (1859), 69, 629. *The Thirty-Third Annual Report of the Baltimore and Ohio Railroad, 1859* (Baltimore, 1859), p. 19, indicates a price of 55 cents a gross ton delivered in the company's cars. At such cost, whatever its quality or the additional repairs necessitated, coal represented a remarkable economy.

burner when the war began. The subsequent sharp increase in expenses induced a considerable shift toward coal that continued until its use was almost universal. Only in the South, with its lighter trains and cheap pine, did many lines continue to burn wood into the 1880's and beyond.[69]

In light of this discussion, it should come as no surprise that the number of coal-burning locomotives was placed at only 350–400 out of an estimated total of 4,000 in 1859; a month earlier the number was put at 250–300.[70] Admittedly the total estimate is too low, but it is doubtful whether the coal burners numbered more than 500. The *Railroad Record*, in discussing the ramifications of railroad influence in 1860, did not see fit to make any allowance for the coal consumed in daily operation: "Another element of great importance is the consumption of wood or fuel. Supposing it to be wood alone (as it is mainly), the cost of fuel is six millions per annum representing 3,000,000 cords of wood." [71] One can find frequent reference to the depredations of the great dragon that was denuding the country of at least 50,000 acres a year by the end of the 1850's, but none to the depletion of our coal reserves owing to the appetite of the iron horse. For good reason: Pennsylvania railroads, with good coal more accessible at low cost than anywhere else, consumed more wood than coal in 1859.[72]

A tolerable estimate of national consumption in 1859 is within our power. Coal-burning locomotives probably made up some 10 percent of the total locomotive stock in 1859, or roughly 500, and could not have averaged more than 20,000 miles of service during the year. This is slightly more than the average mileage on

[69] Two locomotives on the New Orleans, Jackson, and Great Northern got more than 100 miles to the cord — on one trip 164.08 — and wood was quoted along the line of the Western and Atlantic at $.90 a cord. *American Railroad Journal*, XXXII (1859), 597; *American Railway Times*, January 29, 1859; *Tenth Census*, IV, *Transportation*, pp. 586–593.

In my "Productivity and Technological Change," I have estimated a third again as much coal consumption on the national level in 1869 as cordwood, and more than six times as much by 1880.

[70] *American Railway Times*, March 26, 1859, and February 19, 1859.

[71] Reprinted in *De Bow's Review*, XXVII (1860), 243.

[72] *Hunt's Merchants' Magazine*, XLII (1860), 503, reprints the state report which shows that 179,154 tons of coal were consumed, 206,742 cords of wood.

the Pennsylvania Railroad, with one of the highest utilization rates in the country. The national average for all locomotives was probably under 15,000 miles, but since the coal-burning engines were concentrated upon roads with higher than average mileage, the 20,000 figure is more appropriate.[73] The consumption of coal per mile run did not average more than 60 pounds; it is reckoned this high only in deference to the larger freight duties of the coal burners.[74] Thus the total consumption of coal for purposes of railroad fuel in 1859 was slightly less than 270,000 gross tons. By the same token, the amount of cordwood used for locomotive fuel must have come to 2,000,000 cords.[75] Of a total expenditure for fuel and lubricants in 1859 of about $9,000,000, therefore, coal accounted for well less than a tenth. And this was of course higher than in any previous ante-bellum year.

Fully 40 percent of pre-Civil War commodity demands were thus of a patently nonindustrial nature: firewood cannot qualify by any standard. It would be a mistake, moreover, to conclude that the entire residual represents a "new order" of requirements. Among the material inputs in the maintenance of way, ties, of course, figured prominently; our previous discussion on the near universality of wooden bridges establishes a replacement demand for timber for this purpose as well. Even the repair of rolling stock, because of wooden body structures, contributed to a variety of needs.

The computations of Appendix B permit more detail on some of these points. Roughly speaking, outlays for replacement ties

[73] *Fourteenth Annual Report of the Pennsylvania Railroad, 1860* (Philadelphia, 1861), p. 33. The average mileage of 1567 locomotives on 25 railroads was 15,871 in 1858. (*American Railroad Journal,* XXXI [1858], 297.) Since there is a bias on the sample, with some overrepresentation of the largest roads with highest mileages, the mean value for the country as a whole was probably closer to 15,000.

[74] The Baltimore and Ohio in June of 1859 consumed 20 pounds of coal per mile run by passenger engines, and between 55 and 92 pounds per mile for freight locomotives, the highest figure reflecting the steep inclines of the mountain division. On the Philadelphia and Reading, with their heavy loads of coal cars, coal burners consumed as much as 100 pounds per mile. *American Railroad Journal,* XXXII (1859), 486; XXXIII (1860), 90.

[75] Based upon 5,000 locomotives running an average of 13,000 miles a year, with wood yielding between 30 and 40 miles to the cord. The literature already cited indicates that such an average is appropriate. See also *Hunt's Merchants' Magazine,* XLII (1860), 372, for comparative performances on four railroads.

kept almost equal pace with purchases of replacement iron rails; indeed the estimates in the 1840's show expenditures for ties exceeding replacement of rails, but that was an unusual transition period in which part of replacement needs was reflected in construction account. This near equality reflects a shorter useful lifetime for ties than for rails, a divergence that had two effects: the first and more obvious is the greater frequency of renewal for a given period of time; the second and more subtle shows up in the ability of many roads newly built in the 1850's to postpone extensive replacement of rails during the depressed conditions at the end of this decade when they might otherwise have been required. Of importance, too, were the extensive efforts to economize upon replacement of rails. These principally took the form of repairing rails when possible. The Report of the Galena and Chicago Railroad explained as follows: "The repaired rails are those which, being but slightly injured, can be repaired in the Company's shops, by welding new iron over the defect. The cost of this repair is small, and the life of the rail is largely increased thereby." [76] In that year, 1860, 16,522 bars of iron were repaired and only 6,927 newly replaced. A second economy was the purchase of rerolled rails in place of new ones. By taking direct advantage of the scrap value of the existing, worn-out track, the price of replacements could be halved. Such a practice was quite common in the 1850's, according to all indications; the proportion of replacement purchases that took this form was perhaps three-fourths.[77] In combination, these considerations meant replacement expenditures for iron did not dominate those for ties in this period.

The one place where commodity demands conform closely to the ideal of industrial requirements is in the repair of equipment. About three quarters of the cost of repairs of freight cars was

[76] Reprinted in *Hillyer's American Railroad Magazine*, III, no. 1 (1860), 97. Repairing was practical because rails wore primarily at the joint.

[77] This assumption is consistent with the little information available. Samuel H. Daddow and Benjamin Bannon in *Coal, Iron, and Oil* (Pottsville, 1866), p. 683, suggest 56,450 tons were rerolled in 1857. Our replacement requirements in 1856–1857 average something like 85,000 tons from the model spelled out in Appendix B. In addition Fogel cites the *Annual Statistical Report of the American Iron and Steel Association for 1868* (*Railroads*, p. 195), for the information that 78 percent of the worn out rails in 1866 were rerolled.

apparently accounted for by operations upon the truck.[78] This meant demand for wheels, axles, springs, wrought and cast iron, and the like. On the Western and Atlantic Railroad in the 1880's lumber inputs came to less than 10 percent of box car repairs; for cars less than five years old, before their wooden bodies had deteriorated badly, the proportional expenditure was only 5 percent.[79] And although passenger cars required extraneous inputs in the form of upholstery renewal and other repairs of the interior, their contribution to total repairs of equipment was probably less than that of freight cars, even in the ante-bellum period when passenger-miles maintained near equality with ton-miles. The largest part of equipment repairs went for locomotives, in any event, and both the labor and the materials required there did contribute to industrialization. The regular demand for flue sheets, driving wheels, wrought-iron tires, axles, cylinders, pistons, et cetera, nourished and sustained both foundry and rolling mill.[80] Many larger roads developed elaborate facilities, and met such needs themselves, even to the extent of manufacturing their own locomotives. The Philadelphia and Reading Railroad pioneered in this respect. A description of their shops in 1849 would have done other roads proud a score of years later:

. . . they contain every species of machine used in the manufacture and repair of locomotives and cars, some of it very ingenious, useful, and perfect of its kind. . . . There are now employed in these shops, in the repair of engines and cars, about 350 men and 30 boys. . . . The trip hammer shop is put to good use in converting the old materials, that are turned in at better prices than could be otherwise realized, into shafts, axles, tyres, and bar iron for the use of the road and machinery. . . .[81]

A foundry also was attached for the casting of wheels and other necessities. This self-sufficiency did not diminish the effect upon

[78] Wellington, *Location*, p. 167. These results of the 1870's are appropriate to the prewar period as well.

[79] Wellington, p. 162.

[80] Notes of the Secretary of the American Iron Association in the manuscript division of the New York Public Library contain a letter from the superintendent of the Philadelphia and Reading Railroad to the effect that more iron was consumed in other uses than replacement of rails in 1856 (p. 26).

[81] Ringwalt, *Transport Development*, p. 135.

the economy; it merely substituted direct demands for machinery, coal, pig iron, et cetera, for indirect ones.

If the repair of equipment did call forth both skilled labor and industrial production before the Civil War, overall, the record is less satisfactory. Neither in construction nor operation did such demands make up a majority of railroad outlays. Operating requirements are particularly disappointing since about half of material inputs consisted of lumber in one form or another. Total commodity inputs made up only a third of current expenses in any event; as far as employment is concerned, no more than a fourth or so was contributed by such skilled groups as machinists, enginemen, or conductors.[82] Still, the significance of railroad derived demands cannot be dismissed on the basis of this evidence, however much it affords additional perspective. With total expenditures reaching the levels they did in the 1850's, large absolute requirements were necessarily generated. Two further aspects of the matter must therefore be explored: the extent to which such requirements were met by domestic provision and, closely related, the relative proportion of total domestic production taken off by the railroad sector. Neither the unimpressive relative distribution of railroad expenditures nor the more impressive absolute amount of physical requirements tells us what impact the railroad actually had upon American industrialization.

Railroad Requirements and American Industrialization: Iron

From the earliest, the iron industry was recognized as the focal point where railroads would have their greatest impact. Partisans and foes of the innovation alike were in agreement on this issue, if little else. Those who favored canals pointed to the substantial iron requirements as evidence of the impracticality and excessive cost of the new form of transport; those who were committed to railroads "predicted that this unprecedented demand would enormously stimulate the domestic iron industry. The great Philadelphia-to-Pittsburgh railroad would first create this immensely

[82] Based upon the detailed distribution of railroad employees in 1880 reported in the *Tenth Census*, IV, *Transportation*, p. 13, as well as the detailed breakdown of operating costs for the New York railroads in 1859. *Annual Report of the State Engineer and Surveyor on the Railroads of the State of New York for 1859* (Albany, 1860), pp. 334–361.

beneficial state industry and then transport its products cheaply throughout the state and to the west. The railroad's massive iron requirements were nothing but a blessing in disguise." [83]

With the first adoption of the railroad at Baltimore, however, efforts were immediately made to facilitate importation of English iron free of the crippling $37 a ton specific duty enacted in the Tariff of 1828. As evidence, proponents of liberalizing legislation produced replies of various iron masters to the inquiries of the Baltimore and Ohio concerning the availability of domestic supply. The response of J. W. and E. Patterson was typical: "Some years since, we prepared a rolling mill to make bar iron from blooms, and although we are contiguous to the great iron district of this country, we have never been able to procure as many blooms as would make the bar iron necessary to meet the *current* demands of our ordinary business. . . . Nor do we think you will be able to obtain your rails in this country." [84] Only one respondent expressed a willingness to accept a contract, and he only at a price of around $100 a ton. English edge rails were selling for less than £7 and even with duty and shipping charges were cheaper than American strap iron.[85] American production of bar had lagged far behind the British in the 1820's, and in spite of a differential tariff designed to discourage importation from abroad, little development had taken place in the United States. The leading opponent of the tariff relief measure was forced to concede that the current annual output of bar in Pennsylvania, far and away the leading state, was only 21,800 tons against a potential order of between 12,000 and 15,000 tons for this railroad alone.[86]

Although the Baltimore and Ohio request failed of passage in the House after being approved in the Senate, within 2 years the increasing interest in railroads led to a considerable concession. Section 9 of the Tariff of 1830 permitted a drawback from the payment of $37 a ton, subject to various assurances that the iron

[83] Rubin, "Canal or Railroad?", p. 37.

[84] Senate Exec. Doc. No. 192, 20th Congress, 1st Session (Washington, 1828), p. 1.

[85] Senate Exec. Doc. No. 192, 20th Congress, 1st Session, p. 1; the price of English rails in 1831 was £6 17s 6d. John McGregor, *Commercial Statistics of America* (London, 1849), p. 387.

[86] Lewis Haney, *A Congressional History of Railways in the United States to 1850* (Madison, 1908), p. 302.

was used in connection with railroad construction, until the duty should amount to 25 percent *ad valorem*. Since bar iron was selling at less than $50 abroad, the rebate was generous. Only another 2 years elapsed until more favorable terms were offered. Railroad iron, according to the Tariff of 1832, could enter free of any charge. Such a provision continued in force until the Tariff of 1842 went into effect in March of 1843. Indeed, until 1836, when specific disapproval was expressed by Congress, not only the rails but also auxiliary needs like cast-iron chairs, et cetera, were admitted free.[87]

Thus, over the objections of Pennsylvania iron producers, the iron requirements of the railroads did not turn out to be a "blessing in disguise." Free entry meant that American output in the earliest period of the innovation was almost entirely unaffected. For practical purposes all demands were met by import,[88] and well they were. Without such an alternative source of supply, railroad costs would have risen still higher than they soared, and construction surely would have been discouraged.

The first period of significant domestic response to the iron needs of railroads must therefore be dated from 1843 on. A tariff of $25 a ton was levied upon all bar iron, including rails, by the Act of 1842, and under this umbrella of protection there is indication of rising interest by producers in this new market. In 1844, at any rate, we do know of at least one mill turning out U-rail; earlier in the same year, however, it was asserted that ironmasters were unable to satisfy the demand of the Philadelphia and Reading Railroad.[89] The early part of the 1840's was hardly a propitious time to start, of course, when the wreckage from the depression of 1839 precluded any extensive new railroad construction, and older roads in process, aware of the expiration of their privilege of duty-free import as early as 1841, had taken advantage of the interval to accumulate supplies.[90] Also American rolling tech-

---

[87] On this see Haney, *Congressional History to 1850*, pp. 301–307.

[88] There is evidence of some insignificant production of strap iron rails by at least 2 rolling mills, Brady's Bend and the Tredegar Works, in 1837 and 1841. *Hunt's Merchants' Magazine*, XVI (1847), 212, 530. Undoubtedly some American mills also met demand for spikes, and some foundries the demand for chairs.

[89] James M. Swank, *History of the Manufacture of Iron in All Ages* (Philadelphia, 1892), pp. 432–434.

[90] In 1841 an act had been passed levying a duty of 20 percent effective in March,

nology was still far from satisfactory. Experimentation with cast-iron rails was encouraged to bypass this obstacle. A Report of a Select Committee of the Pennsylvania Legislature examined the possibility of using cast-iron rails for renewal of the state railroads in 1842 and reported in its favor: "Here, then, is an interest of vast importance, which may be nurtured and promoted by the adoption of cast-iron rails for railways; and surely the highest considerations of public policy should prompt the authorities of such a state as this, to foster and encourage a leading branch of manufacture." [91] In spite of such sanction, and despite the Philadelphia and Reading's willingness to try cast-iron rails (but only at no risk to the company), nothing came of the idea.[92] Not surprisingly: cast iron was hardly suitable for such use.

Not until later in the 1840's is there much evidence of American rail mills being erected or converted.[93] By 1846, *Hunt's Merchants' Magazine* records a substantial capacity ranging between 60,000 and 119,000 tons, depending upon source.[94] Although some have translated these data equivalently into output they hardly permit of such a direct transition. Not only does capacity differ from actual output, but it is explicitly stated that "nearly all are in operation, except four or five, which are in process of construction and nearly finished." [95] Four or five in this case means a fourth

---

1843. The more stringent Tariff of 1842 superseded this legislation (Haney, *Congressional History to 1850*, pp. 309–310). Remission of duties was particularly large in 1842 and 1843 relative to construction outlays in those years. In part this represented a lag of construction behind importation, but also perhaps a speeding up of track laying in order to qualify for free importation. See Senate Exec. Doc. No. 55, 34th Congress, 3rd Session.

[91] Reprinted in *Journal of the Franklin Institute*, 3rd ser., V (1843), 389.

[92] Swank, *Manufacture of Iron*, p. 433.

[93] Fogel, *Railroads*, pp. 260–261, defends extensive production of strap iron by rolling mills in the early 1840's that went unnoticed because of its similarity to merchant bar production. That little direct evidence of such a phenomenon appears to be available, the rapid shift from strap iron to edge rail as the center of construction moved to New England, as well as the fact of free importation until early 1843, all cause me to continue to dispute this possibility. There are, in addition, the continuing efforts to return to a regime of free importation. Fourteen memorials were presented to the 1843–1844 session of the Senate alone requesting remission of duties. Haney, *Congressional History to 1850*, p. 312. (Fogel's specific criticism of the mileage series used to derive rail consumption for the decade is answered in Appendix B, p. 367, n. 36.)

[94] *Hunt's Merchants' Magazine*, XVI (1847), 593 and 97, respectively.

[95] *Hunt's Merchants' Magazine*, 97. Daddow and Bannon almost always show a

of the mills enumerated. Likewise, a comparison of the two different tabulations, the one for Pennsylvania, and the other for the
entire country, indicates considerable overstatement in the latter.
The capacity for the same mills add up to 44,000 in the first
article, 51,000 in the other. Finally, the same mills rolled plate
as well as rails as part of their production.

Whatever the necessary adjustments, it nevertheless seems
clear that substantial American rail production first began in this
period. One of the factors most responsible for this result was the
increasing substitution of anthracite for charcoal as the principal
fuel. The increased capacity of blast furnaces and the reduction in
cost both encouraged the development of rail mills. Also involved,
it should be pointed out, was the simultaneous rapid increase in
British and continental railway mileage which left an unmistakable imprint upon the price of iron. Imports of English rails were
assessed at $28.68 in the year ending June 30, 1844; $51.01 in
1847; after duty, commission, and shipping were paid, rails in
the latter year easily cost more than $70 delivered; American
rails were quoted at $69.34 in the same year.[96]

In the midst of the expansion, a new tariff had been enacted
in 1846 that liberalized the import duties on bar iron by converting them to a 30 percent *ad valorem* basis. The immediate effect
of this change was hardly noticeable since foreign prices were so
high. Subsequently, however, after English railway investment
peaked in 1847–1848, iron was radically reduced in price. In fiscal
1850 assessed value per ton of imported rails stood at $26.32, the
American price at more than $45. Partly under the influence of
such lower prices, railroad expansion had begun again in significant volume and imports expanded quite rapidly. From a level
of less than 6,000 tons in fiscal 1846, imports increased to 142,000
in fiscal 1850. Meanwhile, American production rapidly dwindled.
When estimates of output first become available, for 1849, pro-

substantial divergence between actual production and capacity in the industry.
See *Coal, Iron, and Oil*, pp. 682–698.

[96] Prices obtained by dividing quantities of imports into declared values. *American Railroad Journal*, XXIX (1856), 490. American prices are those of the American
Iron and Steel Association as reported in *Historical Statistics*, p. 124. The tariff
in 1847 was 30 percent *ad valorem*. The previous specific duty of $25 would have
made imported iron more expensive than the domestic product, and there was much
outcry against the *ad valorem* basis of the new tariff.

duction is indicated at only 21,712 gross tons.[97] Evidence from the *American Railroad Journal* suggests that the turning point in American output came in 1848 when many mills first failed.[98] By the end of 1849 Abram Hewitt wrote: "Of fifteen rail mills only two are in operation, doing partial work, and that only because their inland position secured them against foreign competition for the limited orders of neighboring railroads, and when these are executed not a single rail mill will be at work in the land." [99]

While perhaps not as desperate as Hewitt, or the memorial of the Pennsylvania Iron Manufacturers,[100] made out, the provision of railroad iron had indeed entered a new phase, or perhaps, reverted to the old, in which foreign imports again predominated. Table 13, which displays estimates of American production, and two alternative import series, brings this out clearly. From 1849, when construction began to gather steam in the West, until 1854, when it peaked, importation met 80 percent of American needs. American ironmasters labored under two distinct disadvantages, higher costs and an inability to extend credit. The magnitude of the price differential may be illustrated by a comparison of American and British prices per gross ton of rails — the latter adjusted for duty, ocean shipping, and commission:[101]

Year	British	American
1848	$64.98	$62.25
1849	52.20	53.87
1850	43.16	47.87
1851	42.61	45.62
1852	41.65	48.37
1853	55.38	77.25
1854	66.40	80.12

[97] See Table 13 below.
[98] *American Railroad Journal*, XXII (1849), 184.
[99] Quoted in Swank, *Manufacture of Iron*, pp. 435–436.
[100] Reprinted in the *American Railroad Journal*, XXIII (1850), 514, 529, and 545.
[101] Eleven and a half percent was added for commission, insurance, etc., and $5 for freight to price of imported product. Appendix B discusses this matter, p. 368, n. 39.

TABLE 13.   Iron rail production and consumption (gross tons of 2240 pounds)

	(1) Domestic production	(2) Imports, AISA	(3) Imports, official[a]	(4) Total (1) + (2)	(5) Total (1) + (3)
1840	—	—	27,632	—	—
1841	—	—	23,682	—	—
1842	—	—	21,946	—	—
1843	—	—	14,224	—	—
1844	—	—	18,695	—	—
1845	—	—	13,855	—	—
1846	—	—	9,716	—	—
1847	—	—	21,513	—	—
1848	—	—	49,326	—	—
1849	21,712	—	105,599	—	127,311
1850	39,360	142,036	165,331	181,396	204,691
1851	45,181	202,098	217,125	247,279	262,306
1852	55,784	263,170	272,310	318,954	328,094
1853	78,450	320,352	290,930	398,802	369,380
1854	96,443	303,070	205,191	399,513	301,634
1855	123,816	136,624	141,506	260,440	265,322
1856	160,730	166,602	167,400	327,332	328,130
1857	144,570	192,112	127,525	336,682	272,095
1858	146,171	81,155	72,855	227,326	219,026
1859	174,513	74,962	96,069	249,475	270,582
1860	183,070	130,902	98,332	313,972	281,402

Source: (1) and (2) *Annual Statistical Report of the American Iron and Steel Association for 1875*, p. 182; (3) William M. Grosvenor, *Does Protection Protect?* (New York, 1871), p. 221.
[a] Fiscal year converted to calendar year basis by interpolation.

From a net advantage in 1848, the American position rapidly deteriorated until a maximum differential was reached in 1853, the year of largest importation. But as is obvious from these data, until 1852 the gap was not insurmountable. Moreover, American producers could, and did, emphasize the quality difference between British and American iron to justify a slight differential. What may have made the real difference in the early 1850's was the reciprocal flow of securities and iron. American ironmasters could not afford, because of their limited capital and weak competitive position, to extend long credit, or simpler still, to accept payment in stocks and bonds. On the other hand, "many British iron masters shrewdly sold rails in exchange for railroad bonds, and on this basis drove a flourishing business." [102] The exact magnitude of such trade is difficult to ascertain, but the aggregate figures on capital imports are well correlated with iron imports.

After 1854, security prices declined, reducing considerably British willingness to purchase them, and American prices conformed much more closely to that for imported rails.[103] Both circumstances favored domestic producers. Indeed, the rapid rise in the American price in 1853 and 1854 in part was due to increasing American orders that could be filled abroad only after a substantial delay, and which consequently were diverted to domestic producers; output rose smartly in both years. In addition to these favorable developments, replacement requirements began to mount in importance. By the mid-1850's, the American railway system was already a substantial network whose maintenance alone involved considerable demand for iron. Here the imports of inferior British iron at the beginning of the decade worked to peculiar advantage since it meant more rapid replacement, an area in which Americans could compete profitably. Not only were payments in securities much less relevant for roads already underway, but a sizable proportion of the replacement demand was for rerolled rails, by means of which the value of the scrap iron could be realized directly. Such arrangements were typical, as we may infer from our previous discussion as well as the comment of the *American Railroad Journal* in 1856 that "our domestic rail mills are largely engaged in re-rolling." [104] Thus fortified, American production was almost at parity with imports in 1855 and 1856, and was distinctly ahead in 1858, never again to be headed. Even the reduction of the duty on rails to 24 percent in

[102] Allan Nevins, *Abram S. Hewitt, with Some Account of Peter Cooper* (New York, 1935), p. 104.

[103] Simultaneously, there was an increasing clamor from the western and southern states for reversion to duty-free imports. See Haney, *A Congressional History of Railways in the United States, 1850–1887* (Madison, 1910), pp. 40–46.

[104] XXIX (1856), 490.

1857 did not prevent an increasing American share of the market. The satisfaction of railroad iron requirements thus went through two alternating phases in the ante-bellum period. In the first, imports dominated because of the beneficence of wise legislation, reinforced by the stark realities of American inadequacy in an age of charcoal iron. Between 1844 and 1848, domestic production in substantial quantities was evoked for the first time, but overall, output probably did not exceed 150,000 tons over this interval.[105] It was not that imports cut into the market significantly — they amounted to only 85,000 tons — but rather that railroad construction was being prosecuted vigorously at the time in only one region, New England. After the temporary protection afforded by the English railway mania abated, imports were again resumed as the regular channel of supply. Rapid construction and external provision went together, as before in the 1830's. Finally, at the very end of the period, a strong industry emerged, in large measure a response to replacement demands. Note that it was not a new industry in the end of the 1850's, however. Many of the same rail mills of the 1840's continued through the subsequent hard times by turning to other products and hence constituted the industry at both periods.[106]

That railroad rail consumption was not in fact identical to domestic supply does not close out the question of its relative importance, however much it dilutes its potential effects. There are a variety of comparisons that are of interest in this connection, both quantitative and qualitative. There are also some that are not. One of the most widely used, ironically, falls into the latter category. That is the relationship between pig iron output and total rail production. The reason for its spuriousness should be evident from the earlier discussion of rerolling. Included among the inputs to such a production process were substantial quantities of scrap iron rails as a substitute for pig. Hence any direct

[105] Based upon reported capacities in those years, indicated total consumption between 1840 and 1850, and reported production in 1849 and 1850. See Appendix B, pp. 378–379.

[106] As did the Trenton Iron Co. See Nevins, *Abram S. Hewitt*, pp. 105–110, for information on this mill. See J. P. Lesley, *The Iron Manufacturers' Guide to the Furnaces, Forges, and Rolling Mills of the United States* (New York, 1859), for other instances.

conversion of rail output into a pig iron equivalent will overstate considerably the magnitude of rail demands. Railroads were suppliers as well as demanders of crude iron.

Table 14 takes this into account by stating gross demands for rails less the scrap content of rails replaced and by confining itself to initial requirements for other components. The logic of this subtraction is that although the scrap was not converted directly by railroads, its use somewhere in the economy implied an equal reduction in demands for pig iron.[107] To this extent, Table 14 understates the flow of pig iron into products used by railroads themselves.[108] The divergence is as large as 25 percent in the late 1850's. For although there was a rapid increase in rails replaced, only some three fourths were apparently rerolled. Thus one fourth of the total in line (2) should be multiplied by 1.25 to represent the additional pig iron consumed directly by rail rolling mills. In addition, since it was common practice to introduce new pig iron for the top layer of the rerolled sections, perhaps to the extent of one-third the total weight, demands were further augmented.[109] Similarly, not all repairs of equipment used the old materials in exactly equivalent amounts. At least one report suggests a ratio similar to that observed for rails.[110]

From an economy-wide perspective, however, what matters are the net demands for pig portrayed in Table 14. They tell an interesting tale. In the first instance, there is the solid position of railroad requirements in the 1850's. Something like 20 percent of the net consumption of that decade is explained thereby. Note,

---

[107] The *Iron Masters Journal* commented in 1856: "It is worthy of note, that a large proportion of the old rails taken up is used in *other* manufactures, to which this description of iron is regarded by many as being better adapted. The increasing amount of this stock, which comes into competition with pig, is worthy of special consideration." Reprinted in the *American Railroad Journal*, XXIX (1856), 490 (italics mine).

[108] Another and less important cause is the failure to allow for weight shrinkage of the scrap.

[109] For a description of the rerolling process, see *American Railroad Journal*, XXXI (1858), 476. See, too, the *Railroad Gazette*, III (1871), 444, where J. Dutton Steele criticizes the practice of using slabs of pig iron, but refers to it as a "popular theory among railmakers." A pamphlet describing the Crescent Iron Works at Wheeling also refers to the practice, but cites a higher proportion of crude iron. *Crescent Iron Manufacturing Company* (Boston, 1855), p. 20.

[110] *American Railroad Journal*, XXXIII (1860), 90.

TABLE 14. Railroad derived demands for pig iron (thousands of gross tons)

	1840–1845	1846–1850	1851–1855	1856–1860
(1) Domestic production of rails	62	199	400	809
(2) Rails replaced	17	33	222	391
(3) Net demand	45	166	178	418
(4) Pig iron equivalent	56	208	222	522
(5) Initial demands for spikes & chairs	14	28	95	71
(6) Pig iron equivalent	15	31	104	78
(7) Initial demands for locomotives	5	15	56	39
(8) Pig iron equivalent	6	16	63	43
(9) Initial demands for other equipment	17	47	155	106
(10) Pig iron equivalent	19	53	176	119
(11) Total pig iron equivalent	96	308	565	762
(12) Total domestic production of pig	2059	3580	3039	3700
(13) Total domestic consumption of pig	2153	3886	3568	4022

Source: (1) 1840–1848: 200,000 tons, estimated consumption 1840–1850 minus imports minus known production, 1849 and 1850. See Appendix B, p. 378, for estimated consumption. The allocation to subperiods is approximate and is determined by requirements for new construction plus replacement (Appendix B, pp. 367, 378) and two additional assumptions: inventory decumulation of 10,000 tons in 1840–1845 and accumulation of 20,000 tons in 1846–1850. Three characteristics of the early period point to inventory decumulation of this magnitude: failure of 117 miles of track constructed prior to the period whose rails were then available for resale; contraction of planned construction of at least 100 miles of road in progress, for some of which rails had been obtained; a concentration of completion of road early in 1840 that required previous accumulation of rails. Inventory accumulation is explicable by the increase in mileage added in 1851 as against 1846; the sum required derives from the need to have something like at least the first quarter year's requirements on hand.

(2) 1840–1850: Estimated replacement 1840–1850, Appendix B, p. 378. Original values were multiplied by $\frac{1}{3}$ to reflect lesser weight of scrap relative to iron replaced. Allocated to subperiods by replacement model described in Appendix B, p. 391. 1851–1860: Total consumption from column (5), Table 13, minus requirements for new trackage. Allocated between periods by reference to difference between supply and demand for new construction, Appendix B, p. 392.

(3) (1) minus (2).

(4) (3) multiplied by 1.25.

(5) Seven and one-half tons per mile of new construction. The requirements for spikes and chairs vary pretty much between 5 and 7.5 tons per mile throughout the period, except for early direct imitation of English methods on some New England railroads in the 1830's. See *American Railroad Journal*, XII (1841), 182; *ibid.*, XVII (1845), 775; Appendix, *Missouri Senate Journal* 1858–1859, p. 204; and New York Railroad Commissioners, *Annual Report for 1854-55*, pp. 42–43.

(6) Line (5) multiplied by 1.1 to reflect predominance of cast-iron chairs.

(7) Number of locomotives determined by stock in 1839, 1849, and 1859 as

too, how the rapid increase of domestic rail production toward the end of the decade accounts for almost a third of the increased production of pig iron. Equally clearly, the apparent rapid rise of blast furnaces in the late 1840's had its sources elsewhere. At best railroads absorbed only 17 percent of the total increase in output.[111] If that achievement was the central feature of ante-bellum growth, as Rostow seems to suggest, it was quite independent of simultaneous railroad developments.

The important role of nonrail requirements also may be commented upon. Although much smaller than rail consumption in an absolute sense, because the spikes, wheels, locomotive boilers, et cetera, were constructed out of domestic materials, their effect

[111] Which sectors did absorb this increased output is still something of a mystery and represents the most telling objection to the existing data showing a spurt in output in the 1840's. This uncertainty is heightened by the implication that non-railroad consumption would have had to decline in the early 1850's. Grosvenor makes this point, but does not press it home, in *Protection*, p. 210.

[*Source* notes for Table 14, continued]
estimated in Appendix D. Production for 1850 and 1860 estimated by equipment quantity index in Table 52. This also was used to allocate production by period. Locomotive weights of 20 and 25 tons were used for the 2 decades of which 0.9 represented iron. See Appendix D, Table 56; *Bulletin of the Railway and Locomotive Historical Society*, no. 53 (1940), 64–66; and *American Railroad Journal*, XXVI (1853), 487, 550.

(8) Line (7) multiplied by 1.125 to reflect equal proportions of cast- and wrought-iron requirements.

(9) See line (7). Weights of 5.5 tons and 7.5 tons per passenger car were used for the 1840's and 1850's respectively. Weights of 3.5 tons and 2.0 tons for 8-wheel equivalent freight cars and 4-wheel equivalent coal cars, respectively. On these inputs, see Ringwalt, *Transport Development*, p. 338; Arthur M. Wellington, *The Economic Theory of the Location of Railways*, 6th ed. (New York, 1887), p. 163. A reference to a 7-ton total weight of a passenger car in 1848 can be found in the *American Railroad Journal*, XXI (1848), 149; *Eighth Census, Manufactures*, p. clxxv, indicates a 400–500 pound weight per cast-iron wheel in 1860. The later experience is relevant since car weights changed much less rapidly than capacity.

(10) See line (8).

(11) Sum of lines (4), (6), (8), and (10).

(12) The series of Raymond, based on Carey, was used. It can be found in Frank W. Taussig, "Statistical Appendix," *Quarterly Journal of Economics*, II (1888), 379–382. Fogel has developed a new pig iron series in chap. v of his *Railroads* which is quite similar. The choice of series makes little difference here.

(13) Line (12) plus imports of pig iron, converted to calendar year by averaging. The import series may be found in Grosvenor, *Protection*, p. 221.

upon American pig iron production was proportionally much greater. That they were provided locally is not open to much question. Wheels, axles, springs, and the like were not imported, and neither were spikes or sheet iron in large amounts. At the height of the railroad boom in 1852 imports of spikes amounted to 71,997 *pounds*, in 1854 to the not more substantial sum of 340,529; for the same two years sheet iron imports averaged about 15,000 tons compared to bar imports 3 times as large. There was no opportunity for the completely fabricated foreign product to satisfy demands since all rolling stock was manufactured domestically after the early 1830's, as we shall see. The probable major import for railroad purposes consisted of the excellent Low Moor iron that was particularly well adapted to use in locomotive tires. The Low Moor Company was the only consistent British advertiser in the railroad journals, in any event, and there is some significance in the fact that its sole American agent had offices in Boston rather than New York or Philadelphia, which were the supply centers for the industry. This suggests a limited market.

From these data it is difficult to fault the foresight of Abram Hewitt's suggestion in 1854 that railroad construction, not the tariff, would succor the American iron industry.[112] For economic development the quality of the demands also count. Thus railroad demands contributed heavily to the important transition from charcoal to anthracite, and ultimately, coke, pig. Without a mineral fuel basis the industry could never have grown to the heights it soon reached. The first experimentation with anthracite did precede the railroad age, but it is also true that rail mills could utilize anthracite pig more efficiently than other users, and that much of the consumption took place there. The ultimate lead of anthracite pig in 1855 and the widening margin thereafter was assured by continuing increases in rail production during the decade.[113] Secondly, within the more restrictive, but important

---

[112] Nevins, *Abram S. Hewitt*, pp. 156–157, paraphrases a letter from Hewitt to the Hon. Charles Shelton contained in the Hewitt Papers. Hewitt's sanguine disposition disappeared with the peak of railroad investment in that year, however, and he became an advocate of higher tariffs thereafter.

[113] See Swank, *Manufacture of Iron*, pp. 352–365, 376; and Louis C. Hunter, "Influence of the Market upon Technique in the Iron Industry in Western Pennsylvania up to 1860," *Journal of Economic and Business History*, I (1929), 241–281.

field of rolling, railroads achieved still greater pre-eminence than in their demands for pig iron. In 1860, rails constituted in volume more than 40 percent of all rolled iron.[114] Rail mills were the largest in the country and in the technological van: of a total of six integrated iron works in the United States in 1854, five were rail mills, and the sixth a producer of nails and spikes, and hence possibly connected with the railway interest as well.[115] It comes as no surprise that Kelley's experimentation with the Bessemer process took place at the Cambria Works, a substantial producer of rails, or that the Trenton Works pioneered in structural beams.[116] Subsequently, in the period after the Civil War, the Bessemer process was taken up first for the production of rails. Of the initial ten establishments fitted out for this purpose, seven were formerly iron rail mills.[117]

For perspective, it is well to refer to the later accomplishments of railroad demands in more detail. During the period from 1867 until 1891 rails comprised more than 50 percent of the output of Bessemer steel in *each* year; until 1880 the average ratio exceeded 80 percent. Iron rail output itself had almost tripled between 1860 and 1870, while pig iron doubled.[118] Increasing quantities of scrap were generated in that later period, but with a switch to steel rails, direct pig iron requirements were a larger proportion of output than earlier. The ante-bellum period gave an inkling of what was to come rather than fully accomplishing the ultimate revolution.

Robert W. Fogel's researches into the same question seem to

[114] *Eighth Census, Manufactures*, p. clxxxiii. This excludes the extensive purchases of wrought iron for use in repair of equipment.

[115] Lesley lists 16 rail mills producing 141,555 gross tons in 1856, for an average of about 9,000 gross tons; 7 of the mills produced more than 11,000 tons each. The average size of other rolling mills was less than 2,000 tons (*Guide*, pp. 757, 762). Whitworth and Wallis listed the following 5 rail mills in their 1854 report: Trenton; Reeves, Buck, and Co.; Reeves, Abbot, and Co.; Montour; and Mt. Savage. The 6th was the Fuller and Lord Works in Boonton, New Jersey. Joseph Whitworth and George Wallis, *The Industry of the United States in Machinery, Manufactures, and Useful and Ornamental Arts* (London, 1854), pp. 42–43.

[116] Swank, *Manufacture of Iron*, p. 399; Nevins, *Abram S. Hewitt*, pp. 113–118. Hewitt also experimented with the Bessemer process.

[117] Swank, *Manufacture of Iron*, p. 412.

[118] *Annual Statistical Report of the American Iron and Steel Association for 1894* (Philadelphia, 1895), supplement pp. 8, 10, 11, 13.

deny even this role to the pre-1860 decades. In contrast to the more than doubling of domestic pig iron requirements for rails at the end of the 1850's, displayed in Table 14, he finds a gain of only 40 percent.[119] His result is based primarily upon an increasing supply of scrap rails from 1856 to 1860 that successfully negated the observed growth in production of domestic rail mills. The replacement estimates in turn emanate from a model of rail deterioration asserting that replacement followed a log-normal curve with a mean of 10.5 years and standard deviation of 3. He demonstrates his model not only to be consistent with single observations in the years 1856 and 1866, but also its form and parameters to conform with data culled from the 1880 census.

Despite its careful conception, the method is not without difficulties. In the first instance the use of a relationship between rail wear and time is only a proxy for the functional relationship holding between replacement and cumulative tonnage carried. Over long periods of time, and in a steady state of traffic, the divergence between the two approaches becomes trivial. In the short run, it remains a matter of concern, as can be readily shown. Fogel extends his estimates to 1869 where he estimates total domestic scrap iron consumed in the economy to be less than 370,000 gross tons. But because the Civil War had intervened, with an attendant much greater railroad output per mile of track, replacements at the end of the 1860's were greater. According to the census, in the year 1869–1870 more than 600,000 gross tons of scrap were consumed, and almost 450,000 in rolling mills alone, where rails would find their principal use.[120]

Unfortunately, no similar data are available for 1860. Yet we know that railroad receipts and output per mile of road actually declined at the end of the 1850's owing to the depressed state of

---

[119] A comparison of his Table 5.15, *Railroads*, p. 194, with Table 14 here reveals other differences: the aforementioned excess of pig iron consumption in rail manufacture he finds between 1840 and 1845, and a corresponding shortfall in 1846–1855. The largest absolute difference is to be found at the end of the 1850's, however, and it is also the one which is qualitatively significant. Many of the same arguments relative to the later period apply to the earlier differences too.

[120] U.S. Bureau of the Census, *Ninth Census*, III, *Statistics of Wealth and Industry* (Washington, 1872), pp. 605, 607, 608.

the economy then.[121] Older roads like the Michigan Southern carried less tonnage per mile after 1856 than before;[122] newer roads did not find traffic enough to make up the difference. With rail replacement dependent upon cumulative tonnage carried, the ordinary scrapping that might have been anticipated in the latter 1850's was delayed until later.

A second fundamental objection is the mechanical nature of the model, regardless of the specific form. Rails wear out and are replaced quite independently of the financial context within which such demands occur. In fact, of course, railroads resorted to numerous expedients to avoid the incidence of such heavy outlays. Typically, they temporarily repaired rails rather than replaced them. In the latter 1850's many railroads followed the earlier cited practice of the Galena and Chicago Railroad of welding rather than rerolling.[123] The inconsistency of such automaticity evinces itself at the aggregate level as well as by example. The pattern of rail renewal espoused by Fogel suggests that expenditures for the replaced iron were almost 9 percent of total operating outlays in 1859.[124] Yet in New York and Massachusetts, states whose networks would have to be largely replaced, the observed percentages are about half as great. The *American Railroad Journal*, summing up the results of the varied railroads reporting in its pages generalized to an outlay of from 6 to 7 percent, and this has an upward bias due to almost exclusive reliance upon heavily trafficked roads for the information.[125]

Here precisely lies the difference between the estimates of Table 14 and those of Fogel. The former are rooted directly in the financial expenditures for iron reported by individual roads; the latter in application of long-term homeostatic principles to

[121] See Appendix A, and for a discussion of western railroad fortunes in particular, Chapter IV.

[122] *Railroad Gazette*, III (1871), 444.

[123] *Railroad Gazette*, III, 444, referring to 1869, commented that only half the number of rails formerly repaired "are now mended."

[124] Based upon the purchase of 96,000 net tons of rerolled rails and 60,000 tons of new replacements at a price of $30 for the former (including transport, etc.) and of $50 for the latter, total outlays are $5.9 million relative to operating expenses of $67.3 million.

[125] See for this evidence Appendix B, pp. 374–376.

short-run events. Since the crucial issue turns upon a few years, and abnormal ones at that, I must confess to preference for the expenditure analysis embodied in Table 14.

It is also relevant to note that not all the contemporary evidence on rails scrapped is consistent with Fogel's results. Daddow and Bannon estimate the quantity of rails rerolled in 1857 and 1863 as 56,450 and 146,669 gross tons, respectively.[126] If one interpolates linearly, a procedure that maximizes pre-Civil War totals, rerolled rails from 1856 to 1860 sum to 358,000 tons. Fogel reconciles these data with his model only by assuming the ratio of scrap rails rerolled to total replacement is less than 0.6 before the War, but rises to 0.776 in 1866. No justification for such an assumption is given, and if the later ratio be applied earlier, Fogel's estimate of replacement is too high by a factor of almost 30 percent. Under the same circumstances, mine is still too small by about 15 percent, this continued divergence arising from the previously stated disbelief in a simple linear pattern of increase of rail replacements in 1858 and 1859 during bad times.

Rail replacement is the central difference between Fogel's and my own calculations, accounting for some 200,000 of the total 271,000 ton gap in estimates of pig iron consumption from 1856 to 1860. The residual arises from the asymmetrical fashion in which imports of pig iron are treated. Fogel chooses to subtract from domestic requirements the foreign pig iron presumably directly consumed by rail mills, while at the same time subtracting *all* scrap rails, whether rerolled or not, on the grounds that aggregate pig iron demands were correspondingly reduced. But if the economy-wide perspective is uniformly applied, and total national imports of pig iron are determined by relative price, the allocation of these imports is of no matter. Consumption of imports in rail mills leaves scope for domestic pig iron elsewhere. Only if rail mills uniquely required imports in some fixed proportion does such subtraction make sense; on this substantive point, one is inclined to answer in the negative in light of the sensitivity of the pig iron import series to relative price rather than to rail production.

---

[126] *Coal, Iron, and Oil*, pp. 683, 694–695.

The importance of rails in the market for iron between 1856 and 1860 is thus an unsettled issue. Fogel's model and results require our careful consideration, but not to the exclusion of the different methods and findings advanced here. Nor should the fundamental conclusion of a large and increasing role for railroad demands in the development of the iron industry in the 1850's be obscured. Fogel's own data, if not analysis, corroborate it. Aggregated over all components of railroad construction, his estimated consumption of domestic pig rises by 34 percent between the quinquennia 1851–1855 and 1856–1860; mine, by 35 percent. On average, over the interval 1856–1860, his statistics reveal railway demands absorbed more than 15 percent of American pig iron production; mine, 21 percent.[127] On either basis, railroads were a factor to be reckoned.

Railroad Requirements and American Industrialization: Machinery

The impact of the railroad upon the machinery industry followed different lines. From the beginning, for example, imports played little role in supplying needed rolling stock. Of the 450 locomotives in the United States at the end of 1839, only 117 were imported from England, and of these 78 were brought in before the end of 1835.[128] For other rolling stock there is no evidence of reliance upon foreign producers. On the other hand, at the end of the ante-bellum period there is nothing like the same dominance of railroad demands that was found for iron. The Census of Manufactures in 1860 reported the value of locomotive production as $4,866,900; that of cotton and woolen machinery amounted to a larger $4,902,704. Aggregate production of the machinery sector came to more than $52,000,000 in the same year.[129] Nor is it simply the value comparison instead of a physical one that produces this disparity. Iron rails alone in 1860, as reported by the census, were worth $11,000,000 com-

[127] The various nonrail demands of Table 4.8, *Railroads*, p. 132, have been combined with the contribution of rails stated in col. 10 of Table 5.15, p. 194, to obtain a total comparable with that of Table 14.

[128] Appendix D; *Bulletin of the Railway and Locomotive Historical Society*, no. 20 (1929), pp. 36–44.

[129] *Census*, p. 738.

pared with a total output of the industry of $73,000,000.[130] Were
the other products taken off by the railroad added in, the total
would be much enhanced. The reason for the divergence is substantive. Machinery encompassed a wide range of products that
found use in a wide variety of enterprises: engines for steamboats,
for rice mills, for factories; woodworking equipment; steam ham-
mers for foundries, and so forth. No single demand was pre-
eminent as a consequence.

Rostow has seized upon a different measure of the relative
importance of railroads for the machinery industry than the one
presented above. His point is that the machinery industry grew
out of railroad demands: railways "led on" to the development
of the machinery industry, he says in one place; "brought to life,"
is the expression he uses in another.[131] To prove this contention
the relative position of locomotives in total horsepower generation
is cited. He quotes with approval Paul Cootner's conclusion:
"In 1849, locomotives accounted for 435,000 horsepower or 35
percent of the total. In the course of the next decade, the railroads acquired almost 75 percent of the additional output, and
its total rose to 1,943,000 or 60 percent of the total. In a very
real sense the American engineering industry was a product of
the growth of the railroad. . . ." [132] Unfortunately, Daugherty's
calculations, on which these results are based, are far from accurate. Much better estimates of the horsepower generated by ante-
bellum locomotives are developed in Appendix D. These, when
scaled up by the number of locomotives on railroads at the various dates, yield the following horsepower totals:[133] for 1839,
34,650; for 1849, 170,925; for 1859, 1,015,200. This adjustment

[130] Calculated by taking census production of 235,000 tons times an average price
of $48 reported for that year; See *Eighth Census, Manufactures*, p. clxxxiii, for out-
put; p. 737 for value of all iron products; *Historical Statistics*, p. 124, for price.
[131] Rostow, *Stages*, p. 55; Joint Economic Committee, *United States and Soviet
Economies*, p. 593.
[132] Rostow, "Leading Sectors and the Take-Off," p. 5, n. 1, quoting from Cootner's "Transport Innovation and Economic Development: The Case of the U.S.
Steam Railroads," unpub. diss. Massachusets Institute of Technology, 1953, chap.
iv. The statistics ultimately derive from C. D. Daugherty, "An Index of the
Installation of Machinery in the United States since 1850," *Harvard Business
Review*, VI (1927–1928), 278–292.
[133] See Table 56, Appendix D.

considerably reduces the force of Cootner's, and Rostow's argument.

I dare say, moreover, that Daugherty's totals are equally suspect, but in the other direction, i.e., understated. Consider, for example, the horsepower generated by steam powered vessels. On the basis of estimates of steamboat tonnage on the western rivers and horsepower-tonnage equivalents, we find that this single part of the total steam powered shipping in the country developed 55,728 horsepower in 1840; 425,502 in 1850; and 488,205 in 1860.[134] In addition to such steamboats there was additional service on eastern rivers and bays, and steamers on the lakes: by 1860, steam driven tonnage on the lakes came to 255,449 tons, or about 50 percent more than on the rivers; to this tonnage must be added an additional 97,296 tons engaged in ocean commerce.[135] In sum, the something like 500,000 tons of steam shipping in the United States in 1860 may have generated *more* power than locomotives, not 75 percent less, as Daugherty's data say.[136] The horsepower of steamboats on the western rivers in 1850 alone exceed Daugherty's estimate for ships at that date, and the rapid growth of steam power on the lakes and ocean conspire to make his 1860 estimate for the category less than half of the total probably generated.

The railroad is given additional advantage by such a comparison, since one of the characteristics of locomotives was their relatively long life. Steamboats, by contrast, were notorious for their rapid demise. This meant that the steam engines *built* for shipping exceeded the share indicated by a static count. For example, between 1851 and 1860, Ringwalt estimates construction of more than 730,000 tons of steam vessels with horsepower exceeding that of the 1860 fleet; the locomotives built over that same interval including replacements, came to about 4,600 in

[134] Based upon an equivalent of 2 hp:3 tons in 1840, and 3 hp:1 ton in 1850 and 1860. See Hunter, *Steamboats*, p. 144, and for tonnages, p. 33.

[135] Taylor, *Transportation Revolution*, chaps. iv and vi; pp. 62, 116 for tonnage estimates.

[136] This takes full account of the lower horsepower to tonnage rates of the low pressure ocean and eastern steamships. At a minimum, using a ratio of 1 hp:3 tons, we find total horsepower for steamships at 600,000 in 1860 or at most 40 percent less than that generated by railroads.

number with horsepower of less than 920,000. In the 1840's, the divergence is equally marked. From the standpoint of the demands for the machinery industry, therefore, railroads took second rank to the shipping interest.

Nor is this simply a quantitative judgment. Steamboats used engines much larger than those on locomotives. Horsepower of 1200 was not uncommon on the western rivers, but locomotives of this size awaited the end of the century. In a technical sense, the specific form of railroad steam engines did not provide strategic breakthroughs or develop unique innovations.[137] As far as transmission of skills is concerned, Hunter lists 68 machine shops, employing from 4800 to 4900 men, manufacturing machinery connected with steamboats on the western rivers alone; in the same year locomotive producers employed 4174.[138]

This discussion must be broadened to a second interpretation of Rostow's colorful terminology. What may be asserted is that locomotive production brought into being for the first time a group of specialized engineering firms. The much earlier development of steamboats gives immediate notice of the weakness of this argument. Indeed, the first locomotive built in the United States, the "Best Friend of Charleston," for the South Carolina Railroad, was built by the West Point Foundry, a supplier of marine engines. Rather, instead of creating an engineering industry, the rapid development of domestic production of locomotives in the United States can be explained by the existence of a prior level of skills and technique upon which the industry could call.

Reference to the origins of the first locomotive builders in the United States will illustrate this point concretely. Baldwin was asked to build a model locomotive engine, and ultimately went into large-scale production, because of his prior success in manufacturing stationary steam engines. The parent firm from which Rogers, Ketchum, and Grosvenor emerged was established in 1819 as Clark and Rogers, both to build textile machinery and to spin cotton; machinery for textile firms continued to be turned out even after locomotives were added in 1837. The Locks and Canal Company was nothing more than the machinery company

---

[137] See Hunter, *Steamboats*, chap. iii; Sinclair, *Locomotive Engine, passim*.
[138] Hunter, *Steamboats*, p. 654; *Eighth Census, Manufactures*, p. clxxxix.

for the Lowell mills; in reference to an early contract with the
Philadelphia and Reading, Patrick Jackson told the directors:
"The object in making these contracts is to give profitable employment for our shops and foundry at a time when we have little
else to do." Hinkley had run a machine shop since 1826 before
turning to locomotives in 1840. The major exception to the rule
was the very successful Norris works which passed through difficult times before its position was assured; the Poughkeepsie
plant was less fortunate.[139]
    Not only the early pioneers, but later ventures as well, are
characterized by prior experience gained in other lines. The Manchester plant was established in 1855 by the former head of the
Amoskeag machine shops; Mason, a cotton machinery producer
in Taunton, turned out his first locomotive in 1853; Amoskeag
developed in 1849 from a machine works attached to a manufacturer of cotton and wool founded in 1809; Grant, who set up
in Patterson in 1848, had previously operated a general machine
shop; the founder of Cooke and Company was Rogers, Ketchum,
and Grosvenor's foreman. In the West, too, where in the early
1850's local producers began to multiply, most of those shops
already were in operation, and turned to locomotives to meet the
extraordinary demand posed by the rapid expansion in that
region. Niles and Company of Cincinnati, the largest of the western producers, had just one branch of their business engaged in
locomotives; H. & F. Blandy of Zanesville switched to locomotives in 1851 from other machine work; the Cuyahoga Steam
Furnace Company of Cleveland which was building locomotives
in 1853 was described in 1848 as the leading builder of marine
low pressure engines in the West. The failure of the South to
develop substantial production of locomotives is a reflection of
the lack of already existing machine shop facilities.[140]

[139] *History of the Baldwin Locomotive Works*, p. 9; *Bulletin of the Railway and
Locomotive Historical Society*, no. 8 (1924), 7–23; *ibid.*, no. 79 (1950), *passim; ibid.*,
no. 28 (1931), 6–11; *ibid.*, no. 10 (1925), 54–57. M. N. Forney, *Locomotives and
Locomotive Building* (New York, 1886), pp. 1–3. The quotation is taken from George
Gibb, *The Saco-Lowell Shops* (Cambridge, Mass., 1950), p. 97.
[140] *Bulletin of the Railway and Locomotive Historical Society*, no. 15 (1927), 15–33;
ibid., no. 8 (1924), 24–31; *ibid.*, no. 11 (1926), 23–29; *ibid.*, no. 26 (1931), 9–17;
American Railroad Journal, XXI (1848), 242; *ibid.*, XXVI (1853), 443; George W.
Broome, *The Amoskeag Manufacturing Company* (Manchester, N.H., 1915), p. 77.

The ability of regional producers to mushroom in the first part of the decade and then to disappear as rapidly after the decline of equipment purchases from 1857 on, also testifies to the easy substitution between locomotive and other machine production, at least for short periods. At the same time, it points up the existence of a differentiated industry in which national producers like Baldwin, Norris, and Rogers captured the largest part of the market and allowed the residual to go to local shops satisfying local demands. It was very difficult for later producers to capture a national market for the same reason that foreign producers soon gave way before domestic suppliers.[141] Lack of standardization meant that familiarity with the machinery and a supply of replacement parts were essential. Railroads with large numbers of locomotives from the same producer could satisfy both conditions simultaneously; to buy a small number of engines from a new manufacturer, unless it was a local firm, was irrational. Hence the later firms catered to a narrow demand, making them especially susceptible to business fluctuations and leading them to only a partial commitment to the production of locomotives.

It is not my intention to slight ante-bellum locomotive production; the volume of output in the 1850's compares favorably to that in the 1880's and it may be that as a proportion of the entire machinery industry, locomotives did reach their maximum before 1860.[142] Where the railroad had greatest effect, however, was not so much in the rise of specialized locomotive firms from general machine shops as in the development of elaborate repair facilities on the railroads themselves. Here *was* a powerful force

---

[141] It is often suggested that American displacement of foreign producers was due solely to our excellence as reflected by success in third markets. Thus, Louis C. Hunter writes "so successful were American locomotive builders that their products were being exported to Europe in substantial numbers even before 1840." See his "Heavy Industries before 1860," in Harold F. Williamson, ed., *The Growth of the American Economy*, rev. ed. (New York, 1951), p. 181. Actually, however, exports virtually ceased after 1840 as domestic producers arose in Germany, Austria, etc., to supply their own needs. America was able to export early because the adaptations of the locomotive to fit more primitive conditions made it attractive at first.

[142] In 1869, for example, locomotive production of 1137 units could not have exceeded $15 million in value, while machinery as a whole was $138.5 million. The proportion is not startlingly different from that in 1859. *Ninth Census*, III, *Wealth and Industry*, p. 615.

for the geographic dissemination of skills necessary to an industrial society. Although the South could support only limited
locomotive production, the larger railroads in that region, the
Georgia Railroad, South Carolina, et cetera, all had extensive
shops for the reworking of old metal, renewals of locomotives,
manufacture of rolling stock.[143] Likewise in the West, the repair
shops of the railroads are always included among the local machine shops in any discussion. As well they might: in both Detroit
and Cleveland the railroad shops were among the largest enterprises, and the same was true in other cities. The Michigan Central built all its own cars and even constructed some of its
locomotives.[144]

Such shops were numerous because railroads themselves were
numerous, and the quality of their furnishings was generally of
very high standard. Indeed, if a contemporary English observer,
himself a leading railway engineer, is to be believed, they had
"tools equal or superior to ours in all practical respects." [145] This
is the more remarkable since just three years later, in 1854, one
of the commission sent to the New York Industrial Exhibition
wrote concerning machine shops in general: "The engine tools
employed in the different works are generally similar to those
which were used in England some years ago, being much lighter
and less accurate in their construction, than those now in use,
and turning out less work in consequence." [146] Whether Watkin's
favorable observation was based on a biased sample or not, the
fact is that many railway shops were machine shops in miniature,
with their demands for lathes and other machine tools on the one
hand, and their training of the labor force on the other. If 5 percent of the operating employees on railroads in 1860 were skilled
machinists, and the 1880 census indicated a ratio that large at
the later date, the total number employed by the railroads would
exceed those employed in locomotive works by more than a fifth!
It is this, then, which distinguishes the influence of the railroad

[143] See for example: *Report of the Georgia Railroad and Banking Company, 1843*
(Augusta, 1844), p. 12; *American Railroad Journal*, XXXIII (1860), 12, 841.
[144] *American Railroad Journal*, XXVI (1853), 611–612, 614–615.
[145] E. W. Watkin, quoted in Habakkuk, *Technology*, p. 5.
[146] Whitworth and Wallis, *Industry of the United States*, p. 18.

from steamboats, on the one hand, and from textile requirements on the other. While steamboats may have generated more power, there were limited positive side effects for industrial development, because these were small, individual ventures with less continuing maintenance. And although the output of cotton and wool machinery exceeded locomotive production in 1860, the consequences were felt within narrow regional boundaries and were not extended to the entire country. With the additional repairs of railroad equipment, moreover, total railroad demands probably exceeded those of mills. In 1870, when railroad repairing is explicitly entered in the census for the first time, it comes to 20 percent of the machinery total.[147]

Railroad Requirements and American Industrialization: Coal

Although a reasonable case can be made for the influence of railroad backward linkages before the Civil War in the development of both the iron and machinery sectors, there is little scope for its extension to coal. In 1859, as we have seen, locomotives consumed no more than 270,000 gross tons, of which the largest part was anthracite. Production of anthracite came to more than 9,000,000 tons; total coal, to more than 17,000,000 tons.[148] As a proportion, therefore, direct railroad requirements are an insignificant 2 percent of coal consumption. The impact was to be felt later; in 1880 and 1890 locomotives consumed close to a fifth of total production.[149]

The addition of indirect requirements does not alter the picture appreciably. A good approximation of the coal required by the production and subsequent fabrication of crude iron used in the railroad sector can be derived from the data underlying Table 14. Pig iron used about $2\frac{1}{2}$ tons of coal in its manufacture at this time, wrought iron an additional 1 to 2 tons, and cast iron 1 ton.[150]

[147] *Ninth Census*, III, *Wealth and Industry*, p. 396.
[148] *Historical Statistics*, p. 357, and p. 360, both converted from short to gross tons.
[149] These estimates are based upon my "Productivity and Technological Change."
[150] See Walter Isard, "Some Locational Factors in the Iron and Steel Industry in the Early Nineteenth Century," *Journal of Political Economy*, LVI (1948), 204–208.

At its maximum, therefore, including coal consumed in fabricating scrap, the indirect demand for coal generated by railroads came to something like 4,000,000 tons over the period 1856–1860.[151] Anthracite production over that interval came to 42,374,000 tons, with bituminous scarcely less, making all railroad demands, direct and indirect, about 5 percent of the total, and but slightly more of the anthracite that was primarily used. Two further observations place this result in a more favorable perspective. First, railroad demands for coal were probably the least important of all the derived demands for industrialization. In the ante-bellum economy, coal did not make the engines of industry run as much as it kept the home fires burning. Abundant natural resources, water power and fuel wood, substituted nicely down to 1860 and even beyond. In 1851, when a survey of coal consumption was taken, textile factories required only 200,000 tons; the coal consumed in the manufacture of *all* iron, from the pig through to the final products, was but 1,400,000 tons. Total output exceeded 10,000,000 tons at that time.[152] If coal found primarily nonindustrial markets before the war, it still could not compare with other energy sources in those uses. In 1850, coal was the source of less than 10 percent of the energy consumed in the economy, and still less than 20 percent, ten years later.[153] Yet an impressive development of manufactures occurred in the

---

[151] This total was reached by multiplying rail output by 1.5 tons, and other final demands by 1.25 tons (because of their large cast-iron needs). The consumption of iron in repairs of rolling stock was estimated from total expenditures on repairs. These latter were first adjusted for the differing iron content of repairs from new construction. Replacement of spikes and chairs was derived from the relationship between rail replacement and total production. To the total coal consumed in fabrication, 1,800,000 tons, was added a coal input calculated as 2.5 tons for 762,000 tons of pig iron or 1,900,000 tons in aggregate. A further 25 percent allowance for additional pig actually consumed within the railroad sector in rerolling, etc. brings total coal requirements slightly above the 4,000,000 ton mark.

[152] Howard N. Eavenson, *The First Century and a Quarter of American Coal Industry* (Pittsburgh, 1942), p. 196, for coal consumption in textile mills, and in the manufacture of pig iron, castings, and wrought iron. His source is U.S. Commissioner of Patents, House Doc. No. 102, 32nd Congress, 1st Session (Washington, 1852).

[153] Sam H. Schurr, Bruce C. Netschert, *et al.*, *Energy in the American Economy* (Baltimore, 1960), p. 500.

1840's consistent with this structure. Early industrializations are not necessarily like the later ones.

In the second instance, small as railroad derived demands for coal were, they were about as large a percentage of total output as their demands for such nonindustrial commodities like lumber or fuel wood. Table 15 presents some calculations of lumber requirements from 1840 through 1860, compared with national output over the same intervals. The comparison is not uniform, since ties were hewn rather than produced by saw mills. As a measure of the potential lumber consumed, however, the results are valid. What they disclose are railroad demands accounting for 3 to 4 percent of production during the 1840's, and for 10 percent in the next decade. This stands in sharp contrast to contemporary statements suggesting far more impressive demands: "The consumption of timber on American railroads for the single article of sleepers, is so great as almost to defy calculation." [154] With fuel wood, in spite of frequent comment upon the locomotive's prodigious appetite, the emphasis is even less apt. In 1859, as was shown above, fuel requirements amounted to 2 million cords; a decade earlier, consumption was probably less than a fourth as great. Yet total cordwood consumption for 1850 is indicated at 102 million cords, with 126 million for 1860.[155] As a proportion therefore, the consumption of anthracite coal for locomotive fuel alone in 1859 was more important for that industry than the much larger absolute consumption of cord wood for the forestry sector.[156]

This comparison suggests a further reason for emphasizing the industrial character of railroad demands. Although a minority of total railroad outlays, the industrial requirements made a larger impact on their suppliers than the nonindustrial demands upon theirs. The fortunes of the industrial sectors *did* depend to a greater extent upon railroad purchases than did the economy as a whole. Even though absolutely small, therefore, railroad coal inputs were more influential than their fuel wood or lumber needs.

[154] *Hunt's Merchants' Magazine*, XXXVIII (1858), 384.

[155] Schurr, *et al.*, *Energy*, p. 508.

[156] Owing to the large direct consumption by households, railroad demand as a proportion of total market sales was undoubtedly larger. But it still was of small relative significance, which is the essence of the point.

TABLE 15. Railroad lumber requirements (millions board feet)

Use	1840–1845	1846–1850	1851–1855	1856–1860
Ties (1)	290.2	502.3	1,664.9	2,119.2
Ties (2)	(580.4)	(1,004.6)	(3,329.8)	(4,238.4)
Bridging	48.6	84.0	218.0	277.5
Cars	22.1	53.7	161.7	135.0
Total	360.9	640.0	2,044.6	2,531.7
	(651.1)	(1,142.3)	(3,709.5)	(4,650.9)
Total lumber production	17,408	24,607	32,549	39,664

Source: Ties (1): For replacement demand, see Appendix B. For new requirements decadal mileage times 2200 ties per mile in the 1840's, and 2400 in the 1850's. Size of tie was assumed at 27 board feet in the 1840's and 33 board feet in the 1850's. For confirmation of these assumptions, see Zerah Colburn and Alexander Holley, *The Permanent Way* (New York, 1858), p. 61; also Virginia and New York State reports, the former for 1859 and 1860, the latter for 1856. In 1887, the Department of Agriculture estimated average number of ties at 2640 per mile of size 3 cubic feet, or 36 board feet. Department of Agriculture, Forestry Division Bulletin No. 1, *Report on the Relation of Railroads to Forest Supplies and Forestry* (Washington, 1887), p. 14.

Ties (2): In the same Department bulletin cited above it is recognized that tie production is more wasteful of lumber than other types of requirements: "Each tie represents about 75 feet of good merchantable lumber in the standing timber destroyed for it" (p. 15, n. 1). This is a ratio of 2 feet consumed to 1 used. Accordingly, this second tie series is the first one multiplied by two and provides a better comparison of relative physical demands.

Bridging: Bulletin No. 1 also indicates a consumption for bridging of 2000 cubic feet per mile based on the assumption that bridges comprised 2 percent of the line. Since a sample of Virginia and Massachusetts roads indicates that only 1 percent of line consisted of bridging, one half of this later requirement has been used. Replacement needs were calculated by scaling tie replacements to the lumber consumed in new bridges.

Cars: Number of cars from Appendix D, adjusted for retirements. Lumber consumption was assumed at 6000 feet per passenger car, 3000 feet per freight car, and 1500 feet per coal car. (Wellington, *Location,* p. 163, specifies 4000 feet for an 1883 box car, so these approximations should be reasonably accurate.) Replacement requirements were determined from the ratio of expenditures on repairs of rolling stock to investment in new cars, adjusted for the lower utilization of lumber in repairs than construction. Repairs on cars were calculated as 9 percent of operating expenses, investment in cars as half the total investment in new equipment, and the ratio of lumber use as 0.22. (For the first two assumptions see Appendix B; for the latter, Wellington, *Location,* pp. 163, 164.)

Total Lumber Production: Census benchmarks from *Historical Statistics,* p. 312, linearly interpolated to provide quinquennial sums.

Railroad Expenditures and pre-Civil War Development:
A Final Comment

Railroad outlays possibly exerted more effect upon realized economic change before 1861 than the potential resource saving of lower cost transportation. The large capital-output ratio of the sector caused expenditures to mount up in significance before transport services achieved high levels. The decisive weight of investment was felt by the 1850's as for the first time it governed over-all activity. The relatively early emergence of large expenditures is not unique to railroads. Another major Schumpeterian innovation, and another component of the infrastructure, electric power, partakes of the same properties. The important role currently attributed to social overhead investment depends upon its contribution to output. But the impressive historical contribution of these investments may well reside in their dual function as significant suppliers *and* demanders, with the latter emerging first.

The specific form of railroad requirements, at least, reinforces this conjecture. Not that the ante-bellum period was the scene of their principal triumphs. Only the production of rolling stock took root immediately. Rails continued to be imported through the major part of the boom of the early 1850's, and railroad consumption of coal was modest before the war. Certainly the rise of iron and coal production in the 1840's largely was independent of railroad demands. Subsequently, the potential market became an actual one. By the last part of the pre-war period railroad consumption took off a goodly amount of total domestic iron production. Thereafter derived demands wielded more industrial leverage than before. Bessemer steel production was introduced and almost totally absorbed by railroads. More of the output of the nation's coal mines found its way to the railroad sector than any other. Machine shops and skilled employment multiplied at an increasing pace.

Before the war, however, another aspect of railroad investment may have been more important than either the contribution to demand or the specific requirements. That is the response of other sectors to railway provision. The next set of chapters deal with this subject, beginning with the westward expansion of the 1850's.

Part III

The Nature of the Forward Linkages

CHAPTER IV

The Dynamics of Railroad Extension into the West

Introduction

The rapid pace of American railroad expansion in the 1850's has been noted often in the preceding chapters. No region was so transformed as the West. A few hundred miles of track, the remnant of the disappointed internal improvement schemes of the 1830's, emerged within ten years as a network whose extent surpassed even the most optimistic of those earlier dreams. By 1857 the Mississippi had been bridged and the railhead was on the verge of the Missouri. Iowa and Wisconsin, achieving statehood just prior to the decade, were introduced to the wonders of steam locomotion bare years afterward. The much more densely settled state of Ohio was hardly provided with facilities before it was beset by excess capacity, all within the space of a single ten-year, exciting period.

The magnitude of these changes in the transportation sector was fully matched by changes in other parts of the western economy. Wheat and corn production expanded rapidly, the state of Illinois rising to leadership in both. The old Northwest Territory, plus Iowa, accounted for something like 40 percent of wheat production in 1850, half in 1860; the comparable proportion of corn output increased from 31 to 38 percent. Agrarian prosperity was mirrored in land settlement and increasing land value. Urban settlements more than kept pace, particularly along the lakes. Most impressive of these new cities was Chicago, which almost quadrupled within the course of the decade, and about which a visiting Englishman could already write in 1866: "Chicago has grown to be the largest market in the world for corn, timber, and pork: the three great exports of North America." [1]

This correlation between economic activity and transport improvement did not go unnoticed either by contemporaries or later analysts. A theoretical structure invoking lower transport costs can explain both the increasing agricultural supply area and the centralization of economic functions in urban nodes. The geographic extension of agriculture follows directly from the spatial displacement of the extensive margin. For industry, there is "the reallocation of the market area and the redistribution of industrial production in favor of the most efficient and the best situated firms." Another cause of concentration of industry is "the increased production and mass production economies caused by extending and enlarging the market area." [2]

Such a logical relationship does not establish unequivocal causality, of course. If population migration had already extended the agricultural frontier, if urban agglomerations had already become prominent, transport improvement may have justified and reinforced such developments rather than initiated them. In 1808, Benjamin Latrobe rejected a primitive prototype of the railroad as a practical means of transport because it required much greater densities of population than then existed. Was the enthusiastic acceptance of the railroad in the 1850's the product of an already prospering economy and not its cause?

If one can establish the temporal precedence of railroad construction, the direction of the causal flow becomes unmistakable. Hence the crucial importance of the Schumpeterian notion of construction ahead of demand to his sweeping conclusion that "the Western and Middle Western parts . . . of the United States were, economically speaking, created by the railroad." [3] Such a scheme, while it is consistent with my own notions of the place of railroad expansion in that development, is obviously much too simplified a version of the actual mechanism at work.

[1] S[amuel] Morton Peto, *The Resources and Prospects of America* (London, 1866), p. 93.

[2] Walter Isard, "Transport Development and Building Cycles," *Quarterly Journal of Economics,* LVII (1942), 92–93.

[3] Schumpeter, *Business Cycles,* I, 303.

After all, Ohio qualified for statehood only three years after the turn of the century, almost fifty years before railroads proliferated; more to the point, by the 1840's it ranked among the leading agricultural states. The first part of this chapter therefore subjects the assertion of railroad construction ahead of demand to careful scrutiny. What emerges is a more accurate statement of the dynamics of railroad construction in the West during the 1850's, and the perverse proposition that railroads were *not* constructed ahead of demand. This result does not entirely preclude railroad causality, however. Construction ahead of demand is inadequate because railroad promotion in already settled areas sparked anticipatory population movement to less settled areas. As a consequence, demand was already there when railroads were ultimately built farther west. In a larger sense, therefore, railroads *were* a leading factor. But first let us turn to the Schumpeterian formulation before elaborating upon this other explanation.

Construction Ahead of Demand

"As a rule," wrote an English investment counselor in the 1890's, "the American railroad came in advance of the settlers, and this contrasts with European custom. Apart from being impossible on account of our population density, the prospect of building a line through an unsettled country would be deemed an insane proceeding." [4] Seventy years later, this characterization of American railroad development still has wide currency. Schumpeter's writings, of course, are responsible for much of its persistence. His dictum that many midwestern railroad projects "meant building ahead of demand in the boldest acceptance of that phrase . . ." [5] can be neatly transformed into a theoretical case for the importance of the railroad, as we have seen. [6] Indirectly, too, Carter Goodrich's enlightening studies of the role of government in nineteenth-century American economic development have contributed to the vitality of this interpretation. [7]

[4] S. F. Van Oss, *American Railroads as Investments* (New York, 1893), p. 7.
[5] Schumpeter, *Business Cycles*, I, 328.
[6] Jenks developed the notion in his "Railroads as an Economic Force," pp. 1–20. August C. Bolino has incorporated it in his text, *The Development of the American Economy* (Columbus, Ohio: C. E. Merrill, 1961), p. 172.
[7] See his *Promotion of Canals and Railroads*.

His work can be viewed as an explanation of the viability of such a developmental pattern of construction.

Such later analyses build upon, and accept, the descriptions of contemporaries, like the following:

> Nine-tenths of our roads when first traversed by steam pass through long ranges of woodlands in which the axe has never resounded, cross prairies whose flowery sod has never been turned by the plow, and penetrate valleys as wild as when the first pioneers followed upon the trail of the savage. . . . But no sooner is the great work achieved, then population pours into the rich wilderness, is scattered over the wide sweeping prairies, and settles in the fertile vales. . . . A productive energy is certain to be developed that will finally equal any capacity for business.[8]

Indeed, this sequence of zero population, railroads, and then economic development has become an implicit ideal type of construction ahead of demand. Unfortunately, despite such supposed eyewitness accounts, this specification (and implicit test) of the hypothesis is of little value. The real world bears no resemblance to this idyll: few areas of the country penetrated by railroad in the 1850's were frontier even in 1840, let alone without population altogether. A more general statement of the hypothesis, and less stringent tests, are necessary if the concept is not to be rejected out of hand.

Central to any redefinition must be the notion of an initial disequilibrium that is self-correcting over time not by adjustments along given demand and supply curves, but by induced shifts in the demand schedule. Thus when such projects are first planned or opened, the demand facing them is insufficient to justify them, as reflected by the lack of any profitable price that will clear the market. Over time, however, the sale of these essential services at prices less than full cost encourages income growth in the community so that the altered demand conditions merit the investment, and a profitable equilibrium is eventually attained. If the period involved is sufficiently long the present value of future returns may never exceed the cost of the project. In this instance no investment would have been forthcoming had

---

[8] *American Railroad Journal*, XXXIII (1860), 926, from the *New Orleans Picayune*.

a correct assessment of objective conditions been made; this is the domain of government subsidy or entrepreneurial error. A shorter period of transition introduces a second possibility. Rational investors, after allowance for the risk associated with estimation of expected rather than actual demand, would undertake this class of ventures.

Schumpeter himself tended to stress the first alternative when he asserted that "Middle Western and Western projects could not be expected to pay for themselves within a period such as most investors care to envisage." [9] It is the one, of course, where the market allocates resources inefficiently from a social viewpoint — in the absence either of daring, and not always wise, entrepreneurs or external subsidy. The second set of circumstances, while the private rate may still understate social priorities, will lead to less distortion since the projects will be undertaken in any event. But in both instances, whether ultimate financial success or no, it is the temporal precedence of supply under initially unfavorable conditions that sets the stage for the ultimate shifts in demand.

Three measures of construction ahead of demand emerge from this restatement of the concept. The first is *ex ante* and emphasizes investor anticipations concerning the configuration of demand facing the project. If the capital market absorbed the securities of western railroads without a significant risk premium, this rules out widespread feeling that future returns were so far off that private investors could not participate profitably. Because of the unorganized capital markets of the period and the aggregative nature of our problem, this measure is not easily applied. A ready substitute, the prevalence of government aid, is. Subsidy is simply the limiting case in which the private market values prospects so dimly that funds are not available at any reasonable price. While it may miss intermediate gradations, "building ahead of demand in the boldest acceptance of that phrase" presumably will not be excluded.

But even if the project lures private investors because expectations of future profit are definite enough, construction ahead of demand can not be ruled out. *Ex ante* measures all prove inade-

[9] Schumpeter, *Business Cycles*, I, 328.

quate to the extent that realized operating experience differs from the anticipated. For an analysis of the investment decision they are central; but concern with actual effects requires reference to *ex post* indicators. Profits of the enterprise serve us well here. One of the implications of construction ahead of demand is that initial levels of demand are so low as to yield a less than profitable outcome.[10] A second is that net earnings should increase over time as financial accounts register the supply induced shift of demand. Both implications are subject to test, although the variety of other factors changing over time requires considerable qualification of the second.

While positive and stable profits tend to disprove the hypothesis, negative returns are more difficult to evaluate.[11] They are compatible with a number of cases that one would not choose to label construction ahead of demand.[12] For example, with a positive correlation between railroad construction and economic activity (generated from the side of supply of capital as well as the direct consequences of such building) some projects will reach fruition on the threshold of cyclical economic decline. The general reduction in demand causes such roads to fare badly; otherwise they might have done quite well. In no sense has construction ahead of demand in secular terms occurred. Profits must therefore be adjusted for cyclical variation if they are to be an accurate indicator. Or to take another relevant possibility: if railroads are manipulated as instruments of municipal competition and are unsuccessful, their financial statements as well as the laments of local businessmen will attest to this fact. Still a third factor contributed to poor operating results, namely mismanagement.

[10] Unless the shift in demand is immediate and large enough to make the project immediately profitable. Settlement data indicate precedence of demand, however, and rule out the likelihood of such an interpretation.

[11] Everett E. Hagen's suggestion that lack of profitability could be used as an index of temporal precedence of social overhead capital is thus denied. For the reasons developed in the text for railroads in particular, it is equally unsatisfactory in general. Cf. his "Economic Structure and Economic Growth," in *The Comparative Study of Economic Growth and Structure* (New York: National Bureau of Economic Research, 1958), p. 131.

[12] Schumpeter himself attempted to distinguish between construction ahead of demand and mere creation of excess capacity, but without much success. Cf. *Business Cycles*, I, 158.

One need only read the files of the *American Railroad Journal* at the end of the 1850's to appreciate how pervasive this factor was.

In all these instances, subsequent cyclical recovery, or change of management (or simply experience) may bring profitability. These cases conform to the typical temporal pattern of profit returns of roads constructed ahead of demand, although the circumstances are quite different. For certain purposes it makes no difference. In an aggregate model receiving its developmental impetus solely from the side of demand, the characteristic of investment without immediate output is what counts.[13] But only in the pure case of construction ahead of demand, or development via excess social overhead capacity, is the investment primarily responsible for its ultimate fulfillment.

This identification problem surrounding the use of actual profits cannot be resolved by reference to the statements of individual projects. No railroad, or very few, concede their construction in advance of demand; on the other hand, all proclaim their significance in developing subsequent traffic. Here is a typical example drawn from the promotional literature of the 1850's in the West, the case of the Ohio and Mississippi Railroad. Investors were assured a return of 15.53 percent upon cost and annual dividends of 12 percent, on the most conservative estimates; the potential value of the stock was claimed to be at least double the original subscription price.

That the above is really a minimum I am convinced from a test derived from railway experience, and may be applied by anyone. . . . It must further be remarked in considering the above results, that they have been brought out by calculating the local, direct, and positive trade of this road, and not by including extraneous influence, or even the rapid increase of commerce. . . . In fine, there is more danger that the axial line will not be able to transact the business upon it, than that it will fall short of what its most sanguine projectors have anticipated.[14]

[13] Cf. Conrad's historical adaptation of a growth model *cum* cycles in his "Income Growth and Structural Change."

[14] *Geographical, Geological, and Statistical Relations of the Ohio and Mississippi Railroad* (n.p., n.d.), p. 24.

In 1861, its shares were selling at 1½ (par being 100), and an order for the sale of the eastern division of the road for the benefit of the first mortgage holders was issued by the United States District Court in Ohio.

This asymmetry of the profits measure suggests the need of a third indicator. Population density, serving as a proxy for actual traffic demand, performs this function, but not alone. Some additional information is needed to determine when density is sufficient. To be sure, a population density of more than 90 persons to the square mile — the highest census classification — is obviously large enough to justify the construction of a railroad (but not necessarily many railroads). And at the other extreme, a frontier density of 2 to 6 persons per mile is a dubious source of demand; even geographically isolated mineral resources generated local agglomerations more substantial than this. But what of the intermediate range? Southern Michigan, for example, was largely populated with 18 to 45 persons to the square mile in 1850.[15] The census described such regions as follows: "The third group — 18 to 45 inhabitants to the square mile — almost universally indicates a highly successful agriculture. . . ."[16] Yet Overton refers to the same area in 1846 as a "western wilderness" although no substantial change in population occurred between this date and 1850. He likewise speaks of John Murray Forbes as "fascinated by the prospect of sponsoring a railroad through the Michigan wilderness."[17] Most of the railroad construction of the 1850's took place exactly in areas of such intermediate and questionable densities.

This uncertainty can be resolved. If some railroads in an area of given population density earn satisfactory returns it is evidence that such a region can support railroads even if the recorded profits of other enterprises indicate otherwise. Some railroads in the East were unsuccessful, but the gains of others testify that the territory was not beyond the railroad frontier. Thus, in conjunction with the record of *ex post* profits, population densities are a

---

[15] *Eleventh Census*, I, *Population*, pt. 1, p. 2.

[16] *Eleventh Census*, I, *Population*, p. xxxi.

[17] Richard C. Overton, *Burlington West* (Cambridge, Mass., 1941), pp. 25, 27, n. 50.

useful means of discriminating among doubtful cases of construction ahead of demand. All three tests are utilized in the succeeding sections. Although each has its shortcomings individually, taken together they constitute a rigorous evaluation of the hypothesis. If roads earned profits from the start, did not show an upward trend in net earnings, were built through areas of previous and abundant settlement, and did not receive much government aid, virtually all would agree that construction ahead of demand had not taken place. That these were the typical characteristics of railroad development in the West in the 1850's is exactly what we shall argue. We begin with the relationship of settlement to construction.

The Pattern of Sequential Construction

One of the most striking features of western railroad expansion in the 1850's is the regular progression of mileage added from more to less densely settled areas. Table 16 and the map at page 175 illustrate this tendency. By the end of 1852 Ohio already had one third of the total mileage it was to possess by decade's end. Wisconsin and Iowa at the western extreme had virtually none; even Illinois had barely begun to manifest the railroad fever already gripping states farther east. Such regularity argues for deliberate rationality, with exploitation of opportunities as they became profitable, and postponement of projects in unpromising areas. If western railroads were constructed ahead of demand, why not in some random fashion?

In any event, the very concentration of mileage in Ohio circumscribes the extent of construction ahead of demand. By the early years of the decade, as previously noted, Ohio already "is one of the most important members of that Union, both in wealth and in population, and exercises a degree of influence on our federal councils second only to the great states of New York and Pennsylvania," in the words of De Bow's *Encyclopedia*.[18] It had begun a state-wide canal system in 1825 and completed it some 10 years later; the consequences were rapid agricultural advance

---

[18] J. D. B. De Bow, *Encyclopedia of the Trade and Commerce of the United States*, 2nd ed. (London, 1854), p. 345.

TABLE 16.   Railroad mileage added in midwestern states, 1848–1860

Year	Ohio	Indiana	Illinois	Michigan	Wisconsin	Iowa
Up to 1848	275	86	55	244	0	0
1848	32	0	10	48	0	0
1849	16	0	5	27	0	0
1850	122	106	47	332	0	0
1851	333	152	45	36	20	0
1852	292	376	140	4	42	0
1853	500	379	390	0	18	0
1854	587	251	906	0	52	0
1855	385	226	462	86	156	68
1856	133	218	409[a]	52	107	186
1857	129	123	74	46	291	90
1858	0	111	56	93	120	35
1859	174	60	103	83	78	154
1860	16	0	58	20	7	122
Up to 1861	2,994	2,088	2,760	771	891	655

Source: Paxson, "Railways of the 'Old Northwest,'" pp. 267–274. For Iowa, Poor's Manual, 1868–1869, pp. 20–21.

[a] An error in Paxson's tables has been corrected. Ten miles of the Galena and Chicago Railroad built in 1848 are credited to 1856 in his totals.

and population growth far before the 1850's. Railroads there were clearly not ahead of demand when they expanded rapidly.

Farther west, the 1850 population densities are sufficiently lower in states like Illinois, Iowa, and Wisconsin not to rule out the hypothesis. This is the theater in which such a process had to be staged, if anywhere. Yet even there the tendency previously described in the large, that of sequential development of present opportunities, applies in the small as well. The first railroads in Illinois and Wisconsin were constructed in the rich tiers of counties lying astride the border between the states. The Galena and Chicago Railroad from Chicago, and the Milwaukee and Mississippi from its rival lake port, were both attempts to exploit the surpluses of the Rock River Valley, an area that already had contributed importantly to the large grain export of 1847 and 1848. Other roads in Illinois were built to counties beginning to feel the beneficial effects of the prior opening of the Illinois and Michigan Canal. Prominent among these were the Rock Island,

and the Burlington line. This pattern of searching out the best opportunities first is quantified in Table 17.

TABLE 17. The pattern of railroad construction in Illinois and Wisconsin, 1848–1860

Year	Illinois			Wisconsin	
	Entire state	11 wheat counties[a,c]	8 corn counties[b,c]	Entire state	7 wheat counties[d]
1848	10	10	0	0	0
1849	5	0	0	0	0
1850	47	47	0	0	0
1851	45	36	0	20	20
1852	140	68	72	42	42
1853	390	94	60	18	18
1854	906	146	111	52	34
1855	462	23	21	156	100
1856	409	40	30	107	107
1857	74	0	0	291	75
1858	56	35	0	120	4
1859	103	41	15	78	38
1860	58	0	0	7	0

Source: Paxson, pp. 267–274; U.S. Bureau of the Census, Compendium of the Seventh Census, 1850 (Washington, 1854), pp. 221, 227, 329, 335.

[a] The wheat counties in Illinois are Boone, DeKalb, DuPage, Kane, Lake, Lasalle, McHenry, Ogle, Stephenson, Will, and Winnebago.

[b] The corn counties are Adams, Cass, MacCoupin, McLean, Madison, Morgan, St. Clair, and Sangamon.

[c] Cook County, which includes Chicago, is included in both groups, and mileage constructed there is credited to the group to which it leads.

[d] The Wisconsin counties are Dane, Dodge, Kenosha, Racine, Rock, Walworth, and Waukesha; Milwaukee County is included, however, since it was the terminus of much of the mileage.

Of the total number of miles of railroad built in Illinois by the end of 1853 more than 60 percent were concentrated in the leading 11 wheat counties and the 8 largest corn growing counties, both as measured in 1850. This area was only one fourth of the total land area of the state, and the disproportion of railroad density is clearly due to the existing settlement and economic activity. Illinois railroads do not present a biased picture, as the additional evidence from the Wisconsin experience makes apparent. In that state the 7 largest wheat producing counties plus Milwaukee, with but 10 percent of the total area, contained one half of the state mileage at the end of 1860, and three fourths at the end of 1856.

The less dramatic concentration in Illinois, indicating an earlier shift to construction in less developed areas in that state, is the product of two unusual circumstances. The Illinois Central, one of the two land grant roads completed before 1860, went through the center of the prairie for this reason. Another cause of the divergence is found in the large number of east-west lines that bisected the state. These, numbering among them the Toledo, Wabash and Western; the Ohio and Mississippi; and the Terre Haute and Alton, were built to compete for the through service to the Mississippi River, not to develop local traffic. They were not supported by local interests, and were, on occasion, vehemently opposed; it was with much trouble that the Ohio and Mississippi, connecting St. Louis and Cincinnati, was finally able to secure an Illinois charter. Despite such distortions, the mileage built in counties which had attained importance *before* the railroad era was 31 percent of the total against 25 percent, the expected result if the spatial distribution were completely random.

By the time that the railroad reached into the prairie lands, moreover, that area was far from barren. The use of 1850 densities is misleading in this respect, since the mileage came much later. The migration westward, in full sway by 1852, inevitably led to the cheap and still unsold prairie land. In 1851, the *St. Louis Times* reported, "The emigration into Illinois is immense this season. There are some in every county of the state, but the middle and northern portions are overrun with men in search of new homes." [19] As the northern areas became densely settled, more and more settlers were diverted to the prairie. The Illinois State Census of 1855 bears this out. Those prairie counties with smallest population in density in 1850 achieved a substantial increase in population by 1855; the number of persons per square

---

[19] Quoted in Paul W. Gates, *The Illinois Central and Its Colonization Work* (Cambridge, Mass., 1934), p. 104.

mile increased from four to nine and then to sixteen by 1860.[20]

Between 1849 and 1856, 12 million acres of the public domain of 14 million acres still available in Illinois in 1849, most of it prairie land, had been sold. Some of the land fell into the hands of speculators of course, so total sales do not attest to settlement in the same proportion, but Gates estimates that about half did go to actual farmers.[21] Thus by the time that many prairie railroads were finally completed, even if not in their earliest planning stage, not inconsiderable settlement and economic development had already occurred.

In the case of Iowa, the data confirm this more positively. Table 18 presents the population densities in the railroad counties of Iowa at various dates. The large increase in settlement occurred between 1850 and 1856, not later. Yet virtually no railroad mileage was built before 1856, as Table 16 shows, and it is therefore clear that the principal wave of settlement had markedly preceded the rail network in that state. The location of the Burlington and Missouri's land grant corroborates this conclusion. Although the land was bestowed in 1856, the railroad could not secure any east of Ottumwa, as far as the road reached before the Civil War and about 80 miles into the interior.[22]

Table 18 makes another point: the existence of very much higher densities in the railroad counties than in the rest of the state. Such a circumstance is general and is the reason why state density data are of little value. For Iowa, Wisconsin, and Michigan, the 1860 statistics are 12.2, 14.2, and 13.0 persons per square mile.[23] Coming as they do at the end of the period, these low densities clearly intimate construction ahead of demand in the previous decade. Yet the railroad areas in those states were much more densely populated; in Iowa, densities reached a level

[20] Computed from population data of Illinois State Census of 1855 as reprinted in the *American Railroad Journal*, XXXIII (1860), 1129. The prairie counties used are Champaign, Christian, Grundy, Iroquois, Kankakee, Livingston, Macon, and Piatt. (Kankakee County was formed in 1851 from Will and Iroquois Counties; to derive an appropriate population total for the group, one fourth of the 1850 population of Will County was allocated to Kankakee County.)

[21] Gates, *Illinois Central*, p. 109.

[22] Overton, *Burlington West*, p. 186.

[23] *Eleventh Census*, I, *Population*, p. xxxv.

TABLE 18. Population densities in railroad counties in Iowa (persons per square mile)

	1850	1856	1860
Blackhawk	—	9.6	14.3
Buchanan	0.9	8.9	13.7
Cedar	6.8	16.5	22.4
Clinton	4.0	19.3	27.1
Delaware	3.0	14.1	17.4
Des Moines	31.1	—[a]	47.2
Dubuque	18.0	43.0	51.9
Henry	20.1	35.6	43.1
Iowa	1.4	8.3	13.7
Jefferson	22.1	30.8	34.8
Johnson	7.2	23.4	28.4
Jones	5.2	15.1	23.1
Lee	36.8	51.3	57.0
Linn	7.6	20.4	26.3
Louisa	12.1	23.5	25.4
Muscatine	13.1	28.8	37.6
Scott	13.2	47.3	57.0
Van Buren	25.3	32.9	35.2
Wappello	19.6	30.7	33.6
Washington	8.8	19.6	25.1
State as a whole	3.5	9.3	12.2

Source: Iowa Census for 1880, pp. 200–201.
[a] Not available. The census gives a figure of 19.5 which is undoubtedly incorrect, not only because the reported population for 1856 and 1860 are almost identical, but also because the density for 1850 is 31.1.

more than twice the state average, and a still larger multiple of those in counties without trackage.

This pronounced sequential pattern of western railroad expansion suggests a rational exploitation of opportunity rather than the "insanity" imputed by Van Oss to American entrepreneurs. The absolute population densities, too, are quite respectable prior to railroad operation. The state censuses coming as they do at intermediate dates in the 1850's demonstrate this nicely. In themselves, these results cannot reject the hypothesis of building ahead of demand, however much doubt they cast upon it. It is still possible for the best of unprofitable opportunities to be taken up in order without altering the financial distastefulness of the totality. Because these American densities were unquestionably smaller than those exploited in Europe, and hence not obviously sufficient to support railroad transport, it still remains to be shown that different conditions of construction and operation could transform madness in a European context into profit maximization in the American West.

The Profit Experience

As a starting point, note how the pattern of railroad construction just described clearly suggests satisfactory results upon the early western roads. Suppliers of capital would have soon become discouraged in the face of patently unfavorable operating results on those western lines already completed early in the decade in the most settled areas. The western railroad boom, in fact, continued strongly at least to the beginning of 1855. It was not the result of an absent capital constraint. In spite of the vast amounts of capital allocated to railroad construction, calm and detached judgment was not thrown to the winds. Many projected roads remained precisely in an inchoate stage: "If the elaborate railroad network planned for Illinois by different groups and individuals during the fifties had been constructed, all parts of the state would have been brought within 2 to 5 miles of railroad lines. The only obstacle which prevented the carrying out of these grand schemes was the lack of capital." [24] The capital market rationed resources, albeit imperfectly, between railroads and other enterprises. Hence the early roads could not all have been unprofitable.

These inferences are confirmed by direct evidence upon profits. Some of the early lines were veritable bonanzas. The Galena, for example, paid a dividend of 10 percent less than two years after opening and was a regular income producer throughout the period. Of the early Illinois lines in general, Gates writes, "these roads tapped the rich hinterland of Chicago and prospered at once." [25] It was more than Illinois produce which helped to

[24] Gates, *Illinois Central*, p. 85.
[25] Gates, p. 86.

make such lines as the Galena, the Rock Island, and the Burlington initial and continued successes. The rapidly increasing surpluses of Iowa and Wisconsin sent to a Chicago market contributed to their financial well-being also. The Michigan Central and Michigan Southern to the east benefited from a similar through traffic once they reached Chicago in 1852, as their profit statements vividly show.

Without such extraordinary opportunities as these, other lines did not flourish as conspicuously. Nonetheless, the aggregate record tells a clear tale of success. Table 19 indicates the extent

TABLE 19. Net earnings of western railroads (as a percentage of cost of construction)

State	1849	1855–1856	1859
Ohio	7.5	6.4	3.7
Indiana	6.1	6.2	5.2
Michigan	4.2	10.2	4.6
Illinois	8.7ᵃ	6.8	3.5ᵇ
Wisconsin	—	12.5	3.1ᶜ
Iowa	—	—	3.0
Total West	5.6	7.2	3.7

Source: Net earnings: Appendix A, Tables 42, 43, 44, excluding roads for which gross receipts had to be estimated from mileage;

Cost of construction: summation of unadjusted cost of construction of included roads obtained from same sources as receipts data of Appendix A. For some 1849 roads, higher 1850 census costs had to be used.

ᵃ Cost of construction of Galena and Chicago in proportion to mileage opened in 1849; receipts are for a partial year too.

ᵇ Census of 1860 estimate of cost of Chicago and Northwestern used; if the *American Railroad Journal* total is used, Illinois return is reduced to 3.4 percent.

ᶜ Census of 1860 estimate of cost of La Crosse and Milwaukee used; the *American Railroad Journal* implies a cost greater than $100,000 a mile in 1859; if that is used, Wisconsin return is reduced to 2.0 percent. The appropriateness of the cost figure used is discussed in Appendix B.

to which early returns on western railroads bear out waiting demand.[26] The returns of 5.6 and 7.2 percent in 1849 and 1855–1856, respectively, do not compare unfavorably with profits

[26] The use of net operating earnings divided by cost of construction to measure the rate of profit is obviously open to criticism. There is no doubt that lack of

earned in other sectors. As Conrad and Meyer state, "in contemporary chronicles it is obvious that southerners and northerners alike considered 6–8 percent a reasonable rate of return and a reasonable asking price for loans." [27] More to the point, perhaps, is the loan rate charged western railroads themselves in the capital market. Seven percent bonds with maturities of fifteen years and the like were negotiated in the early 1850's at 85–90 net, a discount that resulted in an effective rate of between 8 and 9 percent. There seems to have been little variation until the tightness of 1854. Despite the veritable deluge of securities seeking placement, frequently of poorer quality than the earlier offerings, prices did not weaken. The market began to take the mind that "western roads are to be our best paying lines, and the great success that has followed the opening of the few roads in that section has done much to confirm this opinion." [28]

Experience corroborated this evaluation. Eastern railroads earned only slightly more in 1849 than those in the West, 6.3 versus 5.6 percent, and by 1855 the sign of the inequality was reversed: the 7.2 percent of western roads exceeded the 6.1 percent of New England and Middle Atlantic mileage. To a large

---

depreciation accounting tended to exaggerate early profits at the expense of later earnings because out-of-pocket costs for renewal and maintenance were small in the first years of the enterprise. Operating in the same direction was the practice of charging to capital account such current expenses as interest obligations. Offsetting this bias is the typically exaggerated cost of construction. Such items as discount on securities, capitalization of interest payments, excessive payments to contractors (detailed in Appendix B), meant that the nominal cost of a road could exceed its resource content by as much as a third, after inclusion of risk in cost.

The net effect of these two tendencies appears to leave a small downward bias in measured early rates of return and a larger downward bias in the 1859 results. On average, it appears that construction accounts were too high by 15 percent (cf. Appendix B). For net earnings to be overstated by a proportional amount, the operating ratio actually reported as 50 percent would have to reach almost 60 percent. On older western roads, where depreciation was currently being met, the average was slightly less. Hence by using unadjusted net earnings and unadjusted construction costs we come close to the true rate of return in the early years, but understate it later when net earnings reflect depreciation more accurately.

[27] Alfred H. Conrad and John R. Meyer, "Economics of Slavery in the Ante-Bellum South," *Journal of Political Economy*, LXVI (1958), 101.

[28] For the reception of western railroad securities the files of the *American Railroad Journal* from 1850 through 1853 are very helpful. A special section dealing with the money market was established in 1851. For this quotation, see XXV (1852), 121.

measure these results reflect the adaptation of western railroads to lesser levels of gross receipts than those in the East. In 1855, western traffic earnings came to about $4800 per mile against $7000 per mile for eastern railroads. But relative to cost, the results are almost identical: 14 cents of receipts per dollar of cost in the West, 15 cents in the East.[29] Western railroads, hastily and cheaply built, were thus perfectly suited to the lower absolute demands found in the West. Galton's contrast of English and American railroads is equally applicable regionally:

The character of American railways, so different in its prominent features from that of railways in this country, is the result of the want which they have been called upon to supply. A means of communication was required which could be laid cheaply and rapidly through forests and cultivated and uncultivated districts. . . .

The practice of constructing the railways in a hasty and imperfect manner has led to the adoption of a form of rolling stock capable of adapting itself to the inequalities of the road; it is also constructed on the principle of diminishing the amount of useless weight carried in a train.[30]

Variation in capacity is an important but absent element in the Schumpeterian framework.

Thus in private, not only social terms, railroads in the early 1850's were already beginning to justify their construction. Only subsequently, and in large measure owing to the panic of 1857, did they become financial burdens rather than blessings. Table 19 describes the transition: despite a more than 33 percent increase

[29] Earnings statistics from Appendix A; Paxson, "Railroads of 'Old Northwest,' " and Poor, *Railroads and Canals*, for mileages; Poor, *ibid.*, and individual reports for cost data.

The lower western gross receipts per mile are not evidence of construction ahead of demand. At such a level they were fully comparable to the gross revenues in the East at the end of the first decade of railroad operation there, and represented a much larger volume of physical output. To assert that western levels in the 1850's are indicative of construction ahead of demand is to imply that eastern railroad development in the 1830's was similarly premature. No one, to my knowledge, has argued that.

[30] Captain Douglass Galton's report to the Board of Trade was published as *Report to the Lords of the Committee of Privy Council for trade and foreign plantations, on the railways of the United States* (London, 1857). It was also reprinted in the *Railway Times of London*, XX (1857), 514–516, 547–549, 593–595, 623–625. This passage appears on p. 548.

in mileage between 1855–1856 and 1859, net earnings showed an $800,000 or 6 percent, decline. These aggregative data do not convey the entire complex development of western railroad fortunes. In particular, even by 1855–1856, declining profits had set in for many railroads in Ohio and Indiana. That is, contrary to the increase in earning capacity over time predicted by the notion of construction ahead of demand, one often finds actual deterioration. Consider the Madison and Indianapolis, the sole Indiana road in operation in 1849 and earning 6.1 percent on its investment at that date. By 1855, its financial condition was far from healthy; its net earnings were absolutely less than those in 1849 and the rate of return was a far smaller 3.3 percent. The cause, although not unassociated with some corporate mismanagement, was primarily the inexorable operation of the market mechanism; initially high returns had encouraged entry and eroded its previous monopolistic position. As the road unfortunately was laid out upon a north-south rather than an east-west axis, its location was soon shown up as an economic liability once other alternatives were available. As early as 1852 the editor of the *Indianapolis State Journal* sagaciously advocated the sale of the stock by the state:

> The Jeffersonville Road will be completed to Columbus early next season — the branch of the New Albany road from Jasper to this city is certain to be made within a short time — and the road . . . to Cincinnati, by way of Lawrenceburg, is also certain to be completed at any early day. All these roads will come in competition with the Madison Road, and, in our opinion will render its stock of very little value. . . .[31]

Not all cases were so dramatic and unambiguous as this. But neither is absolute decline in profits necessary to validate the contentions that returns upon roads in new areas were substantial in the first years of operation, and that there was no marked tendency toward increase over time. Newly opened roads in the farther West did in fact do better on the average than those in operation for a longer period of time in Ohio and Indiana. Thus

[31] Quoted in Wylie J. Daniels, "The Village at the End of the Road: A Chapter in Early Indiana Railroad History," *Indiana Historical Society Publications*, XIII, no. 1 (1938), 84–85.

in 1855–1856 the aggregate return in Wisconsin was more than twice that in the already established states of Ohio and Indiana; Illinois ranks higher as well and would be substantially greater (10.8 percent instead of 6.8 percent) if not for the incomplete, land-grant Illinois Central, which was the exception of railroad development in the decade, not the rule.

In Table 20 we present the rate of return in 1855–1856 as a

TABLE 20.   Number of railroads by rate of return and year of completion, 1855–1856

Year of completion	Rate of return		
	Less than 5 percent	5 to 10 percent	Greater than 10 percent
Incomplete in 1856	5	1	1
1855	2	1	1
1854	3	5	1
1853	2	5	2
1852	2	2	5
1851	2	0	2
1850 or earlier	2	1	0

Source: Rate of return: see Table 19.
Year of completion: Paxson, pp. 267–274; *Report on Finances for 1855–56*, pp. 240–425.

function of the age of the railroad. The rates are those of Table 19, with the dates of completion drawn from the Treasury Report of 1855 and Paxson's study of railroads in the Old Northwest. The hypothesis of independence between the rate of return and the age of the railroad cannot be rejected.[32] This does not necessarily disallow the notion of substantial supply induced shifts in demand over time. These may well have occurred although introduction of new facilities at a rapid rate prevented older roads from realizing the beneficial effects. But it then follows that

[32] A 2 × 2 contingency table was created by combining all railroads with returns over 5 percent, excluding the incomplete railroads, and dividing the years into two groups, one up to and including 1852, the other from 1853 on. χ^2 is then .027. For one degree of freedom, $\chi^2_{.95} = 3.84$ and the hypothesis of independence is upheld by these data by a very decisive margin.

the second, and large, wave of railroads did have demand waiting for them. The results do therefore bear upon the hypothesis. An even more telling *negative* relationship, which I almost would have expected, is denied as well. One reason why it does not appear is the cluster of railroads exhibiting extremely high returns in 1855–1856 and completed in 1852. A closer analysis of four of those five railroads, however, indicates that their returns were high from their inception. This is the key point. Table 21 traces

TABLE 21. Rate of return over time, selected railroads (percent)

Railroad	1852	1853	1854	1855
Michigan Southern	4.6	9.6	6.3	7.5
Michigan Central	7.4	6.6	7.2	8.2
Terre Haute and Richmond	5.4	7.9	10.6	12.2
Cleveland, Columbus, & Cincinnati	13.2	—	12.6	15.9
Cleveland, Painesville, & Ashtabula	—	—	—	—

Source: Compiled from the files of *American Railroad Journal*, XXV (1852)-XXIX (1856).

their path of profits over time. Although some upward trend is apparent for the Michigan Southern and the Terre Haute and Richmond, their initial yields are quite respectable from the start. Note, too, that the two incomplete roads earning 5 percent or better, as shown in Table 20, were both in Wisconsin; railroad development at the geographic margin even for small sections of road was a paying proposition. Although not reflected either in Table 20 or in Table 21, because Iowa railroads do not appear in 1855 and by 1859 the panic had struck, early returns in that state conform to the same favorable pattern.[33]

In sum, there is much truth to Henry Varnum Poor's evaluation in 1855:

[33] The first Iowa railroad, the Mississippi and Missouri, grossed almost $5,000 per mile in 1857 just a year after opening. Its net exceeded $150,000 on an expenditure (for a 67-mile section of the road) estimated to be $2,680,000 — including investment for more equipment than needed for those initial operations. The return thus was 5 percent before the cyclical decline intervened. Cf. *American Railroad Journal*, XXXI (1858), 568–569.

There is no fallacy in the assumption upon which our railroads have been built — that they are adapted to the commercial needs of the country, and that, economically constructed and managed, they can earn a satisfactory income upon their cost. If they prove unproductive, it must be due, consequently, to their excessive cost or bad management. It is owing to *one* of these causes that the holders of unproductive property are without dividends.[34]

But this is not the whole story. An element of overcommitment to railroads that were, and would continue to be, unprofitable does enter. Sometimes roads were built that were unneeded. Competition not only eroded monopoly profits but could be carried to excess as well. A correspondent to the *American Railroad Journal* perceptively foresaw the changes as early as 1853:[35]

By a well contrived and well managed plan a road may perchance be built, that is not wanted, and will never pay, and capitalists saddled with securities that are not better than the road. Certainly great caution is necessary, or the result I have foreshadowed will be realized in more instances than one, in

Ohio and Indianna [*sic*]

By 1855, some of these unhappy consequences were quite apparent in Ohio, just assuming first place among the states in railroad mileage. There the aggregative profits of 6 percent in 1855–1856 present a misleading aspect. Of the twenty reporting railroads, nine earned less than 5 percent; three on the other hand were immensely profitable: the Cleveland, Painesville, and Ashtabula, the Cleveland and Toledo, both components of the lake shore route, and the Cleveland, Columbus, and Cincinnati. If these three be removed, the aggregate return in the state barely exceeds 4 percent. These hard times did not descend owing to construction ahead of demand. They were the product of overextension of railroad mileage in a well-developed territory, an overextension dictated by a conjunction of technology, market structure, and local governmental subsidy.

As mileage initially increased in that state, attempts to arrange combinations, agreements, and formal liaisons began, going as

---

[34] *American Railroad Journal*, XXVIII (1855), 184.
[35] *American Railroad Journal*, XXVI (1853), 613.

far back as 1851. Given high fixed costs, profitability of railroads depended crucially upon the magnitude of receipts; if business was substantial, average costs could be reduced, and returns augmented. The incremental expenditure to subsidize potential allies was thus a rational move for each railroad taken in isolation. Hence the considerable support of eastern trunk lines like the Pennsylvania and the Baltimore and Ohio given to favorite feeders through the state such as the Pittsburgh, Fort Wayne, and Chicago; the Steubenville and Indiana; the Central Ohio; and the Marietta and Cincinnati.[36] Within the state, rivalries led the Little Miami to invest in the Springfield, Mt. Vernon, and Pittsburgh. The Cincinnati, Hamilton, and Dayton saw its defense in the promotion of the Hamilton and Eaton, and the Greenville and Miami. Others did likewise. What was rational for the individual road rebounded to the ultimate disadvantage of all as mileage, and competition, increased. Added to such railroad rivalry was commercial rivalry. Individual towns sought better access to market and encouraged additional construction by subsidy. When competitive construction flagged, the additional device of lower rates was not unfamiliar; such lower prices were promptly met, and, without substantial short-run market elasticity of demand, lower profits for all was the unfailing rule.[37] The problems of Ohio railroads receive succinct and accurate portrayal in the annual report of the *Little Miami* for 1856: "The number of competing routes, and the eagerness of those who control them to procure business, have reduced the prices both of freight and travel below the point of just remuneration, and have obliged us to perform a large amount of service without a corresponding profit." [38]

The distinction here between creation of excess capacity and construction ahead of demand does not depend upon the high

[36] The Pennsylvania Railroad alone was committed to an investment of almost $2,000,000. Special legislative permission was necessary to enable it to purchase, or guarantee, bonds of other railroads in amounts up to 15 percent of its own capital. George H. Burgess and Miles C. Kennedy, *Centennial History of the Pennsylvania Railroad Company* (Philadelphia, 1949), pp. 77–99.

[37] Robert L. Black, *The Little Miami Railroad* (Cincinnati, 1939), contains an account of the competitive struggles of Ohio railroads, focusing on the position of the Little Miami. See also Kohlmeier, *Old Northwest*, chap. vii.

[38] Reprinted in Black, *Little Miami*, p. 119.

level of population density alone, although that is sufficient evidence by itself. It is also true that the railroads in question continued to be unprofitable more than a decade later. The average rate of profit of 10 Ohio railroads yielding low returns in 1855 was 2.5 percent; in 1869 it was barely higher at 2.8 percent and still less than half of the prevailing Ohio return.[39] What was excess capacity earlier was not justified later. For Ohio railroads at least, time was not necessarily a curative for entrepreneurial error.

Confounded with these competitive excesses is the cyclical decline on western roads beginning even before the panic of 1857. Our aggregate data in Table 19 portray the situation from the side of net earnings over the interval 1855–1856 to 1859. To bring the annual pattern of gross receipts per mile of road into full focus, we present in Table 22 the continuous calendar year earnings of so-called "Chicago" railroads, representing almost half of western revenues. Receipts per mile of road fell from a peak of more than $6000 in 1856 to a trough of little more than $4000 in 1859. The aggregate receipts of 1857 were not reached again until the railroad prosperity brought by the Civil War.

This reduction in revenues led to the inevitable series of defaults, receiverships, and reorganizations. In perspective, this first substantial crisis of the railroad age was relatively minor. In 1859 only 2500 miles were in receivership, or about 8 percent of the total; the comparable statistic in 1877 and 1894 was 18 and 20 percent, respectively.[40] Nonetheless, western railroad fortunes were shattered. Security prices plummeted. Cole's index of western stock prices (1853 = 100) shows a decline from 90 in the

---

[39] Four of the railroads were first opened in 1859. Their returns were converted to an 1855 base by the ratio of Ohio earnings of 1855 to those for 1859. The 1869 earnings and cost of construction were calculated from *Poor's Manual* for the same railroads, even if by the later date they had become divisions of some larger unit. The choice of the year is of little importance. The earnings in 1873, at the peak of the boom, averaged only 3.5 percent and the return of other railroads was proportionally higher. (In all of these calculations simple averages have been used since the relevant units are the individual railroads; weighted calculations would make the later upward movement even smaller.)

[40] Henry H. Swain, "Economic Aspects of Railroad Receiverships," *American Economic Association Economic Studies*, III, no. 2 (1898), pp. 66, n.1, and 70.

TABLE 22. Gross receipts, "Chicago railroads"

Year	Gross receipts (thousands of dollars)	Mileage covered[a]	Receipts per mile (dollars)
1855	13,298	2,509	5,300
1856	17,343	2,782	6,200
1857	18,590	3,362	5,500
1858	15,197	3,504	4,300
1859	14,978	3,719	4,000
1860	17,690	3,728	4,700

Source: *Chicago Democratic Press Annual Reviews for 1855–1860*, with the exception of 1858, which is derived from the review reprinted in the *American Railroad Journal*, XXXII (1859), 147.

[a] There may be small errors in total mileage due to changes in the status of leased roads not recorded in the *Annual Review*. The mileages here were secured by summing the mileages reported in the *Review* only for those railroads included in the total receipts tabulation.

spring of 1857 to less than 40 at the end of 1859.[41] By contrast southern railroad investment and receipts continued to increase until the end of the decade. Nor did New England roads feel the burden commensurately.[42]

The great leverage of western railroad capital structures exaggerated the effect upon shareholders.[43] Only 11 of 75 western

[41] Smith and Cole, *Fluctuations*, p. 112.

[42] See Appendix B, Table 53 and Appendix A, Tables 43 and 44.

[43] We should not place excessive weight upon dividends to shareholders as a measure of profits attained. Even when results were poor, many shareholders did receive interest payments during the construction period, and did obtain their equity at a discount, as when contractors received partial payment in stock. Moreover, a levered financial structure — large debt relative to equity — meant that residents along the right of way, most typically the source of equity finance, were able to capture the indirect, spatially fixed benefits such as increased land values for a smaller investment than otherwise. The emphasis upon swindling promoters and hapless farmers is somewhat misplaced accordingly. In Wisconsin the experience *was* unhappy, but only because the railroads were not built as promised. Once in operation, dividends to share capital understate the extent of the return to investors. The slightly smaller return to railroads in aggregate than the loan rate, implying in turn a return to equity less than that to the enterprise, must be interpreted in this light.

(For the ratio of debt to equity, see *Report on Finances for 1855–56*, pp. 422–423. The ratio is 1.2 in the West in 1855–1856, 0.8 in the country as a whole. This under-

railroads were recorded as dividend payers in the bleak days of 1858 and 1859. Some three years earlier the same number of roads declared dividends, but of a many times smaller total of 19. These 11 at the earlier date paid an average dividend of almost 12 percent, reflecting the bonanza character of some of the early railroad investments.[44] Later roads responding to the lure of such profits tended to lack sufficient equity capital, and relying much more heavily upon debt finance, felt the decline in 1857 more severely. In part this reliance upon debt bespeaks excesses, rather than deficiencies, of demand. Often it was necessary, shortly after completion of the road, to invest in additional rolling stock, most easily financed by short-term debt. The Crawfordsville and Wabash was not untypical: "Like most other western railroads it was found on opening the Crawfordsville and Wabash that there had not been provided half enough machinery to do the business offered. . . . The receipts might have been more than doubled had the necessary cars and buildings been provided." [45] The buoyancy of the early years of the decade encouraged railroads to make up the deficiency and thereby expose their financial flank by overextension.[46] In 1857, after the panic, money became scarce at almost any price; renewal of the short-term obligations of western railroads was out of the question even if they had surpassed the hurdle of contractual interest payments. As the Illinois Central Railroad consented to assignment, its Treasurer commented: "The existing derangements in the financial affairs of the country surprised the company with a large floating debt incurred for the completion and equipment of the road. . . . All

---

states the later western ratio since Wisconsin and Iowa railroads report more capital than debt at that early date.)

[44] Tabulated from the share lists of the *American Railroad Journal*, XXIX (1856), 390, and XXXII (1859), 763–766.

[45] Extract from 1852 *Annual Report of New Albany and Salem Railroad*, reprinted in Frank F. Hargrave, *A Pioneer Indiana Railroad* (Indianapolis, 1932), p. 99.

[46] The Illinois railroads reporting to the Secretary of the Treasury in 1855 had capital stock of $16 million, funded debt (with a maturity sometimes as short as five years) of $25 million, and floating debt of $3 million. For all western roads, however, floating debt at that date was only 5 percent of total liabilities as compared to Illinois's 7 percent, and was not significantly different from the national average. This does not indicate equal conservatism in all regions but, instead, a biased sample in the West. *Report on Finances for 1855–56*, pp. 422–423.

usual . . . modes of raising money are well known to be entirely unavailable." [47] Railroad failures in 1857 are perhaps better evidence of prior demand than of precocious development.

This discussion has indicated that early returns to the enterprises in the West were comparable to the returns to be earned in other sectors. Subsequently, the aggregate return was driven downward by excess competition and by cyclical decline. Some western roads, usually those that were profitable from the start, continued to prosper by reason of an erosion-proof monopoly of location. Ironically, it had been the example of these that led to the excess of competitive zeal and helped to reduce the global return. The later, and less satisfactory experience, clearly does not make a case for construction ahead of demand.

This analysis of the *ex post* profitability of western roads does not yet complete the investigation. It is also of interest to determine to what extent these actual gains were foreseen by private investors. We have already hinted at the answer in the previous discussion. A closer examination of the magnitude of governmental aid will confirm the impression that railroad promoters found sufficient funds to pursue their objectives within the context of the market system.

The Pattern of Governmental Assistance

One of the usual concomitants of construction ahead of demand is reliance upon external subsidy. Without such aid, there is little incentive to build where profits are expected to be far distant and uncertain at best. As a result of Carter Goodrich's recent painstaking efforts, the liberal extent of government participation in the development of the nineteenth-century transportation network has been well documented. Thus there exists a prima facie case for the feasibility, though not necessarily the occurrence, of premature construction.

Looked at more closely, however, the structure of aid in the 1850's clearly goes against the hypothesis. All types of assistance, although usually treated identically for their developmental consequences, are not in reality the same. Whereas state and federal

[47] Report dated October 10, 1857, reprinted in part in Carlton J. Corliss, *Mainline of Mid-America* (New York, 1958), p. 94.

subsidies can easily serve as active incentives to initiate railroad construction, local aid is of a more passive character. It is offered subsequent to individual promotion and is often as much extorted by threat as voluntarily given. This difference in entrepreneurial content is reflected by the difference in the financial conditions surrounding the aid. Federal land grants were direct subsidies, state assistance primarily consisted of direct expenditure, but local aid was, as often as not, a loan ultimately to be repaid. Private profits had to loom somewhere on the horizon in the latter case. This distinction is not universally valid. Certain large cities could take the lead in the construction of railroads designed for trade diversion; and federal land grants could be allocated to roads already in process, like the Burlington. Yet, despite such exceptions, the identification of active aid with higher levels of governmental responsibility, and passive aid with the county and town levels, is a useful one.

It is no accident, then, that the period of real construction ahead of demand in the West also witnessed extensive state programs of internal improvement, primarily directly controlled. As a whole, with the exception of the Ohio Canal, these projects were magnificent failures. Illinois had nothing to show for its $4,000,000 investment in railroads but a dilapidated stretch of mileage eventually sold at auction for $21,100.[48] In Ohio and Indiana, where canals were built directly but a small number of railroads were subsidized, continued and elaborate fraud bilked the state of substantial monies without tangible return. Michigan contracted her system sharply to save what she could. The inefficiency of simultaneous construction on a number of projects, poor cyclical timing, and lack of technological know-how all contributed to ultimate failure. But perhaps most relevant was the fact that, by and large, such projects were *planned* by the states as construction ahead of demand and that the anticipated developmental consequences (except in Ohio) never panned out, owing, but also contributing, to the inability to complete the projects in a timely fashion.

In reaction to the large debts left behind by these ventures,

[48] John H. Krenkel, *Illinois Internal Improvements 1818–1848* (Cedar Rapids, 1958), p. 203.

western states typically wrote into their new constitutions of the 1840's prohibitions of further state assistance. Thus when the great wave of expansion of the next decade was underway this source of subsidy was proscribed. As a partial replacement, federal aid was sought and finally achieved in the form of land grants. Yet it is well to asses their *pre*-Civil War significance modestly. Only two western roads were completed within this period through the assistance of such grants, the Illinois Central and the Hannibal and St. Joseph. None of the land voted to Wisconsin and Iowa came into significant play before 1860.[49] In aggregate terms, more than 100,000 acres were given away during the 1860's, and less than 30,000 during the 1850's; and only a fraction of the latter was utilized because two thirds were authorized in 1856 and 1857, on the eve of the crisis. Not much of the western railroad boom is thus explained by federal intervention.

Local funds, rather, played the most important role, exactly as one might anticipate if construction was *not* ahead of demand. The very fact of contributions by towns and counties along the route gives the lie to the existence of an unsettled wilderness. Even in Iowa, where local aid played a larger role in construction than elsewhere, it was still passive and did not often make the difference between construction or not. Sometimes communities sensed this, as when the promoters of the Mississippi and Missouri complained of indifference along the line of the projected route, "[people] feeling that the road would be built along a certain line in any case."[50] Most of the time, they did not, being minor towns "that hoped, by generous stock subscriptions, to assure themselves of places on the main lines of railroads projected through their vicinities."[51]

Not only was governmental assistance in the West limited primarily to local funds, but these themselves were quite small. In Indiana, with more than 2,000 miles of railroad, sixteen counties and ten cities contributed less than $2,000,000 or less than

[49] Individual roads already in progress were recipients of these grants, and only small amounts were raised before the Civil War with the land grant as security.

[50] Earl S. Beard, "Local Aid to Railroads in Iowa," *Iowa Journal of History*, L (1952), 17.

[51] Beard, p. 10.

$1,000 a mile; railroads at a bare minimum cost $25,000 a mile. Illinois, with almost 3,000 miles, had purchased its rail network for only $4,000,000 in local subscriptions.[52] Chicago, the great railroad center not only of the West, but already of the nation as a whole, contributed nothing. It was the lesser towns that paid their tribute, and these rarely found the panacea they had sought.

In Iowa and Wisconsin each, however, it is estimated that local aid exceeded $7 million during the decade.[53] Relative to a cost of construction which stood at $19 million in the former state, and $34 million in the latter, these must be judged quite substantial subsidies, locally originated or not. Coming as they do in those states farthest west and least developed, these grants clearly suggest an element of construction prior to need. In both instances, however, these are aggregative estimates of contemporaries rather than the result of subsequent calculation. Upward bias is therefore likely. These sums probably include pledges, and for sections under construction or projected but not yet completed. Hence the large proportion that aid represents of actual construction is misleading. The magnitude of potential overstatement is by no means inconsequential: at the end of 1861, 2100 miles of railroad were projected in Iowa, but only a third completed; Wisconsin had 2200 miles as a goal of existing companies, of which only 900 were in operation.[54]

The Wisconsin Railroad Commissioners' *Report* for 1874 gives some basis for determining the actual aid to pre-Civil War railroads in that state. The result falls far below the $7 million level now accepted. In the first place, the *cumulative* amount of local aid to 1874 is stated in that report to be less than $7 million; after internal correction, the total comes closer to $8 million, a figure that still probably is an understatement. Most of this sum derives from the period from 1868 to 1873, however. Hence $7 million still seems an exaggerated estimate for the decade of the 1850's alone. Secondly, this aid figure includes not only principal but accumulated interest as well. The addition on this account is

[52] Goodrich, *Promotion of Canals and Railroads*, pp. 141, 144.
[53] Goodrich, pp. 148, 149.
[54] *American Railroad Journal*, XXXV (1862), 14.

considerable: the ratio of the par value of bonds issued to total aid defined inclusive of interest is about one-half. Patently, the total undiscounted flow of repayments of local aid, or obligations to repay, when compared to initial construction cost, will overstate the relative importance of that aid. Thirdly, there is a distinct difference between aid authorized and actual bonds issued; whereas the former stood in 1874 at $7.8 million, bonds issued for railroad use, corrected, total only $5.2 million.[55] Here is another disparity which magnifies contemporary estimates.

So much for criticisms indicating how the Goodrich estimate of $7 million in aid for Wisconsin is likely to be exaggerated. A detailed compilation in Table 23 of assistance to individual railroads under construction or in operation before the Civil War provides positive proof. Only a little more than $3,000,000 of debt was apparently issued, of which $1,614,000 was voted by Milwaukee. Of the latter all but $200,000 (plus accrued interest) was made good by the individual companies.[56] As a proportion of total cost, measured either by the census or the roads themselves, local aid in Wisconsin amounted to less than 10 percent. Moreover, local aid was bestowed relatively more lavishly upon smaller lines like the Kenosha, the Wisconsin Central, the Milwaukee and Horicon, and the Milwaukee and Superior than upon the great through roads like the Milwaukee and Mississippi and the La Crosse and Milwaukee. No part of those small railroads was opened until 1856 and local aid was at least partially in response to the demonstrated financial success of the earlier Wisconsin lines, as well as an attempt to make up for lost time. Local aid clearly did not make a crucial difference to the timing or magnitude of Wisconsin's entrance into the railroad era. One suspects careful study would show much the same for Iowa.

This is not to assert that local investment was totally insignificant or that it was ever unwanted. Beyond a doubt the availability of such funds at an early stage of a project was an

[55] *First Annual Report of the Railroad Commissions of the State of Wisconsin* (Madison, 1874), pt. II, pp. 242–249. The correction is the inclusion in total aid of the repaid Milwaukee loans of the 1850's.

[56] Laurence M. Larson, "A Financial and Administrative History of Milwaukee," *Bulletin of the University of Wisconsin*, Economics and Political Science Series, IV, no. 2 (1908), 74–75, 87–88, 129–130.

TABLE 23. Local aid to Wisconsin railroads

| | | Cost in 1860 | |
Railroad	Amount of aid	Commissioners' report of 1874 (from company reports)	Census of 1860
Milwaukee and Mississippi	$534,000	$ 8,135,674	$7,500,000
La Crosse and Milwaukee	433,000	19,507,222[a]	7,400,000[b]
Milwaukee and Horicon	316,000	1,381,391[c]	1,137,912
Milwaukee and Watertown	221,000	1,520,448	1,498,762
Racine and Mississippi	412,000[d]	3,928,262[a]	2,522,581 (3,802,016)[e]
Wisconsin Central	180,000	507,687[c]	250,000
Kenosha, Rockford, & Rock Island	272,000	898,807	1,069,007
Milwaukee and Chicago	200,000	1,833,695	1,830,073
Chicago and Northwestern	180,000	10,307,037	7,123,282 (10,684,922)[e]
Mineral Point	220,000	1,534,000[c]	1,813,927
Milwaukee and Superior	100,000	158,752[a]	360,000
Beloit and Madison	0	—	350,000
Sheboygan and Fond du Lac	0	826,976	500,000
Manitowac and Mississippi	0	—	200,000
Fox River Valley	50,000	105,885[c]	under construction
Milwaukee and Beloit	100,000	567,075	under construction
Madison and Watertown	33,000	never built	
Total	3,251,000	51,212,911 (51,762,911)[f]	33,555,544 (39,069,579)[e]

Source: First Annual Report of the Railroad Commissioners of the State of Wisconsin, 1874 (Madison, 1874), pt. II, pp. 78–173, 243–251; *Preliminary Report on the Eighth Census*, pp. 228–229.

[a] 1858.

[b] The considerable difference between the census and the company report in this case is due to the scandal-ridden operations of the La Crosse and Milwaukee surrounding its bid for a land grant. The census data more accurately reflect actual cost of construction.

[c] 1859.

[d] Estimated from discount on bonds by assumption of 20% discount at time of sale.

[e] Commensurate with length of road reported in Commissioners' Report.

[f] Using census cost values for the Beloit and Madison and the Manitowac and Mississippi.

important asset when going to the capital market in search of further private funds. Local securities given in exchange for stock also were more marketable than the shares themselves. On the other side, however, it is true that the returns to municipalities from such local assistance, even if negligible financially, were often large. There were too many instances in which towns could be as easily avoided as traversed, and with eager competitors clamoring for relocation of the road, the chance could not be put to the test. Accordingly the "social return" from the investment was almost infinite in opportunity cost terms: in the absence of aid there would likely be only a mournful history of municipal decay and decline. Ironically, although the alternative of not securing the railroad was so baleful, the advantage of having it was limited because other localities all behaved in similar fashion. As a consequence none secured a relative advantage, and the global return was smaller than that to the individual participants. There can be no doubt that local aid contributed to the excess competition prevalent in Ohio by the mid-1850's; the communities of that state alone subscribed about as much as all those in Illinois, Indiana, and Wisconsin put together. The combination of local autonomy, economic decentralization, and rational decision-making led to a bias toward overconstruction to be sure, but not ahead of demand.

The pattern of governmental aid in the West in the 1850's thus adds to the mounting evidence that railroads were not built ahead of demand. Assistance was predominantly local, and relative to total expenditures it was not a major factor. The experience is in sharp contrast to the earlier episode of state aid in the 1830's. More governmental funds were spent to build the thousand-odd miles of western canals and two hundred miles of railroad in the 1830's and 1840's than was expended for the nine thousand miles of railroad between 1850 and 1860. Early in the latter decade Israel Andrews correctly sized up the fundamental difference in economic conditions that brought about that dramatic reversal:

. . . the numerous failures in the first efforts of the new States to construct works of internal improvement were not the result of accident, but a matter of necessity. The schemes were all premature; . . . The country had not been settled a length of time sufficient to designate the sites that were to become the great depots of trade, or the convenient routes for travel and business. . . . Both the old and the new system had its peculiar characteristics. The first proposed in the newly-settled states . . . *anticipated* the wants of the country. . . . The works more recently commenced rest on a very different foundation. They were constructed, and are adapted, to supply wants which *actually* exist.[57]

To which one can only affirm assent.

The Process of Anticipatory Settlement

To recognize the response of individual western railroad projects to present profit opportunities is not completely to deny the causal influence of the railroad in that region's economic expansion in the 1850's. Even if they were not the exogenous force generating that development as suggested by Schumpeter, they obviously extended the range of profitable opportunities once they were constructed. What was profitable previously at the higher transport rates became more so with lower charges, and, in addition, the railroad provided an efficient and rapid medium for personal movement. Thus subsequent development, although not initiated by the railroad, is partially explained by its endogenous, second-round effects. An analogy may clarify this point. An increased demand for steel, say, sets in motion demands for a whole host of other products and the larger production of these other industries generate still further demands. These additional demands, dependent on the internal characteristics of the industries involved, are important to the final result while not themselves the initiating cause of expansion.

It is unnecessary to concede this much. Although the first railroads built in the West in the 1850's were a response to existing economic opportunities, their effects transcended the areas they directly served. The larger, and more undeveloped, part of the West felt the repercussions too. Spatial fixity of rail service did not preclude personal mobility. Once the railroad reached Ohio, settlement in Illinois and Iowa became much more attractive than before. By the time railroads advanced farther west the population and economic development necessary to sustain them were

---

[57] Andrews, *Trade and Commerce*, pp. 357–358 (italics mine).

already there — that is why those railroads were built when they were — so that individual, private projects were feasible. But the reason such settlement was waiting was the railroad itself, considered collectively. Hence the ramifications of early railroad construction exceeded the transport cost reduction it brought to the limited areas served. And although the favorable demand for American agricultural exports generated by the Irish famine is clearly one of the factors influencing the beginning of the boom, the continued westward migration from 1850 through 1853, in the face of unsatisfactory wheat prices and small international demands, testifies strongly to the influence of the railroad in the development of the decade.

This interpretation takes us far from a simple Schumpeterian world. Indeed, it almost turns that model on its head: instead of a heroic role for the railroad investor or even the state, the beneficiary of railroad construction displays the crucial attributes of foresight. The western American farmer was different from his European counterpart or agrarians in underdeveloped countries today, and that difference consisted of a responsiveness to market forces and ubiquity of a profit motive. Only recently has this distinction been given the emphasis it deserves:[58]

> In a very real and profound sense, then, the United States failed to develop . . . a distinctively *rural* culture. If a rural culture means an emotional and craftsmanlike dedication to the soil, a traditional and pre-capitalist outlook, a tradition-directed rather than career-directed type of character, and a village community devoted to ancestral ways and habitually given to communal action, then the prairies and plains never had one. What differentiated the agricultural life of those regions . . . was not simply that it produced for a market, but that it was so speculative, so mobile, so mechanized, so "progressive," so thoroughly imbued with the commercial spirit.

Travelers to the United States were always cognizant of the difference. Birkbeck in 1818, De Tocqueville in the 1830's, and Trollope in the early 1860's, gave it a prominent place in their accounts. The Turnerian idealization of the rural element, with its emphasis upon motivations like "love of wilderness freedom,"

[58] Richard Hofstadter, *The Age of Reform* (New York: Alfred A. Knopf, 1959), p. 43.

has obscured the underlying economic calculus. As Trollope put it, "The Western American has *no* love for his own soil or his own house. The matter with him is simply one of dollars." [59] A recent study of settlement in Trempealeau County, Wisconsin, confirms this restless search for profit. Of 266 farmers reported in the 1860 census, 146 had moved on before 1870, and only 48 persisted to 1880. The group that left were not the economic misfits. There was no appreciable difference in property value between farmers that stayed and those that migrated.[60]

The appreciation of land is central to all of this. The windfall gains accruing to individuals temporarily in advance of the main path of settlement might well outweigh the current incomes derived from production. Farmers were fully cognizant of this possibility. As Curti writes of his Wisconsin sample, "some of our farmers, like some of Bentley's Nebraska farmers, acquired farms with no idea of permanent settlement, but in order to realize on their value as the price of farm land went up." [61] Not only the future gains on land yet to be settled were relevant; past appreciation provided the wherewithal for further migration.

What the railroad brought, of course, was exactly higher land values, and much before its direct benefits mounted up. Speculative excesses insured that. It was the wise man who moved quickly and far. Examples of such anticipatory settlement before the railroad are legion. People did not wait until the first railroad from the East actually entered Chicago in 1852 to recognize the impact upon her future trading area; population and construction were well underway prior to that time. Less prominent sites witnessed the same effects: "In 1854 that town [Mt. Pleasant] had had a population of 1,300; when rail service was opened in 1856, it had already grown to 3,425 and expected 1,000 more people by the end of the year. . . . Even in Ottumwa, *still beyond the railhead*, the demand for lots was so great that two new additions to the town were laid out." [62] The earlier cited evidence from the

[59] Anthony Trollope, *North America* (1861), as reprinted in Guy S. Callender, *Selections from the Economic History of the United States 1765–1860* (Boston, 1909), p. 639.

[60] Merle Curti, *The Making of an American Community* (Stanford, 1959), pp. 69–77, 142.

[61] Curti, p. 66.

[62] Overton, *Burlington West*, p. 72 (italics mine).

Iowa and Illinois censuses provides a similar picture in the aggregate.

The decision for anticipatory settlement apparently was well founded. The Bogues's data on profits of land speculators show the rate of return on Illinois prairie land abruptly increasing from 1855 through 1870 as improved transportation access and war inflation led to rapid rise of land values.[63] The return noticeably starts upward prior to the war, suggesting that the construction of prairie railroads was making its influence felt. By contrast, earlier investments in land in the 1830's were premature (but not irrational) for the planned transport network of that decade never materialized.

Appreciation also had a negative aspect in encouraging anticipatory settlement. Some migrants, able to afford only a small sum for the purchase of land, were driven in the van of the railhead by necessity rather than choice. The editor of the *Burlington Weekly Hawk-Eye* had many perceptive observations to make regarding the relationship between settlement and railroads. With the coming of the latter, he pointed out, Iowa land values had been bid up by speculators who limited the supply flowing out onto the market. As a consequence persons wishing to settle were being discouraged by high prices and diverted to cheap government lands in Missouri, Kansas, and Nebraska. Bitterly he concluded "the first and greatest want of immigrants is cheap land and not railroads." [64] Paul Gates has generalized along these lines. Speculators created "poorly developed rural communities which meant thin farm development, promised little freight for prospective railroads, and made subsidies necessary if they were to be built in such areas." [65]

Evidence of such speculation only confirms the opportunities for profit inherent in anticipatory settlement. But control over supply does not appear to have been carried as far as these statements imply. Had it, migration would have soon halted as land values rose exorbitantly and limited potential profits while at the same time excluding from the market those with little capi-

[63] Allan G. Bogue and Margaret B. Bogue, " 'Profits' and the Frontier Land Speculator," *Journal of Economic History*, XVII (1957), 13.

[64] Quoted in Overton, *Burlington West*, p. 109.

[65] Gates, *Farmer's Age*, p. 91.

tal.[66] Moreover, the settlement of the 1850's was pre-eminently an intensive one, leading to an extension of the productive, rather than the geographic, frontier. The four-state area of Indiana, Illinois, Wisconsin, and Iowa, all well within the geographic frontier, accounted for almost a quarter of the national population increase during the decade. The favorable operating results of railroads and the lack of significant governmental subsidies also make it doubtful that speculation drove settlers too far ahead of actual trackage.

Through the carrot and the stick, western railroad development in the early part of the decade thus set up a continuing flow of westward migration.[67] The profitability of individual projects obscures this mechanism by which railroads, considered collectively in the region as a whole, did create their demand by their initial supply. Whereas disaggregation is the culprit in this instance, aggregation can be equally misleading. In particular, it is on the basis of a national series of railroad mileage added, and total immigration, that Brinley Thomas denies the possibility of extending this influence of the railroad from internal to foreign migration. Only after the Civil War, he argues, were "changes in the rate of inflow of population . . . induced by changes in the general level of investment. . . . In light of this result the generally accepted view that immigration before the war was dominated by the 'pull' of American economic conditions needs to be revised." [68] His evidence is the failure of the aforementioned railroad mileage series, as a proxy for investment, to lead the immigration series.

I would assert, by contrast, that western railroad construction also exerted considerable influence on immigration. To be sure, other forces, the promise of free land, for example, were operative, but the publicity surrounding railroad expansion surely must have attracted many to the profitable opportunities available in the West, in precisely the same way that internal migrants

---

[66] The availability of government land at $1.25 an acre assisted in preventing such a result.

[67] A further, but subsidiary, effect was railroad derived demand for construction labor. At best this could have come to 50,000 laborers annually in the West, a stock that was not continually turned over.

[68] Brinley Thomas, *Migration and Economic Growth* (Cambridge, Eng., 1954), pp. 93–94.

were. Indeed, there were direct encouragements. The trunk lines, in particular, ran special emigrant cars. From a comparison of foreign settlement in the western states and the magnitude of emigrant traffic we can infer that almost all the foreign born reached the West by rail.[69] As a consequence, Illinois and Wisconsin ranked second and third after New York in immigrant settlement during the period.[70] That so many immigrants settled in the West immediately after arrival suggests their awareness of what railroad development meant for economic opportunity. Thomas' opposing view that immigration was exogenous has little to support it. His use of a mileage series as a proxy for total investment, when railroad investment, at any rate, clearly leads trackage, means that his timing is far from exact. Whereas his mileage series peaks in 1856, our new railroad investment series, derived in Appendix B, reaches its maximum in 1853–1854. For that matter, the 1880 census mileage added series peaks in 1854 had Thomas chosen that instead of *Poor's Manual's* version. Causality does not consist of simple temporal priority in any event. While the Irish immigration in the late 1840's was perhaps predominantly pushed (compare J. E. Cairnes's comment that "not far from one in every five of the multitudes who swarmed across the Atlantic had been driven by positive physical violence from his home"),[71] the one million Germans who emigrated from

[69] The Pennsylvania Railroad carried about 20,000 emigrants westward annually, one half ticketed from New York. The New York Central carried 56,883 through emigrant passengers in the fiscal year ending September 30, 1855; 35,000 in the next; and almost 40,000 in 1857. The Erie Railroad transported almost 50,000 emigrants in 1855 and more than 40,000 in the next year. The Baltimore and Ohio, because it lacked direct rail connections in the West and was not a port of entry, did not participate in this business. The total increase in foreign born settlement in the East North Central region plus Iowa between 1850 and 1860 was 731,400 persons. This does not correspond to new immigration since older immigrants migrating internally are included; also there is no adjustment for mortality. Still it does seem to indicate that railroads captured a very large share of the traffic. Data taken from Annual Reports of the respective companies and U.S. Bureau of Census, *Compendium of the Ninth Census* (Washington, 1872), p. 377.
This service was performed at rates about one-half that of first-class travel. The rate of remuneration was so low that the Pennsylvania Railroad participated in it only because the other lines did. (*Tenth Annual Report of the Pennsylvania Railroad Company, 1856* [Philadelphia, 1857], p. 14.)
[70] U.S. Bureau of the Census, *Eighth Census of the United States, 1860, Population*, (Washington, 1864), p. xxix.
[71] Quoted in Thomas, *Migration*, p. 95.

primarily agricultural regions and came in especially large numbers in 1852, 1853, and 1854, could not have been unaware of the new opportunities for agriculture that were being created by railroad expansion. Expectation of future growth based upon the past accumulation and future increments of social overhead capital could easily have caused some lead of immigration ahead of actual economic growth without negating the influence of economic prospects. Pending further analysis, and more is needed, we should not be quick to overthrow the hypothesis advanced by Kuznets and others that the common response of many European countries suggests a single external cause, the state of the American economy.[72] Both through the expenditure effects discussed in Chapter III as well as the extension of profitable opportunities it brought to the West, the railroad was an important determinant of that economy in the 1850's.

Thus far we have argued for a causal role for railroads in the population redistribution, internal and external, that occurred during the decade. In turn, that migration reacted upon railroad development in a significant way. Many western projects earned satisfactory returns from the start only owing to the volume of passenger traffic. As late as the fiscal year 1856, when freight receipts for the country as a whole already exceeded passenger revenues by 20 percent, in the West they were still equal. Net earnings at the same time were eminently satisfactory. Yet in 1859, with western lines carrying considerably more freight than before, earnings were perilously low, both gross and net. The reason was the stagnation of the passenger traffic. Despite a more than 25 percent increase in mileage over the intervening years, passenger receipts in 1859 exceeded those of 1856 by only 5 percent; freight receipts were up by almost a third over the same interval.[73] The absolute data on passenger movement and tonnage tell the same story. On 6 major east-west arteries traversing Ohio the number of through passengers declined from 581,000 in 1857–1858 to 367,000 in 1859–1860; the number of tons carried

[72] Richard A. Easterlin, "Influences in European Overseas Emigration before World War I," *Economic Development and Cultural Change*, IX (April 1961), 341–349, tests and rejects the hypothesis that earlier European natural increase was responsible for the emigration.

[73] See the data in Tables 42, 43, and 44 and the mileage data in Table 16.

increased from 797,000 to 1,026,000.[74] The difference between western and eastern through passengers on lines entering Chicago from the east, a measure of net migration, declined from an estimated 108,000 passengers in 1856 to a mere 10,000 in 1860; total through travel was off from 364,000 passengers to 204,000 between the same years.[75]

The difficulties of western railroads from 1857 on were thus a direct consequence of the break in the flow of migration westward, and not the result of a decline in freight shipments. As the report of the Indianapolis and Cincinnati Railroad sadly announced in 1858: "There will not be, as formerly, a tide of emigration to the West and North to swell our passenger receipts . . ." [76] When railroad prosperity began to return in late 1860 it was on an altered footing from the earlier profitable years and was built upon the firmer base of growing commodity surpluses, not passengers. This transformation in turn mirrors the initial contribution of the railroad in influencing settlement and its subsequent redemption of the promise of lower cost transportation.

Conclusion

This chapter has analyzed the part played by the railroad in western economic development in the 1850's. Theoretically, one would clearly expect the addition of extensive rail facilities to increase the attractiveness of the West vis-à-vis other regions, and foreign countries too, and hence to affect both the regional allocation of resources and the total supply, the latter through immigration. A key issue, however, is whether such railroad influence was primarily exogenous or endogenous, whether railroads first set in motion the forces culminating in the economic development of the decade, or whether arising in response to profitable situations, they played a more passive role.

[74] The lines were the Bellefontaine and Indiana; the Central Ohio; the Cleveland, Painesville, and Ashtabula; the Indianapolis and Cincinnati; the Cleveland and Toledo; and the Ohio and Mississippi. *Second Annual Report of the Ohio Commissioner of Statistics, 1858* (Columbus, 1859), p. 74; *Fourth Annual Report of the Ohio Commissioner of Statistics, 1860* (Columbus, 1861), p. 68.

[75] *Chicago Democratic Press Annual Review for 1860* (Chicago, 1861), p. 53.

[76] *Annual Report of Indianapolis and Cincinnati Railroad for the Year Ending December 31, 1857* (Cincinnati, 1858), p. 16.

Those who have argued most strongly for railroad causality have typically relied upon some notion of construction ahead of demand. Accordingly, this hypothesis became our starting point. It is fair to say, I believe, that the preponderance of evidence denies such a phenomenon before the Civil War.[77] Western railroad enterprises on the whole were initially successful, and some spectacularly so. By and large those that were not continued as poor investments long after and never generated self-fulfilling demand. No matter if we look to population densities, or to the structure of governmental subsidy, or to gross receipts, our impression must be that the expansion was rooted in rationality, not insanity. Even the excesses of construction and consequent rate competition are to be understood as the outcome of logical, and necessary, decisions by individual railroads (and municipalities).

Such results do not necessarily deny an important causal role to the railroad. Rather, they seem to be consistent with an alternative linkage from the railroad construction of the late 1840's and early 1850's to an on-going flow of westward migration that in turn led to continued railroad expansion. We have invoked a process of anticipatory settlement to explain both such a sequence and the vitality of private enterprise. Thus by the time railroads reached Iowa and Wisconsin, existing economic development justified their construction under private auspices, but only because of prior railroad development in Ohio. This newer interpretation may be amended by future research, but at the moment it seems to be a useful way of stating the dynamics of this western railroad expansion.

As far as first causes go, whether it was improved agricultural terms of trade, or lower English iron prices, or increased grain exports that set in motion the initial construction in Ohio, is not a very fruitful question. The process of economic development is too complex, and also too diversified, to permit of unequivocal prime movers. More relevant is the elaboration of mechanisms of diffusion of development, as we have tried to demonstrate here.

[77] A similar set of criteria casually applied to post-Civil War railroad construction in the states farther west suggest that this constituted a true episode of building before demand.

CHAPTER V

The Impact on Western Agriculture

Introduction

The preceding chapter has explored the mutual relationship between railroad extension and western settlement in the 1850's. It has left unanswered the implications of that connection for the pattern of regional and national economic growth. This chapter takes on some of that responsibility by focusing upon the railroad contribution to the transformation and expansion of western agriculture.

Three sets of inquiries are taken up. The first of these is the impact of the railroad upon the geographic structure of land utilization within the West. Traditionally, the railroad is credited with making possible the development of interior, landlocked areas. Leland Jenks elevates such an effect to the major contribution of the innovation; so too does Douglass North in his recent book with his finding that "the highest rate of [population] increase was in the interior counties which the railroad made accessible." [1] Yet while lower cost transportation especially benefited areas bereft of alternatives, it also contributed to the advantage of the already established western production centers. Moreover, as evidenced by the sequential character of western railroad construction, this was an advantage available much sooner, and one which could be turned to immediate expansion of exports. The issue is not only the interesting one of divergent pulls upon agricultural location. If the railroad's major effect was to channel resources to the interior, with an inevitable lag before returns,

[1] Jenks, "Railroads as an Economic Force," pp. 1–20, and Douglass C. North, *The Economic Growth of the United States, 1790–1860* (Englewood Cliffs, N.J., 1961), pp. 146–153, especially p. 150.

then railroad construction was primarily an investment for future decades. If the intensive effects were predominant, the lag was foreshortened, and it was possible for the railroad to have influenced ante-bellum output itself.

Our second objective is to assess how much the total value of farm output in 1859 was increased by western expansion *cum* railroad construction. Three different mechanisms are distinguished. First, expansion onto western soils meant lower capital costs for land preparation. For an equivalent increase in acreage, therefore, the resources actually absorbed in the West were smaller than the alternative inputs that would have been required in the East. The difference is a contribution to output. Second, western soils were more productive so that equivalent yields per acre could be obtained with less labor and capital. The expansion of agriculture there relative to other regions therefore again extended the limits of potential production. Third, the more perfect price equalization accompanying lower transport costs increased farm real incomes in the West. This gain, of course, is nothing more than the sectoral incidence of the direct benefits already calculated in Chapter II.

All these effects can be, and are, quantified (with varying degrees of approximation) in the second section of this chapter. Yet the feasibility of numerical manipulation should not blind us to its partial nature. Inevitably, we must abstract from the dynamics of the situation in order to perform such computations, whether by holding factor supply constant, or by assuming almost as favorable production possibilities elsewhere, or by ignoring demand. To be told that in 1859 farm income without railroads would have been *x* percent smaller than it was in fact, on the basis of the above considerations, does not exhaust the influence of the innovation. Part of the response to the railroad, such as the diversion of additional acreage to cultivation, and an increased supply of labor are not adequately reflected by such calculations.

Equally slighted are the consequences of agricultural expansion for growth in other sectors. Unlike the backward agricultures of certain parts of Europe, the American farm sector was poised to play more than a mere permissive role in the process of industrialization. The existence of unsettled lands and small landholdings joined to make the agricultural sector in the United States a positive and progressive factor in the early period of manufacturing development. The third section of this chapter explores some of these interrelationships.

The Extent and Importance of Interior Development

Despite widespread agreement that a major contribution of the railroad is the access it granted to the interior West, little has been done to substantiate this position for the period before 1860. North's demonstration of a positive association in interior counties between rates of population increase and the occurrence or absence of railroad construction is a recent exception that proves the rule. Such neglect surely cannot be attributed to the self-evident nature of the proposition. Indeed, the first impression in looking at the production data of the western states during the 1850's is the persistence of prerailroad patterns. The concentration of wheat production in northern Illinois and southern Wisconsin was only slightly abated. In Illinois, such counties as Bureau, Lee, Whiteside, and Henry, which first took their places among the leading wheat counties in 1860, were but narrowly removed from the older centers. In Wisconsin the limited geographic extent of the displacement over the decade is equally marked. In Iowa, five of the six leading counties in the production of wheat in 1859 were similarly pre-eminent in 1855 before the railroad ever came. So far as corn is concerned, with such final products as whiskey and livestock easily transportable, interior counties were never so penalized by high transport as with wheat. Even in the central prairie of Illinois, certain counties ranked among the leading producers of corn in 1849, well before the railroad had penetrated.[2]

Such casual empiricism, however, does not controvert the equally casual, but theoretically infallible, conclusion that interior counties were made more attractive by transport cost reduction. A more definitive and encompassing test of the hypothesis is necessary. Tables 24 through 27 provide just that.

[2] Data from *Compendium of the Seventh Census, Eighth Census, Agriculture,* and *Census of Iowa, 1880.*

In these we have classified all counties within the four-state area of Indiana, Illinois, Wisconsin, and Iowa by three characteristics: access to water, above or below average production of wheat (or corn) in 1850, and the state of railroad communication by 1860.[3] The four-state area selected corresponds to a region that was almost entirely without railroad facilities in 1849 but with a substantial network by 1859; hence the realignment to interior areas will better represent the sole effect of the innovation. Also, because the area accounted for 60 percent of the increased wheat production during the 1850's and almost half the national increment in corn, the results are of national significance.

In 1849, as Table 24 indicates, wheat and corn production in the four-state area was concentrated in that part of the region with water access. With about a third of the area, these counties produced almost half of the wheat, and two fifths of the corn. After railroads came, the concentration was reduced: the area accounted for only two fifths of the output of wheat in 1859, and a still smaller proportion of corn. So far so good, for the hypothesis of interior development. The changes are in the right direction, even though the initial concentration is perhaps not as great as might have been anticipated.

[3] Navigable streams were determined by reference to the *Preliminary Report of the Inland Waterways Commission*, pp. 33–93. This source excludes rivers not then navigable and hence tends to understate water access as it actually existed in the 1850's. The distortion is not serious since the smaller streams were not regarded as very satisfactory and were replaced as soon as possible. Counties adjacent to these navigable waterways were considered as having access to water transport, typically involving a maximum overland journey of 30 miles.

Average wheat and corn production in 1850 was not determined by dividing total output by the number of counties, since the large number of very small producers would yield a very low mean. Since the objective is to isolate the leading producers, the average used is the center of gravity of the distribution of output. That is, counties producing outputs equal to or greater than the specified average provide half the total output of all counties. In this instance the proportion is not exact due to rounding. The "average" corn production is calculated as 700,000 bushels, "average" wheat, 150,000 bushels; the corresponding means are approximately 450,000 and 80,000 bushels. The center of gravity definition gives greater scope for expansion in "below average" counties, and hence a more accurate specification of the hypothesis of interior development.

Those counties with railroads by 1860 were determined by reference to the maps in Taylor and Neu, *Railroad Network*. The difference between 1860 and 1861 is negligible in the West and does not affect the results.

TABLE 24. Distribution of output by geographic situation

Geographic situation	Area[a] (thousands of square miles)	Output of wheat		Output of corn	
		(thousands of bushels)			
		1849	1859	1849	1859
Counties with water access[b]	71	9,424	26,451	48,602	87,882
Counties without water access	134	12,021	38,352	72,655	148,810
Total	205	21,445	64,803	121,257	236,692

Source: Compendium of the Seventh Census; Eighth Census, Agriculture.

[a] Computed approximately by assuming homogeneous counties within states, but not among states. Such an assumption is reasonable for this area; the number of counties is so large that any error is minimized.

[b] Defined as those counties that border navigable streams as defined by the *Preliminary Report of the Inland Waterways Commission* (Washington, 1909), and the Great Lakes (excepting Huron).

In part, this lack of early concentration is due to boundaries that are drawn too loosely. Counties that are but slightly removed from water access or market by a short overland journey, such as those of the Rock River Valley, are not equivalent in economic isolation to those more deeply embedded in the interior. We let the market be our guide. Counties without water access but with "above average" production are demonstrably not economically isolated prior to the introduction of the railroad. Table 25, as revised to exclude the latter from the interior group, portrays the initial conditions in terms more favorable to the traditional view. Relative to area, the new subset of interior counties produce only half as much as those with access in 1849, but increase to about two thirds as much in 1859.

Nevertheless, in spite of such improvement, the initial centers of production remain dominant, because the railroads went there with greater certainty, and first. Of 40 counties with above average wheat output in 1849, the railroad enters all but 4 during the decade, and those 4 have water access; of the 60 counties with high corn production in 1849, the railroad goes to 49. The corre-

TABLE 25. Distribution of output by economic situation

Economic situation	Area (thousands of square miles)	Output of wheat (thousands of bushels)		Output of corn (thousands of bushels)	
		1849	1859	1849	1859
"Interior" counties[a]	121	6,146	24,391	36,168	94,949
Other counties	84	15,299	40,412	85,089	141,743
Total	205	21,445	64,803	121,257	236,692

Source: Compendium of the Seventh Census; Eighth Census, Agriculture.
[a] Those counties without water access and below average output in 1849.

sponding results for below average producers of wheat are 145 with railroads, and 166 without; in the instance of corn, 132 with railroads, and 159 without. Even excluding Iowa, where railroad penetration into the interior was slightest, the difference in attractiveness of initially high production areas is statistically significant.[4] The effects of this skewness upon the concentration of production are shown in Table 26, which presents the rate of growth of production, and the proportion of the total decadal increment accounted for by each area. Despite considerably

TABLE 26. The contribution of interior counties, 1850–1860 (in percent)

Economic situation	Wheat production		Corn production	
	Decadal rate of increase	Proportion of regional increment	Decadal rate of increase	Proportion of regional increment
Interior counties	296.8	42.1	162.5	50.9
Other counties	164.1	57.9	66.6	49.1

Source: Calculated from Table 25.

[4] A contingency table testing the positive association between level of output in 1849 and construction of rail facilities yields $\chi^2 = 9.04$ in the case of corn and $\chi^2 = 13.06$ for wheat. These values would occur by chance less than one time in 200 in the former case, less than one time in 1000 in the latter, if these phenomena were actually independent.

higher *rates* of growth, the interior counties do not contribute much more to the *absolute* regional increment in output, and in the case of wheat, significantly less. And this with 50 percent greater area. The large contribution to the growth in corn production is partially spurious, it may be added. The very rapid increase in output is concentrated in the interior Iowa counties astride the Des Moines River. This was a waterway more satisfactory than most, but because it was quickly abandoned in favor of the railroad, it does not figure in the list of subsequently navigable rivers.

This is not to dismiss either the importance of the interior or the contribution of the railroad. The largest proportion of the decadal increment in the output of both corn and wheat does come from those counties simultaneously lacking water access, possessing below average output in 1849, and with railroads by the end of the decade. Table 27 demonstrates the results for

TABLE 27. Sources of increased wheat output, 1850–1860

Area description	With railroads				Without railroads		
	Decadal rate of growth of wheat production (percent)	Proportion of absolute increment (percent)	Proportion of increment relative to proportion of area		Decadal rate of growth of wheat production (percent)	Proportion of absolute increment (percent)	Proportion of increment relative to proportion of area
Above average wheat output and water access	81.5	7.2	1.5		50.0	1.0	0.9
Below average wheat output and water access	246.0	20.4	1.4		402.3	10.6	.8
Above average wheat output; no water access	137.6	18.6	3.0		0.0	0.0	.0
Below average wheat output; no water access	254.4	28.4	1.2		454.0	13.7	.4

Source: See text.

wheat. More than a quarter of increased production, 28.4 percent, emanates from counties with this combination of characteristics. Relative to size, and hence potential, however, this achievement ranks far behind that of the group of counties without water access, above average output in 1849, and with railroad facilities in 1860. Standardizing the absolute increments for area makes this clear. The initially above average region yields two and a half times more per unit area than the below average region. This decisively calls notice to a major contribution of the western railroads before the Civil War: the supply of more efficient transportation to existing centers of production away from water that called forth immediately increasing surpluses for market.

Such a conclusion is reinforced when referred to the investment required to evoke a given increment. Railroad construction seems to have induced less productive settlement per mile in the interior than in the surplus counties. The experience of the Illinois Central is instructive. Only 19 percent of the increase in cultivated acreage in Illinois during the decade 1850–1860 came in those 20 prairie counties to which that road first brought low cost transportation. Since 500 miles of the road, or about one sixth of the total railroad mileage in the state, served this area, the effect upon productive settlement of a mile of road is only slightly higher than the average for the state as a whole. A fairer test should perhaps exclude those 5 counties south of Centralia where the road put forth little effort in colonization. With this adjustment, the ratio of the increase in cultivated acreage to the proportion of railroad mileage does take on a value substantially above unity. But the Illinois Central was not alone. Some 200 miles of east-west line traversed the same area, and with their addition the picture reverts at best to one of average settlement per mile of construction. By contrast, Ogle county in northern Illinois, already a surplus producer in 1849 in spite of its lack of water access, accounted for 2.3 percent of the increase in cultivated acreage with but 1.2 percent of the state's railroad mileage.

Why proportionally more railroad investment should have been required in the interior is suggested by Gates: "A great deal of land in these counties lay between ten and twenty miles from railroads, and as there were practically no navigable rivers to supplement the railroads, the situation for development was not the best. Moreover, on account of poor drainage in this section the dirt roads were impassable for considerable periods of time." [5]

[5] Gates, *Illinois Central*, p. 239.

Less dramatic complementary transport improvements were rendered the more important by railroad penetration of the interior, not the less. This raises the broader issue of the extent of railroad causality in the observed development of the interior. Other influences obviously were operative as well. Some that come readily to mind are technical improvements like an improved plow that did not scour in the prairie soils, and better drainage. In addition, market forces increased the relative price of agricultural output during the decade.[6] Potential diminishing returns on land already in use add another dimension. The previous data bear upon this subject, particularly those of Table 27. There, three measures of change in wheat production over the decade of the 1850's are presented for the four different types of areas in the region, further differentiated by the availability of railroad communication. Thus there is some standardization of other influences that are relevant to the pace of expansion during the period, such as initial production position and ease of water transportation. Uniformly, those regions with railroads provided a larger share of the increased output of wheat over the period, a domination that is not weakened when there is adjustment for size differentials. Only the rates of growth are equivocal. Two of the railroad areas grew less rapidly than those without such communication; one grew more rapidly. The technical explanation for the perversity is the very low initial level of production in the nonrailroad group. More substantively, however, the very high rates of growth confirm that movement to the interior was due to more than rail communication. As commodity prices and land prices rose, those parts of the region formerly underutilized became relatively more attractive independently of transport innovation. Given, additionally, anticipated rail construction and the availability of already completed mileage nearby, it is no wonder that extension into new land went on even in the absence of direct rail links.

The experience of the interior counties where railroads were not built cannot be used to project what would have happened

---

[6] For a discussion of some of the technical advances that eliminated obstacles to prairie farming, see Gates, *Farmer's Age*, pp. 180–183; for the relative rise in agricultural prices, see *Historical Statistics*, pp. 115, 123.

in the total absence of the innovation. Their lesser expansion reflects the obvious relative attractiveness of direct rail communication available elsewhere; on the other hand, settlement was positively influenced to the degree such facilities were close by, if not directly present. Detailed examination of the differential rents accruing to transport access would be required to infer how deep the penetration could have been without railroads. We can suggest, however, the relative strength of some of the forces involved. Rail rates of 3 cents a ton-mile compared to overland freights of 15 cents were equivalent to an increase of almost 20 cents a bushel of wheat to a farmer 50 miles in the interior. The inflationary forces during the decade came to about the same increase in price available irrespective of location. At any point beyond the 50-mile margin, and this probably includes the majority of the interior counties, railroads were the more important influence. Or to put it another way, the exogenous relative increase in price would have bought just 50 additional miles of wagon transportation; extension beyond that point is then the province of the railroad.[7]

The railroad was thus an important factor both in the movement to the interior and in the continuing development of extant surplus areas. About as much more wheat was grown during the decade in interior counties first provided access by railroads as in the counties initially productive and to which track was extended. Since the increment of population in both areas was almost the same, the exports from the interior fully matched those from the other region. Population grew by 546,000 in the interior, production by 12.3 million bushels of wheat, and exportable surplus by 9.6 million bushels. The corresponding statistics for the original production centers are population change of 528,000, increased output of 11.2 million bushels, and exportable surplus of 8.6 million bushels.[8] The rapid development of the first group

[7] This takes the price increase as given and allocates to the railroad, as the variable element, all interaction effects. This is why the result credits the railroad with a greater influence than the preceding evaluation in which both forces are assumed to operate simultaneously.

[8] The per capita consumption has been calculated at 5 bushels. Other reasonable assumptions, while affecting the absolute differences between the two areas, leave the ranking invariant.

is tribute to the process of anticipatory settlement; the latter to the sagacity of railroad promoters in exploiting their most profitable opportunities first.

Taken together, both circumstances meant a supply response to western social overhead investment in the 1850's with shorter lag than in the 1830's. For the earlier period, we have nothing like the later production statistics. Nonetheless, other indications suggest that settlement then was more extensive; that is, migration was motivated less by the opportunity for immediate than for future commercial production. The frontier seems to have moved farther west between 1830 and 1840, for example, than between 1850 and 1860.[9] The first exports of western produce to tidewater did not pass through the Erie Canal until 1836 nor were New Orleans receipts augmented during the period; surplus already awaited the Galena and Chicago Railroad upon its first short trip in 1848.[10] In part, this difference in the length of the lag was due to the failure to complete the planned transportation system of the area in the 1830's as initially projected; in part, it was the consequence of the much smaller settlement of the West in the earlier period. Whatever the causes, the crucial point is that the later railroad expansion led to an immediate economic pay-off in the agricultural sector that earlier western canal innovation had failed to provide.

Railroad Services and Agricultural Incomes

Having satisfied ourselves that the beneficial effects of lower transport costs were not directed simply at a massive redistribution of future production, but made themselves felt in the highly productive areas as well as through immediate returns from the

[9] See the maps of western expansion presented by Randall D. Sale and Edwin D. Karn, *American Expansion: A Book of Maps* (Homewood, Ill., 1962), pp. 12–17, for the visual impression.

[10] Wheat had first come from the western states to be milled at Rochester somewhat earlier in 1831, "but it was not until after 1835 that competition from that area came to be felt to any degree." Even then it was limited. (Neil A. McNall, *An Agricultural History of the Genesee Valley, 1790–1860* [Philadelphia, 1952], p. 124.) For shipments to tidewater see Poor, *Railroads and Canals*, p. 364; for shipments to New Orleans see Table 36, below. The results on the Galena are described in A. T. Andreas, *History of Chicago from the Earliest to the Present Time* (Chicago, 1884), I, 248.

interior, we are still left to wonder at the magnitude of immediate railroad influence. As suggested earlier, transport innovation affected the value of output of the agricultural sector in at least three different ways. First, total costs of land preparation were reduced because acreage expanded in the West rather than the East; second, there was a larger product on the more fertile western soils; and third, agricultural income increased owing to the improved terms of trade between East and West accompanying more perfect price equalization. The size of these effects is now explored.

Suppose, in the first instance, nonrailroad agricultural development would have taken the guise of equivalent expansion of cultivated acreage in the East instead of in the less accessible West. Then investment in preparing the land for cultivation would have cost at least $65 million more than it actually did. The calculations are easily performed. Primack estimates clearing of 18.3 million acres in the West during the decade, of which 13.3 were forested. For the 5.0 million open acres total outlays of $11 per acre were required; the same extension on eastern forested land would have cost $24.[11] This $65 million is a minimum because it equates the cost of preparing eastern and western woodland. At the margin, however, western forested areas were less densely wooded, while those in the East were more so. If Primack's total labor input is applied to eastern land, while the smaller requirement is appropriate to the West, a further differential investment of $214 million is implied.[12]

This $279 million is an upper limit for two reasons. First, it presumes the extremely high cost of $36 for clearing eastern land — while the average value of improved acreage was less than $40 overall in 1860; second, it attributes all western land expansion to the existence of the railroad, when, as we have just noted,

[11] Primack, "Land Clearing under Nineteenth-Century Techniques," pp. 484–497. Although the census indicates clearing of 21 million acres in the Old Northwest Territory states plus Iowa, I use Primack's smaller total consisting of the North Central, Lake, and Prairie regions. The differential costs are discussed earlier, pp. 41–42.

[12] For the first estimate 20 days of labor at $.90 a day are used for woodland; with Primack's 33 days at the same unit cost, an additional $11.70 an acre would have been required in the East for all 18.3 million acres.

other forces would have led inevitably to some movement to lands farther away from the market. At the aggregative level we can approximate this last condition by advancing the alternative that the regional distribution of acreage between East and West would have remained the same in 1860 as in 1850 had railroad construction not been undertaken. This more reasonable statement of railroad influence limits the gain to at most $176 million, but with the same minimum of $65 million, since most of the prairie land would not have been cleared without the railroad.[13] Even the smaller of these two sums is not inconsiderable. The saving could have purchased more than 2000 miles of railroad track, and its annual yield at an interest rate of 7 percent represents an augmentation of agricultural income of $4.5 million. With the larger estimate, these magnitudes are all increased proportionally.

Continuing in this exercise in comparative statics, what were the effects of this more than proportional increase in western acreage upon potential output? If there were no regional differences in productivity the effect would be nil. In fact, however, William Parker's and Judith Klein's research into corn and wheat production indicates that both crops could be grown with smaller inputs of labor upon western soil.[14] Only 1.81 man-hours per bushel were required in preharvest and harvest operations upon the corn crop in the West against an 1840 national average of 3.51; for wheat the differential is a smaller one, 2.84 man-hours versus 3.17, nationally.[15]

[13] The hypothetical alternative consists of 9.5 million acres cleared in the East and 8.8 million in the West. The land shifted to the East is presumed to include all the nonforested type, which is why the $65 million minimum is unaffected. Lesser use of eastern woodland is involved in the maximum estimate, which is why it is correspondingly reduced.

[14] William N. Parker and Judith L. V. Klein, "Productivity Growth in Grain Production in the United States, 1840–60 and 1900–10," *Output, Employment, and Productivity in the United States after 1800*, National Bureau of Economic Research, Inc., Studies in Income and Wealth, vol. 30 (New York, 1965). The man-hour input data are based upon (1) investigation of Carrol Wright's comparison of hand and machine methods (reprinted in *Historical Statistics*, p. 281) using the location of the farms for which the estimates were made; (2) contemporary evidence; and (3) existing twentieth-century data on hand methods still in use.

[15] Parker and Klein, Table 13. These regional man-hour requirements are an average of the entire 1840–1860 period when there was apparently little change in inputs or, in Parker's and Klein's data, yield. The wheat data include preharvest, harvest and postharvest inputs; corn, only the first two.

The reason for western advantage in these 2 crops is the smaller number of man-hours required per acre and not any superiority in yield. Indeed Parker's and Klein's data show smaller yields in the West than in the East. Yet with reports of extraordinary yields per acre on virgin western soil the advantage may have widened in the 1850's on this account, too. Within the region it appears that yields increased as one moved west. Ohio farmers obtained 12 bushels of wheat per acre for the entire decade of the 1850's; and only 10 bushels over the period 1853–1859. In Iowa, farmers were getting an average of 14 bushels in 1855. Wisconsin producers experienced a still higher yield of 16.7 bushels in 1856 and a remarkable 24.5 in 1860. The evidence on corn is more limited. Ohio, even with its excellent bottom lands along the Ohio River, averaged no more than 37 bushels per acre in the first 3 years of the decade, and only 31 bushels from 1853 to 1859. The Iowa Census indicates an output of more than 42 bushels per acre planted.[16] Cost data also seem to affirm a larger advantage for western soils than Parker and Klein find. The survey of the Commissioner of Patents in 1853 turned up the following results: In New York, in Seneca County, the cost per bushel of wheat (excluding interest costs on land) was about 48 cents; in Monroe County, in the Genesee Valley, it averaged nearly 60 cents. In Michigan, the cost similarly calculated was 35 cents. For corn the costs per bushel ranged from less than 7 cents near Peoria, Illinois, and 10 cents in Ohio, to 29 cents in Pennsylvania, and $37\frac{1}{2}$ cents in Virginia.[17]

These fragmentary indications are not proof positive, nor can the smaller weights the outlying areas had in regional output, and hence productivity, be denied. Nonetheless the extrapolation of later yields to the earlier period should be recognized as a possible source of understatement in the regional differentials. In their revised, published paper Parker and Klein now recognize the problem explicitly in a new Appendix B. With the use of their

[16] *Fourth Annual Report of the Ohio Commissioner of Statistics for 1860*, pp.11–14; *Census for Iowa, 1880*, pp. 278 ff.; John G. Thompson, "The Rise and Decline of the Wheat Growing Industry in Wisconsin," *Bulletin of the University of Wisconsin*, Economics and Political Science Series, V, no. 3 (1909), 198.

[17] Commissioner of Patents, *Report on Agriculture for 1853*, House Exec. Doc. No. 39, 33rd Congress, 1st Session (Washington, 1854), pp. 103–153.

TABLE 28. The effect of regional redistribution upon corn production, 1850–1860

Region[a]	(1) Man-hours per acre	(2) Bushels per acre	(3) Man-hours per bushel	(4) Percent distribution of output, 1850	(5) Percent distribution of output, 1860	(6) National average man-hours per bushel, 1850 regional distribution (3) × (4)	(7) National average man-hours per bushel, 1860 regional distribution (3) × (5)
Eastern dairy	111.3	33.5	3.32	9.6	8.1	.32	.27
Middle eastern	62.1	21.8	2.85	31.9	24.3	.91	.69
South	71.6	11.8	6.07	20.8	19.5	1.26	1.18
West	59.2	32.7	1.81	37.7	48.1	.68	.87
Total	—	—	—	100.0	100.0	3.17	3.01

Source: (1–3) Parker and Klein, "Productivity Growth in Grain Production," Table 13. Their methods for deriving these estimates are:
(1) Approximate input for operations on soil derived from pre-1860 information on hand methods, twentieth-century information on hand methods, and regional distribution of farms included in Carrol Wright's study of hand and machine methods in the U.S. Bureau of Labor, *13th Annual Report of the Commissioner of Labor* (Washington, 1899).
(2) Extrapolation backwards of 1866–1876 average yield per acre by state based on stability of yield from 1866 onward.
(3) (1) ÷ (2).
(4, 5) Calculated from *Eighth Census, Agriculture.*
[a] Regional breakdown: Eastern dairy: New England plus New York and Pennsylvania.
Middle eastern: Delaware, Maryland, Virginia, North Carolina, Tennessee, Kentucky.
South: South Carolina, Georgia, Alabama, Florida, Mississippi, Arkansas, Louisiana, Texas.
West: Ohio, Indiana, Illinois, Iowa, Missouri, Michigan, Wisconsin, Minnesota.

text data as they stand, we calculate in Table 28 the output consequences for corn of the accelerated westward expansion of the 1850's. Solely on account of the regional shift in production between 1850 and 1860, when the share of the West increased from more than a third to almost half, the national average number of man-hours required per bushel of corn declined from 3.17 to 3.01. Phrased in terms of output, and neglecting post-harvest labor, the regional shift resulted in an actual corn crop in 1860 about 5 percent larger than it would otherwise have been. That is, had the 1850 regional distribution of acreage prevailed in 1860, and with the same input of man-hours that occurred in 1860, the production of corn would have come to 796.4 million bushels rather than 838.8 million. Stated in terms of increments, regional redistribution accounts for almost a fifth of the increased output during the decade. Use of the alternative Parker and Klein yield series leaves matters unchanged because they increase the yield of the South relatively more than that of the West.

We cannot conclude that total agricultural income was equally sensitive. The effect on wheat output, similarly calculated, comes to less than 1 percent. There is no reason to assume that corn is the more representative example of western superiority. Moreover, a large proportion of national agricultural income was contributed by cotton at this date and was unaffected by the regional shift. Since it is impossible, because of lack of data, to do more with partial analyses to broaden the results, I have experimented with a more aggregative approach to the problem. The principal commodity components of agricultural income for the East and West have been summed into regional agricultural real outputs by applying national prices to the outputs of each area. By dividing these large samples of total agricultural output in each region by the labor force engaged in agriculture in each area, we approximate relative agricultural productivities per man in the respective regions.[18] Although the absolute magnitudes are understated by reason of exclusion of some output, the relative magnitudes are what count in the present context. Then it is possible to calculate the effect of the changed regional distribution of the agricultural labor force between 1850 and 1860 upon output.

As Table 29 indicates, the increase in constant dollar value added per worker between 1850 and 1860 that can be ascribed to such a redistribution is meager indeed, the difference being between an actual $204 and a potential $199. In percentage terms, 1860 agricultural income in the East and West would have been 2 percent smaller if the labor force in that year had been distributed as it was in 1850. Constant 1850 prices, instead of those of 1860, make no difference to the result. In part, this surprisingly small effect is due to the method. The consequences of the westward shift are somewhat understated since there is no allowance

[18] The proportion of output covered is quite large. The selected crops and livestock products make up about 34 percent of the national total of agricultural income in 1850 and about 31 percent in 1860. Since our states made up about one third of the national agricultural labor force in both years, this implies substantial coverage of income in the regions defined, even allowing for productivity differentials between free and slave labor.

TABLE 29. The effect of regional redistribution upon total agricultural income

	East[a]		West[b]		Combined total	
	1850	1860	1850	1860	1850	1860
(1) Sample agricultural income (million current dollars)	115.4	152.4	118.2	264.5	233.6	416.9
(2) Sample agricultural income (million 1860 dollars)	141.9	152.4	154.6	264.5	296.5	416.9
(3) Labor force (thousands)	826	975	713	1066	1539	2041
(4) Output per worker (1860 dollars)	172.0	156.0	217.0	248.0	193.0	204.0
(5) Output per worker, 1850 regional distribution (1860 dollars)	172.0	156.0	217.0	248.0	193.0	199.0
(6) Agricultural output, 1850 regional distribution (million 1860 dollars)	141.9	171.2	154.6	234.7	296.5	405.8

Source: (1) Census production data for wheat, corn, oats, hay, potatoes, cheese, and butter, multiplied by proportion of output entering gross income and then by national price. Gross income fractions from Gallman, "Commodity Output," p. 52; prices from Towne and Rasmussen, "Farm Gross Product and Gross Investment in the Nineteenth Century," pp. 264 ff. The latter source was also used for conversion factors to transform the census inventories of swine and cattle to production flows.

(2) Each quantity component of line (1) times 1860 national price.

(3) Census of occupation data for farmers in 1850 and farmers plus farm laborers in 1860. Laborers were included as farmers in 1850.

(4) Line (2) divided by line (3).

(5) Combined total: Line (4) for each region weighted by 1850 regional distribution of labor force from line (3).

(6) Line (5) multiplied by total labor force in 1860 allocated to regions by 1850 percentages.

[a] New England states plus New York, Pennsylvania, New Jersey, and Delaware.
[b] Ohio, Indiana, Illinois, Michigan, Wisconsin, and Iowa.

for possible diminishing returns in the East, and the possible increasing returns in the West. Between 1850 and 1860, at least, value added per worker, as we have calculated it, moved down in the East and up in the West. Thus the assumption of constancy of productivity at 1860 regional levels independent of the 1860 regional distribution of the labor force biases the calculations downward. More important than this is the virtual absence of any upward movement in labor productivity in our data. Obviously if there was little change, despite the fact that regional redistribution explains it totally, there is little scope for positive effects. By contrast, both Gallman and Towne and Rasmussen have found a substantial increase over the same decade.[19] The divergence is not due to the different price base, but it may come from the difference in coverage. The national data include the southern staple crops. Both cotton and tobacco, which together add up to almost 20 percent of national output, about doubled in volume between 1849 and 1859, while the southern labor force grew much less rapidly.[20] It therefore does not follow with any certainty that our results understate either the total productivity increase in the East and West or the effects of regional redistribution.

On the basis of all the data it appears the westward movement accounts at a minimum for a $14.9 million contribution to 1859 output, the difference of $11.1 million shown in Table 29 scaled up to reflect the partial crop coverage there. This is equivalent to some 3 percent of the decadal increment in national production.[21] To orient the relative importance of such an effect it is useful to compare it with the previously derived estimate of direct benefits. At this minimum level these indirect production effects come to about a tenth of the total social saving in the transport

[19] Towne and Rasmussen find an increase in gross production per worker (in 1910–1914 prices) from $294 to $332; Gallman, an even larger increase (in 1879 prices) from $202 to $240. (Towne and Rasmussen, "Farm Gross Product," p. 269; Gallman, "Commodity Output," p. 31.) This finding is one which is full of implications for the economic history of the ante-bellum period, and which must be explored in greater depth.

[20] Output figures from Lewis C. Gray, *History of Agriculture in the Southern United States to 1860* (Washington, 1933), II, 757, 1026; the lesser rate of growth of the southern labor force shows up in the much smaller rate of increase both of the slave population (about 30 percent) and of white farmers.

[21] The factor, by which the difference between actual 1860 income and 1860 income based upon the 1850 regional distribution of labor is increased, is 1.34. It is the ratio of the national value of the crops and meat products included in Table 29 to total 1859 agricultural production less cotton. The requisite information, as well as the increase in national output over the decade, can be found in Gallman, "Commodity Output," pp. 46–48.

of freight and passengers; relative to the advantages of lower cost transportation of agricultural products, closer to one fourth. That just a single, and understated, indirect effect should be so important justifies the notice to external economies.

Our final influence upon agricultural income is not of this form, however. It is a rehearsal, rather, of the direct benefits seen in another guise. The reduction in transport costs, although previously interpreted as a resource gain, also can be viewed as the purchase of additional specialization with an accordant increase in real income. That is, improved net terms of trade for all parties follow from lower transport costs. We have already observed in Chapter II the improvement in western agricultural prices relative to those in the East during the 1850's as an empirical manifestation of this logical expectation. We reconsider it here to emphasize the relative importance of the railroad to the agricultural sector in particular.

The benefits realized from the railroad transport of agricultural commodities were something like half the total for all freight shipments. If market demand were perfectly elastic for agricultural products, the gains from trade all would have been captured by farmers to the amount of $50 million. Although the market was perhaps not that strong, it is clear from the relative improvement in agricultural prices over the decade that farmers did capture the lion's share of this consumers' surplus, a total further augmented by the opportunity to purchase manufactured commodities at lower prices. Relative to the one-third share of agriculture in national income, this concentration of benefits to the agricultural sector becomes the more pronounced.

This is quite apart from another, but spurious, increase in our usual measures of income gain to farmers in the West. Although the improvement in real income due to increased relative prices pertains only to the proportion of output traded, our valuation of total production naturally will occur at the new, higher prices. Comparing the change in incomes over a period of transport innovation during which price equalization occurs will then overstate the relative gain in the areas initially distant from the market. Thus between 1840 and 1880 agricultural income per worker in the East North Central region grew from $147 to $345, while total income per worker, nationally, increased from $228 to $361, implying a substantial relative improvement for western farmers. Were the incomes properly deflated by regional prices, the relative real income gain would be much smaller: in 1840 the wheat the Ohio farmer consumed was worth much less than the national average price, in the latter period somewhat more. Since agricultural prices varied more, geographically, than those of manufactured articles, care must be observed not to overstate transport induced gains in real incomes of farmers.[22]

So far we have seen that agricultural real incomes probably rose relatively more than those of other sectors, owing to the introduction of the railroad. In addition, we have calculated a capital saving of at least $65 million during the decade owing to greater ease of clearing western soils and something like an annual gain of agricultural output of $14.9 million owing to greater productivity on western land. Common to all these findings is one crucial assumption which limits their usefulness. The terminal period conditions have been assumed to prevail quite independently of transport innovation. Thus the total acreage increment during the decade is taken as the one observed, whether or not railroads were constructed; the number of man-hours at the disposal of the agricultural sector is likewise held constant. In both instances only regional variation has been permitted. This is a simplification that ignores a decisive influence of the railroad. The previous chapter has argued for some positive effects of railroad availability upon immigration. There is good reason to believe, too, that the supply of effort was elastic to the greater rewards provided by improved transport, and that production was more oriented to the market after railroads had been built. Certainly all the demands by settlers for better access to market emphasize this theme, whether in the 1830's or the 1850's. The

[22] For the interregional incomes see Richard A. Easterlin, "Interregional Differences in Per Capita Income, Population, and Total Income, 1840–1950," in *Trends in the American Economy in the Nineteenth Century*, National Bureau of Economic Research, Inc., Studies in Income and Wealth, vol. 24 (Princeton, 1960), pp. 73–140. What I am suggesting is an overstatement of the regional disparity in real incomes in 1840 and a consequent overstatement of convergence of the West by 1880; this also means an understatement of the divergence of the South between the same dates.

following quotation from a description of Iowa of the mid-1850's is typical: "There was little use in raising crops for which no market could be found. . . . Men talked railroads and increased production to any doubtful men they met." [23] Without over-stepping the bounds of credibility, and assuming that only 5 percent of the increased supply of labor, capital, and land in the West during the decade represented a response that would not have been forthcoming without the railroad, we easily double the previously reckoned productivity effect. A reduction of 5 percent in western product as calculated in Table 29 is $13.2 million, and amounts to $17.7 million when adjusted for coverage.

More generally, where the neoclassical full employment model goes astray is in its bias in smoothing the discontinuities of historical change. To every action there corresponds a wide range of only slightly inferior alternatives. In this context it makes little difference whether expansion occurs in sector A or sector B; indeed, there is no room for doubt that expansion will occur somewhere. Yet processes of such automaticity are suspect in a world in which economic growth over long periods is the exception rather than the rule. In the next section we explore some paths by which agricultural expansion, itself a larger beneficiary of railroad advance than our calculations show, affected the growth of income as a whole.

Some Dynamic Sequences

At the most aggregative level one can formulate a model of interaction between agricultural expansion and total income along familiar regional multiplier-accelerator lines. Such descriptions are of questionable value because they lack empirical content. Instead, I elaborate two very concrete, partial dynamic sequences associated with agricultural expansion that have not been extensively treated. One of these is the forward linkage of agriculture to processing industries like flour milling, distilling, tanning, meat packing, and so on.[24] The other is the effect of

[23] Georgia Mills, *West of the River* (Cedar Rapids, 1958), pp. 205–216. Interestingly enough the area in question was close to the Des Moines River but the settlers found it untrustworthy and expensive owing to low water.

[24] I am indebted to Paul David for suggestion and discussion of some of these ideas at a much earlier stage.

agricultural prosperity upon the level of construction activity. That the processing industries grew up to serve agricultural demands is a commonplace. Victor Clark, in his *History of Manufactures*, treats the sequence as self evident: "This group of industries closely correlated with agriculture . . . developed spontaneously, without legislative support or other artificial aids, as a necessary outcome of the nation's productive activities." [25] The tied geographic connection, since the activities were often weight losing, shows up dramatically in the westward shift of the industries with a simultaneous shift of their raw material supplies. The Atlantic Coast states from New York to Virginia produced in value 65 percent of the flour in the country in 1840, but only 57 percent in 1850 and 39 percent in 1860.[26] Meat packing and slaughtering saw a similar shift, not only from East to West, but also from Ohio Valley to the Lake region. Chicago rose to international fame as its pack of pork tripled within the span from 1852 to 1860, while that of beef doubled.[27]

Although the linkage obviously exists, its significance has been neglected or dismissed. Clark, the leading authority on American manufacturing, wastes no time on the processing industry:

> Its annals record no such competitive crises as afflicted textile factories and iron works, no complex interrelations with other industries or with commerce, and no distress due to changes in the processes and mechanism of manufacture. In this uneventful history we may dismiss flour-milling with an allusion to the change in localization earlier described.[28]

This observation affirms the low opinion of these industries held by the contemporary English visitor, Sir S. Morton Peto:

> The people of the United States are taught to think and speak of themselves as a great manufacturing community; but this appears to me a mistake. . . . This aggregate of manufactures includes a vast deal that would not be included in what we call "manufactures." For example one of the principal products of American manufacturing industry is "flour and meal." . . . On this side the Atlantic we

[25] Clark, *History of Manufactures*, I, 479.
[26] Clark, p. 318.
[27] Williamson, ed., *American Economy*, p. 433.
[28] Clark, *History of Manufactures*, I, 479.

should never think of including the product of flour-mills in an estimate of our national manufactures.[29]

Who would guess from Clark's description that as late as 1860 the milling industry ranked as the fourth leading industry in the United States in terms of value added, and first in value of product? Or who would guess from Peto's abrupt remarks that the capital-output ratio in the industry exceeded that of all manufacturing by virtually two to one (2.11 versus 1.18); or that productivity per worker was more than twice as great as that in manufacturing as a whole?[30] The other, unemphasized, side of large material inputs are large capital requirements and high labor productivity.

Peto and Clark are not alone. In Walther Hoffmann's impressive studies of industrialization, his food and drink category (largely inclusive of the processing industries) displays the same properties but he, too, minimizes their importance. On the one hand, the relevant capital requirements are argued to be on a plant basis — which he assumes to be smaller than average in processing — because these are a measure of both the technological and financial difficulties of industrialization. On the other hand, the relative increase in the category in the early stages of industrialization is taken as a reflection only of increasing consumption demand.[31] Yet even accepting the validity of Hoffmann's first point — the relevance of capital requirements on a plant rather than on an industry basis — in the United States in 1859 the average capital per establishment in milling was three times that in boots and shoes, exceeded that in rolling and manufacture of wrought iron, and was not much below that for all industry as a whole. Nor can the discrepancy be laid to large requirements for circulating capital; the importance of plant in total capital, as reported in the 1890 census, for both flour milling

[29] Peto, *Resources and Prospects*, p. 37.
[30] Calculated from *Eighth Census, Manufactures*. The use of reported figures is of course subject to question, but since the comparison is among industries at the same moment in time the objections are somewhat mitigated.
[31] Walther G. Hoffmann, *The Growth of Industrial Economies* (Manchester, Eng.: Manchester University Press, 1958), p. 38. For the underlying data, see the statistical appendix, pp. 163, 169.

and lumber milling exceed the national average.[32] As regards the presumed regular increase of the food and drink group in the process of industrialization, Hoffmann ignores his own data on the subject. During the second stage, nine observations indicate a decline in the proportional importance of the industry, only six an increase. Moreover, these six are almost all countries that began the process of industrialization early.[33]

These processing industries were more important, to American industrialization at least, than has usually been assumed. The high capital-output ratios are not without technological significance. In 1870, the first census to record horsepower revealed the milling industry as the single largest industrial user of power in the United States. Virtually a fourth of the total industrial horsepower was developed by it. But this is not all. It developed 4 times the steam power of the cotton industry and exceeded the iron industry in this respect as well. Of 40,191 steam engines in the country, the mills accounted for 5,358 with a rated horsepower of 168,736. These steam engines in turn were concentrated at western sites, excepting Minneapolis at the Falls of St. Anthony, and so we can infer that the accelerated shift from the East to the interior West in the 1850's brought with it an increased demand for the staple output of the machinery industry, the steam engine.[34]

The higher productivity per worker in processing, coupled with an increasing share of employment in the sector as industrialization progressed, also led to higher aggregate productivity in the economy, and so to higher per capita income. Such an effect is not very important, however. Over the 40-year period from 1850 to 1890 total production would have increased only 1.5 percent from this source, compared with a realized expansion of more than eightfold. Rather, the continued relative growth of processing in the late nineteenth century in the United States is more noteworthy for its spread effects. It immediately disseminated a mod-

[32] Calculated from *Eighth Census, Manufactures*; for 1890, U.S. Bureau of the Census, *Eleventh Census of the United States, Manufactures*, VI, pt. 1 (Washington, 1895), pp. 96–115.

[33] Hoffmann, *Industrial Economies*, p. 138 (Table 36).

[34] These data on consumption of horsepower are taken from *Ninth Census*, III, *Wealth and Industry*.

ern technology to the interior, predominantly agricultural parts of the country. Thus in 1850 in the recently admitted states of Iowa and Wisconsin, processing represented half of the manufacturing sector. It introduced the beginnings of industrialization in a natural and automatic way. Subsequent transition to a more sophisticated industrial structure became the easier. The westward movement of milling, of meat packing, and of tanning in response to shifts in the sources of supply contributed to the rise of such urban areas as Cincinnati, Chicago, St. Louis, Minneapolis-St. Paul, Omaha, and Kansas City. In a context of progressive agriculture, industrialization may be eased rather than hindered by the lure of high returns in farming.

During the 1850's, the specific period with which we are concerned, the processing industries most directly associated with western agriculture grew more rapidly than agriculture itself, and more rapidly than all manufacturing. The sum of the value added in meat packing, distilling, and flour milling increased from 7.2 percent to 7.8 percent of total industrial value added. In the western states the growth was more impressive. While the 5 states of the Old Northwest Territory plus Iowa improved their position in manufacturing from 12.2 percent of the national total value added in 1850 to 15.9 percent, the processing industries more than kept pace, amounting at the end of the period to more than one fifth of western manufacturing. Those states that displayed the most dramatic, recent advances in agricultural production showed corresponding strides in the processing industry. In Illinois, total value added in manufacturing doubled; the value added in processing almost quadrupled. In an older state like Ohio, manufacturing increased 50 percent, but the influence of processing waned.[35] It was in the newer areas that the linkage was both the most potent and the most needed.

The second important indirect influence of agricultural prosperity and the associated westward migration upon the pace of over-all expansion arises from its stimulus to high levels of construction activity. When aggregate demand is not taken for granted, lavish capital outlay rather than frugal abstinence is

[35] Calculated from *Compendium of the Seventh Census*, and *Eighth Census, Manufactures*.

of the essence. The argument to be developed here is that the transport induced migration of the early 1850's was causally associated with a rapid, simultaneous increase in construction expenditures.

A relationship between transport innovation and building activity is nothing new. The very statement of the proposition recalls Walter Isard's pioneering studies a score of years ago.[36] Despite superficial resemblance, the emphasis is really quite different. Isard concentrates in the first instance upon urban and industrial development, with the latter explaining the former. His model starts from the centralizing effects of transport innovation upon industry, and leads to the subsequent increase of population which in turn induces the growth of residentiary activity. An inherent overoptimism perpetuates the boom until overconstruction has occurred, a glut which sets the stage for lower levels of activity until the next innovation.

By contrast, the mechanism that seems to have operated in the 1850's may be described, in equally simplified terms, as follows. The increased opportunities for gain in the West associated with railroad construction, actual and anticipated, promoted a considerable migration into the region. This was primarily an agricultural phenomenon. Urban parts of the West grew not so much in response to industrial opportunity, but to the commercial advantages inherent in distributing the agricultural exports of the region as well as the imports into it. The one major exception is the rise of processing activity, which itself was oriented to the agricultural sector. The level of construction associated with this expansion was increased by the duplication of facilities required in new regions: more fencing went with farm creation than farm extension; additional municipal investment, in the form of paving, public buildings and the like, went with new cities; large outlays for commercial construction, unnecessary in older areas, were required, and so on. While migration continued, the expectations of investors were justified. With its slowing down in the mid-1850's, the pace of induced expansion slowed and the cumu-

---

[36] Cf. Isard's articles "A Neglected Cycle: The Transport Building Cycle," *Review of Economic Statistics*, XXIV (1942), 149–158, and "Transport Development and Building Cycles," pp. 90–112.

lative effects of this pause set in motion a generalized decline. The real resurgence of construction activity was then to await not transport innovation but the next wave of transport induced migration. In all of this, the conditioning role and catalytic effect of the agricultural sector is apparent. Indeed, as we argued earlier, the profitable opportunities for transporting existent surpluses and migrants served to initiate and sustain railroad construction.

Where these two alternative explanations conflict and where their emphases differ, the evidence seems more consistent with this last interpretation. For example, construction expenditure boomed beginning almost with the 1850's, and not the early 1840's as Isard argued from his limited data on building permits. Nonrailroad construction (excluding the value of farm improvements) followed this pattern from 1839 to 1859:[37]

Year	Current dollars (millions)	Quinquennial growth (percent)	Constant (1860) dollars (millions)	Quinquennial growth (percent)
1839	120	—	123	—
1844	128	6.7	139	13.0
1849	173	35.2	181	30.2
1854	323	86.7	339	87.3
1859	330	2.2	337	− 0.6

What we want to explain is not only the increased growth after 1844 but also that remarkable spurt between 1849 and 1854, a spurt that urbanization alone does little to elucidate, for that factor was primarily operative earlier. From 1840 to 1850 the proportion of the population in urban places, i.e., with population of 2500 and above, increased from 10.8 percent to 15.3 percent, while from 1850 to 1860 it showed a lesser gain from 15.3 percent to 19.8 percent. In absolute terms the urban population almost doubled from 1840 to 1850, while increasing by only three fourths from 1850 to 1860.[38] Isard's explanation is better suited to the simultaneous expansion of industrial activity and urbanization

[37] Gallman, "Gross National Product." Since Gallman used my railroad investment estimates, these data are his construction totals less outlay on road.

[38] *Historical Statistics*, p. 14.

in the East in the 1840's, but this unfortunately has little to do with the innovation of the railroad, as is shown in greater detail in the next chapter.[39]

Further support for the views advanced here is the size of the direct investment in farms themselves. Of the some 600,000 families added in the West during the 1850's, more than 40 percent settled on farms. These 250,000 new western farms required the expenditure of considerable sums of resources, as the critical literature dealing with Turner's frontier hypothesis has emphasized, and as our earlier calculations have shown. Almost $400 million must have been invested.

What is noteworthy also about this expansion, and this is not made explicit in most of the writing about farm making costs, is the larger proportion of such capital formation that was market oriented. Capital requirements that can be satisfied by increased individual exertions are no barrier to westward movement, nor do they fairly indicate the impact upon demand (since the acts of savings and investment are performed simultaneously). Prairie settlement, with scant resources of timber available, with soils requiring breaking with specialized equipment, with an incentive to move into commercial production as rapidly as possible, meant monetary agricultural investment, not only self-supply of labor. So elementary an operation as breaking the sod became a commercial matter: "In contrast to the custom in forest-clearing, the practice of contracting out the breaking of prairie sod to specialists for a money payment was a very common one." [40]

Since prairie farms accounted for almost a third of the land cleared in the West, the total investment passing through the market in the shape of demand for materials for residential construction and fencing came to perhaps $50 million during the

[39] One may also comment upon the inadequacy of the usual method of proof of the relationship between construction activity and transport innovation. The use of aggregative data in which the canals or railroads may be in areas totally different from those in which construction occurred is a common failing. So, too, is the failure to relate the magnitude of the transport cost reductions to the subsequent development; the canal and railroad were quite different in this respect as we noted. What this conjunction in the 1840's may show is a relationship between high levels of regional activity and demand for housing, quite apart from transport innovation.

[40] Danhof, "Farm-Making Costs," p. 342.

decade.[41] Lumber entrepôts like Chicago, Davenport, and others, felt the beneficial effects as did railroads like the Illinois Central and the Burlington that were assured a return freight. Not much less than 3 percent of the materials entering into nonrailroad construction during the decade found their way to western farms, in addition to the large direct labor inputs.[42]

Beyond this direct expenditure are the induced outlays. Small towns multiplied in number and size to handle the needs of a commercial agriculture — the distribution of its products, the retailing of manufactured imports, the services of blacksmiths, educational facilities, and the like. Paul Gates surmises that the aggregate population of small towns along the line of the Illinois Central Railroad increased from 12,000 to 70,000 during the decade, or more rapidly than the burgeoning, and hence more obvious, city of Chicago.[43] These smaller towns did not arise and expand in the fashion suggested by Isard's model, that is, as a result of concentration of industry and a geographically widened market area, except in the broadest, and hence misleading, sense. They developed because lower transportation costs encouraged agricultural expansion, and this agricultural expansion required service inputs. It was less a widened than a deepened market area, one in which commercial production took root, that was crucial to their growth. What is true of these smaller towns applies to the larger centers, albeit with reduced force. In cities like Chicago, Milwaukee, St. Louis, which distributed and manufactured agricultural products, the Isard explanation holds more satisfactorily, except that it fails to place sufficient emphasis upon the distributive functions of their economies in their earliest stages.

[41] The cost of the lumber required for fencing is obtained by taking the difference between the typical fencing costs on timbered land of $3 (consisting almost entirely of labor inputs), and on the prairie of $6. Half the building estimate of $4 an acre in the entire area also is attributable to material purchases. Five million acres of open land cleared multiplied by $3, plus $2 times the entire land cleared, gives the $50 million estimate.

[42] Gallman, "Gross National Product," estimates nonrailroad, noncanal, construction investment as twice the materials flow. I have therefore divided the investment during the decade by two to obtain a measure of the decadal consumption of materials. This comes to $1500 million.

[43] Gates, *Illinois Central*, p. 147.

Another distinctive feature of this framework is the emphasis upon the migration component of the construction boom. This is what endows the upswing with a special robustness: more expenditure is required for the expansion of farms, or towns, or cities in the newer region than in the older one. For the farm, the explanation is quite direct. Fencing costs per acre vary inversely with the size of the improved area, and the more the expansion derives from new, small farms, the larger the total expense. In smaller towns, and larger cities, too, the response at low initial levels of both municipal and commercial facilities is more than proportional to the increase in demand. New families settling in Milwaukee, say, call forth an expenditure for a city hall that exceeds the zero expenditure that would have been required had they settled in Philadelphia; the stores likewise are more capital intensive per unit of output because capacity often cannot be efficiently geared to low levels and because, with future growth likely, excess capacity is even desirable. So long as capital requirements and the output of municipal and commercial services are not perfectly and continuously proportional, the wider the geographic distribution of output, the larger the total capital expenditure.

The importance of such nonproportionalities has never been adequately explored. Municipal outlays are probably the least significant. Both the average and the marginal per capita municipal expenditures in the West seem to be lower than in the East. Boston in the 1850's spent more than twice the amounts per capita that Cleveland and Milwaukee did, and increased its per capita expenditures during the decade more rapidly than these cities as well.[44] In the second place, the magnitude of such expenditures in total, coming to perhaps $5 to $10 per capita annually in the largest western cities, of which only a fifth was capital expenditure, does not give them much leverage. It also seems that these expenditures lag behind the initial increase in population, and hence do not reinforce, but run counter to, the

[44] Charles P. Huse, *The Financial History of Boston* (Cambridge, Mass.: Harvard University Press, 1916); Charles C. Williamson, "Finances of Cleveland," *Columbia Studies in History, Economics, and Public Law*, XXV, no. 3 (1924); Larson, "A Financial and Administrative History of Milwaukee."

general move in construction. Consequently the burden of the argument rests upon excess commercial (and industrial) capacity. But it is here that our knowledge is the most inadequate.

Even if it turns out that nonproportionality is much less relevant than has been presumed, it does not render invalid the general criticism of the Isard hypothesis developed here. Urbanization does not explain the timing of the construction boom of the 1850's nor is it adequately descriptive of the mechanism by which transport cost reduction was translated into swings in construction activity in the ante-bellum period.

Summary

This chapter has touched upon a variety of issues. The unifying theme has been the relationship of the railroad to western agricultural developments, and the latter in turn to income growth, overall. The considerable role of the railroad in those parts of the West that were already settled and surplus producing is one that has been inadequately appreciated. Together with the rapid response in the interior accompanying anticipatory settlement it explains the contrast between the results of transport innovation in the 1830's and 1850's. Needless to say, the two together cast further doubt upon the usefulness of viewing western railroad construction as a massive building ahead of demand.

The measurement of some of the indirect effects of railroad induced regional migration also turned up points of interest. The relative importance of lower cost transportation to the income of farmers is one important finding. So too is the rather small effect of regional redistribution upon potential output, and the implied limited gain for railroads via this channel.

To these essentially static considerations, which necessarily bias downward the calculated external economies attributable to railroads, we added a discussion of two indirect sequences which operated to increase the role both of agriculture and railroads. The forward linkage to the processing industries is an example of how westward movement broadened the industrial base and set in motion forces that ultimately led to the great transformation of the West from a predominantly agricultural to a largely industrial economy. The transport-migration cycle elaborated here represented another type of contribution, this time to aggregate demand. These mechanisms were an important part of both the ante-bellum and the later nineteenth-century economy.

The results in western agriculture seem to justify the attention to the indirect effects of social overhead investment in modern growth theory. Even with the limited contribution of regional reallocation, and within a narrow neoclassical framework, increased production of some 2 percent of agricultural income was indicated. This was more than half our annual exports of foodstuffs, and some 10 percent of total shipments. Seen in this way, these are not meager sums, particularly when they are augmented by less easily reckoned indirect effects. An important question is how this impact compares with the stimulus given to manufacturing. The next chapter takes up that tale.

CHAPTER VI

Railroads and Eastern Industrialization in the 1840's

Introduction

After trailing the van of railroad advance in the 1830's, a delay born of technological doubt and lukewarm governmental commitment, New England's rail network blossomed in the 1840's. While the nation as a whole experienced an increase of 211 percent in mileage over the decade, New England trackage expanded at a rate almost twice this. By 1850 the six-state area not only had more mileage per square mile, not surprising considering its size, but double the mileage per person of any other region as well.[1] The transport revolution, when it came, was thorough.

At the same time that New England's rail connections were being forged, the tempo of regional industrial expansion quickened. Whether the criterion be the 175 percent increase in domestic cotton consumption over the course of the decade, the dividends of New England industrial firms, or the statistics of Massachusetts industry, the impression is all of one piece.[2] Within

[1] U.S. Bureau of the Census, *Eleventh Census of the United States, 1890*, XIV, *Transportation* (Washington, 1895), p. 6.

[2] There are a variety of data on domestic cotton consumption. Those of Matthew B. Hammond, *The Cotton Industry* (New York, 1897) show a rise of 175 percent, from 113,000 pounds in 1840 to 280,124 pounds in 1849 (in his appendix). While these data are for the United States as a whole, the proportion in the South was less than a fifth and does not affect the results substantially. A recent unpublished series on physical output developed by Lewis Stettler confirms an increase of almost this magnitude for New England alone. The information on dividends is found in Joseph G. Martin, *A Century of Finance* (Boston, 1898), pp. 128–129. There are state industrial censuses for the years 1836–1837, 1844–1845, and 1854–1855 issued by the Secretary of the Commonwealth, as well as the national censuses of 1840 and 1850.

the Middle Atlantic area the forces of manufacturing were making themselves felt as well. Philadelphia, its dreams of commercial and financial pre-eminence finally buried by the undeniable ascendance of New York, concentrated upon manufactures instead, and emerged with the highest rate of population increase between 1840 and 1850 among America's large cities. This performance was symptomatic of the rising prosperity of the iron and coal industries with which the economy of the Quaker City had become so intimately entwined: capacity of anthracite blast furnaces in eastern Pennsylvania increased more than 5 times between 1840 and 1849, while anthracite production almost quadrupled over the same period.[3]

By contrast, development in the West had come to a pause. To the dizzying heights of land speculation — more than half of federal revenues in 1836 were derived from land sales — the panic of 1837 and subsequent depression beginning in 1839 had provided a sharp corrective. Accompanying the surcease in exploding land values was a radical diminution in migration and frontier exploitation. All that the 1840's were to witness, at least until the exogenous demands generated by the Irish famine in 1847 and 1848, was a gradual growth in real product in the already settled areas, at a rate less than the eastern expansion in manufactures. The public works of the western states, projected on the prospect of continuing boom, suffered badly. As the inflow of capital, primarily from abroad, ceased, the elaborate plans for transport improvement were at first contracted, and then in many instances completely rescinded. Michigan, after using the expedient of land warrants to continue construction on her Central railroad, finally gave up the ghost in 1846 and sold her even then valuable property to eastern capitalists on the condition that the road be completed. Illinois was less fortunate: her Northern Cross railroad, the last vestige of that ambitious improvements scheme of 1836, had no value at all. What little investment there was until the late 1840's — only some 300 miles — was largely limited to completion of extant ventures under private auspices.

Thus the differential rate of railroad construction in East and

[3] For capacity of blast furnaces see Fogel, *Railroads*, pp. 153–158; for anthracite production see *Historical Statistics*, p. 360.

West in the 1840's seems to correspond to fundamental differences in the rate of growth of the two regions. Paul H. Cootner deserves our commendation for being among the first to emphasize this correlation.[4] He argues that causality flowed from the directly productive sectors of the economy to railroad investment, and then back again via the medium of railroad services. For the East, in the 1840's, this means industrial requirements first determined the pace of construction and were then satisfied by better transport conditions: "The eagerness of Massachusetts textile interests to promote the construction of railroads to their mill sites gives . . . evidence of the need for such transportation. The network of rails that covered New England in the forties was an important factor in maintaining textile profits and in keeping cotton cloth . . . as cheap as the Manchester product. . . ."[5] In a recent paper the same argument has been extended to the iron and coal industries of eastern Pennsylvania. Moreover, Cootner now attaches significance to the prior railroad expansion in other regions, the West and South, in cheapening manufacturing inputs.[6] For the West, the converse holds. The lack of present profit potential militated against railroad construction, and development in turn was not benefited.

Three aspects of this regional concentration of railroad investment in the 1840's are explored in this chapter. First we take up the role of industry in sparking the New England railroad boom. We find, unlike Cootner, that no narrow motivational framework suffices to explain the expansion in eastern trackage during the decade. This leads on to the second point, a discussion of the forces that do seem to be responsible for the observed regional variation during the decade. Finally, the contribution of railroad services to the manufacturing development is explored in some detail for three important industries: cotton textiles, wool textiles,

[4] In his "Transport Innovation and Economic Development."

[5] Cootner, chap. iii.

[6] See his "Social Overhead Capital and Economic Growth," in Rostow, *The Economics of Take-Off into Sustained Growth*, pp. 270, 271: ". . . the railroads of New England . . . did not reach their full crescendo until the 1840's . . . The same asymmetric behavior holds in the coal and iron regions of eastern Pennsylvania . . . Coal, iron and textiles formed the basis of the [railroad] growth of the twenties and forties in the already settled areas, whether they were located in the U.S. or the U.K."

and boots and shoes. Again in contrast to the Cootner position, no major effects are apparent. Thus unlike the ever widening ramifications of the initial thrust of western railroad investment at the beginning of the 1850's, the eastern industrial development is largely independent of contemporaneous railroad extension.

The Strength of Industrial Motivation

An important part of Cootner's argument for the decisive role of industrial requirements is his implicit identification of all regional trackage as industrial in function. Granting that, the presumption of industrial motivation is highly plausible even if not fully established. Yet such identification is highly spurious: the disaggregation from national to regional levels must be further extended to particular states and individual railroads. When this is done the hypothetical uniformity of regional mileage rapidly vanishes. Within New England, for example, much of the construction took place in rural Maine, New Hampshire, and Vermont, and even some in Massachusetts was built to compete for passengers, not cloth.

Nowhere does the heterogeneity of interests show up so well as in the 600 miles of railroad — of a regional total of 1900 — conceived as Boston's solution to the long-standing problem of access to the West.[7] In common with the other Atlantic commercial emporia, Boston had reacted in the 1830's to New York's increasing grasp upon the western trade, a command made possible by the Erie Canal. After a period of indecision concerning the relative merits of a canal versus a railroad route, Boston's commercial interests ultimately opted for the Boston and Worcester and Western railroads. Inherently such a route was unsatisfactory because it relied upon the Erie Canal itself and was subject to the disadvantages of higher charges than the Hudson River. Although a significant advantage in time could be achieved by shipping goods bound for Boston via rail directly, the Western Railroad was no means for capturing an export trade for Boston. For that matter, even the largest part of New England grain

<hr/>

[7] Calculated from *Tenth Census*, IV, *Transportation*, pp. 308–315, where mileage added by individual railroads is presented. The routes to the West are discussed in Kirkland, *Men, Cities, and Transportation*, I, chap. 6 especially.

imports continued to come by water. The dissatisfaction with these accomplishments explains the rising interest in the 1840's in a second route to the Lakes through the north. This route would connect directly with the St. Lawrence River at Ogdensburg, bypassing the Erie Canal completely, where, as an optimistic railroad engineer, James Hayward, had observed in 1831, "it [could] strike boldly for the commerce of the great lakes, a world within itself." [8] On the way, New York would be dealt another blow by the diversion of the Lake Champlain traffic. Such were the dreams and the promises of railroad prospectuses.

They were illusory. Despite a more favorable grade than the Western, the northern route included a longer rail and shorter water trip at a necessarily greater cost. If the Western could not dent the superiority of New York, a fortiori neither could the route to the lakes. Financial insolvency rewarded the attempt. The affairs of the Vermont Central, in particular, made that road a notorious symbol for fraud and mismanagement. These are not matters which concern us here, however. What does, is the fact that here is a considerable part of New England railroad investment flowing into a scheme primarily for commercial, not industrial exploitation. In spite of the expanding textile interests of New England, commerce was not yet dead. Boston, after all, still ranked second to New York as a port of entry.

These six hundred miles are the largest single bloc of "non-industrial" mileage easily identified. They do not exhaust the total. Portland also succumbed to the lure of a share in the commerce of the West via a connection with Montreal. The results were less disappointing than those of Boston's northern route, but the debacle of the *Great Eastern* scheme symbolizes how far short the actual achievement fell. The western market was an attraction in the creation of even apparently local roads. "Places like New Haven, Bridgeport, Norwich, New London, Providence, and Fall River, and a host of lesser communities were not passive. They had ambitions and needs of their own. Like their bigger brethren, they dreamed of a route to the West. . . ." [9]

Beyond such attempts, there were roads, particularly in Maine,

[8] Quoted in Kirkland, I, 161.
[9] Kirkland, I, 256–257.

whose design was to encourage primary activities. The Androscoggin and Kennebec and the Kennebec and Portland fit into such a niche, as do many of the component parts of the route to the lakes. When it came to explain the difficulties besetting New England railroads in 1850, the *American Railroad Journal* commented: "Here too many competing lines have been pushed into unproductive parts of the country which had little surplus to send to market." [10] This does not tally with Cootner's picture of clamoring mill owners. Within the industrialized as well as the undeveloped part of the region, not every railroad was oriented toward a manufacturing clientele. Most of the newly built railroads were dependent for the largest part of their revenues upon passenger traffic; the ratio on the New York and New Haven was five to one in favor of passenger receipts. The Old Colony even deliberately bypassed the major shoe centers of the South Shore in the selection of its route, in order better to compete for passenger traffic.[11]

If New England railroads were not uniformly and conspicuously the instruments of manufacturing expansion, how much more mythical are the so-called Pennsylvania railroads designed to exploit iron and coal production. Beyond some twenty-five miles or so of miscellaneous additions to existing projects, and a single private gravity line, the 1840's are a distinct blank. Indeed, the actual circumstances of railroad penetration of the coal regions are quite the reverse of what Cootner suggests.[12] In the late 1820's and during the 1830's more than a dozen small feeder lines were built from the mines to existing water outlets such as the Union Canal, the North Branch, the Schuylkill Navigation, and the Lehigh Navigation. So prominent was this development that Michel Chevalier, in classifying the railroads of the country during his visit from 1833 to 1835, included "works connected with coal mines" as one of his five major groups.[13] Only one railroad to

---

[10] *American Railroad Journal*, XXIII (1850), 584.

[11] "When the road was actually constructed, it elected a route which left aside some of the larger shoe centers, and located the track so that no part was more than twelve miles from the ocean." Kirkland, *Men, Cities, and Transportation*, I, 252.

[12] For the dates of charter, construction, and completion of the Pennsylvania railroads, see Poor, *Railroads and Canals*, pp. 414–518.

[13] His valuable description of the communications system of the United States

bring coal directly from the anthracite region to market was carried through to completion, the Philadelphia and Reading. In the 1850's, after the victory of the Reading over the Schuylkill Navigation, and the demonstration that railroads could compete effectively even in the carriage of bulk commodities, other long distance roads were constructed to deliver coal directly from the fields to an expanding market. These include the Delaware, Lackawanna and Western, the Lehigh Valley, and the Catawissa, Williamsport, and Erie. The decade also saw for the first time a significant attempt to develop feeders to the bituminous fields. Although the Blossburg and Corning (completed in 1840) had traversed a small coal bearing area, it, too, was not successfully rebuilt until the later period, in company with new lines like the Bellefonte and Snowshoe, the Huntington and Broad Top Mountain, and a few others.

The story with regard to the exploitation of iron ores is the same. The furnaces and mills in the anthracite region were located quite close to both coal and ore supplies and had easy access to them through the existing feeder railroads, rivers, and canals. These facilities eliminated most of the difficulty in distribution of the final product too. Transportation of the final product was a less serious concern in any event, because of the greater value per unit of weight and the lack of weight loss.[14] The charcoal furnaces of central and western Pennsylvania depended upon proximity of the raw materials for their success even more. The finished blooms were sent on to Pittsburgh to the rolling mills there for final processing, with the assistance of the rivers or the Pennsylvania Canal.[15] While one may disparage the usefulness

---

may be found in English in Chevalier, *Society, Manners, and Politics*, pp. 219–261. Of the 7 connections from the region to market, 5 were canals, one the Philadelphia and Reading, and one the Pottsville and Danville, partially completed and allowed to decay until rebuilt in the 1850's.

[14] In at least one instance rails were delivered to the Erie Railroad from Scranton via teams to the Delaware and Hudson Railroad, then by canal to a junction in New York where they were again transported overland. This indicates both the availability of nonrailroad substitutes as well as the ability of the product to bear transport costs. (For details of this episode see Mott, *Ocean and Lakes*, p. 91.)

[15] For the location of furnaces and rolling mills (including abandoned ones of the 1840's), see Lesley, *Guide*, pp. 1–263. Substantial quantities of pig iron were imported into Pittsburgh by canal. See J. D. B. De Bow, *Industrial Resources of the Western and Southern States* (New Orleans, 1853), II, 376.

of the State Works as an interregional carrier, it served quite well for intrastate commerce of this sort.[16]

Going beyond Pennsylvania to other states where iron and coal expanded rapidly, one finds much the same picture. To be sure, the completion of the Baltimore and Ohio Railroad in 1842 set up a rapid percentage increase in Maryland shipments — almost a fifteenfold increase by 1849 — but at the latter date these represented barely 2 percent of national production. Ohio was a more considerable factor in both coal and iron, ranking second, but far distant, to Pennsylvania in production of both commodities. Yet not until 1852 was a coal company railroad built in that state. In West Virginia, the leading county in the production of coal was Kanawha, with exit to the Ohio River by the river of the same name.[17]

These criticisms do not deny the quickened tempo of railroad investment in the East in the 1840's relative to earlier and later periods, or its correlation with industrial activity. Nor is the association simply spurious. But the nexus seems to lie in the conditions of capital supply rather than in direct industrial requirements. Rising profits in textiles and other manufactures first increased the supply of loanable funds available for investment in other sectors. Under this impetus local promoters were quick to rejuvenate old schemes and initiate new ones. Investment was limited to the immediate region for a number of reasons. Among the most important of these was the appeal of most railroads to the indirect returns from improved transportation, indirect returns that could be appropriated only by proximity to the route. As Thelma Kistler points out, the "appeals were characteristically phrased in terms of 'incidental advantages' rather than in terms of profitability." [18] They were successful. An analysis of subscribers to various New England projects of this period clearly

---

[16] During the 1840's the tolls collected on shipments of iron and coal varied from $\frac{1}{4}$ to over $\frac{1}{3}$ of the total. In 1847, a peak year of grain shipments, tolls from iron and coal were more than twice as great as receipts from flour and grain. See Pennsylvania Board of Canal Commissioners, *Annual Reports*, 1843–1849 (Harrisburg, 1844–1850).

[17] Eavenson, *American Coal Industry*, pp. 407, 518–519; 414, 500; 503, 507–509.

[18] Thelma Kistler, "The Rise of Railroads in the Connecticut River Valley," *Smith College Studies in History*, XXXII (1938), 80, 83. See her entire chap. v.

shows that the shares were taken by those along the road.[19] The appearance of individual industrialists on the rolls of investors does not imply that the external economies to manufacturers were the dominant force after all. These leaders almost invariably had other interests to defend as well, interests inextricably entwined with the fate of their individual communities. The variety of interests of the Boston Associates — "merchants, bankers, legislators, manufacturers, railroad builders" — held true for less prominent entrepreneurs too.[20]

Less influential probably, but still operative, were the factors that militated against investment in the West. The excesses of the boom of the 1830's could hardly be forgotten as long as the funded obligations of the western states, let alone individual enterprises, had poor credit ratings. However large the potential profits of a railroad there, they were apt to be heavily discounted in light of past experience. This was the more so since New England investors were geared to equity rather than debt participation in railroad ventures, as the capital structure of New England roads testifies. Then there was the fact that Boston was a local rather than a national capital market by this time. Western railroads like the West itself, found themselves much more closely attached to New York; when the tremendous expansion of the 1850's occurred, it was New York that financed the surge.[21] Of the few western railroads that were prosecuted earlier, at least two did obtain funds from the Boston financial community. These cases were the outright purchase of the Michigan Central in 1846 and the 1845 loan to the Little Miami.[22] A more aggressive western interest by Boston entrepreneurs or a more perfect capital market might have led to a more efficient allocation of funds, considering the poor performance of the New England railroads

[19] Kistler, Appendix A.

[20] Vera Shlakman, "Economic History of a Factory Town," *Smith College Studies in History*, XX (1935), chap. ii and Appendix A.

[21] Alfred Chandler, "Patterns of American Railroad Finance, 1830–1850," *Business History Review*, XXVIII (1954), 254.

[22] John Murray Forbes was the leader in the Boston syndicate obtaining control of the Michigan Central after being approached by Frank Joy, then a Detroit lawyer. The negotiations for the Little Miami loan are described in the Third Annual Report of the company reprinted in the *American Railroad Journal*, XIX (1846), 218–219.

actually built and the favorable results on the early western roads.[23]

Table 30 presents data that bear upon some of these observa-

TABLE 30.   Massachusetts railroad investment and industrial profits

Flow of funds: (millions of dollars)	1840–1843	1844	1845	1846	1847	1848	1849	1850	1851	1852
Capital stock	5018	1238	2681	4123	6240	7536	3545	2373	1281	1157
Funded debt	2198	88	106	292	1447	658	1450	1901	1229	− 182
Floating debt	1000	700	0	1054	1071	963	− 414	− 1799	− 441	512
Total[a]	8217	2026	2788	5469	8758	9157	4581	2474	2069	1487
Rate of profit[b] (percent)	5.8	13.7	15.5	14.4	10.1	5.9	6.4	6.6	4.0	5.1

Source: Massachusetts Committee on Railways and Canals, Annual Reports of the Railroad Corporations of Massachusetts, 1840–1852; Joseph G. Martin, A Century of Finance (Boston, 1898), pp. 128–129.

a May not add to total due to rounding.

b Unweighted annual dividends as a percent of par value of New England manufacturing companies. Firms reporting dividends in absolute dollars or paying stock dividends are not reckoned, nor new firms not reporting for the entire year.

tions. The flow of funds into Massachusetts railroads is shown to lag perceptibly behind the rate of profit of manufacturing enterprises, as measured by the dividends declared.[24] This is consistent with the explanation just advanced. If industrial motivation had been dominant, a much shorter lag or even a reversal in timing would be anticipated. Table 30 also points up the important position of share capital in total finance and hence the ease of

[23] Vermont railroads yielded less than 3 percent on cost during the 1850's. New Hampshire properties earned less than 5 percent on the average, including the profitable Concord Railroad. The better results in Massachusetts are partially spurious because they reflect the high rates of return on roads built during the 1830's. Thus instead of the 6 percent earned by all roads in 1849, the newer ones built after 1839 returned only 4.5 percent. (Calculated from Poor, Railroads and Canals, pp. 40, 71, 93.) Western railroads earned 5.6 percent in 1849, as shown in Table 19.

[24] In Appendix B, Miss Shlakman, "Economic History of a Factory Town," presents data that indicate a good correlation between operating profits and dividends that therefore make the latter a reasonable proxy for the former. The use of par rather than market value is desirable since some measure of return on physical investment is what is relevant. Lewis Stettler's series of absolute dollar profit of a sample of New England firms also peaks in 1845.

local support. Only after New England railroads were well in process, and in deep financial troubles, were floating and funded debt used to bail out the floundering project — usually unsuccessfully.

This appeal to conditions of capital supply does not eliminate the role of prosperity in biasing expectations upward, nor its effect of improving actual prospects. But it does seem that financial markets deserve more emphasis in explaining the regional variation of railroad construction in the 1840's than they have thus far received. Even in the later transition to western investment, more than a mere improvement in prospects of western railroads was involved. Absolute capital requirements of western railroads also diminished at just that time owing to the remarkable decline of prices of imported iron rails as an aftermath of the British railway boom; assessed value per ton fell from $51.01 in 1847 to $26.32 in 1850.[25] Expenditures for rails were about 20 percent of total costs at this time. But as a proportion of monetary outlay they were much larger. Subscribers could and did contribute work services directly. With the fall in rail prices local interests could afford to undertake construction without external financing, financing that sometimes had been previously refused. The supply of funds to western railroads over the range of initial requirements was simply nonexistent. The very large profits, once partially underway, of such roads as the Galena, the Cleveland, Columbus and Cincinnati, and the Cleveland and Toledo both attracted additional support for themselves and spurred further construction. Then the process became self-justifying in the manner that Chapter IV suggests. It was not only a sudden advance in the anticipated receipts of western railroads that called forth construction, therefore. Costs fell too, and these, because of the imperfect capital market, were important in getting the boom underway.[26]

[25] *American Railroad Journal*, XXIX (1856), 490.

[26] This point has rarely been given the emphasis it deserves. But the *Report of the Commissioner of Agriculture for the Year 1862*, House Doc. No. 78, 37th Congress, 3rd Session (Washington, 1863), p. 69, mentions it explicitly: ". . . events in England made railroad iron cheap and in great abundance, and with its characteristic energy the west was not slow to avail itself of the inducements proffered."

248 RAILROADS AND ANTE-BELLUM ECONOMY

The Magnitude of the Forward Linkages

Whatever the motivation leading to their initial construction, the consequences of the eastern railroads for industrial expansion are worth pursuing. Of course, the previous discussion is not without relevance. If railroads did not appear as a response to pressing industrial requirements, the less likely their considerable achievement within this sphere. As Table 30 has emphasized, too, there certainly was no sudden prosperity in the New England mills that can be traced to the *completion* of the region's communications system in the late 1840's. Profits had peaked long before, because they led the flow of funds, and railroad operations in turn lagged behind these. More than twice as much New England mileage was completed in 1848 and 1849 than in all the years from 1843 through 1847.[27] It is rather awkward for those who believe the New England railroads made a significant contribution that the system largely came into being just as manufactures entered their time of troubles; absolute dollar profits for a sizable sample of textile firms were larger in the period 1843–1847 than in any other contiguous five years before the war.[28]

The favorable influence of prior construction in other regions, while immune to this criticism, has little to support it. The southern railroads were prostrated by the depression beginning in 1839 and by 1850 the mileage in Mississippi and Alabama barely exceeded 100 miles, although almost a thousand had been projected. Yet by 1849, without the benefit of improved overland transport, these two states produced almost half the cotton crop. By contrast, the two southern states that early succeeded in completing good sized portions of their rail systems, Georgia and South Carolina, increased their production by lesser amounts. The reduction in the price of cotton in the 1840's was not due to improved transport, but to a slower rate of growth of foreign demand relative to capacity. Freight charges (including insurance) amounted to no more, probably, than $2.00 per bale for domestic shipment within the South, and this is a generous maxi-

[27] This is true irrespective of whether the 1880 census on transportation or the *Poor's Manual* mileage series is used.

[28] Based on the unpublished data of Lewis Stettler covering 12 New England mills.

mum.[29] This meant that if zero freight rates prevailed in the South, the price of cotton would be reduced by less than one-half cent per pound! The unweighted average price in the 1830's was 11.2 cents per pound, in the 1840's 7.6 cents, and in the 1850's 11.2 cents again.[30] When we go beyond this potential influence of southern railroads, it is difficult to imagine other interregional linkages. Western railroads were sufficiently few and isolated to have no impact upon the flow of foodstuffs eastward, and there were no trunk line connections until 1851. Raw wool was often a local raw material, a fact that goes to explain the geographic decentralization of the industry. When imported eastward, it came via the Erie Canal. Coal and iron were found together within the East so it is the eastern railroad network that is of interest there. The conclusion is clear: the eastern industrialization emerging in the aftermath of 1839 was not supported or sustained by the prior railroad (or canal) investment in other regions.

The contribution of the eastern roads themselves was circumscribed by the late completion of many roads, as we have pointed out. The carrying function of existing lines was utilized, however. As a consequence, railroad operations expanded rapidly. In Massachusetts, for example, freight revenues increased from less than $400,000 in 1840 to more than $2,500,000 in 1849.[31] Declining freight rates meant a still greater increase in ton-mileage. Table 31 indicates the substantial magnitude of this output rise between 1846 and 1849, only a third of the decade. Such statistics are subtly deceptive. First, these accomplishments do not necessarily reflect increasing industrial utilization. The discontinuity in 1847, at a high point of the textile prosperity, is totally unrelated to it, for example. It is the increased volume of grain for export over the lines of the Western and Boston and Worcester railroads that is primarily responsible. As David M. Balfour commented in his article on Massachusetts railroads, "the result is varied by the extraordinary circumstances of the year 1847, in which an un-

[29] See Gray, *History of Agriculture*, II, 715–716. Gray cites a range of $2.50 to $4.00 a bale for freight, packing, *and* commissions. The last two factors were probably ⅔ of the total cost.
[30] Calculated from the prices given in Gray, II, 1027.
[31] Poor, *Railroads and Canals*, p. 43.

TABLE 31.   Output of Massachusetts railroads, 1846–1849

Year	Ton-miles (thousands)	Passenger miles
1846	40,634	84,251
1847	66,188	103,037
1848	67,022	126,371
1849	70,848	144,305

Source: De Bow's Review, XIII (1852), 576.

usual quantity of farm produce sought the seaboards, by every possible channel, regardless of expense, on its way to Europe, where exorbitant prices remunerated every means of transport." [32] Under these unusual conditions, which abated only gradually in succeeding years, even the Boston route to the West prospered. Of more fundamental importance, however, than the varied character of the freight, is the small margin of superiority that went with railroad services. So long as they were cheaper, railroads naturally won an increasing share of the growing transport market; but this does not imply that the industrial growth of the 1840's would have been stymied by their absence.

One hardly expects it. Relative to the selling price of manufactured goods the cost of transportation is a small matter. Hence both the demand and the supply of manufactured commodities are less sensitive to variations in transport efficiency than are the demand and supply of primary products. Nor were New England railroads particularly noteworthy for the transport cost reductions they brought. As Appendix A shows, the average rate on New England railroads was among the highest in the country. More generally, our previous results indicate a minor reduction in distribution costs of finished goods as a consequence even of the some 28,000 miles of road built by 1859. Nonagricultural commodities of *all* sorts, excluding coal, were moved by rail in 1859 at savings of less than $50 million. This is about 5 percent of the value added in manufactures in the same year, and about

[32] In De Bow's Review, XIII (1852), 576.

half as much of total value of product.[33] The influence of improved transport on coal mining was obviously greater owing to the low price per unit of weight. But the major role was played by primitive feeder lines, often without steam locomotion, using inclined planes, et cetera. The technology of the 1820's would have been adequate for these purposes; the steam railroad was not required.

Despite this evidence of meager influence on manufactures, it will shed additional light to take up briefly the effects of the railroad on the fortunes of some of the leading New England industries — cotton, wool, and boots and shoes — of the period.

The Textile Industries and Railroad Innovation

Before the Civil War textiles were the foremost industrial product in the United States. From the earliest and imperfect Census of 1810 to the far more informative Census of 1860 the value added in the manufacture of yarn and cloth outstripped that of all competitors. Within the textile group, cotton manufacturing stood out as the most important and progressive. Innovations of technology and organization such as the power loom and the dormitory system, not to mention those of distribution, developed first in this branch. By the Civil War the large average size of the individual enterprise and market regional concentration were additional evidence of the premier rank of cotton manufacturers in the industrial hierarchy. Wool lagged behind in the United States, as in Great Britain, but its absolute importance still made it a factor in the process of industrialization.

The vigorous growth of the cotton industry in the 1820's is evidence that railroad expansion was not a necessary factor at its inception. The locational characteristics of the industry suggest the same conclusion for the later period. Within New England, by 1859, 41 firms accounted for about half the total capital invested in the country, and these firms were localized at a handful of sites: Saco-Biddeford, Lowell, Lawrence, Nashua, Manchester,

[33] Gallman, "Commodity Output," p. 43, for value added. The direct benefits are calculated in Chapter II.

Chicopee, Fall River, and Providence.[34] All of these cities possess a common asset, simultaneous access to both water power and navigation. All except one, Lawrence, had been developed prior to the railroad era, before reduction in land transport rates was a relevant factor. Even Lawrence was valued more for its water power than its extant rail connections; not until 1848, 3 years after initial development, did the Boston and Maine relocate its main line to serve the city.[35]

As convincing as these considerations is a comparative study of the location of the industry within New England before and after the completion of the regional rail network. If lower transport costs were an effective force in making new water power sites available in the interior, as Cootner alleges, one would anticipate a significant change in the locational distribution of production between 1840, say, and the 1850's. Table 32, based upon the

TABLE 32. The location of cotton cloth manufacture in Massachusetts

Counties and townships	Percentage of total Massachusetts value of output			Percentage of total number of yards of cloth produced in Massachusetts		
	1837	1845	1855	1837	1845	1855
Middlesex County	45.7	39.0	32.0	42.0	45.3	34.0
Lowell	41.6	35.0	30.8	38.4	42.2	31.3
Worcester County	15.2	17.8	20.3	16.1	17.0	16.5
Bristol County	12.8	11.8	9.8	14.6	10.9	11.2
Fall River	5.1	4.3	4.9	6.2	4.0	6.0
Hampden County	11.5	16.0	15.3	12.0	13.9	16.3
Chicopee	8.3	12.0	6.2	8.8	10.2	8.2
Essex County	2.8	6.3	14.7	1.8	3.8	12.3
Lawrence	0.0	0.0	7.8	0.0	0.0	6.3

Source: Massachusetts Secretary of the Commonwealth, *Statistical Information Relating to Certain Branches of Industry*, for the years ending April 1, 1837; April 1, 1845; and June 1, 1855.

[34] Evelyn H. Knowlton, *Pepperell's Progress: History of a Cotton Textile Company, 1844-1945* (Cambridge, Mass., 1948), pp. 6, 32.
[35] George P. Baker, *The Formation of the New England Railroad Systems: A Study in the Nineteenth Century* (Cambridge, Mass., 1937), p. 147.

Massachusetts Censuses of 1837, 1845, and 1855, refutes such a possibility. The two coastal counties of Middlesex and Essex together account for almost half the output of cloth in both 1837 and 1855, with no significant change over the intervening years. The relative decline of Lowell was compensated by the rise of Lawrence close by, and there was no burst of activity at any interior site. Although the output of Worcester County did increase slightly more than proportionally over the period, it was not owing to the emergence of any new center — Fitchburg in 1855 accounted for only 1 percent of the total Massachusetts value of output — and did not involve any reorientation of the industry. Moreover, if one includes the manufacture of calico and the processes of bleaching and coloring, the apparent relative decline of Lowell and Middlesex County is completely eliminated. With this broader classification, the latter's share actually increases from 38 to 42 percent of total value over the interval from 1837 to 1855, indicating the success with which the older center made the transition to new activities. Similarly, because of its specialization in printing, Fall River is a much more significant part of the expanded industry at all dates. In short, the industry needed no interior sites before the Civil War, a result brought home to the promoters of Holyoke, where water power went begging despite its service by the Connecticut River Railroad.[36] Indeed, when the industry subsequently was constrained by water power limitations, it relocated along the seaboard at Fall River and New Bedford, where delivery of coal for steam power could be secured most cheaply. It did *not* follow the railroad to the interior.[37]

The minor significance of improved land transportation can be traced to the technological and institutional characteristics of the industry. In the first instance, raw material supply was largely unaffected by the railroad. The movement of raw cotton in the South before 1860 was dependent upon the abundant waterways of that region, a circumstance that naturally led to the ascendance of the coastal trade in interregional shipment. As late as 1860, of total arrivals of 382,000 bales of cotton in Boston, less

[36] Constance M. Green, *Holyoke, Massachusetts* (New Haven, 1939), chap. ii.
[37] See J. Herbert Burgy, *The New England Textile Industry* (Baltimore, 1932) chap. i.

than 23,000 arrived by rail.[38] The Pepperell mills at Biddeford, in spite of a direct rail connection to Boston, continued to obtain their cotton requirements by schooner from that port until 1859.[39] The limited amount of coal needed was at first imported from abroad and then later received from Philadelphia and New York by sea. Little else was needed.

From information that is easily available, it is possible to calculate the specific savings in costs the railroad contributed to the Lowell mills, a not unsubstantial part of the entire industry. In 1845, the Lowell mills consumed a little more than 12,000 tons of cotton (61,100 bales according to one account, 24,180,000 pounds according to another), in excess of 30,000 tons of coal and charcoal, and perhaps another 1,000 tons of starch, flour, oil, and so on.[40] Altogether, therefore, around 45,000 tons of inputs were received and a little more than 10,000 tons of merchandise shipped, primarily to Boston. Supposing that overland transport were at the rate of 20 cents a ton-mile, it would have cost a total of $330,000 to ship by wagon in both directions; the difference between wagon and railroad was perhaps half as great. The total valuation of the output of cotton cloths in Lowell in 1845 was in excess of $4,000,000. Some of the inputs enumerated above went into the production of woolens, and cotton prices in that year were unusually low. Consequently it seems safe to affirm that the impact of the railroad over the 1840's was probably no more than a reduction of 3 percent in costs. Given the locational concentration of the entire industry near the coast, the proportion is not inappropriate for the industry as a whole. A once and for all change of this magnitude hardly can have been instrumental in the boom. Much more significant increases occurred continuously in productivity. Thus between 1840–1844 and 1845–1849, the average number of pounds of cloth produced per worker increased from 8.93 to 10.22, or just about 15 percent.[41]

[38] *Seventh Annual Report of the Boston Board of Trade* (Boston, 1861), pp. 66–67.
[39] Knowlton, *Pepperell's Progress*, p. 47.
[40] Henry A. Miles, *Lowell, As It Was, And As It Is* (Lowell, 1845), pp. 59–60; John Hayward, *A Gazetteer of Massachusetts* (Boston, 1847), p. 188.
[41] Robert G. Layer, *Earnings of Cotton Mill Operatives, 1825–1914* (Cambridge, Mass., 1955), p. 54.

The foregoing assigns no significance to the contribution of the railroad in the distribution of the product beyond Boston. The omission is deliberate. Sales agencies located in the large coastal cities were the usual channel for marketing the final product.[42] This meant that interior linkage from the mills direct to the retailer was not of crucial importance then or until far later. Since the largest cities in the interior were located on navigable waterways, the hinterland was economically accessible without railroads. A measure of this accessibility is the rapid growth of the industry before an *interregional* rail system was a factor at all. The New England rail network was not linked into any all-rail distribution system until the mid-1850's. Although this later impact of the railroad probably lowered the total costs by more than the 3 percent specified above, this still was not a major advantage — because imports shared it — nor relevant to the prior rapid growth of the industry.

The poverty of market effects realizable in the 1840's also is brought out by the limited extent of home manufacture by that time. Although domestic manufacture of cotton and linen cloths in New York declined from almost 3,000,000 yards in 1845 to about 300,000 in 1855, the increase in the total market was small indeed. The reduction was 4 percent of 1855 New York output; or to put the matter slightly differently, the increment in production between the two dates was 10 times the reduction in home manufactures.[43] Had the transport cost reductions of the railroad been responsible for the entire displacement, which it was not since declining relative prices of cloth occurred quite independently, it still would not have had a major impact.

Such a conclusion applies to the manufacture of woolens as well. There are many similarities here, as one would anticipate. The industry experienced the same rapid growth between 1843 and 1849. Whether measured by capital invested, value of product, employment, or raw material consumption, that decade is

[42] Caroline F. Ware, *The Early New England Cotton Manufacture* (Boston, 1931), chap. vii; Knowlton, *Pepperell's Progress*, p. 83.

[43] Secretary of State, *Census of the State of New York for 1855* (Albany, 1856), p. lx. It was necessary to estimate the yards of cloth produced in 1855 from the value data since no physical quantities were given. The Massachusetts average price of the same year was used for the transformation.

comparable only to the remarkable record of the wartorn 1860's when cotton was in such short supply.[44] During that period there is no evidence of any relocation of production in Massachusetts. The only significant change is the establishment of Lawrence as a center. Earlier, between 1837 and 1845, Berkshire County did double its share of output, which amounted to about 25 percent in value at the latter date. This perhaps is to be ascribed to the beneficial effect of the Western Railroad, but I suspect other factors, such as the shifting sources of wool supply, were also operative. Pittsfield, for example, although directly served by that railroad declined in its share from 1837 to 1845, while North Adams, not linked by rail transport until December, 1846, showed the largest increase.[45]

Again transport costs were necessarily limited in the role they could play. Raw material and final product both were more expensive per unit weight than cotton. As a consequence, the one-cent reduction per pound realized in shipping wool from Illinois to the East between 1843 and 1860 came to only 3 percent of its average selling price.[46] The proportional reduction in the cost of the final product was hardly more, given twice the value at half the weight.

Only the abrupt decline in home manufactures of woolens in New York between 1845 and 1855, more than sufficient to account for the entire increase in factory output in that state, argues for the relevance of transport cost reductions to the rapid growth experienced.[47] For a number of reasons this evidence is not decisive. The New York experience cannot be generalized to New England owing to the divergence in urbanization: more than half

[44] Arthur H. Cole, *The American Wool Manufacture* (Cambridge, Mass., 1926), I, 268, summarizes the census statistics for the development of the industry over this period.

[45] Percentage shares calculated from the Secretary of the Commonwealth, *Statistics of Massachusetts Industry*, 1837, 1845, and 1855 (Boston, 1838, 1846, and 1856).

[46] Chester W. Wright, *Wool-Growing and the Tariff* (Boston, 1910), p. 151.

[47] *Census of State of New York for 1855*, p. lv, gives the figures for domestic manufactures. It also gives factory manufactures for 1845 on p. lx and for 1855 on p. 434. While domestic manufacture declines from 4.3 million yards in 1845 to 0.6 million yards in 1855, factory manufacture holds constant at 4.8–4.9 million yards. The 1855 figure is undoubtedly a severe understatement, since both 1850 and 1860 Federal censuses indicate outputs above the 1855 level.

of the Massachusetts population lived in places with more than 2000 persons in 1840, fewer than a quarter of that in New York.[48] Domestic manufacture had already largely disappeared in the former at that date. And in the western states, understandably, the rapid diminution in household manufactures comes in the 1850's and so is unable to explain the rapid growth of the earlier decade.[49] Finally, even within New York, it is by no means obvious that railroads are the explanatory variable. The early railroad pattern in that state did not reduce transport costs significantly. Little railroad mileage was constructed outside the canal counties where it might have made a difference.[50] According to Cole, what explains the decline is the "establishment . . . of many wool-manufacturing concerns, especially small enterprises dependent upon a strictly *local* market for their goods." [51] If this is the case, railroad influence is negligible. The sources of the rapid growth of woolen manufactures, like those of cotton, must be sought elsewhere.

Railroad Forward Linkages and the Boot and Shoe Industry

Another leading ante-bellum industry was boots and shoes. Nationally its 1860 value added ranked it third among all industries, but it held first position in employment. In Massachusetts, it was leader by both criteria. Despite this position, its expansion in the 1840's was much less marked than that of the cotton industry. Output of shoes increased only from 15 to 17 million pairs between 1837 and 1845 while the yards of cotton produced showed a 40 percent expansion in the same interval. Subsequently, from 1845 to 1855, output of boots and shoes doubled while the cotton industry could manage only 80 percent growth.[52] The industry thus followed a slightly different pattern of advance

[48] George Tucker, *Progress of the United States* (New York, 1843), p. 132.

[49] Cole, *Wool Manufacture*, I, 284, presents the census statistics of home manufactures in per capita form.

[50] Of the 768 miles opened in New York between 1840 and 1849, 439 were in counties bordering the Erie Canal, its branches, or the Hudson River. The only exceptions were the Erie and Long Island Railroads. Calculated from *Tenth Census*, IV, *Transportation*, pp. 318–345.

[51] Cole, *Wool Manufacture*, I, 282 (my italics).

[52] Data from *Statistics of Massachusetts Industry*, 1837, 1845, and 1855.

than the other of the New England basic industries, one more closely tied to agricultural development outside of the region. This may be due to the lack of competition from imports as the market expanded, a boon denied to cottons and woolens. Be that as it may, a brief survey will reassure that the already completed rail network had little to do with the magnitude or timing of the expansion of production.

The prewar organization of the manufacture of boots and shoes allowed little latitude for large effects from the side of transportation. Tanning and shoe manufactures were found close together in eastern Massachusetts for much of the period, minimizing the delivery expense of leather. It was not until the 1850's that leather deliveries increased relative to hides, as the local supplies of bark were giving way. Even so the coasting trade was prominent. One third of the leather received at Boston came by ship, and two thirds by railroad, usually only a short distance from interior Massachusetts. Hides came almost entirely by ship — 90 percent by 1860 — as befits both a raw material and a commodity largely imported.[53] Finally, the industry was heavily concentrated in eastern Massachusetts: virtually the entire output of that state, about half that for the country as a whole, was produced within a forty-mile radius of Boston. Thus the overland distance to market the product or to secure supplies was not an insuperable handicap. Randolph, second only to Lynn and Haverhill in the value of output, and Boston "were not then [1857] linked by railroad. Stage coach and expresses were transporting passengers and freight. The various boot and shoe firms had their own express wagons or employed private expresses as a rule. One, Cole's, was for the general public to use."[54] We have already seen how the South Shore Railroad detoured completely around the shoe centers south of Boston, with no apparent fatal blow to their prosperity.

It is true, of course, that shipments of shoes out of Boston did go predominantly by rail; in the later 1850's, when the Board of

[53] Data on shipments from *Sixth Annual Report of the Boston Board of Trade* (Boston, 1860), pp. 67, 70. *Seventh Annual Report of the Boston Board of Trade,* pp. 77, 81.
[54] Blanche E. Hazard, *Organization of the Boot and Shoe Industry in Massachusetts before 1875* (Cambridge, Mass., 1921), p. 103.

Trade reports begin, 70 percent of the volume was shipped this way. Earlier, though, with the southern market relatively more important than the western, the coasting trade may have been more vital. The number of cases cleared by the Custom House in 1845 relative to total production of boots and shoes reported by the State Census of that year, does not validate these expectations.[55] All this may indicate is rail shipment to New York and subsequent transshipment to the South by packet. Boston's direct connections with that market certainly left something to be desired. Paradoxically, too, the evidence that boots and shoes were delivered by rail demonstrates in part the insignificance of the railroad: only highly valued manufactures could afford such a luxury, but these were the same commodities for which even the much higher wagon rates would have made little difference.

In production, as well as distribution, there was little scope for railroad influence. Power supplies were irrelevant. Boots and shoes were produced most frequently under a putting-out system until virtually the end of the prewar period. Individual sewing machines were the limit of mechanical advance before the war, and not until 1860 was steam power just introduced in the larger establishments.[56] In any event, power requirements were never a major locational factor. The industry centered from the first on the North and South Shores near Boston and remained there long after the railroad network was laid down.

Some Final Comments

The *American Railroad Journal* spoke as follows in 1850 of the link between railroads and manufacturing development:[57]

The increase of population in the Eastern and Middle States is almost entirely owing to their progress in these branches of industry. The growth of manufacturing establishments, as a natural consequence, stimulated the construction of means of transportation, and these, by opening access to the natural resources of the country, its water power, coal, iron ores, etc., etc., operated powerfully to the development of these resources. Manufacturing and the construction

[55] Data on clearances from *De Bow's Review*, XIV (1853), 257.
[56] Hazard, *Boot and Shoe Industry*, p. 124.
[57] *American Railroad Journal*, XXIII (1850), 648.

of works to cheapen transportation have gone hand in hand; the latter being absolutely essential to success in the former pursuits.

Our discussion has been addressed exactly to this point, and the conclusions have been found wanting. There is little reason to suppose that the rapid rise of ante-bellum manufacturing in the 1840's evoked, except in a general way, the construction of railroads, or that it depended crucially upon completion of the rail network. In the 1850's, with an expanding market due to better transportation of agricultural products, manufactures might then have received a positive stimulus. But it did not come then because imports captured an increasing share of the market.

The rapid industrial growth, rather, was due to a variety of circumstances.[58] Low cotton prices meant high profits for cotton manufacturers, even if woe for southern planters. The very substantial net protection provided woolen manufacturers by the Tariff of 1842, and almost eliminated in 1846, partially explains the rise and subsequent decline there. For both textiles lagging technological changes vis-à-vis the English in the next decade contributed to the greater success of foreign imports, as the home market grew. It was increasing demand for a standardized product in the 1850's that contributed to the transformation of the boot and shoe industry. Iron manufacturers, on the other hand, benefited from the English railway mania that kept foreign supplies scanty and expensive. The coal industry was stimulated by the increase in mineral smelting and also by greater use of coal as fuel in a period of increasing urbanization. Railroads were neither a common nor a significant element in these developments.

The absolute levels of production reached in all these branches (except coal) in the 1840's compare favorably with the outputs of the 1850's. From the production side, therefore, there is no evidence of a real or potential absolute constraint removed by railroad expansion. The rising trend of coal mined is not a damaging counter indication. It is true that railroads of a sort performed a valuable feeder function from mine to ultimate carrier. But they did so in a most modest fashion: using horses for locomotion,

[58] Cf. the specific industry histories by Ware, Cole, and Hazard.

inclined planes, stationary engines, strap iron rails, and so forth. This is not what we mean when we speak of the impact of the railroad. Water channels continued to carry half the coal for final delivery on the eve of the war. I do not overlook the existence of interactions and dynamic sequences. The expenditure effect of railroad construction, for example, did aid eastern prosperity somewhat. And cost reductions even of a limited sort might have set in motion a chain of cumulative response far beyond its initial importance. But there is no evidence that such was the case, while there are abundant indications that it was improbable. One could write an independent history of manufactures and railroads in the 1840's; one could not do the same for western expansion and railroads in the 1850's. This contrast is the important point.

CHAPTER VII

The Influence of Pre-Civil War Railroads on the Patterns of Domestic Commerce

The railroad expansion of the 1850's, due more to its sheer size than conscious design, marked the beginning of a national network. Where traffic patterns before that decade had been exclusively local, afterward there was continuous communication between seaboard and interior, if not between North and South. The 1860 census celebrated this transition by calling attention to the great "trunks or base lines upon which is erected the vast system that now overspreads the country." [1] To be sure, from a later vantage point such enthusiasm can only appear premature. Not until the later waves of consolidation and the acceptance of standardization of gauge and interchange of rolling stock would a deliberate and rational system emerge. But compared to what went before, the decade witnessed a striking change.

Railroad integration was not neutral in its effects. The east-west linkage stood in sharp contrast to the north-south direction of the rivers and canals of the West and the coastal route. Transport cost reductions thus encouraged firmer bonds between East and West at the expense of the South. The Census of Agriculture called attention to one important consequence, what it termed a "revolution . . . in the grain trade of the west. The trade and commerce of the Mississippi River, so far as related to grain and other produce, has not kept pace. . . ." [2] Equally noteworthy was the rapid growth of a reverse flow of manufactures from the East.

Internal commerce has come to the fore recently as a deter-

---

[1] *Preliminary Report of the Eighth Census*, p. 104.
[2] *Eighth Census, Agriculture*, p. clvii.

mining factor in the growth of the ante-bellum economy.[3] An investigation of the impact of railroad expansion upon both its volume and its direction is therefore all the more relevant. In this chapter, then, the search for railroad indirect benefits moves to the realm of domestic trade. In the course of the discussion we derive some new estimates of the monetary flows among the regions and treat the controversial question of the exchange between West and South. After this framework has been developed, it becomes clearer what the railroad did, and did not, do.

Railroads and the Trade Between East and West

The appendix to Chapter II has already discussed the salient aspects of the competition between the four great trunk lines and the Erie Canal. What was shown there was the continued dominance of the canal route in total tonnage: fully 60 percent of freight moved by water, and an even higher proportion of the eastbound through shipments.[4] Due to specialization, however, the role of the railroad was greater than such aggregate magnitudes suggest.

Thus, although almost the entire bulk grain trade of the West found its way to tidewater by lake and canal, the railroad, even before the Civil War, had emerged triumphant in the contest for flour. Table 33 demonstrates this. All-rail shipment, however, was considerably smaller than total trunk line shipments. The lake trade brought far the largest part of the flour to the New York lines. Of the 542,765 barrels received by the Erie at Dunkirk, only a little more than a tenth were received from the Buffalo and Erie Railroad. Only 600,000 of the 2,000,000 barrels

---

[3] North, *Economic Growth.*

[4] There are two incorrect (but influential) sources on this matter that the reader should be warned against. The 1860 Census of Agriculture (p. clxvi) asserts that railroads were carrying two-thirds the tonnage between East and West in 1862 or a far larger proportion than we have maintained. Their error is in the inclusion of *all* tonnage, way and through, as indicative of interregional commerce. Since railroads had large amounts of the former — due partially to increasing coal shipments — the result is arithmetically correct, but not indicative of railroad dominance in the trade between the two regions. Louis B. Schmidt's "The Internal Grain Trade of the United States, 1850–1860," *Iowa Journal of History and Politics*, XVIII (1920), 121, errs in the opposite direction. He finds that the canal brought 16,769,000 tons to tidewater in 1860, far more than railroads carried. His error is the use of *cumulative* tonnage from 1836 through 1860 rather than the annual flow of the latter year.

TABLE 33. Routes of direct West-East grain shipments, 1860 (shipments in thousands)

Route	Wheat (bushels)	Flour (barrels)	Corn, rye, oats, barley (bushels)	Total[a] (tons)
New York Central[b]	1,500	2,000	1,000	273
Erie	501	543	653	87
Pennsylvania	500[c]	427	364[c]	68
Baltimore and Ohio	80[c]	352	46[c]	38
Total railroads	2,581	3,322	2,063	467
Erie Canal[d]	19,673	901	18,779	1,180

Source: Statistics of Foreign and Domestic Commerce, pp. 159, 169; Eighth Census, Agriculture, 1860, p. cli; Kohlmeier, Old Northwest, p. 191.

[a] Flour is converted to tons at a final weight ratio of 10 barrels per ton. Wheat is reckoned at 60 pounds per bushel, corn and rye at 56, barley at 48, and oats at 32. Based on the experience of the Erie Railroad, all railroad shipments except wheat and flour have been treated as corn.

[b] Estimated as sum of receipts at Suspension Bridge (with wheat separated from total grain shipments by use of 1859 ratio) plus the residual difference between receipts of produce at Buffalo and shipments by the Erie Canal. The proportion of residual wheat assumed to be shipped directly is about one fifth, with the remainder assumed to be shipped as flour; all the residual flour is assumed to have gone by rail. See American Railroad Journal, XXXI (1858), 283, for comparable estimates for 1858.

This method of calculation almost certainly overstates the amount of railroad carriage since the implied tonnage of western produce accounts for 85 percent of the total tonnage of vegetable food, way and through, reported by the railroad. On the Erie Railroad, the proportion of total vegetable food accounted for by the entry in the Table is less than half. Since the New York Central traversed a region that might be expected to supply larger amounts of local produce of flour and wheat, this comparison almost conclusively suggests some kind of overstatement.

[c] Direct statistics on wheat and other grains separately are unavailable. Kohlmeier's estimate of total wheat shipments over the two roads combined has been allocated in proportion to total grain movement on each.

[d] Shipments east from Buffalo and Black Rock plus adjusted receipts at Oswego. Black Rock tonnage of wheat and flour was probably all wheat, and was so converted. One half of the Oswego receipts of wheat have been assumed to be shipped on directly by canal, the other half milled, of which only two thirds was subsequently shipped by canal. These calculations are based upon similar ratios prevailing in 1858. (Hunt's Merchants' Magazine, XL, 1859, 548–549.)

credited to the New York Central came via the Grand Trunk of Canada. In turn, the Pennsylvania and the Baltimore and Ohio must have depended upon the Ohio River for almost half their tonnage.[5] In all, of the total volume of flour delivered to the eastern ports by rail, perhaps a third was carried the entire distance overland before 1860. By 1876, more than three fourths of all grain shipments (including bulk) followed an all-rail route.[6] Integration was primarily a postwar phenomenon.

One area of specialization where the through railroads did alter the structure of interregional trade before the Civil War was the shipment of livestock and animal products. Table 34 provides a basis for this observation.[7] While grain continued to follow a water course, provisions almost entirely were sent by rail, even in 1862 when western railroad capacity was taxed. Livestock had never gone by water to any significant extent, but substantial numbers had been driven overland before the railroad. What the table shows, imperfectly, is the increased ratio of shipments of livestock relative to salt meat; this does not emerge clearly due to the wartime conditions. Such was the broader trend, however. Railroads made a distinct bid for transport of livestock by offering additional inducements like special stock cars with sleeping accommodations for drovers, and stock yards; and their efforts were rewarded by a predominant share of the market.

It was in the westward commerce that the trunk lines really excelled. Dry goods and groceries were the staples of this trade, with prominent differences among the various port cities. Philadelphia, for example, shipped far more textiles than Baltimore,

[5] *A Statement of the Operations of the New York and Erie Railroad under the Receivership* (New York, 1862), p. 9; *Fourth Annual Report of the Pittsburgh, Ft. Wayne, and Chicago Railroad* (Pittsburgh, 1861), p. 42.

[6] For 1876 proportion see U.S. Treasury Department, Bureau of Statistics, *Report on the Internal Commerce of the United States for 1876* (Washington, 1877), p. 102. The 1860 figure is calculated from Table 33. In 1865 the proportion of all-rail carriage was lower than in 1860. The Civil War did nothing to enhance the role of the railroad in the grain trades; and the diversion of trade to Canadian ports may have delayed the ascendance of overland shipments.

[7] It also points up the lack of extensive excess capacity on the western railroads of the 1850's. The proportional and absolute changes in grain carried by lake far exceed the increases on railroads. This substantiates as well our claim that water routes had sufficient capacity to handle the actual ante-bellum railroad traffic.

TABLE 34.   Chicago rail and lake exports of selected agricultural products, 1860 and 1862

Commodities	Railroad[a]		Lake		Percentage by rail	
	1860	1862	1860	1862	1860	1862
Flour (barrels)	408,082[b]	672,971[b]	218,741	1,057,803	65.1	38.8
Wheat (bushels)	377,647	288,213	11,817,476	13,466,325	3.1	2.1
Corn (bushels)	577,611	125,162	13,063,043	29,248,677	4.2	0.4
Cattle	94,544	107,231	1,129	735	98.8	99.3
Hogs: Live	186,038	443,786	160	449	99.9	99.9
Dressed	35,130	44,578	0	0	100.0	100.0
Beef (barrels)	69,226	127,493	6,701	22,345	91.2	85.1
Pork (barrels)	83,256	83,814	4,672	108,735	94.6	43.5
Lard (pounds)	9,809,880	54,422,303	139,600	34,120	98.5	100.0

Source: Chicago Board of Trade, *Third Annual Statement of the Trade and Commerce of Chicago* (Chicago, 1861), pp. 17, 33, 35, 39; *Fifth Annual Statement . . .* (Chicago, 1863), pp. 17, 34, 37, 38.

[a] These include the shipments by the Michigan Central, the Michigan Southern and the Pittsburgh, Fort Wayne, and Chicago. There were additional minor rail shipments other than eastward.

[b] Not all flour was shipped through. There were transshipments at Toledo and Detroit of perhaps half the railroad receipts.

while the latter handled large tonnages of coffee and sugar, as befitted a textile center and South American trade center, respectively. Equivalent detail for the New York lines is unavailable but one suspects imported merchandise loomed significantly there; 91 percent of the westward through freight on the New York Central was merchandise.[8] In contrast to this, the Erie Canal carried far less — a sixth — and far more inexpensive commodities. Sugar and iron made up more than a third of total through tonnage in 1860.[9] Even such a disparity understates the dominance of the railroad. For what started by rail tended to

[8] See the commodity descriptions of freight in the *Fourteenth Annual Report of the Pennsylvania Railroad, 1860,* pp. 108–109; *Thirty-Fourth Annual Report of the Baltimore and Ohio Railroad* (Baltimore, 1860), pp. 110–114; *Annual Report of the New York State Engineer and Surveyor on Railroads for the Year Ending September 30, 1860* (Albany, 1861), pp. 152–156, 176.

[9] *Statistics of Foreign and Domestic Commerce,* p. 129.

complete its journey by rail. Only a third of the tonnage delivered by the Erie to Dunkirk was sent on by lake; the Pittsburgh, Fort Wayne, and Chicago stood ready to carry the goods brought to Pittsburgh by the Pennsylvania, as did the Buffalo and State Line for the New York Central; and even though the Baltimore and Ohio was more dependent upon waterways than the others, western railroads took off more than half the goods delivered to Wheeling and Parkersburg.[10] On the other hand, a substantial proportion of the canal shipments must ultimately have been delivered by railroad.

Specialization was necessary to capture traffic from the highly competitive canal route. Only as a consequence of it did direct benefits as large as the $11.6 million calculated in Chapter II emerge in the through trade. Almost all of this reduction in transport costs can be attributed to special advantages in the transport of livestock and flour, and still more to the avoidance of such charges as interest and insurance costs whose magnitude depended upon the value of the goods shipped. What such specialization also meant was a clear dominance in the proportion of interregional trade these lines carried, as measured in value. One official estimate, utilizing 1862 tonnages of the various trunk lines and the canal, placed East-West trade at more than $1 billion, of which railroads transported more than 90 percent.[11] Even after correction for the use of way tonnage in this estimate, the total exchange is $800 million, and the railroad share 85 percent. A comparable estimate for 1860, when trade was much smaller, comes to more than $500 million, with an equivalent railroad proportion. Although this total may be too large because of an overly generous valuation for merchandise shipments, an alternative estimate based on more modest assumptions still exceeds $300 million.[12] It is no wonder, therefore, that contemporaries ranked the contribution of the railroad far above the direct benefits we have calculated. The imposing size and power of the

---

[10] Kohlmeier, *Old Northwest*, pp. 206–208.

[11] *Statistics of Foreign and Domestic Commerce*, p. 129.

[12] See my "Antebellum Interregional Trade Reconsidered," *American Economic Review*, LIV (May 1964), 352–364, and the technical appendix especially, where estimates for all the axes of interregional trade are given for six selected years from 1839 to 1860.

RAILROADS AND ANTE-BELLUM ECONOMY

giant trunk lines — the commercial interests of the great Atlantic ports were crucially dependent upon them — did nothing to dispel such an impression.

This is not to admit that the limited direct benefits exhaust the contribution of these railroads engaged in the commerce between East and West. The large reduction in Erie Canal rates during the 1850's, for example, is quite clearly related to railroad competition. Nor can we really separate the contribution of the through lines from that of their intraregional feeders. As the census described, they were base lines, and other roads grew up around them. The trunks often assisted such a process directly. The Pennsylvania and the Baltimore and Ohio, especially the former, aided the construction of feeder lines directly to the extent of some 900 miles, or a tenth of midwestern mileage added between 1850 and 1860. A more subtle demonstration effect prevailed with even greater pervasiveness. The small interior lines conceived of themselves as part of some great through route to the East; few accepted roles as feeders of local traffic. It is exactly the period of extension of the trunks when the great railway boom in the West gathers force. The new railroads, more and more, were constructed as feeders to other railroads, not, as before, as north-south feeders to the Ohio River or the Great Lakes. The Indianapolis and Bellefontaine, "which if constructed, must become one of the great thoroughfares for the transportation of the immense business between the Atlantic cities . . . and the centre of this great Valley," was promoted with just such a prospect before it.[13] The trunk lines stretched with beckoning gestures from the East, and the lines to meet them from the West multiplied in response. Those interior lines did make a difference both in their transport cost reductions and in indirect benefits.

Beyond such impulses, and also not fully reckoned in the direct benefits, is an advantage like diminished seasonality of prices. The costs of holding inventories do not do full justice to the rail-

---

[13] *Indiana State Sentinel*, April 6, 1848, quoted in Daniels, "The Village at the End of the Road," p. 57. Note also the following statement in the *Sentinel* of October 30, 1847: "We need more railroads, especially some eligible outlet *northwardly*, so that we can reach New York next year, by way of the New York and Erie railroad, in three days." (*Sentinel*, in Daniels, p. 45.) Even north-south lines were a response to the prospect of direct rail connections.

road's contribution if only because they presume ready availability of the necessary floating capital. Western money markets hardly conformed to such an ideal. In fact, price seasonality in the Cincinnati market perceptibly diminished in those commodities being shipped east by railroad. Some fluctuation remained, but it was a predictable ebb and flow of an agricultural export region, not an erratic, violent record governed by the stages of the river.[14] An industrializing economy can only gather strength from such stability.

Speed, too, had its indirect aspects: shippers could choose the most favorable market and increase their own returns while at the same time evening costs to consumers. It is no accident that Cincinnati and eastern prices first began to converge in the 1850's, although transport costs were really not much altered.[15] A direct and rapid line of communication by railroad narrowed price differentials. Since eastern prices were more responsive to both foreign and domestic demands — for, as we shall see, the East was the food deficient region, not the South — this represented a gain to western producers. The very existence of a wider range of choice of alternative eastern markets afforded by the multiplicity of railroads reinforced such a consequence.

All of these effects, operative in a dynamic context, place the through lines in a more favorable perspective. Further, there is their contribution to trade diversion. But before we can move on to this matter, it is necessary to broaden the discussion of domestic commerce to its other dimensions.

The Trade Between North and South

In the important exchange between North and South, the ocean served as the principal highway of commerce. Not that a parallel rail route was lacking. One of the first discernible axes of railroad construction in the 1830's ran north to south linking together the leading commercial cities of the country, and based upon existing passenger traffic. By 1840, it was possible to travel south from New York all the way to North Carolina by rail, with some discontinuities, of course. These roads were never as much

[14] Berry, *Western Prices*, pp. 129–135.
[15] Berry, pp. 106, 108–109.

utilized for the transportation of freight as for passengers, however. Even in 1859, the aggregate freight earnings of the coastal group came to $2.3 million, passenger earnings to $4.0 million. Earlier, passenger earnings had been a much larger percentage. The total 1859 ton-mileage implied by these receipts is approximately 60,000,000, of which only a small proportion represented *through* commerce. For example, the Richmond and Petersburg, a central link in the chain, earned but a fifth of its freight revenues from through freight although it was only 27 miles in length.[16] Such a result cannot compare with the 400,000,000 ton-miles of exclusively through commodities carried by the trunk lines.

This meager performance partly reflects inefficient integration of the individual lines: gauge differences prevented continuous shipment from North to South, and vice versa, and even when these did not impede traffic, the variety of other breaks in the supposedly "continuous" rail line did. With a large number of independent roads, transshipments were frequent and often separated by considerable distances. There was a more basic flaw, however. Long hauls over a water route were far cheaper than by rail since many of the charges by ship were fixed — loading, insurance, commission, and the like were largely independent of distance.

Nowhere does water dominance emerge so clearly as in the substantial cotton trade, the South's major interregional and international export. All of the cotton to supply New England's textile mills before the Civil War came by water. The railroad did carry northward 7,661 bales in 1855 and 108,676 bales in 1860 but these were for reshipment to foreign markets. The coastal trade carried *nine* times more cotton than railroads to the Atlantic ports in 1860, of which the largest part went to Boston for redistribution to the interior. There was no direct overland transportation of cotton to sites of domestic consumption in the North until 1867.[17]

The return trade from the North included textiles, boots and shoes, and other manufactures. Philadelphia, in particular among the northern cities, seems to have cultivated the southern market

---

[16] Dozier, *Atlantic Coast Line*, p. 87.
[17] *Report on Internal Commerce for 1876*, pp. 142, 147, 180.

and to have exported large amounts of industrial commodities.[18] By all indications from the traffic reports of the sole railroad leading southward from the city, the Philadelphia, Wilmington, and Baltimore, these went by water, probably from New York. That city clearly handled the largest share of commerce southward, even if it originated elsewhere. New York's pre-eminence is mirrored in the heavy incidence of bankruptcy due to the loss of southern accounts after the outbreak of hostilities, and in the friendliness of its press toward the South. Boston did not even have a line of steamships running south of Baltimore, and merchants in that city were eager to establish one just before the war. "It is utterly idle, to suppose that buyers of the best credit will continue to come to Boston, when we confess our inferiority to New York, by gratuitous carriage of merchandise to that city, for shipment thence to our Southern ports in steam-vessels." [19]

The magnitude of the total exchange between the North and South has never been measured. The volume of shipping is not a good indicator. Although the total tonnage employed in the coasting trade was more than twice the capacity of the shipping upon the lakes and western rivers in 1860, much of the trade was between the North Atlantic ports themselves, often in coal.[20] Nevertheless, it seems that such interregional exchange was quite important until at least the early 1850's: Andrews estimated in 1852 that the coasting trade accounted for half the total flow of internal commerce in both tonnage and value.[21]

A contemporary estimate places northern sales in the South in 1859 at $240,000,000. Foreign imports sent down from the North are an additional $106,000,000, with still further outlays of

<hr/>

[18] See Edwin T. Freedley, *Philadelphia and Its Manufactures* (Philadelphia, 1859), pp. 467, 490, for illustrative comments on the prevalence of a southern market for Philadelphia manufactures.

[19] *Steam Communication between Boston and New Orleans. Appeal of the Board of Trade, to the Retired Capitalists and the Owners of Real Estate* (Boston, 1860), p. 6. Reprinted and italicized in Kirkland, *Men, Cities, and Transportation*, II, 174.

[20] The tonnage figures in that year are 2,014,005 in the coasting trade, 450,726 upon the lakes, and 369,014 on the rivers. The rate of growth of the tonnage in the coasting trade during the 1850's is larger than that for river tonnage, although smaller than that of lake shipping. North, *Economic Growth*, pp. 252–253.

[21] Andrews, *Trade and Commerce*, p. 905.

$116,000,000 for northern financial services and travel.[22] Despite Douglass North's acquiescence, these calculations cannot be accepted as they stand. It is easy to show why. Central to the estimate of the exchange of goods are the two following assumptions: (1) Per capita (white) consumption of manufactures in the South in 1850 was $50, in the North $60, in the West $40, whence it follows (subtracting southern production) that in 1850, imports of $146,000,000 of manufactures from the North were required. Since industrial output in the North expanded between 1850 and 1859 by 50 percent, manufactured imports in the latter year were "easily" $240,000,000![23] (2) "The annual report of the Secretary of the Treasury for the year 1856 . . . gives the amount of imported goods consumed in the United States in 1850 at . . . $7.02 per head of the whole population. The distribution of that amount was to the South, $43,000,000; West, $35,000,000; North, $85,180,000. In the past year these importations have risen to . . . $10.59 per head, which would give, to the same proportion, for Southern consumption, $106,000,000; for Western, $63,000,000; and for the North and East, $149,000,000." [24]

Apart from the arbitrariness of the assumptions, Kettell's method does not even yield his results. The technique for deriving imports of northern manufactures applied to 1860 census data, produces a sum of $320 million, or a result a third greater than Kettell's estimate. Since this is embarrassingly inconsistent with the other items in the balance of payments, we may conclude that either the method, or the estimation of the other entries, or both, are at fault. The last alternative is most probable. The direct quotation indicating the method of deriving imports is shot through with error. The actual 1859 regional proportions are totally dissimilar to the 1850 ones presumably used. Nor does Kettell allow for the more than $30 million of total imports that went directly to the southern states without intermediate distribution.

There is therefore little reason to accept this estimate of a

[22] Thomas P. Kettell, *Southern Wealth and Northern Profits* (New York, 1860), p. 75. The data are quoted as being indicative "of the likely magnitudes" by North, *Economic Growth*, p. 114.

[23] Kettell, *Southern Wealth*, pp. 59–60, 74.

[24] Kettell, p. 74.

biased observer whose sole intent was to emphasize the importance of the southern market for northern businessmen. The task
is not a hopeless one, however. The earnings of southern export
staples plus capital inflows give southern import capacity and
hence a measure of trade. To his credit, Kettell does not ignore
this possibility. Where he goes awry is his refusal to accept the
results; he doubles the indicated proceeds by reference to "other
produce" that "swell the figures." This other produce is not only
much smaller in volume than he assumes, but also consists almost exclusively of *western* products transshipped via New
Orleans.

A more correct calculation starts only from the shipments of
cotton, tobacco, rice, naval stores, sugar, and molasses. This
covers the gamut of southern earnings rather completely. The
understatement caused by the exclusion of the flow of grain
northward from Virginia, for example, is a minor affair. For 1860,
a peak year of cotton revenues, the export potential of the South
is indicated in Table 35: at the end of the ante-bellum period,
the South was earning about $275 million of goods and services
from other areas plus any additional purchases financed by capital inflows. These latter were probably not considerable in the
late 1850's. One of the perversities of southern pride was the
claimed finance of southern railroads by local capital rather than
by export of securities as the West had done.[25] Although this
contention must be qualified by the external flow of governmental
securities marketed to support the railroads "locally," I doubt
that capital inflows in 1860 were sufficiently large to alter matters
significantly.

Against these earnings, something like $30 million of imports of
commodities from abroad and between $5 and $10 million of imports of specie must be balanced. Likewise, imports from the
West of almost $40 million must be reckoned.[26] This leaves for
northern manufactures and imports channeled through the North
a maximum of $200 million. Some northern services in connection
with the export trade are not included, however, since wholesale

---

[25] See, for example, Kettell, *Southern Wealth*, pp. 86–88. Because of his bias he
might be expected to emphasize the possibility of northern investment in the South.

[26] This estimate is derived by applying the fraction of western foodstuffs consumed in the South (Table 39) to total receipts of western products (Table 36).

TABLE 35.   Southern export potential, 1860

	Production	Export	Average price (dollars)	Value of exports (millions of dollars)
Cotton (million pounds)	2,275	2,188	0.108	237.4
Tobacco (million pounds)	300	—	0.078	23.4
Rice (million pounds)	—	44	0.032	1.4
Naval Stores	—	—	—	2.0
Sugar (thousand hogsheads)	222	161	82.00	13.2
Molasses (thousand gallons)	24,888	9,642	0.35	3.4
Total	—	—	—	280.8

Source: Cotton: Production, Hammond, *Cotton Industry*, Appendix I; export is production less estimated southern consumption, as derived from the ratio of cotton taken by southern mills to that taken by northern mills in *Report on Internal Commerce for 1886*, pp. LXII and LXXII; price is export price derived from *Report on Commerce and Navigation for 1860*.

Tobacco: Total production in southern states (excluding Maryland and Delaware) for census year extrapolated to 1860 by use of ratio of exports for fiscal 1861 to fiscal 1860. No allowance is made for southern consumption to compensate for the excluded value added of manufactured tobacco exported from Virginia. Average price from Gray, *History of Agriculture*, II, 1038.

Rice: Total American exports calculated from Gray, II, 1030; relatively little production was exported for northern consumption.

Naval Stores: Total American exports from *Report on Commerce and Navigation for 1860*, p. 54. Foreign exports from the North and domestic imports into that region from the South partially cancel.

Sugar: Total Louisiana production and exports to the interior from the review of the sugar trade in the *New Orleans Price Current*, August 31, 1861. Coastwise shipments to northern cities from the same source were added to interior exports. The price is the New Orleans price.

Molasses: Shipments to northern cities as above plus estimated shipments to the interior derived from the 1857 ratio of sugar and molasses tonnages times 1860 sugar tonnage, given in Kohlmeier, *Old Northwest*.

For fuller description see the discussion accompanying Tables A-6 and A-7 in the technical appendix to my "Antebellum Trade."

prices, f.o.b., were used to value quantities. Consequently, we do not capture the entire range of trade between the two sections, but what we do get is a measure comparable to the previous estimate of the exchange between East and West. In any event, the total magnitude of these commissions and other services is undoubtedly far smaller than the $63 million Kettell estimates and North approves, at least in light of the typical commissions cited by Gray.[27]

That trade between East and West, as we have noted above, ran to some $175 million at a minimum and possibly to as much as $300 million before its rapid wartime growth. As such it was approximately equal in magnitude to, or greater than, the North-South flow. It was not always so. The prior development of the South made it an unquestionably superior market at the beginning of the period. In 1839 the South was absorbing perhaps four times as much as the West, a dominance that disappeared finally only at the end of the 1850's.[28] If, as has often been suggested, the consumption of foreign imports was more highly concentrated in the South, the rapid rise of the western market may well have prevented a slowing down in the rate of growth of domestic manufactures.

This is not to discount the importance of the southern market. Throughout the ante-bellum period the demand for negro cloth, brogans, machinery, and other commodities, undoubtedly affected the process of American industrialization favorably. As the Treasury stated in 1864: "The manufactures and machinery produced in all the New England States, New York, Pennsylvania, New Jersey, Delaware, and Maryland, have been carried coastwise to the entire south, from the Delaware bay to Texas. The value of these manufactures has always been large." [29] Nevertheless, by the end of the 1850's, the relative importance of those demands had diminished.

The Trade Between West and South

Thus far we have analyzed two of the channels of internal trade between America's three major pre-1860 regions. It remains only to consider the flow between the West and the South. The traditional view is that because the South was producing staple crops

[27] Gray, *History of Agriculture*, II, 715–716. It is doubtful if northern services could have come to one-fourth the export value of the cotton crop, especially since the *purchaser* paid the largest share of costs. See the evidence presented by North, *Economic Growth*, p. 115.

[28] See my "Antebellum Trade" and its technical appendix.

[29] *Statistics of Foreign and Domestic Commerce*, p. 121.

for export it was acquiring its foodstuffs from the West, whose comparative advantage conveniently lay along these lines. As Schmidt has summarized, and North recently reiterated:[30]

The rise of internal commerce after 1815 made possible a territorial division of labor between the three great sections of the Union — the West, the South, and the East. . . . Each section tended to devote itself more exclusively to the production of those commodities for which it was best able to provide. . . . The South was thereby enabled to devote itself in particular to the production of a few plantation staples contributing a large and growing surplus for the foreign markets and depending on the West for a large part of its food supply . . .

Such a model is simple, internally consistent, and not lacking the support of contemporary observation. Russell, one of many foreign visitors, noted the existence of specialization: "The bacon is almost entirely imported from the Northern States, as well as a considerable quantity of Indian Corn." Christy, a southern defender of slavery, emphasized the solidarity of western and southern commercial interests and commented in a like vein: "The West . . . had its attention now [after 1815] turned to the South, as the most certain and convenient mart for the sale of its products — the planters affording to the farmers the markets they had in vain sought from the manufacturers." [31] The increasing flow of receipts at New Orleans often is used as evidence of the continuity of such exchange to a later period.

Such a position has come under recent attack.[32] Richard Easterlin's review of North's book points to the production statistics of the southern states as evidence of substantial self-sufficiency in foodstuffs.[33] The number of swine and bushels of corn produced

[30] Louis B. Schmidt, "Internal Commerce and the Development of a National Economy before 1860," *Journal of Political Economy*, XLVII (1939), 811. Cited by North, *Economic Growth*, p. 103.

[31] Both quotations in Callendar, *Economic History, 1765–1860*, pp. 292, 296.

[32] Although his is a far better study than Schmidt's brief summary, Isaac Lippincott's opposing views have not achieved wide circulation. See his "Internal Trade of the United States, 1700–1860," *Washington University Studies*, IV, pt. II, no. 1 (1916), 63–150. For the discussion of the trade between West and South, see pp. 130–132.

[33] *Journal of Economic History*, XXII (1962), 125. See also Donald L. Kemmerer, "The Pre-Civil War South's Leading Crop, Corn," *Agricultural History*, XXIII (1949), 236–239.

per capita in the South from 1840 through 1860 were higher than the national average, for example. So too, the number of cattle, and the quantity of peas and beans produced. In this tally, the border states contribute more than proportionally, suggesting a flow of trade between different parts of the South, and not inter-regionally. The southern social structure, with large numbers of land owners with few or no slaves at all, also indirectly testifies to an economic structure with self-sufficiency and local produc-tion of foodstuffs for sale to nearby plantations.[34] Intrasouthern trade of some significance, apart from that with the border states, is a distinct possibility that has not yet been fully explored.

Although these data are obviously relevant to the question of southern dependence upon the West, their impact is dulled be-cause they do not bear directly upon exchange between the two regions. It is necessary to focus upon such exchange if the matter is to be resolved. A good place to begin is with the receipts at New Orleans. Since the Ohio and Mississippi Rivers formed a continuous channel the largest volume of western produce for southern consumption passed to this market. So, too, however, did a large quantity of southern staples, which means that gross receipts at New Orleans are not a valid measure, absolute or relative, of the West-South trade. In Table 36, New Orleans re-ceipts are separated into two components, one consisting of the southern staples, the other a residual comprising western prod-ucts. These latter were largely foodstuffs, although lead was also important at the beginning of the period. From 1842 on these values are exact; for the earlier period they are estimates for the components, and exact for the totals. Included in Table 36, too, is a weighted index of physical receipts of western foodstuffs at New Orleans compiled by Thomas S. Berry.

These data yield two important conclusions. First, for the entire period, western products, and therefore western foodstuffs, make up less than half of New Orleans receipts. The very rapid

---

[34] For the number of slaveholders and slaves, see *Eighth Census, Agriculture,* p. 247. For a discussion of the different types of farmers in the context of a single plantation state see Herbert Weaver, *Mississippi Farmers, 1850–1860* (Nashville, 1945), especially chap. ii. Kenneth Stampp, *The Peculiar Institution* (New York: Alfred A. Knopf, 1956), pp. 51–53, also presents scattered evidence on self-suffi-ciency.

TABLE 36.   Average annual receipts at New Orleans, 1823–1860

Years ending Aug. 1	Cotton	Tobacco	Sugar	Molasses	Other commodities	Total[a]	Index of receipts of western foodstuffs at New Orleans (base — 1810–62 average)
			(millions of dollars)				
1823–1825	7.9	1.0	2.0	—	5.3	16.2	11
1826–1830	10.1	1.3	—	—	10.2	21.6	21
1831–1835	18.0	1.8	—	—	8.9	28.7	40
1836–1840	29.6	3.4	—	—	11.1	44.1	58
1841–1845	28.1	5.5	5.8	0.5	14.4	53.3	112
1846–1850	34.8	4.2	10.2	1.9	34.0	85.2	237
1851–1855	54.5	6.8	14.7	3.6	36.9	116.3	212
1856–1860	89.2	10.2	17.0	4.9	44.1	165.6	212

Source: 1842–1849, except 1843: Annual reports of New Orleans Commerce reprinted in the October issue of Hunt's Merchants' Magazine for the respective years.
1850–1860 and Total for 1823–1841: U.S. Treasury Department, Bureau of Statistics, Report on Internal Commerce for 1887 (Washington, 1888), pp. 191, 209.
1823–1841, 1843: Cotton: Receipts in bales at New Orleans, Hunt's Merchants' Magazine, XXI (1849), 557; average New Orleans price per pound given in Gray, History of Agriculture, II, 1027, multiplied by an assumed 500-pound bale. These values were reduced by 13 percent, the average overstatement produced by the method during the period covered by exact values and predicted ones in the 1840's. Values were further reduced for the earlier periods in proportion to the ratio of bale size in the given years and that prevailing in the 1840's. (Data on bale size from Gray, History, II, 705.)
Tobacco: Receipts at New Orleans, Hunt's Merchants' Magazine, XXI (1849), 557; average New Orleans price from Gray, II, 1038. Value of receipts inflated by 13 percent (average understatement in 1840's) to compensate for the exclusion of shipments by containers other than hogsheads and also for an understatement of price due to shipment of some higher valued tobaccos.
Sugar: Total values, 1843, Gray, II, 1033. Production, 1823, Hunt's Merchants' Magazine, XXI (1849), 557; 1824–1825, Gray, II, 1033. Prices, Gray, p. 1034. Receipts at New Orleans from 1826–40 exclude sugar entirely.
Molasses: In "Other commodities," 1823–1840; 1841, 1843 extrapolated from actual values of other years.
Index of western receipts at New Orleans: Berry, Western Prices, p. 581. An apparent typographical error in the entry for 1830 has been corrected although the same error is repeated in the text. With all components declining, the index goes up by 60 percent according to the printed version.
[a] May not add due to rounding.

rise in Berry's index between 1826–1830 and 1831–1835 does not contradict the simultaneously declining value of receipts that is the basis for this observation. Not prices, but the declining trend of lead receipts is responsible for the divergence. With foodstuffs only a fraction of the 1826–1830 values and almost the complete 1831–1835 total, they could have gone up sharply, as Berry's index suggests, consistent with a small decline in value of all western products. To find a dominance of western products, therefore, it is necessary to go back before the depression of 1819 when the Southwest was not yet producing substantial quantities of cotton. In 1816–1818, Berry's index stands at 10 or at about its 1823–1825 level. Western prices were higher than in 1823–1825, and the total values of New Orleans receipts only $10 million a year.[35] Only at that early date did the share of western products exceed 50 percent of the value of New Orleans receipts.

A second noteworthy result is the *absolute* decline in western shipments in the 1850's. The physical index brings this out nicely as do the value data once the rapid increase in the prices of agricultural products over the period is appreciated: bacon, pork, and lard, more than doubled in price between 1850 and 1857, flour was up by 25 percent, beef by 67 percent, and so on.[36] Since the South was expanding its cotton production rapidly exactly over this interval — output doubling — this is presumably when imports of western products should have shown a rapid increase! This disparity, and the seeming rapid growth in imports in the late 1840's, in part results from an inadequacy of these data that has not been fully recognized. Receipts of western produce at New Orleans were not entirely consumed but were also re-exported either to foreign or coastwise ports.

It is surprising that so little attention has been paid to this link in the argument. After all, the entire discussion of trade diversion in *De Bow's Review* revolved exactly upon the issue of whether it was cheaper to ship to the East via New Orleans or eastward by canal or railroad. Contemporaries clearly attributed

[35] *Report on the Internal Commerce of the United States for 1887*, pp. 191, 215; Berry, *Western Prices*, p. 580.

[36] According to the valuations of western produce at New Orleans published along with the annual summaries of the trade of that city in the October number of *Hunt's Merchants' Magazine* for the respective years.

the decline in receipts of western produce in the 1850's to the loss of transshipment, not to lesser southern consumption. A simple comparison in Table 37 of the total value of receipts of produce

TABLE 37. Retained receipts at New Orleans (thousands of dollars)

Years ending Aug. 1	Receipts from interior (1)	Foreign exports (2)	Coastwise exports (3)	Residual (1)–(2)–(3)
1832–1833	28,238	16,133	9,058	3,047
1836–1837	43,515	31,546	15,116	− 3,147
1841–1842	45,716	27,427	19,444	− 1,155
1845–1846	77,193	30,748	19,150	27,295
1850–1851	106,924	53,968	27,229	25,727
1855–1856	144,256	80,550	28,031	33,175

Source: *Report on the Internal Commerce of the United States for 1887*, pp. 199, 215, 285–286, 377.

at New Orleans with the volume of all exports, foreign and coastwise, emphasizes how little was retained, at least until the mid-1840's. Of the subsequent growth in the residual a good part consists of sugar and molasses either consumed directly in the South or exported up-river to Ohio Valley points. With annual value of sugar and molasses production at level of $20 million by the 1850's, and with coastwise exports of these not much more than half of output, the significance of this distortion is readily apparent.

Fortunately, over the very interval in which there is some doubt concerning an increase in consumption of western foodstuffs, it is possible to be more precise. The records kept at New Orleans from 1842 on include re-exports of western produce to both foreign and coastwise ports; these compared with total receipts of such foodstuffs, give an exact notion of the quantity retained. Table 38 presents these data for the interval 1842–1861. From it we can see that the value of produce either retained at New Orleans or shipped coastwise to other southern ports approached one half of total receipts only toward the end of the

TABLE 38. Southern consumption of western foodstuffs (annual average)

	Flour (barrels)	Pork (barrels)	Bacon (hogs-heads)	Lard (kegs)	Corn (sacks)	Whiskey (barrels)	Beef (barrels)	Value (thousands of dollars)
1842–1845[a]								
Receipts[b]	491,836	333,232	30,856	654,063	490,169	81,537	36,023	8,275
Exports[c]	245,542	244,115	8,012	575,974	189,573	7,274	19,835	4,823
Consumption[d]	246,294	89,117	22,844	78,089	300,596	74,263	16,188	3,452
Cons./Rec.	0.50	0.27	0.74	0.12	0.61	0.91	0.45	0.42
1846–1849								
Receipts[b]	1,043,949	507,219	57,760	1,204,501	1,887,984	126,005	18,393	20,824
Exports[c]	726,399	308,492	25,303	1,064,975	1,446,457	15,948	49,417	13,830
Consumption[d]	317,550	198,727	32,457	139,526	441,527	110,057	28,976	6,994
Cons./Rec.	0.30	0.39	0.56	0.12	0.23	0.87	0.37	0.34
1850–1853								
Receipts[b]	817,244	441,235	87,378	1,005,985	1,306,799	140,090	69,446	22,211
Exports[c]	304,836	234,578	30,232	910,169	496,277	8,970	49,624	10,803
Consumption[d]	512,408	206,657	57,146	95,816	810,522	131,120	19,822	11,408
Cons./Rec.	0.63	0.47	0.65	0.10	0.62	0.94	0.29	0.51
1854–1857								
Receipts[b]	989,735	325,243	67,658	702,801	1,588,001	141,424	48,433	26,300
Exports[c]	529,863	139,447	16,127	724,726	820,267	7,179	28,340	13,053
Consumption[d]	459,872	185,796	51,531	− 21,925	767,734	134,245	20,093	13,247
Cons./Rec.	0.46	0.57	0.76	− 0.03	0.48	0.95	0.41	0.50
1858–1861								
Receipts[b]	1,149,695	275,246	63,910	448,381	1,820,616	139,129	42,287	24,984
Exports[c]	425,542	39,543	4,907	405,351	410,004	4,425	15,051	6,873
Consumption[d]	724,153	235,703	59,003	43,030	1,410,612	134,704	27,236	18,111
Cons./Rec.	0.63	0.86	0.92	0.10	0.77	0.97	0.64	0.72

Source: Hunt's Merchants' Magazine, VI(1842), 391–392; XI(1844), 419–421; XIII(1845), 370–372; XV(1846), 406–409; XVII(1847), 413–414; XIX(1848), 511–516; XXI(1849), 554–556; XXIII(1850), 536–537; XXV(1851), 602–605; XXVII(1852), 489–492; XXIX(1853), 624–629; XXXI(1854), 475–477; XXXIII(1855), 601–604; XXXV(1856), 474; New Orleans Price Current, Sept. 1, 1856; Hunt's, XXXVII(1857), 603–607; New Orleans Price Current, Sept. 1, 1858; Sept. 1, 1859; DeBow's Review, XXIX(1860), 521; New Orleans Price Current, Aug. 31, 1861.
  a 1843 values were unavailable.
  b Calculated in homogeneous physical units by dividing total value of receipts by price of specified physical unit.
  c Foreign exports plus coastwise shipments to Boston, New York, Philadelphia, and Baltimore. Unspecified coastwise shipments were credited to southern ports, and hence consumption.
  d Consumption equals receipts minus exports.

period, finally reaching a fraction of almost three fourths in 1858–1861. In years of particularly large receipts, 1849 is a good example, the proportion consumed moves inversely, clearly indicating the re-export function of New Orleans. Only in the 1850's, moreover, do coastwise shipments to other southern ports begin to amount to a large fraction of total consumption. In 1842, the value of the produce retained at New Orleans is $1.9 million; that shipped to southern ports is $0.4 million. But in 1854 the corresponding values are $7.7 and $3.5 million.[37] This means that the small residual in New Orleans commerce before 1846 found in Table 37 may be taken as indicative of little *total* southern consumption, not only little consumption at New Orleans.

Such an aggregate result conceals substantial variation in the consumption of particular commodities. Despite some fluctuation, it seems on average about as much flour was sent on as was consumed, with possibly a slight upward trend. In the instance of provisions, on the other hand, an upward trend in consumption is obvious. So, too, do receipts of corn at New Orleans come more and more to represent southern needs. Yet both of these last commodities probably originated in Kentucky and Tennessee in large quantities and hence do not fully represent interregional trade. The consumption of lard and whiskey shows little variation over time — the former being almost wholly re-exported, the latter completely retained. The net result of these divergent patterns was to cushion consumption somewhat against the absolutely declining receipts of western produce at New Orleans in the 1850's. Nevertheless, the consumption data tell a tale similar to Berry's physical receipts index: substantial growth in the 1840's and much more modest advance in the 1850's. Consumption in 1850 dollars was $4.6 million in 1842–1845, $10.0 million in 1850–1853, and $12.3 million in 1858–1861. Even as its staple production proceeded apace the South was not becoming absolutely more reliant upon the West, and, relatively, less so.

These new consumption data permit us now to re-examine the West-South trade with respect to three basic characteristics: its absolute magnitude vis-à-vis other interregional trade, the relative importance of the exports to the West, and the relative importance of the imports to the South. First, we can conclude rather assuredly that the trade was relatively quite small. The $18 million consumption of foodstuffs in 1858–1861, although

[37] Calculated from the data underlying Table 38.

possibly augmented by imports of other western produce of equivalent size — as suggested by Table 36 — is only a third of the exchange between West and East, and for that matter, a smaller proportion of the shipments from the North to the South.[38] Before the 1850's, the small residual receipts at New Orleans contradict an appreciable exchange. It therefore does not appear that southern demands for foodstuffs were an important mechanism by which increasing exports of staples from the South transmitted a dynamic impulse to the West.

More direct evidence on this point, namely the proportion of selected western exports taken off by the South is available for the period after 1839. As Table 39 brings out, southern demands for every western product except whiskey were in a substantial minority by 1849. When weighted by relative values the meager extent of the southern market is yet more obvious. As early as 1839, at its peak, southern demands took off less than a fifth of western exports of foodstuffs. When receipts at New Orleans rallied owing to favorable river conditions or export demands, as they did both in 1849 and 1857, they were offset by increasing exports. That, after all, was the significance of New Orleans — as a gateway, not a terminal. Moreover, in the one important area in which southern demands held to a high level, provisions, the border states came to play a larger part. In 1853 Louisville contributed a fifth of the pork and bacon received at New Orleans, with additional amounts from the Cumberland and Tennessee rivers; in 1860 the share of Louisville alone increased to a third.[39]

If relatively unimportant to the West, the imports were minute compared with production of foodstuffs within the South itself. The 1842 corn consumption of 241,049 sacks (= 2 bushels each) may be compared with an 1839 crop in the South of 225,000,000 bushels; or the 1850 consumption of 763,014 sacks with 1849 production of almost 300,000,000 bushels; or 1860 consumption of 1,590,131 sacks against 1859 output of more than 340,000,000

[38] In "Antebellum Trade," eastern consumption of western products is estimated at $108 million. This is after an allowance for export of foodstuffs abroad; the gross flow is a larger $146 million.
[39] Kohlmeier, *Old Northwest*, pp. 118, 202.

TABLE 39. The importance of the southern market to the West (percent)

Commodity	Proportion of western exports shipped via New Orleans						Proportion of receipts of western produce at New Orleans consumed in the South						Proportion of western exports consumed in the South					
	1839	1844	1849	1853	1857	1860	1842	1844	1849	1853	1857	1860	1839a	1844	1849	1853	1857	1860
Flour	53	30	31	27	34	22	42	50	30	60	41	86	22	16	9	14	14	19
Meat products	51	6	50	38	28	24	41	31	34	62	69	95	21	19	17	24	19	23
Corn	98	90	39	37	32	19	46	70	21	44	65	91	45	63	8	16	21	17
Whiskey	96	95	67	53	48	40	80	95	89	90	93	98	77	90	60	48	45	39
Total foodstuffs	49	44	40	31	27	17	37	38	29	52	52	85	13	17	12	16	14	14

Source: Proportion of western exports shipped via New Orleans: Kohlmeier, *Old Northwest*, pp. 33, 52–53, 83–85, 116–117, 146–148, 191–193, 248–249. Meat products include livestock (estimated for 1839–1853 as described in the technical appendix to "Antebellum Trade"). Some of the percentages deviate from Kohlmeier's text declarations due to divergence between those and absolute quantities separately given; the differences are small. Total foodstuffs include wheat, which is not shown separately. Current western prices have been used to weight the specific commodities.

Proportion of New Orleans receipts consumed in the South: Table 38. Meat products here are the weighted sum of bacon, pork, and beef. Total foodstuffs include lard and whiskey, but exclude wheat. This incomparability with panel 1 is not important.

Proportion of western exports consumed in the South: Panel 1 times panel 2.

a Exports for 1839 via New Orleans times 1842 retention ratio.

bushels. Domestic production was augmented by imports to the extent of less than 1 percent in each of these years. Wheat imports represented a larger addition to productive capacity, to be sure, but still a modest one in absolute terms. Entering principally as flour (reckoned at 5 bushels to the barrel), imports of wheat amounted to 960,000 bushels in 1842, 2,600,000 in 1850, and 4,250,000 in 1860. Output reached 25,000,000 bushels in 1839, 20,000,000 in 1849, and 38,000,000 in 1859. At best, due to the poor crop of 1849, imports supplemented production by 13 percent; but by 1860, due to a resurgence in southern wheat output during the simultaneous cotton boom, the ratio actually declined slightly to 11 percent. In meat products, the relative importance of external supplies is akin to the independence displayed in the case of corn. The 1850 census credited to the South more than $45,000,000 in slaughtered animals, an estimate that must be raised beyond $100,000,000 to compensate for understatement. The year 1850 saw imports of pork, bacon, and beef amounting to only $3,600,000. In 1860 the ratio of imports, similarly calculated, managed to climb only to the 5 percent mark.[40]

Only one possibility remains to refute these contentions. That would be a substantial flow of western produce directly to southern sites bypassing New Orleans. It certainly does not seem to have occurred on the western rivers. The proportion of shipments from Cincinnati to downriver ports other than New Orleans is of no significance. In 1848–1850 less than 1 percent of the provisions shipped to New Orleans were destined to such other ports; of corn the ratio is 10 percent, but Cincinnati was not the leading forwarder; of flour, another growing export of St. Louis, the proportion is about 20 percent on average.[41] On the other side of the transaction, receipts at other southern cities do not appear to

[40] Census data for corn and wheat as reprinted in Gray, *History of Agriculture*, II, 1040. Delaware, Maryland, and Missouri are excluded in the totals given in the text. Value of slaughtered meat products from *Eighth Census, Agriculture*, pp. 187, 191. Wheat was converted to flour at 5 bushels to the barrel after an allowance of 12.5 percent of the crop for seed. The relationship between reported and actual values is derived from the national totals estimated by Gallman, "Commodity Output," p. 46.
[41] Calculated from *Hunt's Merchants' Magazine*, XXIII (1850), 542.

be substantial. Kohlmeier comments about shipments up the Cumberland and Tennessee rivers in the following vein: "they supplied a local market in western Kentucky and were comparatively limited in quantity." [42] The Vicksburg and Jackson Railroad is reported to have carried 297,119 pounds of meat from the river city to the interior in 1850.[43] This is equivalent to 371 hogsheads compared to receipts of 250,000 hogsheads at New Orleans in the same year. The Memphis and Charleston Railroad reported receipts from through freight eastward as $35,573.13. Converting to tons carried, this is only about 4,000 tons, an insignificant quantity.[44]

The underlying economics make shipment via New Orleans far more probable. With a predominantly downstream commerce, the trip upstream was necessary in any event and back haulage was presumably accommodated at low rates. The very marketing of the cotton in New Orleans also meant that factors could easily purchase the required foodstuffs there. In this instance, logic seems to have a counterpart in fact. The *Report on Internal Commerce for 1887* remarks: "There was no trade between the Western cities and the Southern plantations, very little even with the towns; it all paid tribute to New Orleans. . . . Of these shipments up-stream over 75 percent, strange to say, were articles which had previously been sent down-stream." [45]

Finally, this was before efficient rail contact had been established between West and South. Gauge differences, lack of bridging, and actual physical breaks meant that southern railroads were "completely without rail connections with any other part of the nation." [46] Thus the range of alternative direct marketing routes from the West to the South was quite limited. While the Western and Atlantic Railroad could conceivably have received some shipments via a complicated routing on the Cumberland

---

[42] Kohlmeier, *Old Northwest*, p. 202.

[43] From a contemporary account quoted in John H. Moore, *Agriculture in Ante-Bellum Mississippi* (New York, 1958), p. 111.

[44] *American Railroad Journal*, XXXIII (1860), 840–841. The receipts were converted to tons on the assumption of a 3- to 4-cent ton-mile charge and a length of road of 271 miles.

[45] *Report on Internal Commerce for 1887*, p. 205.

[46] Taylor and Neu, *Railroad Network*, p. 48.

River, and then the Nashville and Chattanooga Railroad, the commerce was necessarily small because water shipments up the Cumberland were limited. In describing the increase in flour and grain brought to Charleston after 1852 by the South Carolina Railroad, Derrick explains the result as a consequence of more efficient rail connections not to the West, but to northern Georgia, Alabama, and Tennessee.[47]

One further path bypassing New Orleans, namely coastal re-exports from northern cities, has recently been suggested as a challenge to these findings.[48] Although a possibility, it is not one that should be given undue weight. In the first instance, the growing shipments from New Orleans to other southern ports during the 1850's are indicative of increasing reliance upon a New Orleans route rather than the reverse. Secondly, there were actual exports to the North of corn and flour from Norfolk and Charleston during the decade, a situation which would lead to the belief that the return flow was limited and partially canceled, in any event.[49] Finally, the magnitude of the shipments required to alter the condition of substantial southern self-sufficiency would be quite large. In 1860, Baltimore, probably the prime source of supply to South Atlantic cities, exported 1,358,033 bushels of corn coastwise, 120,000 barrels of flour, and 562,339 bushels of wheat. Even if all went South — which we know from Boston receipts a goodly part did not — total imports of western corn would have supplemented output by less than $1\frac{1}{2}$ percent, and reliance upon external supplies of wheat would not have exceeded 15 percent.[50] Some additional exports to the South beyond

[47] Samuel M. Derrick, *Centennial History of the South Carolina Railroad* (Columbia, S.C., 1930), pp. 211–212.

[48] Fogel raised the point in his discussion of my "Antebellum Trade," in the *American Economic Review*, XIV (May 1964), 377–389. For a fuller reply see my "Postscript," in Ralph Andreano's forthcoming *New Perspectives on American Economic Development*.

[49] See the Boston Board of Trade reports at the end of the 1850's for some receipts of corn and flour from southern ports. For exports from Charleston and Norfolk see *De Bow's Review*, XXIX (1860), 526, and *Hunt's Merchants' Magazine*, XLII (1860), 480.

[50] For Baltimore exports see the *Eleventh Annual Report of the Baltimore Board of Trade for 1860* (Baltimore, 1861), pp. 21–56. From the Boston reports it appears that perhaps as much as half of the Baltimore flour and a quarter of the corn found their way to that city.

those received via New Orleans are certain, but it is doubtful whether they were large enough to matter.

Railroad Expansion, Trade Diversion, and its Consequences

A basic conclusion following from this discussion of internal commerce is the limited contribution of the railroad before 1860 in two of the three major axes of trade. Only in the flow between East and West, and to a smaller degree in the opposite direction, did the trunk lines carry a large volume of traffic, and even these with minor benefits. Almost all the trade emanating from or destined for the South was quite independent of developments in the railroad sector, in part because the overland connections between that region and the others were poorest, but more fundamentally, because competitive water routes represented barriers so formidable that integration would have made little difference and hence received little attention. Much later, in the mid-1880's, when the railway mileage in the country had tripled, it still could be commented: "Eastern business has been done until very lately, it may be said, entirely by the steamship lines running from those points. Even at this date the movement via all-rail lines is very small . . ." And the flow of western agricultural produce by river to New Orleans exceeded *all* tonnage by railroad from the West to the entire South at least until the early 1880's.[51]

Yet, if the railroad influenced only the movement between the seaboard and the interior, its ramifications extended beyond that immediate route. Both in diverting traffic that had followed a river and ocean route to the East and also in contributing to more rapid development of the West and eclipse of the southern market, the great trunk lines were of national significance. In this section we analyze the shift in markets in the 1850's, and its effects.

Table 39 has portrayed this transformation in concrete terms. From a third of the western exports of flour in 1849 (of which two thirds was shipped onward), the share going to New Orleans dwindled to a fifth in 1860, of which almost all was intended for southern consumption. In provisions, the decline was still more

[51] *Report on the Internal Commerce of the United States for 1886* (Washington, 1887), pp. 679–738.

precipitous. Not only did the share of exports taken by the southern gateway decline from 80 percent to 38 percent, but a rising share of southern consumption meant that the river route no longer represented passage to the East or to Europe. More extreme still was the declining share of exports of corn. Not only did it plummet from 60 percent to less than 20 percent, but the 1860 magnitude almost totally represents southern requirements. These data clearly affirm the reality of a "revolution . . . in the grain trade of the west." What was so special about it was the absolute decline in western receipts at New Orleans while the flow to the East was increasing dramatically. The 1850's did not witness the first erosion of the southern position: the Erie Canal by its successful breach of the Appalachian barrier had accomplished that long before. More than a decade earlier, well in advance of railroad influence, more flour was shipped east than south. But the accelerated pace of the later southern demise, to which the railroads did contribute, stands out as an equally impressive achievement.

This gross shift in trade flows is usefully viewed as the resultant of two separate components, one the variation in output in a given supply area, the other, changes in the boundaries of those areas. Thus one of the reasons flour shipments eastward increased between 1839 and 1849 was the more rapid development of the area north of the National Road and tributary to the lakes. Specifically, production of wheat in the northern parts of Ohio, Indiana, and Illinois more than doubled between 1839 and 1849, increasing the exportable surplus from 3 or 4 million bushels to 12 million. The southern parts of the same states witnessed a decline from a 5-million bushel surplus to a 1-million export over the same interval.[52] If it had not been for the increased production area tributary to the river in 1849, therefore, exports to New Orleans would have fallen far more.

Neither of these components exclusively measures trade diversion caused by transport innovation. Variations in growth of pro-

[52] Data taken from Kohlmeier, *Old Northwest*, pp. 95–96, who divided the census data into northern and southern divisions of the states. The surplus has been calculated on the assumption of per capita consumption of five bushels, not the eight bushels assumed by Kohlmeier. Whichever assumption is made, the conclusions are invariant.

ductive capacity reflect better marketing opportunities just as do shifting boundaries; as we have seen, railroads were intimately associated with settlement decisions. The more painful of the two causes of diversion, however, is clearly constriction of supply areas. So long as the hinterland remains intact, absolute decline is unlikely. Once erosion begins, it is difficult to check.

Exactly such a shift in supply areas lies at the heart of the reduced volume of flour shipments and complete disappearance of wheat exports to New Orleans between 1849 and 1860. This may seem surprising in view of the very rapid growth of wheat output in the northern parts of the western states. Nonetheless, the *relative* change in surplus was all in favor of New Orleans, primarily owing to increased output in southwestern Ohio. The area south of the National Road in 1849 could do little more than feed its own inhabitants in 1849, but in 1859 the potential surplus came to almost 10 million bushels. Between 1849 and 1860 there occurred a radical diminution of New Orleans' share of the surplus product of the northern part of the region as well as a rapidly loosening grip on the area formerly completely tributary to the river. In 1849, "about a million bushels each from Iowa, from the Illinois river and Rock river in northern Illinois, and from the middle Wabash river in northern Indiana found its way to the southern gateway." [53] Not only was this source of supply lost, but in 1860 the proportion of flour flowing upstream from Cincinnati or shipped by railway and canal was 90 percent, against a downriver proportion of 97 percent mentioned in the Andrews report.[54] Had both 1849 proportions been carried over to 1860, New Orleans' share of the export of flour would actually have increased over that interval. Had the South retained only the Cincinnati trade at the 1849 rates, its decline would have been more than halved!

In the weaning of the Ohio Valley, the contribution of the inter-regional railroads emerges rather convincingly. Both the Baltimore and Ohio and the Pennsylvania railroads directly served the region from 1853 on. In 1860 they took what must have been 500,000 barrels of flour eastward to Philadelphia and Baltimore,

[53] Kohlmeier, p. 84.
[54] Andrews, *Trade and Commerce*, p. 711; Berry, *Western Prices*, p. 168.

more than half of which came upstream by boat to Wheeling and Pittsburgh.[55] So effective competitors were the railroads that in 1857, when New Orleans attracted a large inflow of flour from the West for re-export east owing to favorable river conditions and low freight rates, Cincinnati continued to divert her shipments upriver or by rail. A clear contrast with the former pattern emerges here. The shift away from New Orleans between 1849 and 1860 is exactly matched by the increased flow to Philadelphia and Baltimore, while New York's share remained constant. The loss of allegiance in the northern part of the region just as clearly was due to the interposition of the railroad. But in this instance it was the feeder roads that counted most, east-west feeder roads that siphoned off a commerce whose more profitable previous alternative lay with the southward flowing rivers that drained the West. Since only a third of total flour shipments to the East followed an all-rail route, the feeders to lake cities like Milwaukee and Chicago were especially important in accomplishing this result.

In all of this, one should be mindful of the fluidity of the trade pattern. In 1856–1857, with the trunk lines and their feeders operative, 30 percent of the flour shipped to New Orleans was destined for the northern coastal ports, against 5 percent in 1853–1854 when the rail net was less extensive.[56] In the tripartite competition of canal, railroad, and river, the railroad's supremacy in the carriage of flour was far from conclusive before the war.

An analysis of the shifting export of meat products suggests a conclusion similar to that reached for flour. The two southernmost trunk lines again diverted the trade of the Ohio Valley in significant amounts. Of the 42 percentage point decline in New Orleans receipts of provisions indicated by Table 39, Philadelphia and Baltimore accounted for 22 points, New York for 19.[57] Cincinnati is once more a sensitive indicator. In 1850–1852 only 7 percent of the barreled pork moved upstream or via railway and canal; in 1859–1861, 42 percent. Beef packed in barrels showed a more modest change, but had less weight in the total. The pro-

[55] Kohlmeier, *Old Northwest*, pp. 199, 201.
[56] *Hunt's Merchants' Magazine*, XXXI (1854), 477; XXXVII (1857), 607.
[57] Kohlmeier, *Old Northwest*, pp. 85, 192.

portion going downriver fell from 92 percent of Cincinnati exports to 71 percent. Most dramatic shift of all was in tierces of beef destined for export to England: from 92 percent downriver in 1850–1852 to 96 percent by river or canal directly east.[58]

More than before, however, production effects are discernible The decade witnessed a relative reduction of swine in the Ohio Valley, and an increase in the lake area. Swine in the latter region increased from less than three million in 1849 to more than four million in 1859; in the area of Ohio, Indiana, and Illinois south of the National Road there was a lesser growth from 3.3 to 3.6 million swine, not to mention the absolute reduction in Kentucky from 2.9 to 2.3 million.[59] With Cincinnati drawing some of its supplies from northern Kentucky and Louisville, of course, this last is a matter of some relevance. According to Kohlmeier's calculations — without any allowance for the decline in Kentucky — the swine surplus in the river region declined by 70 thousand while that in the north rose by 40 thousand. Yet had Cincinnati continued to ship proportionally as much provisions downriver in 1860 as in 1849, New Orleans would have represented an outlet for about 50 percent of the salt meat rather than 38 percent.[60]

Shifting affiliation was thus a significant part of the story. It appears in another guise too. With the introduction of through railroad facilities, animals were exported live rather than as provisions. Not all railroad traffic in livestock should be viewed this way since some rail carriage substituted for overland driving that would have gone on in any event. This was more true for cattle than swine. A goodly part of the hogs that were shipped from the West in 1860 undoubtedly would have appeared as pork and bacon a decade earlier and potentially could have gone to New Orleans. The river route never was in position to compete for

<hr/>

[58] Berry, *Western Prices*, p. 91.

[59] Kohlmeier, *Old Northwest*, p. 204, as computed from the census for the parts of Ohio, Indiana, and Illinois lying north and south of the National Road. The Kentucky production, reprinted from the census, is conveniently found in Gray, *History of Agriculture*, II, 1042.

[60] Computed from information on Cincinnati trade in *Hunt's Merchants' Magazine*, XXIII (1850), 542–543.

the commerce in livestock and the railroads made their diverting influence felt in this indirect fashion.[61]

Because it is a case where railroad generated diversion was less conspicuous, the decline in corn shipments to New Orleans is instructive. Increased production in the northern areas of Illinois and Ohio, and Iowa's entrance as a large-scale supplier, tipped the balance in favor of the lakes. Improved feeder connections to the north encouraged such a response and assured an eastward flow. Without railroads, Iowa's surplus would have been shipped to St. Louis and thence to New Orleans. With the Burlington Railroad meeting the river at Davenport, an alternative path was provided. Even more significant than the railroads were the newly completed canals. The Illinois and Michigan Canal diverted northward production from the Illinois River region that had formerly been tributary to St. Louis. The Wabash and Erie Canal had the same effect in the Wabash Valley in southern Indiana. The canals were more prominent in deliveries of corn than the railroads. Although feeder roads participated in the traffic, declining southern consumption and the increasing attractiveness of a lake and canal voyage to the East were what counted.

In sum, the east-west railroad linkage of the 1850's did reduce the flow of trade through New Orleans. But it did not do so by affording the first route to market other than the river, as is often asserted.[62] The Erie Canal long before had done that. Rather, it was in the Ohio Valley that the railroad scored its most conspicuous success. The capriciousness of the river in the 1850's was of valuable assistance there. Berry writes, "severe droughts in 1854 and 1856 tied the rivers up for such long periods as to damage steamboat traffic in flour and certain other products beyond recovery. At such times the railbound traffic was so heavy that some westerners were afraid to ship by train." [63] The specific

---

[61] It is relevant that while there was undoubtedly an expansion in the eastern consumption of pork products from 1853 to 1861, the number of hogs packed in the West was roughly constant over that period (Berry, *Western Prices*, p. 223).

[62] For example: "Until the development of through lines . . . the only outlet for the produce of the Mississippi Valley was by way of the river through New Orleans." Harold G. Moulton, *Waterways Versus Railways* (Boston, 1926), p. 85.

[63] Berry, *Western Prices*, p. 90.

contribution of *through* rail connections was largely limited to that theater. By 1849 the northern part of the West was already fairly free of New Orleans influence; where it was not, the feeder canal and rail connections to the lakes made the difference, not the trunk lines.

Of what economic significance was such trade diversion? The reduction in transport costs associated with eastward rather than southward shipment was undoubtedly small, else New Orleans would not have done as well as it did in 1857, nor would there have been lingering proofs by leaders like De Bow of lower rates through the southern gateway. The marginal direct benefits of the trunk lines also speak to this. The substitution of the eastern for the southern market did reduce price seasonality and improve the terms of trade by closer convergence of price, however. These indirect effects have already been discussed. Here I want to explore a different linkage. Did the altered export flow also alter the flow of imports to the West and thus broaden the market for eastern manufactures? Victor Clark has argued that it did:

. . . the traffic of the Great Lakes country was drawn to the Mississippi highway. This diversion of commerce to a southern port was a disadvantage to eastern manufacturers in the northwestern market, for our heaviest foreign shipments were of cotton, and from the cotton metropolis trade routes, freights, exchanges, and mercantile connections favored the importation of European goods. As rapidly as railways supplanted rivers and canals, and made tributary to the northern lakes the trade that formerly had gone down the Mississippi, they placed eastern factories intermediate on the route from Europe to these markets, instead of at the end of a branch line almost equally distant from them.[64]

Clark is very wrong — both on the mechanics of trade diversion and the effects.

Trade had begun to flow eastward by lake long before the regional feeder railroads, or the trunk lines, had been constructed. When the accelerated pace of diversion occurred in the 1850's it was not a simple matter of railways supplanting canals and bringing the surplus to the lakes. Canals remained significant in the

[64] Clark, *History of Manufactures*, I, 352.

transportation of corn, for example; and provisions never became tributary to the lakes. More fundamentally, the initial conditions postulated by Clark, large-scale import of manufactures via New Orleans, never prevailed. Thus there was no scope for a process consisting of a shift in ports of entry and ultimate import substitution. From the earliest, even before the Erie Canal, with the exception of imports of sugar and coffee, the West received her supplies from the East. High valued manufactures always could bear the burdensome overland transport costs from the East; it was western produce that could not absorb the charges eastward.

In 1821, when the import data by customs districts begin, New York was already the leading American port, followed closely by Boston. Philadelphia and Baltimore each surpassed New Orleans in total trade. In exports, New York still led New Orleans at this date.[65] Not until the boom of the 1830's did New Orleans attain supremacy in exports, and by that time New York imported four times as much. Indeed, New Orleans was unable to supplant Boston as the second leading city in import volume. There never was any diversion of imports to the northern ports from New Orleans. The southern advocates of direct trade immediately prior to the Civil War were calling for a new regime of international trade, not a return to the old.

What imports New Orleans received were largely noncompetitive with American manufactures: coffee was always a leading commodity owing to the city's proximity to the Latin American market. In 1856 it represented more than a third of imports and was five times greater than imports of cotton and wool manufactures.[66] Earlier there is no easily accessible record, but results could not be far different. Regardless of the composition of foreign imports, what we do know is that before 1856 virtually no manufactures were shipped upriver. In 1835, of the 66,000 tons estimated to have been shipped northward from New Orleans to the West, more than half was salt, a third, sugar, a sixth, coffee. All the merchandise came from the East, as well as some salt. Merchandise alone amounted to 30,000 tons — approximately what was carried overland annually between 1818–1824 before the Erie

[65] *Compendium of the Seventh Census*, pp. 186–187.
[66] *Report on Internal Commerce for 1887*, p. 382.

296 RAILROADS AND ANTE-BELLUM ECONOMY

Canal was completed![67] It was no hypothetical trade for which the merchants of eastern cities were competing with their variety of transport innovations in the 1820's.

The lessened downriver trade of the 1850's did affect upriver returns, but not in manufactures. It was the South's distribution of sugar, salt, and coffee that suffered. While total imports into the West increased from 360,000 to 900,000 tons between 1849 and 1860, the imports forwarded by New Orleans showed a more modest rise from 125,000 to 200,000 tons. Almost as much coffee was shipped in 1849 as in 1860; sales of sugar registered an insignificant increase during an interval when western population and income were expanding at a great rate.[68] Although southern and western commercial interests were rapidly going their separate ways, the significance of this dissolving relationship to the national economy was probably less than to political union.

A. L. Kohlmeier has concluded from his analysis of changing interregional trade patterns that "the Ohio Valley was in 1860 as closely connected economically with the South as in 1835." [69] His case is weak in light of the foregoing discussion. Both direct southern consumption as well as re-exports were demonstrably smaller at the later than the initial date. The diversion in the Cincinnati trade is obvious. His *deus ex machina* is large river shipments from the West to the South bypassing New Orleans: "To the Northwest New Orleans was relatively a little less important than formerly, but the South as a whole was as important as ever." [70] As we have seen, there is no evidence to support such a position, nor any basis to claim that New Orleans was only a "little less important"; it was dramatically less important, particularly for the Ohio Valley. Southern leaders were not myopic in visualizing an independent economic status in the late 1850's. 1860 was not 1835 when Hayne could be excited with the prospect of a Charleston to Cincinnati rail connection. That chance had

[67] Kohlmeier, *Old Northwest*, pp. 7, 21.
[68] Kohlmeier, pp. 92–93, 205–208. Southern exports to the West in 1860 were amplified beyond Kohlmeier's account in the manner described in the technical appendix to "Antebellum Trade."
[69] Kohlmeier, *Old Northwest*, p. 213.
[70] *Old Northwest*, p. 213. Kohlmeier himself gives little credence to such an argument earlier. Cf. his p. 202.

irretrievably passed. The South was virtually self-sufficient in foodstuffs on the eve of the Civil War, and the re-export trade had dwindled to insignificant proportions. Political overtures to the West were without economic content. Although the Ohio Valley suffered from disruption at the outbreak of war, increasing government contracts and adequate transport capacity eastward allayed discontent. The real point is not that the Old Northwest needed the South in 1861, but that it could not do without the East.

Final Comments

Although the railroad patently did not create interregional flows, it left a major imprint upon their direction and magnitude even before 1860. The two regions bound together by rail, the East and West, expanded their trade rapidly while exchange with the South dwindled relatively. The through lines from the seaboard to the interior were not responsible alone for that accomplishment. It was the product of all the railroads, interregional and intraregional, and the total harvest of all their effects, direct and indirect. The diversion of trade from New Orleans to the East illustrates the multiplicity of causal elements nicely. The through lines increasingly absorbed the surplus of the Ohio Valley directly, even as feeder railroads in northern Illinois and Wisconsin were delivering large quantities of grain, not to the Mississippi, but to the lakes. The rapid growth of the lake area in turn reflects the attractiveness of a region with ample, and alternative, routes to market.

What railroads did *not* do before the Civil War was to forge a national market. The primitive state of physical integration not only prevented it, but probably also testifies to its unimportance. There were too few economies of scale in production, or distribution, to be reaped from direct rail contact and that is one reason why overtures in that direction were so limited. This was still a period before interchange of parts was universal, before standard products were marketed, before the full effects of industrialization were apparent, let alone realized. There was time enough for such things in the future. Not until the 1880's was a single, standard gauge established. Before 1860 what mattered more was extension of agricultural capacity and greater realization of its potential, and for this the more limited interchange that existed was sufficient, if not fully efficient. The railroad expansion of the 1850's opened to many individual farmers a choice not only of final destination, but various routings to that point. As a consequence, marketing patterns changed radically, but purchasing patterns much less so.

All in all, what this chapter has shown is a further dynamic aspect of railroadization. Like many of the other benefits, the contribution of a nascent railroad network and through connections was one that future generations enjoyed more than the ante-bellum economy. But there is no doubt that the latter, too, was affected by it.

Part IV

Concluding Observations

CHAPTER VIII

Some Implications for the Theory of Social Overhead Capital

Recapitulation

In 1859, inspired by the continuing railroad influenced depression, a contemporary economic commentator of note, Henry Carey Baird, bitterly assailed the innovation: "Our railroad system has cost more than $1,000,000 and has brought ruin upon nearly everyone connected with it, the nation included. What power would not the one-half portion of the amount expended in railways give to us if directed to the development of our mining, manufacturing, and mechanical resources." [1] Two years earlier, still in the flush of a railroad influenced prosperity, another correspondent had concluded far differently: "As a whole the railroads of the country are a success; they have developed the resources of the interior in a most wonderful manner; they have built up towns and villages in what, but for them, would have been a wilderness. . . ." [2] From the perspective of more than a century later, the latter view is the more accurate.

Our calculations have shown how railroad returns to capital, in the shape of net earnings and transport cost savings alone, fully justified the investment even before 1860. Fifteen percent per annum on the investment despite the arbitrary time horizon, and the limited calculation of returns, is impressive. It is difficult to imagine the country doing much better than that in any reasonable alternative. The immediate stream of private profits — for as enterprises they earned an early and satisfactory return — means that only if the harvest of indirect, social gains were

---

[1] *Hunt's Merchants' Magazine*, XLI (1859), 69.
[2] *Hunt's Merchants' Magazine*, XXXVII (1857), 326.

greater elsewhere could the ante-bellum economy have done as well in their absence. Yet railroad accomplishments in this sphere are exactly what stand out before 1861.

Quite apart from the benefits of lower cost transportation, there are the strong influences from the side of demand in the 1850's. Baird's reaction, ironically, testifies exactly how much railroads had come to mean for realized aggregate income. Beyond the magnitude of the investment itself, there is the induced sequence of migration and expansion of western agriculture that left its imprint on the decade in the form of an unmistakable construction boom. Other expenditures may have filled the gap, but this is by no means certain. Even if it be objected that these developments are secondary to the trend growth of supply, the railroad investment of the 1850's retains an important role. It was responsible directly for the largest part of the capital inflow from abroad during the period, and the induced investment it evoked may have arisen from changed preferences for the future rather than from a constant and independent supply of savings.[3]

At the sectoral level, railroad demands display their distinctive qualities more clearly. The nationwide dissemination of industrial skills through the on-going repair and replacement requirements of the growing network stands as an important accomplishment. So, too, does the impetus rail requirements afforded to the emergence of a modern, mineral fuel oriented iron industry and to a more advanced rolling mill technology. Although supply forces clearly were involved in each of these changes, the interdependence with demand requires that the latter not be ignored, particularly in light of the growing domestic rail industry through the 1850's. This is not to condone the exaggerations that have surrounded the backward linkages. Coal consumption, whether direct or indirect, was insignificant before the war, nor were railroad horsepower requirements dominant among industrial uses. And the role of railroads as suppliers of scrap as well as demanders

---

[3] Gallman, "Gross National Product," shows an increase in the share of capital formation in gross national product from 11 to 14 percent between the decades 1839–1848 and 1849–1858. Although it is impossible to attribute this observed increase to the railroad, the direction of the change is consistent with railroad influence in this sphere.

of pig iron must be explicitly recognized. Withal, this was an area where railroad expansion left its mark.

The prime beneficiary during the ante-bellum period was not industry, however, but agriculture. In this evaluation I diverge sharply from the position taken by Rostow, who has asserted: "Railroadization was well underway in the United States in the 1840's . . . ; and it was the industrial rather than agricultural consequences . . . that created the take-off." [4] Derived demands, a favored Rostow linkage, although they had positive effects by the 1850's as railroad investment increased, were an insignificant influence earlier. In particular, railroad demands for iron were independent of the rapid growth of the domestic industry in the 1840's. Nor do the inducements afforded manufacturing by lower transport costs seem capable of explaining the observed industrial surge of that decade. Distribution costs were a small fraction of total expenses, and it is possible to identify other factors, like lower cotton prices, tariff protection, and the large English demands for iron, that were more significant to the initiation and continuation of that expansion. By the time the New England railroads were completed the peak in production already had been attained, and imports captured an increasing share of the market in the 1850's despite improved interregional communication.

Whereas the causes underlying this industrial breakthrough seem to be independent of the railroad, the agricultural expansion of the 1850's owes much more to it. This is exactly what one would expect from a sector whose products were of low value relative to weight — a ton of wheat sold for $30, a ton of cloth for perhaps 15 times as much; whose products traveled farther to an ultimate market; and whose transport alternatives included a mix involving more overland haulage on much worse roads. Although exogenous forces, in the shape of the exports induced by the Irish famine at the end of the 1840's, help to account for reviving prosperity then, continued migration and agricultural investment in the face of falling prices and demand speak for the role of the railroad in influencing supply. It did so both by making the interior more attractive and by encouraging further surpluses

---

[4] Rostow, "Leading Sectors and the Take-Off," p. 14.

in the areas originally settled. Because the population largely anticipated railroad construction to the interior, there was little lag between social overhead investment and increased output there, and of course the same was true of the settled regions. This anticipatory migration in turn made it possible for railroad expansion to occur under private auspices to serve present needs, and obviated widespread building ahead of demand.

The direct contribution to potential supply from the westward movement of agriculture during the decade seems to be rather small, perhaps a tenth as large as the benefits to the economy from reduced transport costs. But coupled with the large incidence of these cost savings to agriculture, as well as the difficult-to-measure gains deriving from the induced sequence identified above, there seems little doubt that agriculture, not industry, felt the prime effects of the innovation. In a larger sense also, Rostow errs when he links railroads to industry and thence to the take-off. One of the distinctive features of American development is a progressive and commercial agriculture amidst abundant land. Rapid growth in this environment did not take the same form as in older countries and, in particular, was not dependent solely upon advances in the manufacturing sector.

As between the relative significance of direct benefits and other external economies it is more difficult to choose. Numerically, the decision is clearly in favor of the former. But this may be a reflection more of our limited abilities for quantification than of the state of the world. Although we can identify induced developmental sequences, whether arising from derived demands or forward linkages, it is a herculean task to assign values to them because the alternative path of growth is largely unknown. How much of the pig iron actually consumed by railroads would have been absorbed in other uses? What proportion of actual railroad investment would have been replaced by other outlays? To what extent would migration to the West have continued without the railroad's influence? Over what range of economies of scale did railroad extension of the market operate? Only in the case of direct benefits is the alternative clearly defined by the structure of the nonrailroad transportation system. Or, to put the matter another way, at the present time comparative statics are much easier to quantify than dynamics. Yet, as we have seen, minimal effects upon variables like labor supply, foreign capital inflow, et cetera, redound to large consequences upon output. Specifically, beyond the minimum $14.9 million calculated as the annual gain associated with the redistribution of the agricultural labor force between 1850 and 1860, a mere absolute reduction of 5 percent in the size of that western labor force adds another $17.7 million. Again, if half of the foreign capital made available for railroad construction had not been diverted to other projects, total savings and hence investment would have been 1 percent smaller between 1849 and 1860. Cumulated, a decline in 1859 income of almost $25 million might be expected.[5] The potential effects from the side of aggregate demand were still greater as railroad investment climbed to more than 15 percent of total capital formation in the 1850's. Because of the wide variety of consequences, extending to all industries and inclusive of many inducements to expansion, such a calculus inevitably is partial. At the risk of exaggeration, I am inclined, therefore, to come down on the side of larger indirect effects, if only because of the deferment of direct benefits to the end of the period when they were at least partially offset by resource redundancy. Up through 1855, as railroad transport services remained secondary, a decision in favor of the induced sequences seems certain, and the superiority probably applies to the ante-bellum period as a whole. This allocation suggests a social rate of return to railroad investment well above 20 percent, and, indeed, close to 30 percent.

Such an affirmation of the importance of the railroad does not imply that it was singularly crucial to the increased pace of economic activity before the Civil War. Without the innovation, growth would surely have been slower, but the country would not have withered: 5 percent, or even 10 percent, of 1859 income is a small sum in this context. Few innovations can be expected to become indispensable within brief years of their introduction. Certainly the steam engine, or electric power, did no such thing. For that matter, the range of potential solutions to specific prob-

[5] This has been calculated on the assumption that the actual annual compound growth rate of 5.37 percent was correspondingly lowered by 1 percent. The discussion of the role of railroads in securing foreign loans occurs in Chap. III, p. 117.

lems may be so large that no individual response is ever really essential. Thus, in the absence of railroads a concerted program of canal and road investment might have reduced the effects still further as Professor Fogel has alleged. Still, from the standpoint of historical fact, it was the railroad that actually brought the lower transport costs and the induced sequences, and these must be credited to it.

Implications

In a broader sense, this has been a case study of social overhead investment in an economy just about to emerge, or recently launched, into sustained, long-run growth. As such, these observations have an interest beyond their immediate historical setting.

The major emphasis of the theory of social overhead investment is the induced sequences it evokes. As Hirschman states it, "Investment in SOC [social overhead capital] is advocated not because of its direct effect on final output, but because it permits and, in fact invites DPA [directly productive activities] to come in." [6] In the ante-bellum United States such expectations were realized, but in a manner that casts a shadow upon overly optimistic anticipations in many underdeveloped countries in the contemporary world. The region in the United States with least industrialization, the South, had substantial railroad mileage in 1860, much of it newly opened. But the hoped for impetus to diversification did not come, despite conscious efforts to bring it about.[7] In part, the pattern of construction from interior to ports is to blame; but in larger measure it was the continuing profitability of the export staple economy. Equally relevant is the character of the success story in the West. There it was largely an agricultural response to social overhead provision that was prominent. The ability of an infrastructure to alter the economic environment in favor of industrialization is perhaps weaker than we appreciate.

[6] Albert O. Hirschman, *The Strategy of Economic Development* (New Haven, 1958), p. 84.
[7] See a typical prediction of "diversions of labor and capital, which must be greatly beneficial to the South," in *De Bow's Review*, XII (1852), 499.

What social overhead theory largely ignores are the direct benefits. It does so out of preoccupation with the obstacles and barriers to growth and low levels of existent activity. It is not far from such a focus to the theorem that social overhead projects must precede private investment. The American railroad experience did not conform to these conditions. In part this was because the natural waterways and canals represented an already extant transport network. But many countries today also have progressed well beyond a primitive state of communication. For these the American lesson that the process of development can create its infrastructure and can achieve direct gains as it goes along is of relevance. Hirschman's development strategy of inducing such simultaneity has better historical basis than the theoretical preconception that social overhead investment must always come first.

Another doubtful preconception is the necessity of large governmental subsidies, whether social overhead investment precedes *or* follows. What justifies such aid are technical characteristics of the overhead capital — long gestation periods, durability, indivisibility — that add up to low private rates of return. Extensive external economies in turn mean great social profitability. So long as the social return exceeds the private gain, and decisions are determined by the latter, insufficient investment is the inevitable result. Government recognition of broader advantages can redress the balance.

Yet Americans did not lack for railroads before the Civil War despite the generous extent to which market response determined the pace and timing of the construction of the rail network. Only in the 1830's was aid both prominent and unsuccessful; the recent useful destruction of the myth of ideological laissez-faire in the United States must not give rise to the equally erroneous impression of all-embracing, and essential, public promotion.

Two sets of factors produced this happy consequence in the ante-bellum United States. First, the private return on most projects was sufficient to evoke investor support. The practice of building behind demand was largely responsible for this, and this was possible in turn because the technological and financial barriers did not operate with anything like the force they are currently thought to have possessed. Gestation periods were fore-shortened by the practice of opening small sections of line as they were completed. Engineering considerations always ranked second to early completion, as the small extent of tunneling and double tracking, among other characteristics, bear witness. The financial analogue consisted of a large number of local projects substituted for a single, coordinated enterprise with much more concentrated capital requirements. Such division may have reduced the over-all efficiency of the transport system, but it did considerably ease access to funds in an imperfect and fragmented capital market. Both adaptations limited the adverse consequences of indivisibility. Rostow's example of the incidence of lumpiness is particularly ill chosen as a result: "You either build the line from, say, Chicago to San Francisco or you do not: an incomplete railway line is of limited use. . . ."[8] The first railroad built westward from Chicago was the Galena in 1848. It opened its first ten-mile section to Harlem and immediately became one of the most profitable enterprises in the West.

Beyond these adjustments of timing and allocation, American technological ingenuity found ways to economize on the absolute quantities of capital needed. Durability was sacrificed for lower capital costs long after the abortive solutions of strap iron rails and lumber piling were discarded. Foreign visitors to the United States never failed to be impressed by the differences between American and continental practices. One of these, David Stevenson, assented to reissue in the 1850's of his *Sketch of the Civil Engineering of North America*, originally written in the late 1830's, with the explanation by the publisher "that he has [done so] chiefly in view of its application to new countries" like India.[9]

Favorable private returns thus led to substantial investment. The question remains whether it was sufficient in light of the additional social gain not reckoned by individual decision makers. There are reasons to believe that it was, and these constitute the second part of our explanation of the satisfactory operation of the American market mechanism. First, investors did not re-

[8] Rostow, *Stages of Economic Growth*, p. 25.
[9] David Stevenson, *Sketch of the Civil Engineering of North America*, 2nd ed. (London, 1859), note opposite p. x.

spond simply to current evidences of private profitability. The demonstrated divergence between social and private returns in the investment process arises in part from the assumption that they did. Take what has become the classic illustration of the incidence of dynamic external economies:[10]

> Investment in industry A will cheapen its product; . . . the profits of industry B, created by the lower price of factor A, call for investment and expansion in industry B, one result of which will be an increase in industry B's demand for industry A's product . . . equilibrium is reached only when successive doses of investment and expansion in the two industries have led to simultaneous elimination of profits in both. . . . We can conclude, therefore, that when an investment gives rise to pecuniary external economies, its private profitability understates its social desirability.

This sequence involves not only the absence of perfect foresight, but virtual exclusion of foresight altogether. Expectations do exist, however, and in the instance of American railroad investment, they were typically optimistic, sometimes to later sorrow. This was reasonable. One characteristic of social overhead capital is its intermediateness to a large range of final activities. So much better, therefore, is the opportunity to recoup some gain from the dynamic sequence initially set in motion. From the earliest this was well understood. The first annual report of the Norwich and Worcester Railroad, in an already settled region, recognizes that "in regard to transportation of merchandise, etc. there is abundant reason to be satisfied that it will equal our highest anticipations, and *like all similar undertakings greatly increase the business upon its line.*" [11]

Beyond such reckoning of an ultimate financial gain, there was further cause for conformity to the signals given by the social return. That was the ubiquity of local investment, particularly in equity. Although many of the indirect effects of railroads inevitably were external to the enterprise, they could accrue to the

[10] Tibor Scitovsky, "Two Concepts of External Economies, " *Journal of Political Economy*, LXII (April 1954), 198.
[11] Massachusetts Committee [of the General Court] on Railways and Canals, *Annual Report of the Railroad Corporations of Massachusetts, 1837* (Boston, 1838), p. 51 (italics mine).

owners of that enterprise. Thus land owners invested in railroads not for the private return the projects earned, but for the indirect transport advantages that ultimately raised his land value. The manufacturer contributed, not only for the dividends he received, but for the additional profits he could subsequently earn. Appeals were always phrased in such terms, and the long rolls of investors proximate to the line testify to their success. This method of internalization enabled the private market response nonetheless to reflect envisioned external economies.

America before the Civil War thus did not suffer from a deficiency of railroad investment despite the private nature of its provision. Indeed, when government intervened, it more often than not led to excess and wasteful construction. The response of cities and towns to the large potential loss of not having a railroad typically was to subsidize extensions. The actual returns from the facility were far smaller than the loss from not having it, because everybody acted in similar fashion and any relative advantage was offset. Competition of individual railroads encouraged defensive investment in much the same way. The lurking danger in the United States always was excessive investment in poorly situated railroads that would never earn a return, private or social, and not insufficient accumulation.

A further divergence between the theory and the American experience is the neglect of expenditure effects in the a priori model. This is understandable. Within the chronically inflationary underdeveloped countries today, aggregate demand is not likely to prove inadequate. For the pre-1860 United States there were no such guarantees. Hence there was abundant scope for influence from the side of large total investment. That the theory fails to discuss specific backward linkages also is understandable. It is not easy to generalize about the derived demands of the broad gamut of social overhead projects — ranging from investment in irrigation to that in education. Some will involve substantial construction outlays, others relatively little; some will require skilled personnel, others unskilled labor. Only to the extent that all represent a modern technology in common may one predict some positive, ultimate impetus from the side of demand. By contrast, one of the most impressive features of railroad development in the United States and elsewhere was the compelling backward linkages set in motion.

Indeed, the very generality of social overhead theory weakens its descriptive relevance. It fails completely to render the *composite* character of nineteenth-century American railroad investment that made it so potent a historical force. It was not only owing to the induced sequences that railroads were important, but also to their more efficient substitution for other transport agencies and their industrially biased mix of demands. Such a package of potentially large influences on both demand and supply is rare enough. What made the innovation so beneficial in fact was the specific American historical context. At every turn the circumstances of the American success were a far cry from the initial conditions in the low income countries today. The extensive role of private investment bespeaks a responsiveness to market forces, a pool of local capital, a foresight — properties that go far to explain the substantial gains reaped from lower cost transportation. The concentration of those benefits in agriculture, moreover, testifies to an economy with abundant fertile land, farmers that were profit motivated and market oriented, and a population that was geographically mobile. Underdeveloped countries, wracked with large and unproductive agricultural sectors, illiteracy, concentrations of wealth, frequently wasteful governmental intervention, can take scant hope from the efficacy of railroad investment in the United States before the Civil War.

Appendixes

Selected Bibliography

Index

APPENDIX A

The Derivation of Output Estimates

Published statistics of railroad receipts and output before the Civil War are both sparse and unreliable. The principal ones have been brought together in Table 40. Column (1), which is the longest and most continuous series, alas is also the most untrustworthy. With the exception of 1860, these data have been calculated by taking 12 percent of another series on cost of construction. Since the costs are nothing more than a mileage series multiplied by a constant $35,000 per mile, the equivalent and more direct assumption is that every mile of road in operation from 1848 to 1858 yielded in every year gross revenue of $4,200. No wonder the regular rise the series exhibits. The receipts for 1860 are also apparently based upon a "12 percent rule," but applied to the *American Railroad Journal* estimate of cost for that year rather than a scaled mileage series.

Column (2) contains the single receipts statistic for the period derived by aggregation over individual railroads. The Secretary of the Treasury conducted a survey of all railroads in the spring of 1856 and requested a variety of information, including total receipts for the nearest fiscal year. These returns were published in the fall of that year in the *Report on Finances*. The coverage was surprisingly complete, although key omissions like the Michigan Southern Railroad (with almost two million dollars of receipts) and certain other large roads cause it to understate the total, and particularly the regional subtotal in the West. This estimate even as it stands, however, refutes the mechanical technique underlying the first series.

Found in column (3) are the pre-1860 statistics reported by the

TABLE 40. Ante-bellum railway output statistics

Year	Gross receipts (thousands of dollars)				Ton-miles (millions)	
	(1)	(2)	(3)	(4)	(5)	(6)
1848	22,113	—	—	—	—	—
1849	26,026	—	—	—	—	—
1850	31,290	—	—	—	—	—
1851	37,615	—	39,566	—	—	—
1852	45,980	—	—	—	1,101	—
1853	56,463	—	—	—	1,158	—
1854	65,681	—	—	—	1,490	—
1855	77,580	91,183	84,250	—	1,719	3,402 (1,404)
1856	87,017	—	—	132,000	2,193	—
1857	98,950	—	—	—	2,200	—
1858	106,014	—	—	—	2,306	—
1859	—	—	—	100,000	2,521	—
1860	140,000	—	—	120,000	3,282	—

Source: (1) American Railroad Journal, XXXI (1858), 377; for 1860, ibid., XXXIV (1861), 17.

(2) Report on the Finances for 1855–56, Senate Exec. Doc. No. 2, 34th Congress, 2nd Session, p. 423. Estimate refers to year 1855–1856.

(3) Interstate Commerce Commission, Railway Statistics before 1890 (Statement No. 32151, 1932), p. 8.

(4) 1856: American Railroad Journal, XXX (1857), 1. 1859: Hillyer's American Railroad Magazine, I (1859), 548. 1860: Reprint from Railroad Record in De Bow's Review, XXVII (1860), 243. Estimate refers to year 1859–1860.

(5) Carl Snyder, Business Cycles and Business Measurements (New York: Macmillan Co., 1927), p. 238.

(6) See (2) and text.

Interstate Commerce Commission in its publication, Railway Statistics before 1890. There is no further explanation of their source than the declaration that they "have been copied for convenient use from the various annual issues of Poor's Manual of Railroads for the years 1869 to 1900." Other evidence suggests that the 1855 figure is based upon the aforementioned Report on Finances. These data have the widest circulation since they appear in the census Historical Statistics volume.

The final three receipts estimates in column (4) are informed contemporary judgments. The 1860 result is explicitly stated to be an extrapolation of sample results upon "certain leading roads." Other estimates of a similar sort also were current in the railroad literature. Although they agree in rough orders of magnitude, that is all.

Moving now to physical output, column (5) contains a continuous series of railroad ton-mileage between 1852 and 1860. Carl Snyder first presented them in his *Business Cycles and Business Measurements*, and they were subsequently reprinted in Schumpeter's *Business Cycles* and from there, elsewhere. Uncritical use is not to be recommended, however. For 1852 and 1853, one railroad only, the New York and Erie, is the basis for the national total; in 1854 the New York Central enters the sample; in 1855, the Pennsylvania, and in 1857, the Pittsburgh, Fort Wayne, and Chicago. The maximum content of the sample is thus four railroads, accounting in 1860 for 532 million ton-miles, or one sixth of Snyder's total. It is hardly necessary to stress the hazards in extrapolating national ton-mileage by this means.

The final column in Table 40 presents 2 ton-mileage totals from the *Report on Finances*. The 3.4 billion figure is the result actually printed in the report. It is subject to gross error as it stands. One New York railroad 100 miles long and with receipts of less than $200,000 is duly credited with more than *2 billion* ton-miles in fiscal 1855. Two thirds of national freight service is thus presumably contributed by a railroad not only modest in size, but one forced to default upon its interest payments in the very year it appears so central to American internal commerce. The ton-mileage for this road given in the New York report for that year is a more appropriate 2.4 million ton-miles, a substitution which explains the parenthetical 1.4 billion figure in column (6). This latter unfortunately is not a much better guide than the original estimate, because it suffers from understatement. The queries on passenger- and ton-mileage in the Treasury survey were answered far less frequently than those on receipts.

Related information on net receipts also could be tabulated. Not surprisingly the inventor of column (1) easily derives such a series by multiplying his gross receipts by a constant 42 percent. There are net revenue analogues to columns (2) and (3) as well. Likewise, the *Report on Finances* contains a passenger-mile estimate. Such further detail is unnecessary. The discussion has already made plain the uncertain basis of all existing quantitative information on these subjects, not to mention the almost complete absence of national data on passenger and freight revenues. This appendix is designed to remedy this undesirable state of affairs. New series of gross receipts, net receipts, passenger earnings, freight earnings, ton-miles, and passenger-miles have been constructed for four separate years spaced from 1839 to 1859. Tables 41 through 44 present the results, by state, for 1839, 1849, 1855–1856, and 1859, respectively. These benchmark dates not only are sufficient for trend analyses, but the location of one in the middle of the decade when railroad output was growing most rapidly gives us further detail when it is most useful.

Certain general observations pertinent to all the Tables may be helpful before individual discussion of each. All receipts series for the eastern states for 1839, 1849, and 1859 come from Henry V. Poor's summaries in his *History of the Railroads and Canals of the United States*, published in 1860. Since the accuracy of this source has come into recent question, a few words in its defense are required.[1] Although it is true that Poor's data are subject to omissions, let alone occasional arithmetical and typographical errors, the fact remains that short of recalculation of hundreds of individual reports they are by far the best we have; moreover, I am convinced from a comparison with State reports that the effort of redoing his work would not yield a very much different set of results. The major weakness of his summary tables is his practice of entering a road only upon completion and not during construction. This admittedly distorts the cost of construction totals to the point where they cannot be differenced to obtain annual investment flows. But because earnings are negligible until operation of a sizable part of the line, this discontinuity of Poor's tabulations does not lead to similar difficulty with his data on receipts.

A comparison of Poor's summary results with our 1855–1856 state totals, which were laboriously built up from individual rail-

---

[1] See Wicker, "Railroad Investment before the Civil War," *Trends in the American Economy in the Nineteenth Century* and also George Roger Taylor's "Comment" in the same volume.

road reports in the *Report on Finances*, Poor's *Railroads and Canals* and the *American Railroad Journal*, yields the following results:

	(1) Poor (thousands of dollars)	(2) Table 43 (thousands of dollars)	(3) (1) ÷ (2) × 100
Me.	1,394.0	1,540.9	90.5
N.H.	2,012.6	1,960.9	102.7
Vt.	1,587.0	1,552.9	102.1
Mass.	9,290.3	9,178.5	101.2
Conn.	3,093.6	3,224.9	95.9
R.I.	286.6	264.8	92.5
N.Y.	19,695.2	18,822.1	104.5
N.J.	3,541.9	3,367.2	105.0
Penn.	14,126.8	15,013.3	94.1
Del.	68.9	0.0	—
Md.	4,771.1	4,848.0	98.5
Total	60,762.4	59,773.5	101.7

In total, Poor's results are only 1.7 percent higher for the same group of eastern states. Such aggregate conformity is reassuring, as is closer examination of the individual states. One of the greatest percentage deviations occurs in Maine, which has little weight in the total.[2] Two thirds of the difference there is explained by our inclusion of an estimate of earnings of the Portland and Kennebec Railroad for part of the year (on the basis of an 18-month overlapping figure supplied by Poor himself). Of the $147,000 divergence, $29,000 is explained by the different fiscal year of the reports filed with the Treasury Department, and only $20,000 is explained by outright omissions. I submit that this comparison verifies an earlier assessment of the quality of Poor's

[2] The discrepancy in Delaware is actually the largest percentage deviation, but it is too small in absolute terms to merit much attention. It is brought about by Poor's double count of the receipts of the Newcastle and Frenchtown Railroad, which are already included in the revenues of the Philadelphia, Wilmington, and Baltimore.

work: "Poor's 'history,' considered as an assemblage of financial statistics relating to the railroads of the country in their formative period and as a bibliography of early American railway law, is a product of care, thoroughness and labor." [3]

A second comment relevant to all the estimates concerns dating. Pre-Civil War railroad fiscal years varied widely in individual roads and states. New York railroads, for example, reported for a fiscal year ending September 30; Massachusetts roads, November 30. Others kept their books in any number of different ways. No attempt has been made here to adjust all railroads to a comparable reporting period; such a task would be hopeless. In general, the fiscal year with the most months in the specified calendar year has been used. In Table 43, however, so much of the data refers to a fiscal year ending sometime in 1856 that the joint dating 1855–1856 is used to reflect this difference. What we get, therefore, is not a flow corresponding to any exact calendar year but a flow centered in it, with some reports extending forward, others back. This limitation does not seriously impair the utility of the information.

There is one final point on coverage. The general rule has been exclusion of receipts on city passenger lines as well as subsidiary feeders to canals in the Pennsylvania anthracite region. The former is a matter of choice, the latter of necessity. It is impossible to segregate the railroad operations of the canal companies from total transportation and occasionally even from total sales of coal. Thus, although the investment in such lines is included in Appendix B — because they employed steam power — they typically are not counted here. From the tonnage of the affected canals the approximate distortion can be determined. It amounts to less than 40 million ton-miles in 1859 or no more than 1.5 percent of railroad freight output. Not only are the exclusions small, but also, for the calculation of general purpose railroad transport services, they may be desirable.

1839 Output

With these introductory remarks out of the way, we can move on to the specific tables. First, Table 41 for 1839. The limited

[3] Dunbar, *History of Travel*, IV, 1381–1382.

railroad mileage in operation in the West and South at this date relative to later years means that the large bulk of the receipts data come directly from Poor's *Railroads and Canals*. Thus, although the information on non-Eastern railroads is sparser for this year than any other, it also affects less the accuracy of the aggregate. This is evident from the fact that the sum of receipts estimated for those railroads for which inadequate direct information exists amounts to considerably less than 10 percent of the total. No more than $510,000 of total earnings (including entries for which some indirect evidence serves as the basis) falls into this category, as well as proportional amounts of the other series. The decision to exclude certain railroads which Gerstner reported as operating in 1839 does not affect this conclusion. This mileage was principally in the southern states and much of it either opened late in 1839 or subsequently failed. Even if all the questionable mileage was included, the percentage deviation from the total reported in Table 41 would only amount to about 2 percent.

These relatively firm earnings data stand in contrast to the less certain passenger- and ton-mile statistics that can be derived from them. No state breakdown at all is attempted for these and so they are not presented in the table proper. The estimates are based upon Gerstner's comments upon typical freight and passenger charges. In summarizing the financial returns "upon those railroads which I have inspected," the generalization was made that "passenger fares were set at five cents per mile and the tonnage rate at seven and a half cents per mile." [4] Since Gerstner visited a substantial sample of the operating roads, his report on rates must be given careful consideration. This is particularly true since the independent estimate of receipts in Table 41 approaches rather closely the slightly more than $3000 of revenue per mile assumed by Gerstner in the same discussion.

There is other evidence of such high average charges, moreover. For example, in 1838 the directors of the South Carolina Railroad sought authorization for higher maximum rates from the state

---

[4] Franz Anton von Gerstner, "Letters on Internal Improvements in the United States," *Journal of the Franklin Institute*, n.s., XXIV (1840), 295. The accuracy of Gerstner's work is discussed in Appendix B where it is relied upon extensively in connection with the investment estimates for the 1830's.

TABLE 41. Railway output, 1839

	Total receipts	Net earnings	Passenger receipts	Freight receipts
			(thousands of dollars)	
Me.	19.7	5.2	9.5	10.2
N.H.	0.0	0.0	0.0	0.0
Vt.	.0	.0	.0	.0
Mass.	1073.3	486.9	696.0	337.6
Conn.	31.9	20.4	20.0	10.0
R.I.	100.0	50.0	74.0	20.0
New England	1224.9	562.5	799.5	377.8
N.Y.	1088.9	573.1	976.7	60.9
N.J.	997.1	451.6	661.3	272.2
Pa.	1470.0	602.1	738.9	617.9
Del.[a]	0.0	0.0	0.0	0.0
Md.	722.2	210.3	430.2	283.3
Middle Atlantic	4278.2	1837.1	2807.1	1234.3
Va.	599.6	170.3	261.3	288.2
N.C.	151.8	50.0	110.0	25.0
S.C.	403.0	88.7	179.3	195.3
Ga.	298.6	150.8	99.5	182.1
Fla.	21.0	6.3	13.0	7.0
South	1474.0	466.1	663.1	697.6
Ky.	28.0	8.4	16.0	10.0
Tenn.	0.0	0.0	0.0	0.0
Ala.	46.0	13.8	23.0	20.0
Miss.	18.5	5.6	10.0	8.5
La.	124.0	50.0	93.0	31.0
Tex.	0.0	0.0	0.0	0.0
Southwest	216.5	77.8	142.0	69.5
Ohio	15.0	7.5	4.0	11.0
Ind.	10.0	3.0	3.0	7.0
Ill.	0.0	0.0	0.0	0.0
Mich.	150.0	80.0	85.0	65.0
Wisc.	0.0	0.0	0.0	0.0
West	175.0	90.5	92.0	83.0
Total	7368.6	3034.0	4503.7	2462.2

legislature. In December new rates of $7\frac{1}{2}$ cents per passenger-mile and 10 cents per ton-mile were approved.[5] Similarly, the *Tenth Annual Report of the Baltimore and Ohio Railroad* (1836), in emphasizing the uneconomical cheapness of its own rates of 3 cents per passenger-mile and $4\frac{1}{2}$ cents per ton-mile, compared charges on other roads. These included the following:

	Passenger rate	Freight rate
	(cents per mile)	
Petersburg Railroad (Va.)	5	10
Winchester and Potomac (Va.)	6	7

[5] Derrick, *Centennial History*, p. 114.

Source: *Receipts and Net Earnings:* Me. through Md., except R. I.: Poor, *Railroads and Canals, passim.*

R.I.: 50 miles at $2000 per mile for gross earnings based on Report of Providence and Stonington for year ending August 31, 1840, reprinted in *Hazard's United States Commercial and Statistical Register* III (1841), 394; net earnings inferred from same source and receipts distributed between passenger and freight like those of Boston and Providence Railroad.

Va.: *American Railroad Journal* XXXIII (1860), 973.

N.C.: Cecil K. Brown, *A State Movement in Railroad Development* (Chapel Hill, 1928), pp. 31–44, 50. Raleigh and Gaston total receipts distributed like experience of 1840's on that road. Wilmington and Weldon gross receipts estimated at $100,000, and net at $50,000 on basis of report of 1840 operations; distributed according to this later report.

S.C.: Derrick, *Centennial History*, p. 160. Fiscal years 1839 and 1840 averaged. Net earnings estimated from 1839 ratio (slightly modified for better fiscal 1840 experience) derived by multiplying Derrick's average operating cost per mile run (p. 111) by miles run given in Phillips, *History of Transportation*, p. 160.

Ga.: Phillips, *History of Transportation*, pp. 244, 264. Receipts on Georgia Central distributed like those on Georgia Railroad.

La.: Based upon operating information for Pontchatrain Railroad presented in Franz Anton von Gerstner, *Die Innern Communicationen der Vereinigten Staaten von Nord Amerika* (Vienna, 1842–1843), II, 303. An additional allowance of $2000 per mile has been made for 12 miles of the Carrolton and Lake Borgne railroads then in operation.

Mich.: Gerstner, *Die Innern Communicationen*, II, 24, 32, for information on the Erie and Kalamazoo and the Michigan Central.

Ohio: Gerstner, *Die Innern Communicationen*, II, 354, for information on the Mad River Railroad. Similar operating results assumed for the Sandusky and Mansfield.

All others: Mileage of railroads in operation (derived from Gerstner, but not identical to his totals for reasons discussed in text) multiplied by $1000 per mile, except $500 in case of Indiana.

[a] New Castle and Frenchtown Railroad included in report of the Philadelphia, Wilmington, and Baltimore.

	Passenger rate	Freight rate
	(cents per mile)	
Portsmouth and Roanoke (Va.)	6	8
Boston and Providence (Mass.)	5	10
Boston and Lowell (Mass.)	3.5	7
Mohawk and Hudson (N.Y.)	5	8

The conclusion that "there are but few railroads in the Union upon which the charges are not higher than those on the B & O" was obviously correct, and the legislature authorized an increase of one cent in the former passenger mile rate.[6]

The passenger- and ton-mile totals for the United States implied by Gerstner's rates and the receipts data are 32.8 million ton-miles and 90.1 million passenger-miles. In addition to these estimates, upper bounds of 60.3 million ton-miles and 155.3 million passenger-miles have been computed by using the passenger and freight rates prevailing in 1849. The 1849 charges of 2.9 cents per passenger-mile and 4.0 cents per ton-mile undoubtedly understate 1839 rates by a good margin and hence overstate traffic service. In all likelihood, therefore, ton-miles did not exceed 40 million in number nor did passenger-miles climb beyond the 100-million mark by the end of the first decade of railroad operation in the United States.

1849 Output

Table 42 portrays the situation ten years later. Again eastern railroads, for which information is most complete, predominate. The number of completed southern and western lines is still small and their operations account for an insignificant proportion of national revenue. This potential source of error is further limited by better data for noneastern railroads at this later date. As a result, Table 42 is quite exact. Railroads whose direct reports were unavailable contribute less than 2 percent of gross receipts; the proportion is only marginally greater for passenger and freight earnings and for the net revenue.

Although the receipts and earnings data for 1849 have a firm basis in railroad reports, again the same does not hold for the passenger- and ton-mileage estimates. Few railroads kept records of physical output at this early date. The procedure used in deriv-

[6] Quoted in Hungerford, *Baltimore and Ohio*, I, 187–188.

ing the 1839 estimates has therefore been applied again; that is, average passenger and freight rates have been divided into the appropriate receipts to yield the output figures. Here, however, the rates are far better grounded. They come from a survey of charges covering almost all operating railroads in 1848 and were published in the *American Railroad Journal*, XXI (1848), 467. There is enough information to permit a regional breakdown, helpful in light of the substantial variation in rates in different parts of the country. In certain instances, when the variation within the region was large, state rates were used for greater accuracy. The average rates actually used are the following:

	Passenger rate	*Freight rate*
	(cents per mile)	
New England	2.5	4.5
Middle Atlantic	3.0	
N.Y.		4.0
N.J.		6.0
Penn.		3.5
Md.		3.0
South	4.3	4.5
Southwest	5.0	7.0
West	3.0	4.0

These are not simple averages of the quoted rates, but are best guesses of the charges prevailing. For example, the first and second class freight rates credited to Mississippi and Alabama railroads are well over ten cents per mile; it is doubtful whether the *revenue ton-mile rate*, which is a weighted average of all classes of freight, was in fact so large.

Despite this problem, the resulting passenger- and ton-mile aggregates probably represent railroad output in that year within a small margin of error. Upper bounds based upon regional 1855–1856 rates indicate maximums about 25 percent larger than the actual estimates. The divergence is greater for ton-miles than passenger-miles because freight rates declined much more rapidly than the already low passenger rates. No set of lower bounds is included in Table 42 although they can be determined from the 1839 rates. The minimum of 272 million passenger-miles and 187

TABLE 42. Railway output, 1849

	Total receipts	Net earnings	Passenger receipts	Freight receipts	Passenger-miles 1849	Passenger-miles Upper bound	Ton-miles 1849	Ton-miles Upper bound
		(thousands of dollars)				(thousands)		
Me.	185.0	103.7	149.3	32.4				
N.H.	1,100.8	511.6	486.3	546.6				
Vt.	57.3	33.6	25.1	32.2				
Mass.	6,271.6	3,002.1	3,379.1	2,589.5				
Conn.	1,036.5	563.7	502.8	470.7				
R.I.	181.0	95.8	117.8	56.5				
New England	8,832.2	4,310.5	4,660.4	3,727.9	186,416.0	186,416.0	82,842.2	104,716.2
N.Y.	5,986.2	3,317.9	3,231.9	2,472.9				
N.J.	2,127.3	896.0	1,402.1	621.5				
Pa.	4,547.8	2,258.4	1,361.9	2,881.7				
Del.ᵃ	—	—	—	—				
Md.	1,809.9	804.5	644.6	1,065.8				
Middle Atlantic	14,471.2	7,276.8	6,640.5	7,041.9	221,350.0	296,450.8	190,041.7	283,947.7
Va.	749.1	267.4	314.2	362.8				
N.C.	330.4	64.7	169.1	67.0				
S.C.	892.4	428.5	223.3	622.0				
Ga.	1,625.8	894.6	368.0	1,187.4				
Fla.	21.0	6.3	13.0	7.0				
South	3,618.7	1,661.5	1,087.6	2,246.2	25,293.0	58,498.3	49,915.6	62,813.2
Ky.	66.0	32.0	40.0	23.0				
Tenn.	—	—	—	—				
Ala.	167.0	71.0	90.0	55.0				
Miss.	120.0	60.0	68.0	46.0				
La.	179.0	70.0	130.0	45.0				
Tex.	—	—	—	—				
Southwest	532.0	243.0	328.0	169.0	6,560.0	9,398.3	2,414.3	4,884.4
Ohio	770.1	399.9	403.9	345.1				
Ind.	243.2	109.2	78.0	158.0				
Ill.	55.5	19.3	25.0	30.0				
Mich.	728.0	357.4	349.0	339.0				
Wisc.	—	—	—	—				
West	1,796.8	885.8	855.9	872.1	28,530.0	33,696.9	21,802.5	27,083.9
Total	29,250.9	14,367.6	13,572.4	14,057.1	468,149.0	584,481.1	347,016.3	483,445.4

Source: Me. through Md.: Poor, *Railroads and Canals.*

Va.: *American Railroad Journal*, XXXIII (1860), 1017.

N.C.: Dozier, *Atlantic Coast Line Railroad*, p. 170. Raleigh and Gaston receipts are estimated at $20,000 on basis of literary evidence in Brown, *A State Movement in Railroad Development*, pp. 56–57, and distributed equally between freight and passenger earnings on basis of operations in 1851 reported in *American Railroad Journal*, XXIX (1856), 506; zero net earnings were credited.

S.C.: Derrick, *Centennial History*, pp. 209, 210.

Ga.: Phillips, *History of Transportation*, pp. 244, 320. *American Railroad Journal*, XXIII (1850), 55, 517, 805; Milton S. Heath, *Constructive Liberalism: The Role of the State in Economic Development in Georgia to 1860* (Cambridge, Mass., 1954), p. 273. All data are exact with the exception of allocation of receipts of Western and Atlantic, for which the semiannual report in *American Railroad Journal* was used.

Fla.: With no additional evidence available, the Tallahassee Railroad is assigned the same receipts, etc., as in 1839.

Ky.: Receipts, earnings and distribution of receipts for the Lexington and Frankfort and the Louisville and Frankfort (under construction at the time) are inferred from operational reports for the years 1850 and 1851 published in the *American Railroad Journal*, XXIII (1850), 725, and XXIV (1851), 455 and 419. The receipts on the former are estimated at $2,000 per mile with an operating ratio of 50 percent; on the latter earnings of $10,000 are used for 1849 of which $4,000 represents net proceeds.

Ala.: Montgomery and West Point Railroad report for year ending March 1, 1850, reprinted in *American Railroad Journal*, XXIII (1850), 247. Receipts are distributed in proportion to 1851 report appearing *ibid.*, XXIV (1851), 282. Earnings of the Tuscumbia and Decatur, 46 miles, are estimated at $1000 per mile, and allocated to freight and passenger earnings in proportion to those of Montgomery and West Point; net receipts assumed to be only 10 percent since the road was not profitable.

Miss.: Gross receipts computed by taking 60 miles of Vicksburg and Brandon Railroad (Southern Railroad) at $2000 per mile on basis of indirect report of operations for the late 1840's in *American Railroad Journal*, XXI (1848), 417–418; distributed like other southern railroads.

La.: Same receipts as 1839 with allowance for additional 55 miles of railroad at $1000 per mile. See *De Bow's Review*, XIV (1853), 168, for evidence of no trend.

Ohio: The Little Miami report is reprinted in *American Railroad Journal*, XXIV (1851), 67; net returns are estimated using 1850 operating ratio. The Mad River and the Mansfield, Sandusky, and Newark reports are summarized *ibid.*, XXVIII (1855), 339, 340.

Ind.: The report of the Madison and Indianapolis is found in *American Railroad Journal*, XXIII (1850), 132; receipts are allocated in accord with 1850 operating results reported *ibid.*, XXV (1852), 246.

Ill.: Receipts of Galena and Chicago Railroad are those for calendar 1849 with the same operating ratio which prevailed over fiscal year: *American Railroad Journal*, XXIII (1850), 425. The Springfield and Meredosia earnings are estimated at $500 per mile for 55 miles, allocated like those of the Galena, except that net earnings are only 10 percent of receipts.

Mich.: Michigan Central report in *American Railroad Journal*, XXIII (1850), 5. The Michigan Southern estimate for 1849 is based upon report of operations for 1850 in *American Railroad Journal*, XXV (1852), 184. These are scaled down by about 40 percent in consideration of the improvement and extension of the road over the interval. An operating ratio of 50 percent is used. Receipts for the Detroit and Pontiac railroad, 25 miles, are estimated at $1000 per mile, equally distributed between freight and passengers, with net earnings of 50 percent.

ª New Castle and Frenchtown Railroad reported in earnings of the Philadelphia, Wilmington, and Baltimore.

million ton-miles suggest much too large a range of uncertainty because we know rates declined rapidly between 1839 and 1849.

1855–1856 Output

Table 43 summarizes the relevant data for 1855–1856. The totals for this fiscal year have been obtained by summation over individual roads, including, for the first time, actual ton- and passenger-mile reports. Table 43 thus differs markedly from the other estimates. Such a procedure is feasible only because of the efforts of the Secretary of the Treasury, James Guthrie (whose railroad interests led him shortly to the presidency of the Louisville and Nashville Railroad), to collect information in 1856 upon cost, capitalization, revenues, interest payments, and so forth, from every railroad in the United States. For certain of these magnitudes, he was surprisingly successful. Thus the complete gross receipts are $102.3 million; the Treasury report indicates a national total of $91.2 million or only 10 percent less.[7] The coverage of net earnings is comparable. For the other magnitudes

[7] Note, however, that one reason the report comes off so well is the existence of arithmetic mistakes that inflate the indicated total beyond the sum of the entries.

TABLE 43. Railway output, 1855–1856

	Total receipts	Net earnings	Passenger receipts	Freight receipts	Passenger-miles	Ton-miles
			(thousands of dollars)		(thousands)	
Me.	1,540.9	570.2	761.0	721.4	27,130.4	17,745.0
N.H.	1,960.9	773.8	671.8	1,216.2	18,792.1	38,476.8
Vt.	1,552.9	434.4	568.0	949.1	19,018.8	35,104.1
Mass.	9,178.5	3,042.4	4,741.3	3,977.2	187,581.5	105,341.8
Conn.	3,224.9	1,208.1	1,923.3	1,145.0	93,712.2	28,537.8
R.I.	264.8	109.0	157.3	97.5	5,926.8	2,292.7
New Eng.	17,722.9	6,137.9	8,822.7	8,106.4	352,161.8	227,498.1
N.Y.	18,822.1	8,010.0	8,559.9	9,689.8	425,682.6	344,039.4
N.J.	3,367.2	1,474.1	2,117.9	992.2	95,826.6	19,097.6
Pa.	15,013.3	7,770.5	4,055.1	10,835.4	144,760.3	462,632.1
Del.	0.0	0.0	0.0	0.0	0.0	0.0
Md.	4,848.0	2,240.9	1,012.6	3,835.0	36,672.3	196,720.2
Mid. Atl.	42,050.6	19,495.5	15,745.5	25,352.4	702,941.8	1,022,489.3
Va.	2,500.4	1,085.6	997.6	1,309.5	30,891.0	33,400.6
N.C.	1,318.0	632.9	737.9	450.9	22,455.5	12,591.9
S.C.	2,150.4	1,196.0	608.6	1,499.3	23,663.5	43,495.1
Ga.	4,584.0	2,470.2	1,377.2	2,957.4	43,316.1	84,355.3
Fla.	21.0	10.7	7.0	11.7	231.0	332.3
South	10,573.8	5,395.4	3,728.3	6,228.8	120,557.1	174,175.2
Ky.	761.3	379.4	354.1	375.1	11,352.9	13,079.6
Tenn.	1,055.4	542.9	426.6	567.1	13,673.0	18,903.3
Ala.	640.0	272.3	259.3	339.0	6,938.3	7,470.0
Miss.	259.4	113.8	142.6	104.9	3,556.1	2,346.7
La.	539.0	198.1	283.2	247.9	6,581.4	5,612.3
Tex.	62.0	31.6	25.0	34.0	623.4	760.6
Southwest	3,317.1	1,538.1	1,490.8	1,668.0	42,725.1	48,172.5
Ohio	9,927.1	5,217.0	4,739.6	4,853.5	190,173.1	154,218.2
Ind.	3,350.1	1,677.7	1,797.4	1,418.4	66,863.6	44,463.9
Ill.	8,267.8	3,871.6	3,619.7	4,317.7	141,504.2	131,193.4
Mich.	5,581.5	2,522.9	2,978.4	2,416.6	117,259.8	75,755.4
Wisc.	1,268.5	682.6	476.3	784.0	18,751.9	24,576.7
Mo.	163.1	34.1	65.1	98.5	3,115.4	1,409.3
West	28,558.1	14,005.9	13,676.5	13,888.7	537,668.0	431,616.9
Total	102,222.5	46,572.8	43,463.8	55,244.3	1,756,053.8	1,903,952.0

Source: See text.

the *Report on Finances* is less satisfactory. Omissions and implausible returns (of which there were more than the one cited earlier), make the ton- and passenger-mile totals quite unreliable. In addition, separate passenger and freight receipts were not requested. For these four series considerable supplementary material and estimation were required.

Tables 43a through 43e demonstrate both the methods and the extent of estimation involved in these four series. Table 43a contains those passenger- and ton-miles observed directly, from the *Report on Finances* for the most part, with additional information from the New York and Massachusetts state reports for railroads in those two states. All of the state totals are calculated by summing over individual railroads. Something like 60 percent of the final passenger- and ton-mile totals are derived in this way. Table 43a also contains the passenger and freight receipts for the same railroads, collected directly from Poor's *Railroads and Canals*, reports reprinted in the *American Railroad Journal*, and histories of individual roads. In combination, these two sets of information yield revenue ton- and passenger-mile rates which become important inputs for the next stage of the process.

This next stage is represented by Table 43b. From directly reported passenger and freight receipts passenger- and ton-miles are estimated. The procedure is the already familiar one of using average rates to make the conversion. The difference here is the now far more accurate information on rates. Table 43e shows both the rates computed from Table 43a and those actually used. The difference between the two is explained by extraneous information concerning the biased nature of the sample for individual states. Between Tables 43a and 43b we account for about four fifths of the national totals with a maximum of reliability.

Table 43c takes up most of the residual. Here estimated passenger and freight receipts are converted to outputs the same way that directly reported revenues were in Table 43b. Typically, the allocation of total receipts to freight and passenger components has been accomplished by the use of the state or regional average. Occasionally, for important railroads, a comparable railroad served as the model. This procedure was followed for the Michigan Southern whose operations were similar to those of the Mich-

Railway output, 1855–1856, directly reported

	Passenger receipts	Freight receipts	Passenger-miles	Ton-miles
	(thousands of dollars)		(thousands)	
Me.	213.7	61.3	9,001.2	1,300.0
N.H.	546.9	1,023.5	15,223.6	32,240.6
Vt.	510.5	788.6	17,089.8	29,159.8
Mass.	4,741.3	3,928.1	187,581.5	104,034.8
Conn.	1,250.9	893.3	59,052.5	22,165.7
R.I.	13.0	1.1	333.8	8.3
New England	7,276.3	6,695.9	288,282.4	188,909.2
N.Y.	8,039.4	9,098.8	399,786.6	323,082.0
N.J.	987.2	352.8	44,663.5	6,184.6
Pa.	2,680.2	7,835.9	95,655.5	326,853.4
Del.	0.0	0.0	0.0	0.0
Md.	1,003.9	3,713.0	36,357.1	194,019.2
Middle Atlantic	12,710.7	21,000.5	576,462.7	850,139.2
Va.	100.0	135.2	2,649.1	2,656.3
N.C.	212.1	120.3	5,102.5	3,200.0
S.C.	500.8	1,105.1	20,105.8	32,296.4
Ga.	243.2	942.1	6,907.9	27,102.6
Fla.	0.0	0.0	0.0	0.0
South	1,056.1	2,302.7	34,765.3	65,255.3
Ky.	343.5	364.0	11,013.2	12,709.6
Tenn.	0.0	0.0	0.0	0.0
Ala.	245.6	179.5	6,596.7	3,901.7
Miss.	0.0	0.0	0.0	0.0
La.	81.8	118.9	1,560.0	2,760.0
Tex.	0.0	0.0	0.0	0.0
Southwest	670.9	662.4	19,169.9	19,371.3
Ohio	1,416.0	1,544.5	60,604.9	52,310.3
Ind.	545.3	0.0	19,349.4	0.0
Ill.	859.0	1,429.0	30,791.2	40,913.2
Mich.	0.0	0.0	0.0	0.0
Mo.	65.1	98.5	3,115.4	1,409.3
Wisc.	0.0	0.0	0.0	0.0
West	2,885.4	3,072.0	113,860.9	94,632.8
Total	24,599.4	33,733.5	1,032,541.2	1,218,307.8

Source: See text.

	Passenger receipts	Freight receipts	Passenger-miles	Ton-miles
	(thousands of dollars)		(thousands)	
Me.	538.0	652.1	17,933.3	16,302.5
N.H.	97.6	146.3	2,788.5	4,734.6
Vt.	0.0	97.1	0.0	3,596.2
Mass.	.0	49.1	.0	1,307.0
Conn.	672.4	251.7	34,659.7	6,372.1
R.I.	144.3	96.4	5,593.0	2,284.3
New England	1,452.3	1,292.7	60,974.5	34,596.7
N.Y.	520.5	591.0	25,896.0	20,957.4
N.J.	219.3	149.1	9,923.0	2,982.0
Pa.	596.9	1,247.5	21,317.9	52,196.6
Del.	0.0	0.0	0.0	0.0
Md.	.0	103.3	.0	2,266.0
Middle Atlantic	1,336.7	2,100.9	57,136.9	78,402.0
Va.	353.1	571.2	11,653.4	16,227.2
N.C.	268.0	214.1	8,844.8	6,082.3
S.C.	0.0	213.6	0.0	6,068.1
Ga.	322.5	109.2	10,643.5	3,102.2
Fla.	0.0	0.0	0.0	0.0
South	943.6	1,108.1	31,141.7	31,479.8
Ky.	0.0	0.0	0.0	0.0
Tenn.	286.3	416.5	9,176.2	13,883.3
Ala.	0.0	149.4	0.0	3,342.3
Miss.	.0	0.0	.0	0.0
La.	.0	.0	.0	.0
Tex.	.0	.0	.0	.0
Southwest	286.3	565.9	9,176.2	17,225.6
Ohio	1,551.2	1,458.7	61,070.8	45,727.2
Ind.	366.1	608.4	14,413.3	19,072.1
Ill.	1,873.8	2,077.7	73,771.6	65,131.6
Mich.	1,540.0	1,241.0	60,629.9	38,902.8
Wisc.	208.1	483.7	8,192.9	15,163.0
West	5,539.2	5,869.5	078.5	183, 218,978.7
Total	9,558.1	10,937.1	376,507.8	345,700.8

Source: See text.

TABLE 43c. Railway output, 1855–1856, receipts allocated, passenger- and ton-miles estimated

	Passenger receipts	Freight receipts	Passenger-miles	Ton-miles
	(thousands of dollars)		(thousands)	
Me.	4.4	4.2	146.6	105.0
N.H.	27.3	46.4	780.0	1,501.6
Vt.	57.5	63.4	1,929.0	2,348.1
Mass.	0.0	0.0	0.0	0.0
Conn.	.0	.0	.0	.0
R.I.	.0	.0	.0	.0
New England	89.2	114.0	2,855.6	3,954.7
N.Y.	0.0	0.0	0.0	0.0
N.J.	908.9	465.3	41,126.6	9,306.0
Pa.	240.4	703.2	8,585.7	29,422.0
Del.	0.0	0.0	0.0	0.0
Md.	8.7	8.7	315.2	435.0
Middle Atlantic	1,158.0	1,177.2	50,027.5	39,163.0
Va.	269.6	172.2	8,897.6	4,892.0
N.C.	257.8	116.5	8,508.2	3,309.6
S.C.	107.8	180.6	3,557.7	5,130.6
Ga.	536.6	1,298.0	17,709.5	36,875.0
Fla.	7.0	11.7	231.0	332.3
South	1,178.8	1,779.0	38,904.0	50,539.5
Ky.	10.6	11.1	339.7	370.0
Tenn.	140.3	150.6	4,496.8	5,020.0
Ala.	13.7	10.1	341.6	226.0
Miss.	142.6	104.9	3,556.1	2,346.7
La.	143.6	69.9	3,581.0	1,563.0
Tex.	25.0	34.0	623.4	760.6
Southwest	475.8	380.6	12,938.6	10,286.3
Ohio	1,269.3	1,379.7	49,972.4	43,250.7
Ind.	732.8	810.5	28,850.3	25,391.8
Ill.	696.3	756.0	27,413.3	23,699.0
Mich.	1,438.4	1,175.6	56,629.9	36,852.6
Wisc.	268.2	300.3	10,559.0	9,413.7
West	4,405.0	4,421.6	173,424.9	138,607.8
Total	7,306.8	7,872.4	278,150.6	242,551.3

Source: See text.

	Passenger receipts	Freight receipts	Passenger-miles	Ton-miles
	(thousands of dollars)		(thousands)	
Me.	4.9	3.8	49.3	37.5
N.H.	0.0	0.0	0.0	0.0
Vt.	.0	.0	.0	.0
Mass.	.0	.0	.0	.0
Conn.	.0	.0	.0	.0
R.I.	.0	.0	.0	.0
New England	4.9	3.8	49.3	37.5
N.Y.	0.0	0.0	0.0	0.0
N.J.	2.5	25.0	113.5	625.0
Pa.	537.6	1,048.8	19,201.2	54,160.1
Del.	0.0	0.0	0.0	0.0
Md.	.0	.0	.0	.0
Middle Atlantic	540.1	1,073.8	19,314.7	54,785.1
Va.	274.9	430.9	7,690.9	9,625.1
N.C.	0.0	0.0	0.0	0.0
S.C.	.0	.0	.0	.0
Ga.	274.9	608.1	8,055.2	17,275.5
Fla.	0.0	0.0	0.0	0.0
South	549.8	1,039.0	15,746.1	26,900.6
Ky.	0.0	0.0	0.0	0.0
Tenn.	.0	.0	.0	.0
Ala.	.0	.0	.0	.0
Miss.	.0	.0	.0	.0
La.	57.8	59.1	1,440.4	1,289.3
Tex.	0.0	0.0	0.0	0.0
Southwest	57.8	59.1	1,440.4	1,289.3
Ohio	503.1	470.6	18,525.0	12,930.0
Ind.	153.2	0.0	4,250.6	0.0
Ill.	190.6	55.0	9,528.1	1,449.6
Mich.	0.0	0.0	0.0	0.0
Wisc.	.0	.0	.0	.0
West	846.9	525.6	32,303.7	14,379.6
Total	1,999.5	2,701.3	68,854.2	97,392.1

Source: See text.

TABLE 43e. Railway output, 1855–1856, passenger and freight rates (cents per mile)

	Implicit rates derived from Table 43a		Rates used to derive Tables 43b, 43c	
	Passenger	Freight	Passenger	Freight
Me.	2.37	4.71	3.00	4.00
N.H.	3.50	3.09	3.50	3.09
Vt.	2.98	2.70	—	2.70
Mass.	2.58	3.76	—	3.76
Conn.	1.94	3.95	1.94	3.95
R.I.	2.58	4.22	2.58	4.22
N.Y.	2.01	2.82	2.01	2.82
N.J.	2.21	5.70	2.21	5.00
Pa.	2.80	2.39	2.80	2.39
Del.	—	—	—	—
Md.	2.76	1.91	—	5.00
South	3.03	3.52	3.03	3.52
Ky.	3.12	2.86	3.12	3.00
Tenn.	—	—	3.12	3.00
Ala.	3.72	4.54	4.01	4.47
Miss.	—	—	4.01	4.47
La.	5.24	4.31	4.01	4.47
Tex.	—	—	4.01	4.47
West	2.54	3.19	2.54	3.19

Source: See text.

igan Central, for which we had all the information. The largest share of entries in Table 43c relate to the West and South, since Poor's projected volumes summarizing the financial statistics for those regions never appeared, and the *American Railroad Journal* did not secure all company reports.

The final section, Table 43d, contains the directly observed ton- and passenger-miles of the *Report on Finances* for which the corresponding freight and passenger earnings were not available. Estimation in this instance proceeds from physical output to receipts. The rates of Table 43e could not be used here, except in a relative sense, since the estimates of component earnings were subject to the constraint of total receipts. Often, therefore, the implied rates of Table 43d diverge radically from those of Table 43e. Because the receipts so estimated are a very small part of the total, the internal inconsistency is not a serious matter.

The sum of Tables 43a and 43d gives total ton- and passenger-miles observed directly, while the sum of Tables 43a and 43b gives the corresponding total for passenger and freight receipts. Not surprisingly, the ratio of the latter to their aggregate is greater than the ratio of directly observed ton- and passenger-miles to their total. To focus more sharply upon the quality of these statistics, as well as those of gross and net receipts, we reproduce below, by region, the percentages of the various 1855–1856 totals which were tabulated directly and not estimated.

	Gross receipts	Net earnings	Pass. receipts	Freight receipts	Pass.-miles	Ton-miles
New England	100.0	100.0	98.9	98.5	81.9	83.1
Middle Atlantic	100.0	98.9	89.2	91.1	84.8	88.5
South	99.0	98.9	53.6	54.6	41.9	52.9
Southwest	91.0	90.2	63.4	73.4	47.7	42.8
West	92.5	87.2	61.6	64.3	27.2	25.2
Total	97.5	95.2	78.5	80.8	62.7	69.1
					(84.1)	(87.2)

Despite substantial regional variation, the results are heartening. Moreover, the data contain much less potential error than the above proportions suggest. If we include the passenger- and ton-miles estimated from known passenger and freight receipts, the national percentages increase markedly, as the figures in parentheses show. The improvement in the West, in particular, is notable if this less stringent criterion be adopted; the fraction of tabulated passenger- and ton-miles to the regional total increases to about two thirds.

No bounds have been provided with these data since such a large proportion has been obtained by addition rather than assumption. Moreover, the rates used for 1859 have been influenced by the rates obtained for 1855–1856 and hence are not independent. The 1849 rates are not very relevant since a major reduction in transport costs occurred between the two dates. In principle, the variance in the rates of individual roads within a given state or region could be used to calculate bounds in Tables 43b and 43c, but the additional information does not justify this additional labor.

1859 Output

Again in 1859, we revert to a more aggregative approach. With the 1855–1856 rates as benchmarks, however, the conversion of receipts to output in 1859 is less subject to error than in either 1839 or 1849. Table 44 brings together the relevant final data. No state by state source detail is presented because of the large number of individual railroads by this time. In addition, the sources for the receipts data are already familiar — Poor's *Railroads and Canals* for the eastern states (except for New York and Massachusetts where state reports were available), the *American Railroad Journal* and the individual histories — with one major addition. That is Burgess' *Railway Directory for 1861*,[8] which despite its title, refers primarily to a fiscal year ending either early in 1860 or late in 1859. It served as a valuable addition to the other sources and reduced substantially the estimation required. Its data, of course, were checked against the other sources when possible, and they were always comparable.

Although both gross and net receipts achieve a very high degree of direct coverage, passenger and freight earnings fall slightly short of this standard. Burgess did not provide such detail, although it was possible in many instances to use the allocation for a previous or succeeding year, where such evidence was available and reasonable stability prevailed in the traffic pattern. The estimation involved, for all receipts categories, is spelled out in Table 44a. Roughly 10 percent of the passenger and freight receipts are estimated,[9] compared to 6 percent of net earnings and

---

[8] Josiah J. Burgess, *Railway Directory for 1861* (New York, 1861). The author compiled the results from official reports requested of the individual railroads. In addition to gross receipts, there are data on cost, distribution of liabilities, gauge of road, names of officers and directors, and date of annual meetings.

[9] Estimated passenger and freight receipts are those obtained by use of a state average when specific information about the individual road was unavailable. When

TABLE 44. Railway output, 1859

	Total receipts	Net earnings	Passenger receipts (thousands of dollars)	Freight receipts	Passenger-miles 1859	lower bound (thousands)	Ton-miles 1859	lower bound
Me.	1,416.5	586.1	573.4	765.1				
N.H.	1,667.2	714.5	509.4	1,068.2				
Vt.	1,618.6	451.5	479.5	1,051.2				
Mass.	8,787.8	4,064.6	3,894.2	4,291.6				
Conn.	3,163.1	1,281.9	1,692.2	1,206.3				
R.I.	284.9	121.2	166.6	110.6				
New England	16,938.1	7,219.8	7,315.3	8,493.0	319,063.9	291,446.2	253,991.7	238,567.4
N.Y.	17,370.6	6,947.1	6,869.2	9,789.3				
N.J.	4,914.2	2,594.4	2,379.4	2,033.3				
Pa.	15,889.8	7,107.7	3,993.3	11,019.4				
Del.	108.8	39.2	75.0	25.0				
Md.	5,009.4	2,470.6	1,252.3	3,574.8				
Middle Atlantic	43,292.8	19,159.0	14,569.2	26,441.8	649,029.1	650,410.7	1,159,541.6	1,066,201.6
Va.	4,094.2	1,977.9	1,761.8	2,112.9				
N.C.	1,694.0	804.8	787.6	769.8				
S.C.	2,775.0	1,181.1	888.6	1,714.9				
Ga.	5,573.1	2,994.2	1,698.2	3,620.9				
Fla.	276.4	152.5	84.2	180.0				
South	14,412.7	7,110.5	5,220.4	8,398.5	193,348.1	168,944.9	248,476.3	234,594.9
Ky.	1,169.0	566.3	519.3	595.9				
Tenn.	3,244.8	1,748.9	1,749.7	1,289.1				
Ala.	2,063.7	1,106.7	685.2	1,290.7				
Miss.	1,026.6	575.4	447.0	513.2				
La.	1,699.9	651.3	617.4	1,009.0				
Tex.	315.5	219.4	150.0	150.0				
Southwest	9,519.5	4,868.0	4,168.6	4,847.9	138,953.3	119,444.1	123,043.1	140,112.7
Ohio	12,927.1	4,923.6	5,679.1	6,447.1				
Ind.	2,998.8	1,360.3	1,319.7	1,518.2				
Ill.	9,855.3	3,081.7	3,734.9	5,626.4				
Mich.	4,034.5	1,751.9	1,798.2	2,020.1				
Wisc.	2,179.4	840.2	735.8	1,362.7				
Mo.	1,914.4	836.9	943.9	882.1				
Iowa	598.6	272.6	230.6	344.9				
West	34,508.1	13,067.2	14,442.2	18,201.5	577,688.0	568,590.8	791,369.5	565,263.9
Calif.	174.5	92.8	76.7	94.5	1,534.0	1,534.0	1,260.0	1,260.0
Total	118,845.7	51,517.3	45,792.4	66,477.2	1,879,616.4	1,800,370.7	2,577,682.2	2,246,000.5

Source: See text.

less than 2 percent of gross receipts. Given the typical inade-
quacies of historical data, these results need no apology, even for

data upon gross receipts were available from Burgess, say, and a previous or subsequent year's distribution of receipts, such passenger and freight receipts are not
included in Table 44a.

TABLE 44a. Railway output, 1859, estimated receipts (thousands of dollars)

	Total	Net	Passenger	Freight
New England				
Middle Atlantic				
Va.				
N.C.			86.3	172.4
S.C.	91.0	69.3	196.0	367.6
Ga.	44.0	280.2	116.4	280.0
Fla.	154.0	85.0	84.2	180.0
South	289.0	454.5	482.9	1000.0
Ky.	17.0	8.2	7.6	8.7
Tenn.	0.0	0.6	0.0	0.0
Ala.	.0	.0	78.3	147.6
Miss.	15.0	8.4	6.5	7.5
La.	182.0	552.3	163.5	127.0
Tex.	0.0	0.0	0.0	0.0
Southwest	214.0	569.5	255.9	290.8
Ohio	100.0	423.8	1000.1	1587.8
Ind.	856.0	388.0	529.6	620.6
Ill.	276.0	471.3	898.7	1354.0
Mich.	0.0	0.0	254.6	260.3
Wisc.	142.0	149.1	512.0	808.1
Iowa	0.0	195.4	44.1	67.2
Mo.	10.0	777.5	468.4	451.0
West	1384.0	2405.1	3707.5	5149.0
Calif.	0.0	92.8	0.0	0.0
Total	1887.0	3501.9	4446.3	6439.8

Source: See text.

the allocations of passenger and freight earnings, upon which the accuracy of the physical output series depend.

The rates used to convert these receipts are the following:[10]

[10] Note that passenger- and ton-miles of all railroads in New York and Massachusetts were tabulated directly from the state reports; the outputs of the Pennsylvania and the Baltimore and Ohio railroads were also recorded directly.

	Passenger rate	Freight rate
	(cents per mile)	
Northern New England	2.75	2.70
Southern New England	2.00	3.69
Middle Atlantic	2.50	2.50
South	2.70	3.38
Southwest	3.00	3.94
West	2.50	2.30
California	5.00	7.50

By and large these freight rates represent crude extrapolation of the 1855–1856 information on the basis of the rate trends of an admittedly small number of roads.[11] The trend is downward for the trunk lines and their midwestern extensions and stable for the New England roads. Passenger rates by region are virtually unchanged from those reported in Table 43e with the exception of slight reductions in the South and Southwest where charges were far above average at the earlier date.

Because the interval from 1855–1856 to 1859 is so short, there can be little quarrel over the order of magnitude of the 1859 rates. On the other hand, it is embarrassingly true that small absolute changes in rates yield substantial absolute differences in the final estimates of passenger- and ton-miles. The use of 1855–1856 rates as they stand contradicts the possibility of substantial upward bias to the 1859 results. Against an actual 1.9 billion passenger-miles, the lower bound is 1.8 billion; for ton-miles the comparison stands 2.6 to 2.2 billion. Another independent test suggests that the estimates are not too low. Frickey's indexes of tonnage and passengers increase 57.5 and 10.3 percent respectively from fiscal 1855 to fiscal 1859.[12] Applying those same factors of increase to ton- and passenger-mileage yields aggregate estimates of 3.0 billion ton-miles and 1.9 billion passenger-miles. The latter is only 3 percent larger than our estimate, but the former almost 20 percent larger. The greater discrepancy in ton-miles is due to two

[11] *Wholesale Prices, Wages, and Transportation*, Senate Report No. 1394, 52nd Congress, 2nd Session, pp. 615–616.

[12] Edwin Frickey, *Production in the United States, 1860–1914* (Cambridge, Mass., 1947), p. 100.

causes: first, tonnage on the sample roads increased about 20 percent more rapidly than their own ton-mileage;[13] second, the appropriate base for comparison with our results in Table 43 is probably an average of fiscal 1855 and fiscal 1856 for reasons indicated earlier. If an adjustment is made for the first of these factors, the estimate is reduced to approximately 2.85 billion ton-miles, now about 10 percent larger than our total. If both adjustments are made, the resultant ton-mileage is within 1 per-cent of our estimate.

[13] Frickey, p. 91.

APPENDIX B

The Derivation of Capital Formation Estimates

This appendix describes the methods used to estimate annual railroad investment for the period 1828–1860. The principal feature is reliance upon values of the capital stock at original cost at three different points during the interval: 1839, 1850, and 1860. These are so spaced that first differences, after some adjustment, yield decadal investment flows spanning the period. To these quasi-net investment flows, so called because railroad cost of construction accounts conformed more closely to a net capital concept than to cumulative gross outlays, are added allowances for replacement expenditures charged to current account. These gross decadal totals are then distributed annually by two different techniques. For 1828–1839 a disaggregated approach is feasible, and annual expenditures of individual railroads form the basis of the national totals. These annual investment data either are compiled directly from company reports or are estimated by allocating outlays over the gestation period by reference to a construction profile developed from a sample of roads providing the needed information. For 1840–1860 the proliferation of railroads renders such a tack impracticable. Therefore a measure of relative annual expenditures, the product of a mileage in process index and a cost index, is substituted as a means of distributing the decadal totals. These annual gross investment estimates in current dollars are cast in regional as well as national terms. In addition, annual net flows and constant dollar variants of both gross and net investment are developed. The subsequent discussion will elaborate upon each of these steps, starting with the nature of the cost of construction information.

The Reliability of the Cost Data

Our approach obviously places great weight upon the underlying cost of construction aggregates. It does so at the expense of differing sharply with George Rogers Taylor concerning their utility. Despite the abundant data on construction cost before the Civil War, and hence frequent estimates of the capital stock valued at historical cost, Taylor has recently concluded that nothing much could be done with them:

> None of these early cost summaries can be taken very seriously. At least we should not consider them to be any more reliable than did informed contemporary observers. The *American Railroad Journal* stated in 1852 that it was impossible to represent the cost of building the railroads "with any accuracy." Moreover the rough agreement among the various series cannot be taken as proof of their reliability. . . . Even if they were not copied from each other . . . the statistics had a common source in the annual reports of the railroad companies and the state governments.[1]

Such a pessimistic evaluation was established by reference to the inconsistencies in a variety of ante-bellum cost estimates he had assembled for the purpose;[2] many of these, with some addition and alteration, appear here in Table 45.

At first glance, Taylor's judgment is readily confirmed. For example, from 1850 to 1852 the series in column (1) shows an increase from $313 million to $471 million; the change over the same interval in column (2) is almost half again as much. Such divergence is not nearly so troubling as Taylor believes, however, because the data are not of the same quality and do not merit equal consideration. The estimates in column (1) are nothing

---

[1] "Comment," pp. 537–538.

[2] Note that Taylor does not claim widespread false reporting. ("Comment," pp. 543–544.) There were colorful instances of this, like the New York railroad that charged to construction account the repairs to the road resulting from an accident with a wandering cow and the value of the cow too, because "the cow got upon the track in consequence of the fences not being built, and hence . . . as the accident arose in consequence of incomplete construction, the damage done should be charged to that account." *Annual Report of the State Engineer and Surveyor on the Railroads of the State of New York for 1854* (Albany, 1855), p. 7. And Poor did inveigh in the *American Railroad Journal* in the late 1850's against manipulation of the capital account. But relative to the great sweep of new construction, questionable practices were insignificant.

TABLE 45. Cost of construction of United States railroads (thousands of dollars)

End of year	(1) Extrapolated mileage	(2) Cumulated reports	(3) Census estimates
1847	184,275	—	—
1848	216,895	—	—
1849	260,750	—	—
1850	313,460	302,590	296,660
1851	385,230	—	—
1852	470,525	400,714	—
1853	547,385	489,603[a]	—
1854	654,830	616,766	—
1855	750,715	—	—
1856	850,150	—	—
1857	917,350	919,991	—
1858	—	961,047	—
1859	—	1,118,921	—
1860	—	1,177,994	1,151,561

Source: (1) Hunt's Merchants' Magazine, XXXIX (1858), 378.
(2) 1850, Ibid., XXV (1851), 121.
1852, Ibid., XXVIII (1853), 115.
1853, Ibid., XXX (1854), 129.
1854, Ibid., XXXII (1855), 131.
1857, American Railroad Journal, XXXI (1858), 4.
1858, Ibid., XXXII (1859), 4.
1859, Ibid., XXXIII (1860), 2.
1860, Ibid., XXXIV (1861), 6.
(3) Preliminary Report on the Eighth Census, p. 231.
[a] Reprinted in Compendium of the Seventh Census, p. 189, as estimate for 1854 without specifying that it refers to January 1 of that year.

more than a mileage series multiplied by an assumed constant cost of $35,000 per mile; columns (2) and (3) on the other hand, contain estimates derived by aggregation over individual railroad reports. That column (1) differs from the others is no measure of *their* inaccuracy.

In the second instance, we must recognize that the reliability of the data is not independent of their use. The shorter the period for which the flows are calculated the more they are subject to error. If we wanted to find annual investment in 1858, the answer from the data of column (2) would be $41 million. Similarly, the flow during the years 1853–1858 is $560 million. It turns out, in fact, that our 1858 figure of $961 million is off by exactly $100 million owing to errors in addition; further errors of reporting, etc., enter in unknown ways and amounts. Supposing for the moment that $1061 million is the true figure, note the hierarchy of error: 10 percent in the 1858 cost estimate, 15 percent in the flow from 1853 through 1858, 70 percent in 1858 annual investment. The less exacting the demands upon the data, the more "reliable" they are. In general, the larger the absolute value of the cost magnitude, the smaller the proportional error. Differences between cost estimates taken over long periods have the further advantage that error components in each stock figure may cancel out and leave the flow correct. In the case at hand, it is exactly differences over decadal intervals that are relevant, and hence Taylor's indictment must be softened.

The more so since the data we use are the census estimates of column (3). These are free from many of the objections to which the other summaries are vulnerable. Although reaching aggregate cost in the same fashion as the contemporary *American Railroad Journal*, by a summation of individual construction accounts, and although also apparently compiled by Henry V. Poor, editor of the *Journal*, the census possesses important advantages over its competitors. The census summary was compiled during the year 1861 when the railroad reports for 1860 were already complete. Poor as editor, on the other hand, had to meet a deadline that required the 1860 cost total to appear in the first issue of 1861. One sees the result: the *Journal* was forced to rely on the 1858 report of the Illinois Central to get its 1860 total; the census used the correct 1860 report, $3,000,000 larger. A second difference is scope. The census did not cover roads in process, the *Journal* tried to. Although the latter method is desirable from the standpoint of total construction expenditure, such coverage could be had only at a price. Thus, unable to find any firm data on Minnesota railroads, Poor guessed at $2 million as a likely sum; similarly, but less defensible, one New York railroad is shown as having spent $3,500,000 whereas the state report credits it with only $300,000.[3] The consistent undercoverage by exclusion of works in process can be dealt with once it is recognized. Such an adjustment is more desirable than the inclusion of rank guesses.

A simple test of the census data is provided by a comparison of Taylor's own careful estimate of railroad investment in Maine with one based upon the census materials. At first blush, the results turn out rather badly. Taylor's total flow from 1851 to 1860 comes to $7.7 million (after adjustment for definitional consistency with the census); the census yields $9.6 million. Initial impressions are misleading, however. The largest part of the divergence is explained by a census geographical allocation of costs for the Atlantic and St. Lawrence Railroad that differs from Taylor's. The road passed through 3 different states, and a total estimate including all would not be subject to this type of error. In the second place, the comparability of the flow data is not complete. The census data must first be adjusted for the different amount of road in process in 1850 and 1860, since neither year includes any allowance for such expenditure. More mileage was underway in 1850 than in 1860, and allowance for this narrows the gap to an insignificant level.

A comparison of 1860 costs in Wisconsin also turns out favorably. Table 21 in Chapter IV has already presented both the census cost and an alternative estimate derived from individual company reports. Once again, the reported totals, $33,600,000 versus $51,200,000, argue against my position. Even after correction for out of state construction included in the company reports, the differential still remains. The cause is the La Crosse and Milwaukee, the "Erie Railroad" of the West, whose involvement in scandal and inflation of cost account led it down the familiar path of bankruptcy and reorganization. Whereupon, the cost of $100,000 per mile originally carried in the accounts was reduced to a more reasonable $35,000 per mile, which is the basis for the census figure. After this correction, the two totals are within 1 percent of each other.

The retention of the census data is important not only because

[3] *American Railroad Journal*, XXXIX (1861), 6. The New York railroad is the Lake Ontario and Hudson River. It allocated proportionally to construction account $2,500,000, which was the cost of breaking its contract.

they provide a consistent means of measuring the expenditure flow over a single decade, the 1850's, but also because they can be used, in conjunction with a cost estimate for 1839, to span the entire period. These 1839 data come from one of the many studies of the American railroad system made by foreign engineers in the 1830's. Franz Anton von Gerstner, engineer on the pioneer European railroad from the Moldau to the Danube, came to the United States in the fall of 1838 and visited most of the mileage built or underway. His untimely death prevented him from completing more than a few brief articles on the railroad system, but his companion, Ludwig Klein, posthumously published a complete series of articles in English that appeared in 1840–1841, as well as a two-volume book that appeared in 1842–1843. These latter stand as the most complete study of early American railroad development, excelling even Michel Chevalier's able volumes on the same subject.[4]

One of Gerstner's principal interests was the cost of construction of the various works, and he made every effort to secure the official figures as presented in the company's own reports. A check of his data against independent accounts in the Virginia, Massachusetts, Illinois, and Michigan state documents shows that he succeeded admirably in most cases. Where direct information was unavailable we may presume that he used an informed judgment in preparing his cost estimate.[5] Accordingly, his results are the principal source for our 1839 cost estimate.

Table 46 presents this estimate, developed by additional refer-

---

[4] The articles by Klein appeared in both the *Journal of the Franklin Institute* and the *American Railroad Journal* and have been cited in Chapter I, n. 4. They are usually credited to Gerstner. Some of the latter's own letters on American internal improvements are to be found in the *Journal of the Franklin Institute*, n.s., XXVI (1840), 217, 289, and 361, in the same number as Klein's articles. The book is entitled *Die Innern Communicationen der Vereinigten Staaten von Nord Amerika* (Vienna, 1842–1843).

Michel Chevalier's work is *Voies de Communications aux Etats-Unis* (Paris, 1840–1841). An abridged discussion of American internal improvements as well as his other valuable comments upon the United States is in English in *Society, Manners, and Politics in the United States*, already referred to earlier.

[5] In one of Gerstner's articles comparing Belgian and American railroads he commented: "the Presidents . . . gave me not only all their printed reports, but laid before me . . . their books and accounts." *Hazard's United States Statistical and Commercial Register*, II (1840), 119.

ence to other source materials,[6] and compares it with the Gerstner results. Of the latter, there are actually two. The first are those published in the book; the second derives from the series of summary articles. The principal difference between them is the inclusion of construction in process in the articles, whereas the book was more restrictive in its coverage. Column (3) contains the final estimates which had the advantage not only of Gerstner's efforts but also of the additional materials detailed in the notes to the table. Sometimes it was a matter almost of sheer guesswork to determine which of the various costs reported in different sources were the more accurate. More frequently, however, there was excellent agreement, and on balance the results compare favorably with the accuracy of the later census tabulations. A last refinement is the exclusion from the cost estimates of those primitive railroads on which only horsepower was employed *and* which did not subsequently convert to steam locomotion. All of the early Pennsylvania coal railroads are included, with one exception, since they did adopt locomotives later. That exception is the Mauch Chunk, which never progressed beyond reliance upon gravity and inclined planes. Thus, ironically, the first two "railroads" in the United States, the Mauch Chunk and the Quincy, which did much to convince skeptics of the practicality of the innovation, find no place in our railroad investment series.

The combination of this 1839 estimate with those of the census for 1850 and 1860 yields expenditure flows for roughly each of the first three decades of the railroad era. For such utilization the underlying cost data are robust enough. The greater challenge is the conversion of such outlays to investment, as currently defined. As they stand they are far from such a magnitude owing to the vagaries of railroad accounting. This is the next task.

From Construction Costs to Quasi-Net Investment

The most direct approach to the reconciliation is an analysis of the composition of construction costs. Then we can see where

[6] Comment here is in order upon one recent source, Wicker, "Railroad Investment before the Civil War." His limited construction data are not always correct. Thus he excludes expenditure for iron rails in Michigan, and his Illinois railroads include one turnpike. Likewise, his data on Virginia railroads are often in error. I have used only his Illinois results (after a further check).

TABLE 46. Alternative railroad cost of construction estimates, 1839 (thousands of dollars)

	(1)	(2)	(3)	(4)
Me.	150.0	200.0	254	254
N.H.	10.0	610.0	200[a]	200[a]
Mass.	11,142.7	11,100.0	10,800	10,740
R.I.	2,500.0	2,500.0	2,500	2,500
Conn.	2,610.5	1,905.0	2,568	2,568
N.Y.	11,144.3	11,311.8	11,165	10,986
N.J.	5,582.9	5,547.0	5,647[b]	5,647[b]
Penn.	22,379.9	18,070.0	23,098	22,658
Del.	550.0	400.0	550	550
Md.	8,999.2	12,400.0[c]	9,057	9,057
Va.	4,840.4	5,201.0	4,935	4,935
N.C.	2,782.0	3,163.0	2,799[b]	2,795[b]
S.C.	2,330.7	3,200.0	3,070	3,070
Ga.	5,300.0	5,458.0	4,766	4,766
Fla.	790.0	1,420.0	820	820
Ala.	1,435.0	1,222.0	1,510	1,510
La.	2,430.0	2,862.0	2,652	2,602
Miss.	3,510.0	3,490.0	3,495	3,495
Tenn.	200.0	1,100.0	400	400
Ky.	947.0	947.0	757	745
Ohio	420.1	420.1	355	315
Ind.	1,150.0	1,375.0	1,200	1,200
Mich.	1,936.0	1,896.0	2,042	1,975
Ill.	1,875.0	1,832.5	2,356	2,314
	94,975.7	97,630.4	96,996	96,102

Source: (1) Gerstner, *Die Innern Communicationen, passim.*

(2) Gerstner (Ludwig Klein), "Railroads in the United States," *Journal of the Franklin Institute,* n.s., XXVI (1840), 89–102; 227–230; 301–307.

(3) The above two sources, as well as Poor, *Railroads and Canals,* provide most of the material for the eastern states. There is occasional information in the early issues of the *American Railroad Journal.* In addition, for the specified states the following additional works have been used:

Me.: Taylor, "Comment," p. 540.

Mass.: Annual reports of railroad companies published in the Massachusetts Committee on Railways and Canals, *Annual Reports of the Railroad Corporations in the State of Massachusetts,* 1836–1840.

Conn.: Annual reports of Hartford and New Haven Railroad.

such costs diverge from the concept of investment and to what extent. Table 47 presents cost distributions derived from samples of railroads built in each of the three pre-Civil War decades. The large standard deviations (presented in parentheses beneath the means) indicate the substantial variability among the individual railroads in the samples. Responsible for this range are not only natural factors like difference in terrain, but also variations in

---

N.Y.: Stevens, *Beginnings of the New York Central Railroad*, pp. 113, 124–130, 155, 175–176; Mott, *Oceans and Lakes*, pp. 38, 41–43, 46, 49.

Penn.: *Annual Reports of the Commissioner of Internal Improvements* directly, and also as reprinted in *Hazard's Statistical Register;* occasional annual reports of the following roads: Harrisburg, Portsmouth, Mt. Joy, and Lancaster; Philadelphia and Reading; Philadelphia, Germantown, and Norristown; and Philadelphia, Wilmington, and Baltimore.

Md.: Annual reports of the Baltimore and Ohio Railroad, 1827–1840.

Va.: *Journals of the Virginia House of Delegates; American Railroad Journal,* XXXIII (1860), 973.

N.C.: Brown, *A State Movement in Railroad Development*, pp. 36, 46–48.

S.C.: Annual reports of the South Carolina Railroad, 1833–1840.

Ga.: Heath, *Constructive Liberalism*, p. 273. House Exec. Doc. No. 172, 26th Congress, 1st Session (Washington, 1840), pp. 420–423. (The latter is a report on the condition of state banks in 1838 and 1839, but because many southern railroads had banking privileges, the cost of construction of such railroads is also given.)

La.: Merl E. Reed, "Government Investment and Economic Growth: Louisiana's Ante Bellum Railroads," *Journal of Southern History*, XXVIII, no. 2 (1962), 183–201, only for Carrolton Railroad. His other data are largely estimated. Also House Exec. Doc. No. 172, p. 483, for West Feliciana Railroad.

Miss.: House Exec. Doc. No. 172, pp. 551, 638; Mississippi Legislative Journals, 1840 and 1841. Milton S. Heath, "Public Cooperation in Railroad Construction in the Southern United States to 1861," unpub. diss., Harvard University, 1937.

Tenn.: Stanley J. Folmsbee, *Sectionalism and Internal Improvements in Tennessee, 1796–1845* (Philadelphia, 1939), pp. 185–191.

Ky.: McGill, *et al.*, *Transportation before 1860*, pp. 468–469.

Ohio: Black, *Little Miami Railroad.*

Ind.: Logan Esarey, "Internal Improvements in Early Indiana," *Indiana Historical Society Publications*, V, no. 2 (1912), 115–116; *American Railroad Journal*, XXVIII (1855), 246.

Mich.: *Annual Reports of the Michigan Board of Internal Improvement*, 1839, 1840, 1841.

Ill.: Krenkel, *Illinois Internal Improvements;* Wicker, "Railroad Investment before the Civil War," p. 523.

(4) Same as Col. 3, with subtraction for horsedrawn railroads.

[a] Eastern of New Hampshire included in Eastern of Massachusetts.

[b] Explicitly excludes steamboat properties, coal lands, etc.

[c] Includes the Philadelphia, Wilmington, and Baltimore Railroad.

technique. Despite the variability, Table 47 conveys an accurate impression of the changing content of construction cost in the ante-bellum period. Nevertheless, the data are further adjusted in Table 48 to reflect more adequately the distribution of actual aggregate construction expenditure. Because the sample underlying Table 47 is far from random and special circumstances like the double tracking of New York railroads intervened in the 1840's, this additional step is necessary.

TABLE 47. Distribution of construction expenditures (percent)

Type of expenditure	1828–1839	1840–1850	1851–1860
Graduation and masonry ⎫	38.4	32.8 (12.4)	39.4
Bridging ⎭	(14.4)	2.9 (1.6)	(9.3)
Superstructure	30.8 (11.0)	28.8 (9.6)	25.9 (7.3)
Equipment	7.1 (2.6)	9.2 (3.5)	8.2 (3.8)
Buildings and machinery	4.8 (2.6)	4.6 (2.9)	3.5 (2.5)
Engineering	4.7 (2.2)	3.4 (2.6)	2.8 (1.5)
Land, including fencing	9.8 (7.4)	10.5 (2.1)	4.3 (3.5)
Miscellaneous (primarily interest payments and discount on securities)	4.9 (5.5)	7.8 (15.4)	15.8 (11.4)

Source: Unweighted arithmetic averages of from 12 to 23 roads in the first decade, 21 in the second, and 18 in the third. The variation in number in the first period is due to the fact that not all roads reported all items.

Information on type of expenditure was obtained as follows:

1828–1839: *Annual Reports of the Railroad Corporations in the State of Massachusetts*, 1835–1839; Gerstner, *Die Innern Communicationen; American Railroad Journal*, X (1840), 27.

1840–1850: *Annual Reports of the Railroad Corporations in the State of Massachusetts*, 1847–1850; *Annual Report of the State Engineer and Surveyor on the Railroads of the State of New York*, 1847–1851; Annual reports of individual railroads.

1859–1860: *Annual Reports of the Railroads of the State of Virginia to the Board of Public Works*, 1857–1861; *Annual Report of the State Engineer and Surveyor on the Railroads of the State of New York*, 1857; Annual reports of individual railroads

TABLE 48. Adjusted distribution of construction expenditures (percent)

Type of expenditure	1828–1839	1840–1850	1851–1860
Graduation, masonry, bridging (including fencing)	42	37	37
Superstructure	30	30	28
Equipment	7	9	9
Buildings and machinery	4	5	4
Engineering	4	3	3
Land, excluding fencing[a]	7	8	3
Miscellaneous	4	8	16
Legal expenses, nonrailroad expenditures, etc.	1–2	1–2	1–2
Interest and discount	3–2	7–6	15–14

Source: Table 47, altered to reflect underrepresentation of western and southern roads in 1850's, relaying of iron on New York roads in the 1840's, the lack of completion of many roads in the 1830's (which increased the proportion of expenses going to graduation), etc. All changes are well within the ranges of the standard deviations of Table 47.

[a] Fencing, if undertaken completely on both sides of the track for all roads (which it was not) could not have amounted to much more than 2 percent of total costs. Since a fence on both sides of the right of way could have been built for no more than $800 a mile, relative to total costs of $30,000 a mile, this comes to only slightly more than 2 percent. But since roads were not on average so well fenced, particularly in the South and West, a 1–2 percent subtraction from land costs including fencing is quite ample. Expenditure for fencing is added to the graduation and masonry account. For fencing costs see Danhof, "Farm-Making Costs," and also his "The Fencing Problem."

A first and obvious difference between investment and construction costs emerging as significant in Table 48 is the inclusion of land costs in railroad accounts. Although such outlay is an expense to the individual road, to the economy as a whole it is only a transfer expenditure since the transaction involves no production. Accordingly, a rather substantial part of railroad expenditures in the 1830's and 1840's, a little less than a tenth, and a smaller proportion in the 1850's (reflecting the shift of construction to less densely settled areas), fall outside the scope of an investment series.

The second important divergence is less obvious. This is contained in the interest and discount account that appears as the largest proportion of the miscellaneous account in later years.

After a residual allowance of 1 to 2 percent, say, for legal expenses, other nonrailroad assets held by some companies, et cetera, the remainder of the miscellaneous account consisted of the two components, interest and discount. The former consisted of cumulated payments of interest on capital during the period of construction, before operating revenues were available to meet such current obligations. Some roads, however, continued to charge payments of interest to capital account even after completion when they could not be financed out of current receipts, and there is even one instance when a road included all payments of interest in excess of the legal maximum of 6 percent.[7] The upward trend in interest paid is due to an increasing debt-equity ratio, and to the spreading practice of guaranteeing interest payments on equity during the gestation period, something lacking earlier. Discount is the difference between par value of securities and the actual payments received. As roads competed for funds in the 1850's, securities, particularly bonds, were sold at less than par to offer a dual incentive to investors: the prospect of capital gain by guaranteed redemption at par and a higher effective rate of interest than the nominal face rate. The growth of both the interest and discount accounts, therefore, perfectly reflects the financial accommodations accompanying the substantial railroad boom after 1849.

Each of these expenditures represented an increase in liabilities unmatched by any physical increase in road and equipment. This is most obvious in the case of discount since the corporation was liable for the face amount of the security, but had received in payment thereof only a fraction of par value with which to construct the railroad. Interest payments did not directly build mileage either. Faced with this divergence, and the immutable accounting identity of assets and liabilities, the choice before the railroad companies was either to increase construction account by transforming liabilities simultaneously into assets or to reduce other liabilities directly, that is, net worth. The first, not sur-

[7] An example of the former is the Illinois Central. See its financial history in *American Railroad Journal*, XXXIV (1861), 561–565. The Cape Cod Railroad in Massachusetts capitalized what it considered "excess" current charges. *Annual Reports of the Railroad Corporations in the State of Massachusetts, 1849* (Boston, 1850), p. 41.

prisingly, was the course actually followed in the treatment of both interest and discount.

The decision with regard to the disposition of the interest account has merit. Interest paid during construction is payment for two real inputs in the construction process, namely time and risk. So long as the gestation period is not artificially lengthened, therefore, interest payments are a cost as relevant as the payments for iron rails: given two roads, identical in all respects, the one that takes longer to complete costs more to the economy; given two roads with identical gestation periods, the one that pays a higher risk premium also costs more to the economy. The Pennsylvania Railroad was showing an appreciation of classical economics, as well as justifying its profits, when it contended that "interest is an element in the cost of construction and must be added to capital expended." [8] The Interstate Commerce Commission regulations embody the same recognition, and current railroad investment data include either actual payments of interest during the period of construction or imputed interest if financed internally.[9] Hence, apart from inappropriate charges to this account, interest is both an element of cost of construction and also part of investment expenditure, whether actually paid or not. To be consistent, therefore, interest should be computed on the entire capital flow. This makes it necessary to impute interest on share capital which bestowed no immediate return. In the 1830's and early 1840's interest was rarely paid, and yet at the same time share capital formed the preponderant part of finance, so that imputation is not an unimportant adjustment.

Discount on securities, in spite of its intimate connection with interest account, is another matter. Although discount is an indirect way of offering a higher rate of interest than the nominal rate, and hence an alternative to paying a higher nominal rate, the *total* amount of the reduction in price cannot apply to the construction account. The increase in effective yield due to dis-

[8] *First Annual Report of the Pennsylvania Railroad Company, 1847* (Philadelphia, 1848), p. 12.

[9] Primary Account No. 76 of the 1914 ICC classification of Investment in Road and Equipment allows for inclusion of interest payments on debt instruments during the period of construction as well as "reasonable charges for interest . . . on the carrier's own funds expended for construction purposes."

count consists of two components: the larger ratio of absolute interest payments to purchase price and the present value of the capital gain accruing at maturity. Since the interest account already registers the absolute charges during the gestation period, only the latter element is neglected. Moreover, not the total difference in price is relevant. A small portion, rather, represents the neglected interest cost paid *during the period of construction* and is admissible. Any other rule is equivalent to charging such interest costs over the entire life of the debt to capital account. The Interstate Commerce Commission, after initially dismissing discount altogether, conceded in 1914 that some part might legitimately be charged to construction. The permissible proportion is determined by the ratio of the period of construction to the maturity period of the security. Appropriately, since equity has an infinite life, no discount on share capital is recognized. If a forty-year bond is sold at a 20 percent discount to finance construction taking two years, the ICC regulations permit only 1 percent discount to be included in cost.[10]

With growing sales of securities at less than par in the 1850's to the point where many roads had 10 percent and more of their costs attributed to discount, this adjustment obviously affects a final investment estimate considerably. In addition to this explicit discount, of whose magnitude we have some idea from the distribution in Table 48 (approximately half of the interest and discount account in the 1850's), there is implicit discount buried in the construction account itself. This arose from the practice of paying contractors and suppliers in securities apparently accepted at par. Few participants in such arrangements did not reciprocate by raising their contract prices in proportion to the discount from par actually prevailing in the market. In this way, the charges for superstructure account, masonry work, etc., were simply escalated in proportion to the loss the contractor would have suffered by accepting the securities at par. Data for the North Missouri Railroad are illustrative. The prices of the prime contractor,

[10] This method is only an approximation. The value of the discount during the construction period, i.e., the portion of interest not charged, also depends upon the interest rate.

Sanger and Company, deviated from those actually paid in cash
to the subcontractors in the following proportions:[11]

	Sanger and Co.	Subcontractors
Earth excavation, per cubic yard	$ 0.28	$ 0.18 – 0.225
Hauling stone, per yard, per mile	0.50	0.40
First-class masonry, per cubic yard	11.00	8.00 – 9.00
Crossties	0.50	0.325– 0.505
Tracklaying, per mile	400.00	300.00 –325.00
Bridges, per lineal foot	20.00	12.00

The weighted difference came to 35 percent. The State Report
conceded that the prices were "probably too large by the amount
of discount in the bonds which were paid by the company to the
contractors at par." [12]

   This was presumably not an isolated instance as the practice
of building roads under contract grew more prevalent, particularly in the West and South. *De Bow's Review* noted the existence
of a dual price system early in the 1850's. Fifteen to sixteen cents
per cubic yard of excavation was the price if the transaction was
entirely for cash; twenty-five cents if securities were accepted for
as much as half the work.[13] Still more subtle methods of disguising
discount in the cost account were evolved. Quality deterioration
was another way of equating the value of services performed to
the payments received. Shoddy bridges, weak embankments, and
other examples of inferior workmanship are to be found on roads
built under contract.[14] The exchange of poor British iron for

[11] *Missouri Senate Journal*, Twentieth General Assembly, 1st Session (1858), appendix, p. 288.
[12] *Missouri Senate Journal*, 1858, appendix, p. 157.
[13] *De Bow's Review*, XVIII (1855), 405.
[14] See, for example, the report of the Board of Public Works investigating engineer on the condition of the Hannibal and St. Joseph. *Missouri Senate Journal, 1858*, appendix, pp. 219 ff. The road required the contractor to accept one-third payment in stocks and bonds.

questionable securities is only one such trade that became famous owing to its international setting.[15] It was repeated countless times domestically.

Hidden discount should not be accorded any different treatment than the explicit variety: the means of marketing securities, whether via contractors or directly, does not affect resources embodied in railroad capital formation. While the principle is clear, its application is difficult. That implicit discount was important is suggested by this statement of the Ohio Commissioner of Statistics: "Traced up to the actual receipt and expenditure of cash, probably not more than two-thirds of the nominal *cost* of our roads is represented by *money*. The other third is represented by discounts, exchange, and interest." [16] But this is meager basis for determining exactly what adjustment is required.

In the next section we attempt to ascertain more carefully the approximate discount, explicit and implicit, by which railroad accounts were in fact bloated. For now it is sufficient to have pointed out that railroad cost of construction and the concept of investment are by no means identical. Although no other substantial differences separate the two, Table 48 testifies that adjustments for land damages, discount, and imputed interest can come to as much as 20 percent of construction costs. A fortuitous identity between construction expenditures and investment does hold through the 1830's, because additions for imputed interest and deductions for land damages almost exactly offset each other. This is only historical accident. By the end of the period, the net distortion becomes considerable. The case of the United States is not unique, moreover. The oft-cited extreme construction costs in England reflect such noninvestment categories as

[15] *Herapath's Railroad Journal*, an English publication, even conceded its occurrence: "It is, no doubt, the fact, that the rails of American lines generally are indifferent stuff. The iron had to come from this country; and being paid for in bonds, it is said the iron-masters took advantage of their position and palmed off on the 'Yankees' inferior material." *Herapath's* need not have been so confident that the English came out ahead; the bonds eventually turned out to be rather "indifferent stuff" too. Quoted in the *Journal of the Franklin Institute*, 3rd ser. XXXVII (1859), 372.

[16] *Third Annual Report of the Ohio Commissioner of Statistics* (Columbus, 1860), p. 43. The Commissioner was Edwin Mansfield, former editor of the *Railroad Record*, and well acquainted with western railroad affairs during the period.

Parliamentary expenditures, land damages, and some discount on securities as well. In France and Germany the situation is similar. All railroad cost statements must be treated with caution.

The result of making the indicated corrections is what I term a quasi-net investment series. As the title suggests, it comes close to a net investment concept without quite being identical to it. It is not gross because the railroad cost accounts did not include replacement expenditures, as they were made over a number of years. On the other hand it exceeds a net investment concept because it is partially inclusive of depreciation. Railroads asserted, and continued to assert until the formal institution of depreciation accounting in 1907, that their replacement and maintenance expenditures exactly equaled depreciation so that no additional subtraction was required from construction accounts to reach net asset value of the roads. If this were true and the distribution of replacement and maintenance expenditures over time accorded with the physical deterioration of the assets, then a series based on cost accounts, and adjusted for land damages, imputed interest, and discount, would be exactly equal to a net investment series. Since railroads understated obsolescence, and because the time distributions of expenditures and deterioration did not coincide, the result is a quasi-net rather than a net series.

A Quasi-Net Investment Series

With the adjustments required to transform cost of construction now firmly in mind, and with the discussion concerning the reliability of the cost aggregates concluded, we may now proceed to the derivation of the specific decadal flows. Table 49 summarizes the results and should be referred to in connection with the following description.

In line (1) the cost aggregates referring to the end of 1839, 1850, and 1860, respectively, are given. The first of these was derived in Table 46, and the 1850 and 1860 figures are adjusted census values from Table 45. These last adjustments were minor, being limited to the subtraction of the Mauch Chunk at both dates and the addition of five excluded railroads to the 1850 totals: the West Feliciana in Louisiana, and the Catawissa, the Williams-

TABLE 49.   Quasi-net investment, by decade (millions of dollars)

	1827[a]	1839[a]	1850[a]	1860[a]
(1) Cumulative cost of construction	0	96.1	301.0	1151.2
(2) Expenditure flow				
(between terminal dates)		96.1	218.9	846.4
less:				
(3) Land purchases		6.7	17.5	25.4
(4) Discount and excess interest		0.0	0.0	127.0
plus:				
(5) Net imputed interest payments		7.2	2.2	0.0
(6) Quasi-net investment		96.6	203.6	694.0

Source: See text.
[a] End of year.

port and Elmira, the Little Schuylkill, and the Union Canal Company, all in Pennsylvania.[17] Relative to the absolute census magnitudes these 1850 changes come to little more than one percent.

Line (2) gives the expenditure flows between the indicated terminal dates. In principle, these should be equal to the differences between the cumulative cost totals of line (1); in fact they are not. There are two reasons why this is so. First, the cumulative construction costs do not represent cumulative asset values at all dates. Because roads failed in large numbers after 1839, they were not included in the 1850 tabulation although their expenditures are comprehended in the 1839 total. A simple difference between the two dates then understates the actual expenditure on new construction during the interval. Second, and applicable to all dates, the amount of mileage under construction is not the same at the end of each decade. Since the census totals

---

[17] The asymmetry between the treatment of railroad adjuncts of canals in Appendix A and here should be noted. We count them fully, even a private gravity road like the Pennsylvania Coal Company, for two reasons: the similarity in expenditures to other railroads; and their eventual incorporation into steam railroad companies. Private mine roads like the Mauch Chunk and some additional 150 miles measured by Daddow and Bannon are excluded because they do not fully satisfy the second condition, and equally to the point, cost information is almost totally lacking. (Daddow and Bannon, *Coal, Iron, and Oil,* p. 729.)

excluded roads in process, it is necessary to make some allowance for expenditures upon uncompleted projects that occurred in the decade before the mileage was opened.

The first of these factors increases substantially the estimated expenditure flow from 1840 through 1850. A tally of railroad failures, meaning either complete discontinuation such as occurred on ill-fated ventures like the New Orleans and Nashville, or radical write-downs of assets like that on the Northern Cross, whose more than $1,000,000 of construction cost brought less than $25,000 at auction, totals $8,400,000 of the cumulative 1839 cost.[18] This sum is therefore added to the difference between the 1850 and 1839 cumulants of line (1). In later periods failures were proportionally much less significant. The *American Railroad Journal*, writing in the aftermath of the panic of 1857, to be sure, claimed "the increased investment would have been considerably larger but for the reduced capital of many companies consequent upon a reorganization of their affairs." [19] But the construction accounts of such prominent roads thrown into receivership as the Pittsburgh, Fort Wayne, and Chicago, the Chicago, Alton, and St. Louis, and the Ohio and Mississippi, do not validate this contention. In most instances where the change was considerable, like the La Crosse and Milwaukee reorganization cited earlier, the write-down brought cost of construction into much closer alignment with an investment magnitude. Accordingly, no correction for later failures was deemed necessary.

The number of miles underway in 1850 but excluded from the census tabulation for that year is larger than at either of the other two terminal dates. Consequently it is necessary to increase the expenditure flow from 1840 to 1850 and to reduce that from 1850 to 1860. Although the census of 1880 mileage series indicates that 1,200 miles were added in 1851, some 800 of these accrued to corporations already included in the 1850 census; for these no compensation is required since the construction accounts include the outlays. The residual 375 miles is estimated to have already cost $15,000 per mile during the period up to and including 1850

[18] The criterion is failure to appear in the 1850 census tabulation or appearance at a much reduced cost. The list of railroads is too extensive to enumerate here.

[19] *American Railroad Journal*, XXXIV (1861), 17.

and a sum of $5,600,000 was therefore added to the 1840–1850 flow. No adjustment was made for mileage underway in 1839 since the totals for that year include expenditures on roads in process. For the 1851–1860 interval a smaller net difference is involved. Of more than 1,000 miles of road opened in 1861 only 126 miles seem to be excluded from the purview of the 1860 census. Most of the mileage brought to completion in that year was built by already existent corporations and consequently the work done on them up to the end of 1860 was included in the 1860 cost figure. A difference of construction in process in favor of 1850 of some 250 miles therefore exists; the direct 1851–1860 flow accordingly has to be reduced by $3,750,000 (at the same estimated $15,000 a mile).

These corrected expenditures in line (2) now must undergo the adjustments described in the previous section to convert them to properly defined investment flows. For each decade the estimated percentage of expenditure for right of way is taken from Table 48 and the corresponding absolute level determined. These are given in line (3).

The subtractions for discount and for interest paid after the close of the construction period are less easily ascertained. Fortunately the category of legitimate interest costs provides a fruitful entry to the subject. For since we have a fairly good notion of what railroads actually charged to their interest and discount accounts, any excess over warranted interest payments is then explicit discount and inflated (or, if negative, imputed) interest payments.[20] Allowable interest expense can be measured indirectly. Suppose that all capital needed for construction during a year was obtained at its very beginning. Then the appropriate interest charges would be iC, where i is equal to the rate of interest and C the annual cost of construction (inclusive of interest payments and discount); if it took two years to complete, and expenditures were distributed evenly, charges would be $iC/2$ in the first year and $i(C/2 + C/2)$ in the second, since the first year's obligations must still be met until operation is underway. More

[20] The symmetrical treatment of discount and excess (or imputed) interest leads to a slight error. Interest paid beyond the gestation period should be subtracted in full while some discount should be allocated to construction. With the sums involved the maximum error thus introduced is far less than 1 percent of investment.

generally, under these assumptions, the allowable charge is equal
to $\sum_{n=0}^{k} (k - n)iC/k$, where k is the length of the gestation period.
For the case where the flow of capital coincides exactly with the
smooth expenditure profile, the interest costs are lower and equal
to $\sum_{n=0}^{k} (k - n - 1/2)iC/k$. The percentage of allowable interest
expense to total cost follows by simple division by C. The result
then is a simple function of the length of the gestation period, the
nature of finance, and the prevailing rate of interest. For a two-
year construction period the proportional amount of interest cost
is the interest rate itself when the capital is obtained continuously; for the discrete case it is $1.5i$. For three years, the solutions are $1.5i$ and $2i$ respectively. Under the more realistic circumstances of smaller costs in the first years of construction, the
correct percentage would be somewhat lower, but not enough
to invalidate the formula.

With the American practice of opening sections of road as
rapidly as possible, and the inclusion in cost of later expenditures
for equipment and capital improvements (outlays with effectively
no gestation period), and with interest rates of 7 to 9 percent
actually paid, the percentage of cost accounted for by interest
varies between 7 and 10 percent over the three decades, being
larger at the beginning owing to longer gestation periods.

This result, together with Table 48, provides a basis for filling
in the rest of the entries.[21] In the 1830's we know from the percentage distribution of costs that only 2 to 3 percent of expenditure probably resulted from payments of interest or discounts on
securities. The appropriate charges for interest alone would have
involved something like 10 percent with a 3-year construction
period and a charge of 7 percent for funds. The difference, or 7
percent of the total corrected expenditure flow, is added on line
(5).[22] During the period 1840–1850 6 to 7 percent of costs con-

[21] Admittedly, given the large standard errors calculated for the interest and
discount portion of costs, the degree of potential inaccuracy in this procedure is
almost intolerably high. For this type of correction I doubt that much improvement
is possible.
[22] The total interest on line (5) is slightly more than $0.07 \times \$96.1$ million since
the corrected figure must include the imputed interest costs themselves. The correct
factor is 0.0753.

sisted of interest payments and discount. Probably 7 to 8 percent would be the correct proportion of interest charges taken by themselves, reflecting a lower rate of interest and a shorter length of construction. The 1 percent plus correction factor is entered on line (5) too.

In the 1850's, for the first time, the charges in the railroad accounts themselves exceed the permissible interest costs. Hence, it is necessary to switch to subtraction. But it is not sufficient merely to subtract the appropriate proportion of interest payments from the total interest and discount actually reported. Implicit escalation of costs is also a factor, as we have seen. The Ohio Commissioner's assertion that interest and discount, implicit and explicit, made up about one third of costs suggests, now that we know what interest costs are allowable, that excess interest plus discount was about 25 percent of cost of construction. Henry Varnum Poor, writing in 1868, can be quoted to the same effect: "It is not probable that the stocks and bonds issued by all the companies have produced more than seventy five cents on the dollar." [23]

This is probably too large a discount, however. It suggests implicit discount was fully 3 times as prevalent as explicit. More direct evidence than this implausible implication can be mustered. At the time the Ohio Commissioner was stating his views, the capital structure of Ohio railroads looked like the following: [24]

First mortgages	$30,590,550
Second mortgages	17,235,250
Third mortgages	8,129,300
Income bonds, floating debt, and other mortgages	13,332,395
Total bonds	69,287,495
Share capital	56,290,122

If first mortgage bonds sold at a 10 percent discount, all other debt at 20 percent less than par, and even shares at a 20 percent

[23] *Poor's Manual, 1868–69*, p. 24.
[24] Tabulated from *Second Annual Report of Ohio Commissioner of Statistics* (Columbus, 1859), pp. 71, 73.

discount, the aggregate discount is only 18 percent. In fact with shares sold to subscribers along the right of way, it is doubtful whether such an average reduction for stock prevailed. For securities actually sold in the market, we know from the discussion in Chapter IV that western railroads regularly negotiated bonds at discounts no greater than 10 to 15 percent during the period of peak construction. Southern railroads, making up the bulk of later construction, were largely financed by state securities that did not fall much more below par than this. The Tennessee Road Commissioner in his annual report for 1857 termed a discount of 20 percent unusually heavy. He did so with good reason. Comparison of cash received with par value of bonds sold for Tennessee railroads in 1858–1859 indicates an average discount only of 91. Shares were invariably recorded at par.[25] In the East, for much construction occurred there as well during the 1850's, discount was probably still less prevalent. Older, well-established railroads like the Baltimore and Ohio found a market for second mortgage bonds at more than 91 in 1853.[26] More striking evidence is the average discount of bonds of New York railroads of only 12 percent in 1855. It was also reported that 30 percent of the total cost of railroads providing the necessary information was paid for directly by stock issues. Thus even if implicit discount of 20 percent was embedded in construction account by this means, aggregate discount of less than 15 percent is certain.[27]

On the strength of this evidence, 15 percent has been deducted from the expenditure flow of 1851–1860 in Table 49 to compensate for the unwarranted exaggeration of contemporary construction accounts. This implies a somewhat greater amount of actual discount — say, 16.5 percent — some small portion of which is correctly charged as investment. Nothing much more exact is

[25] *American Railroad Journal*, XXX (1857), 741, for the reprinted extract of the 1857 report. For 1858–1859 data see Tennessee Commissioner of Roads, *Report to the General Assembly on the Condition of Railroads in Tennessee for 1858–1859* (Nashville, 1859).

[26] *American Railroad Journal*, XXVI (1853), 153.

[27] *American Railroad Journal*, XXIX (1856), 737. If stock issues to contractors were 30 percent of the total cost of construction, they in turn represented half of the equity. With half the shares selling for 20 percent discount, the other half at 10 percent, and all bonds at 12 percent, total discount is still less than 14 percent. If all other shares brought par receipts, the discount is barely above 10 percent.

possible at such an aggregative level. But while not precise, the final series is a far better measure of investment than the initial crude expenditure flows.

These results are subject to a commodity flow check. The total expenditure for iron rails in each decade, as independently determined by the physical requirements for mileage constructed and by prevailing delivered prices, when multiplied by the reciprocal of the percentage that iron outlays represented of total investment, should yield results identical to those just developed. This method has particular attraction in the 1850's since the use of quoted market prices completely bypasses the problem of implicit discount as it arose from inflated contracts. It also has certain weaknesses. Since the only magnitude that is observed is the percentage of rail purchases to total *expenditure*, the derived ratio of iron outlays to *investment* necessarily builds into the check the prior adjustments for explicit discount, imputed interest, and land purchases. Note, too, that the very large standard error associated with the observed percentage makes for very wide variation in the estimate of the multiplier. Finally, the valuation of the number of tons of rails consumed in new construction poses problems: for the 1830's there is no consistent series of American prices, and in the 1850's the annual variation in price is large enough that substantial leads of rail delivery ahead of emplacement could lead to error. Despite these shortcomings, which after all is the reason for not placing primary reliance upon the commodity flow approach, it is not an unuseful exercise. At the very least it tests the rough consistency of 4 different sets of information: the cost distribution of Table 48, the consumption of iron rails, rail prices, and aggregate construction outlays.

We start with the 1830's. The thorough researches of Gerstner provide a basis for the estimate of iron required for new construction. Of the 3,229 completed miles represented by the expenditures reckoned in Table 46, about 35 percent were laid with edge rail of various sorts, the prototypes of the soon to be universal T-rail.[28] Two thousand miles, including almost the entire construction in the South and West plus some eastern roads, had

---

[28] This mileage total includes 387 miles completed early in 1840, since the largest part of the expenditures for this construction date to 1839 or before.

nothing more for rails than simple plates of iron, ranging between $\frac{1}{2}$ and 1 inch in thickness and 2 and $2\frac{1}{2}$ inches in width, spiked to wooden bases. Early edge rail varied in weight from the $25\frac{1}{2}$ pounds per yard of the South Carolina Railroad to the 58 pounds of the Boston and Providence, or from 40 to 91 gross tons per mile. The average weight of iron on all railroads so constructed was 69.5 gross tons per mile.[29] Strap iron, too, showed substantial variation: Stevenson spoke of 13 pounds a yard, or 20 tons a mile, as usual; on the Philadelphia and Columbia 23 tons were used, with 30 tons on the Syracuse and Utica; at the other extreme Gerstner found some southern roads using less than 10 pounds per yard.[30] An average of 25 gross tons per mile for strap iron is probably not far from the mark.[31] These average weights and the mileages indicated above, plus a small (5 percent) allowance for sidings and double tracking, yield an estimate of total consumption for the decade of almost 140,000 gross tons.

Although we can be reasonably certain of the number of tons consumed, the relevant delivered cost is much less sure. Those iron price series we have for the period have reasonably uniform movements over time, but their absolute levels are often substantially different. And it is the absolute level that is crucial here.[32] We have used two of these series to indicate the range of difference involved, one of English railroad iron prices to which have been added allowances for commission, insurance, ocean freight, and domestic delivery, the other of merchant bar prices in New York to which only domestic delivery charges have been

[29] Gerstner also described the type of rail and superstructure. These mileages and weights have been calculated from his full series of articles on American railways. The Baltimore and Ohio and the Philadelphia and Columbia railroads both are credited with edge rail on their complete distance, although some strap iron was still used on them.

[30] David Stevenson, *Sketch of the Civil Engineering of North America*, 1st ed. (London, 1838), p. 242; Ringwalt, *Transport Development*, p. 84; Stevens, *Beginnings of the New York Central* p. 154; Gerstner, "Internal Improvements in the United States," *Journal of the Franklin Institute*, n.s., XXVI (1840), 292.

[31] Since this section has been completed, Robert W. Fogel (*Railroads*, p. 179), has converted Gerstner's specifications of size of strap iron to weight and his calculated average is almost identical to the 25 gross tons used here.

[32] Extrapolation back of a known later absolute price is no real solution since it embodies the assumption that the later relative differences between the series prevailed earlier. This is by no means obvious.

added.[33] The railroad iron series gives an estimate of aggregate expenditure on iron over the period of $8.7 million; the merchant bar series, $12.4 million.[34] Had the American Iron and Steel Association merchant bar prices been used, the total would have been even higher. The bar iron prices probably overstate the cost of strap iron, but they understate the cost of edge rail since the latter was relatively more expensive then, although cheaper subsequently.

The final step in the procedure is the calculation of the proper multiplier by which to scale up these iron expenditures to total railroad investment. In Table 48 it is seen that superstructure costs represented about 30 percent of total expenditures over the decade of the 1830's. The iron component must have accounted for 40 percent of this subtotal, or 12 percent of the aggregate.[35]

---

[33] MacGregor, *Commercial Statistics of America*, p. 387, presents an English railroad iron price series from 1831 on, reprinted from *Hunt's Merchants' Magazine*, XII (1845), 233. This was converted to dollars at the rate of $5 = 1£. It was extrapolated back to 1829 by a merchant bar series. 10 percent for commission, 1.5 percent for insurance, $5 for ocean freight and $3 for domestic freight were all added to obtain a reasonable facsimile of delivered price.

The commission and insurance rates were taken from J. D. De Bow, *Encyclopedia*, p. 397; their magnitude is confirmed by independent evidence in Fred M. Jones, "Middlemen in the Domestic Trade of the United States, 1800–1860," *Illinois Studies in the Social Sciences*, XXI, no. 3 (1938), 20, 23. Freight rates of about $5 are confirmed by De Bow, p. 397; MacGregor, pp. 387, 884; and less directly, by Robert G. Albion, *Square Riggers on Schedule* (Princeton, 1938), p. 268. For actual charges paid by the Erie Railroad in 1840 confirming these magnitudes see Mott, *Ocean and Lakes*, p. 329. Domestic delivery charges embody the assumption of average inland shipment of 75 miles at 4 cents a ton-mile. No annual changes could be incorporated into either of these shipping costs.

Duty of $37 was added prior to 1830, 25 percent *ad valorem* for 1830 and 1831, and none thereafter since iron was placed on the free list. The merchant bar price series was collected by the Secretary of the Treasury in 1863 and reprinted in Grosvenor, *Protection*, p. 221.

[34] Annual variations were taken into account by constructing a decadal average price weighted by mileage put in place in the following year to allow for the lead of purchases. The 1880 census mileage series was used in preference to the series implicit in Gerstner since he does not indicate the completion of specific sections of road.

[35] Since land costs and additional imputed interest virtually cancel each other, the proportion of superstructure to reported costs and to investment is the same. For the proportion of iron to superstructure see the description of various superstructures in Ringwalt, *Transport Development*, pp. 84–85, and also the discussions in Benjamin Latrobe, "Description of a New Form of Rail . . ." in *American Railroad Journal*, XII (1841), 182.

The correct multiplier is therefore about 8.5. Application of this figure to the above expenditures yields the two alternative estimates of $74.0 and $105.4 million, results that bound the $95.6 million entered in line (6) of Table 49.

The check obtained in the 1840's is equally consistent. Iron rail requirements for the 5,545 miles of road represented in the expenditure flow from 1840 to 1850 come to just about 550,000 gross tons.[36] The average weight over the decade used for this mileage is 83 gross tons per mile, i.e., 53-pound-rail, exclusive of sidings, yard track, et cetera. This over-all average is the result of different patterns of construction in the two halves of the decade. In the first years, as the projects begun or planned in the 1830's were brought to fruition, lighter rails were usual; in the last part of the period, new construction in Massachusetts and New York utilizing heavier rails dominated. Of the mileage added between 1840 and 1845, inclusive, 31 percent was in the South; between 1846 and 1850, less than 20 percent. According to Gerstner, the rail being placed in such lines varied between strap iron and light edge rail weighing scarcely less than 40 pounds. Even newly built eastern lines like the Attica and Buffalo used strap iron in 1842, and the Baltimore and Ohio was using light bridge rail of about 50 pounds. By contrast, at the end of the decade, construction was almost exclusively employing edge rail — and heavy weights at that. No road in New York was relying upon sections weighing less than 56 pounds a yard for their main track, and the Massachusetts roads displayed the same practice. The weight of rails for the 1902 miles constructed through 1845 accordingly is taken at 70 tons; for the mileage thereafter 90 tons is used.[37]

[36] This mileage estimate is the adjusted difference between the earlier mileage total of the 1830's and the 1860 census total for 1850 of 8590 miles. Additions of 117 miles for failed road that disappeared were necessary plus 67 miles of net inclusions. (Note, in light of Fogel's demonstration in his book, that the 1839 Gerstner total cannot be used in conjunction with the 1880 census figure for 1850, that the *1860* census is the source employed here, with the specified changes to assure comparability. Interpolation of this 5545 miles by the adjusted 1880 census series (see n. 70), yields a total of 1902 from 1840 to 1845, and 3643 from 1846 to 1850. The corresponding figures directly from the census are 2345 and 3961 miles.)

[37] At the latter part of the decade, even western roads like the Little Miami were planning upon rail weighing 90 tons. *American Railroad Journal,* XIX (1846), 729.

To such requirements for main track, we add an allowance for 10 percent additional trackage for sidings, at weights of 50 and 70 tons, respectively. We know from the Massachusetts and New York state reports that such additional trackage amounted to 11 percent of the 1850 mileage in the former state, and to 15 percent in the latter. The average elsewhere was probably lower, however, so that 10 percent in aggregate is a reasonable approximation. Finally, we allow for 600 miles of double track built in the latter half of the decade. New York and Massachusetts railroads directly account for 422 miles, and the Philadelphia and Reading for another 94; an additional 84 miles on the variety of railways then in operation is a plausible safeguard against undercounting.[38]

Two price series are used once more to value physical consumption. One is derived by dividing declared value of imports of railroad iron by the reported quantities; such a price has the advantage of being properly weighted through the year and referring distinctly to newly produced iron going for the most part into new construction. The second is the continuation of the merchant bar series used in the 1830's. As before, the average decadal price is determined by using the mileage added data of the 1880 census as annual weights. The domestic merchant bar series gives the higher expenditure estimate of $38.2 million versus $34.3 million for the imported railroad iron series.[39]

[38] *Annual Reports of the Railroad Corporations in the State of Massachusetts, 1850* (Boston, 1851), *passim* (no summary tables published); *Annual Report of the State Engineer and Surveyor on the Railroads of the State of New York for 1850* (Albany, 1851), p. 7, and appended Table A.

[39] The series on imports of railroad iron and declared values cannot be traced to the Congressional Documents since these do not separate bar and railroad iron on a regular basis until 1855. The reported quantities and values for railroad iron apparently come from a Treasury tabulation made at the behest of the American Iron Association and published in their *Bulletin* for 1856, to which Robert W. Fogel directed me. The railroad iron import series up to 1855 is in the *American Railroad Journal*, XXIX (1856), 490, reprinted from the *Iron Masters' Journal*. It also is in Benjamin French, *History of the Iron Trade of the United States* (New York, 1858), p. 70 and in Grosvenor, *Protection*, p. 221.

The same additions for commission, etc., are made as in the 1830's with the exception that domestic delivery charges are $1 a ton from 1840 to 1846 and $3 thereafter. The lower initial charges reflect improved transport to the nearby, inland points where construction was occurring early in the decade. Since the import price series refers to a fiscal year (ending June 30 beginning in 1844) it was not lagged additionally. Iron was free until 1843 when a specific duty of $25 was imposed, and a duty of 30 percent by the Tariff of 1846.

The multiplier appropriate to this second decade of railroad investment is smaller than the statistic used in the 1830's. Although superstructure costs are the same percentage of reported railroad costs in both decades, iron rails form a larger proportion of railroad investment in the 1840's as a result both of the heavier weight of iron and the different ratio of investment to actual expenditures. Excluding land and including imputed interest, superstructure costs come to a little less than a third of total investment, and railroad iron is perhaps 65 percent of this, or about 21 percent overall.[40] In order to find investment, it is necessary therefore to multiply expenditures on iron by a factor of 4.8. This operation yields estimates of $179.5 and $161.0 million, respectively. Our estimate in Table 49, $203.0 million, patently lies outside of this range.

The discrepancy can be explained. Many older roads correctly charged to construction account the extra expenditure incurred in laying down edge rail in replacement of strap iron during the 1840's. The New York roads, and the Baltimore and Ohio, even went so far as to enter *all* expenditures, less the scrap value of the old rails, on capital account. These specific examples accounted for 400 miles of retracking during the decade. Here, alone, therefore, are an additional 36,000 tons of iron whose inclusion increases the previous estimates to $191.2 and $171.5 million. The disparity is no longer as prominent, nor is it improbable that further instances of such practice are to be found. No blatant inconsistency is discovered; rather, only the necessity of adapting the commodity flow technique to special circumstances. In this regard, it should be noted that the proportion allocated to superstructure in Table 48 was increased from the observation in Table 47 exactly to reflect this reconstruction; alternatively, applying the greater multiplier appropriate to new construction to the initial iron outlays will also make the two sets of estimates consistent.

During the 1850's, 22,111 miles of construction generate the expenditure flow of Table 49. A number of indications point to a

[40] The proportion of iron to total superstructure is almost always in the range 60–70 percent on either actual or projected construction during the decade. See for example, *American Railroad Journal*, XVIII (1845), 458–459, 760; XIX (1846), 630; XX (1847), 28; XXI (1848), 72, 119, 771.

slightly increased weight of at least 90 gross tons per mile for this decade owing to the final disappearance of strap iron and light edge rail. A compilation of reports of 61 railroads by the American Iron Association in 1856 indicates an average weight of 91.3 tons per mile. These railroads totaled 5,840 miles and thus constitute perhaps a 25 percent sample of all railroads in the country. Since plans for an additional 573 miles for extensions and sidings are reported, it is clear that this average has relevance to the marginal weight as well.[41] More conclusive evidence is the actual weight used on construction in that decade in two southern states that together accounted for some 10 percent of the national decadal increment. For 1,383 miles of Tennessee railroads there was an average (weighted) of 60.6 pounds per yard; 1,021 miles of Virginia trackage used rails weighing only slightly less, 55.8 pounds.[42] These, converted to gross tons per mile, are, respectively, 95.2 and 87.8 tons. Since we might expect southern mileage to fall below a national average, these heavy weights are more significant evidence in favor of a 90-ton mean than the well known large weights on eastern railroads.[43] First track thus accounts for consumption of almost 2,000,000 tons. Double track of 1,700 miles represents 153,000 tons more, and with an allowance for sidings amounting to 8 percent of mileage at the lower weight of 80 tons, total consumption amounts to 2,300,000 tons.[44]

[41] *Bulletin of the American Iron Association*, 1856, p. 35.

[42] *Annual Reports of the Railroads of the State of Virginia to Board of Public Works, 1858–1859* (Richmond, 1860); *Report to the General Assembly on the Condition of Railroads in Tennessee for 1858–1859*. There are also indications that railroads in other southern states behaved similarly. *The Sixth Annual Report of the Mississippi Central Railroad* (Memphis, 1858) indicates use of iron rails of 56 to 58 pounds per yard.

[43] New York railroads in 1855 used an average of 93 gross tons per mile of all track, including sidings and branches. *Annual Report of the Board of Railroad Commissioners of the State of New York for 1855* (Albany, 1856), pp. 32–33. Weights as high as 70 and 75 pounds per yard were reported on railroads like the Hudson River and the Erie, which built extensively during the decade.

[44] Sidings were reduced to 8 percent of mileage in deference to the extensive construction in the West and South where lesser density of traffic required less ancillary construction. The Tennessee and Virginia reports indicate ratios of 5.2 and 5.9 percent, respectively. With regard to double tracking, there was an increase over 1850 of almost 1200 miles in the 3 states of Massachusetts, New York, and Pennsylvania alone. (*Returns of the Railroad Corporations in Massachusetts, 1860* [Boston, 1861]; *Annual Report of the State Engineer and Surveyor on the Railroads of the State*

Once more, two price series are used. One is the continuation of the railroad iron import series used in the 1840's. The other is the comparable American series on railroad iron prices quoted in the Philadelphia market, available beginning in 1847. The mileage added series of the 1880 census is used as a means of weighting the annual iron prices into a suitable decadal average. In this instance, because the prices both relate to rails, the divergence between the two series is quite small, the import series leading to an average price during the decade of $61.09 a ton and the lagged American series to $64.13.[45]

The corresponding cumulated expenditures are $139.6 and $146.5 million. The relevant multiplier is obtained as before from Table 48 where expenditures for superstructure in the 1850's are indicated as 28 percent of total railroad costs; subtracting land and explicit discount, which together make up some 10 percent of railroad accounts, means that superstructure is increased to about 31 percent of investment. With iron amounting to about 70 percent of the account by this date it follows that the proportion of total costs going to the purchase of iron was slightly less than 22 percent, or that the multiplier is 4.6.[46] Estimates of total expenditure of $642.2 and $673.9 million result.

---

of New York for 1860, in which the increase in double track *and* sidings was allocated by using a 10 percent proportion of sidings to total mileage; and the Pennsylvania Report of the Auditor General as reprinted in *Hunt's Merchants' Magazine,* XLII [1860], 502–503.) The Baltimore and Ohio had double track of 100 miles or so, and the Hartford and New Haven, the Concord, and the Galena and Chicago meant almost another 200 miles. All in all 1700 miles is about right, since those roads with double track were also those about which we have the most information.

[45] The import iron series was increased by duty (first 30 and then 24 percent beginning in 1857) and the same delivery charges, etc., as in the late 1840's. There is some confirmation for these delivery charges. Freights from England to the interior varied from about $7.50 to Toledo and Detroit to $10.50 to Cincinnati; at another place it is stated that total costs, including commissions, to Cleveland are $9.14. Our $8 in the former case and our $11 in the latter compare quite favorably (*American Railroad Journal,* XXIV [1851], 232, 273, 665). The American iron series is published in the bulletins of the Iron and Steel Association and appears in the Aldrich Report as well as most accessibly in *Historical Statistics,* p. 124.

[46] For the 70 percent for iron rails see the annual report of the Illinois Central for 1857 and that of the New Orleans, Jackson, and Great Northern for 1858, where the proportion was 69 percent and 76 percent, respectively; on the Hannibal and St. Joseph it was two thirds and slightly more on the St. Louis and Iron Mountain (*Missouri Senate Journal,* 1858, appendix, pp. 204, 248); in Virginia, with

The lower extimate falls only 7.5 percent below the $694.6 million estimate of Table 49, the higher but 3 percent. The validity of the extensive adjustments to the crude expenditure flows is thus affirmed. A bias to underestimation is to be expected when there already exists a sizable bloc of mileage of earlier vintage to which a variety of capital improvements constantly is being made. Construction accounts more adequately record such expenditures than a commodity flow analysis based upon a single, albeit important, input. A similar phenomenon occurs when the method is applied to the 1840's. Accordingly, the lesser commodity flow estimates are indicative not of too niggardly a subtraction for discount, but rather of an appropriate allowance.

Replacement Expenditures

The series of original investment expenditure, having thus been corroborated, must now be further adjusted to a gross level. Quasi-net investment derived from railroad construction accounts exclude all replacement outlays, and these charges to current account — although numerically insignificant in a period of initial capital formation — should be counted. There is some question, however, as to whether all replacement qualifies. The current definition of railroad gross investment excludes renewals of ties and rails; Ulmer has done the same in his estimates of capital formation beginning in 1870.[47] The rationale for such a definition is the much lesser degree of substitutability over time such expenditure is deemed to possess. If there is little latitude the outlays become more akin to repairs than investment. Only the gross magnitudes are affected by such a decision, it must be emphasized. Depreciation and repairs are inversely correlated; hence, the larger the sums attributed to maintenance, the smaller is the allowance for capital consumption, and so net investment remains the same.

If we adopt this accounting rule in our historical work, our

almost 5 percent of the decadal increase in mileage expenditure on iron rails, spikes and chairs ranged between 70 and 76 percent of total cost of superstructure (*Annual Reports of the Railroads of the State of Virginia to Board of Public Works, 1859–1860, passim*).
[47] Ulmer, *Capital in Transportation.*

additions to the quasi-net figures of Table 49 will be minor indeed. With equipment a small part of total investment in those early years, and with continuing purchases primarily for expansion rather than replacement, understatement on this account is limited. The exclusion of renewals of ties and rails before 1860 is not as obvious as in the twentieth century, however. Flexibility quite definitely applied earlier. In the 1840's the Raleigh and Gaston Railroad found it possible to continue operations even in the absence of a continuous track;[48] other railroads probably showed similar variation, if not to this extent. In the late 1850's, evidence points to delay of replacements of rails and substitution of repairs, instead, due to straitened financial circumstances. Before the era of state railroad commissions and enforcible safety regulations, mechanical response to requirements is not a likelihood. In deference to the logic of temporal consistency, however, although the totals are presented inclusive of renewals of ties and rails, the data are disaggregated so that one can choose among the alternative definitions according to his preference.[49]

As before, to estimate replacements we start with the railroad accounts, but this time with the operating rather than the capital component. After the appropriate decadal flows are derived, these are checked, where possible, by reference to other methods. Ties and rails, responsible for the largest part of renewals, are considered first.

By the end of the pre-Civil War period, maintenance of way amounted to just about a fourth of total operating expenses. Contemporary testimony and new statistical calculations both concur in this estimate.[50] A sample of fifty railroad reports for the years 1858 and 1859 from all regions of the country yields an unweighted average of 27 percent; moreover, despite a slightly

[48] See the description in Brown, *A State Movement in Railroad Development*, p. 57.

[49] A second reason for including such renewals is no longer valid. Until Robert E. Gallman's new estimates of gross capital formation that segregate railroad and nonrailroad investment in "Gross National Product," the commodity flow estimates marking up all construction materials implicitly included renewals of ties and rails in total investment. Then any comparison such as Ulmer performed understated the railroad contribution.

[50] For the former, see *American Railroad Journal*, XXXII (1859), 585, and Colburn and Holley, *Permanent Way*, p. 7; for the latter, see Chap. III, p. 124, n. 61.

higher percentage on southern railroads (owing to smaller proportional outlays for fuel), the difference is not statistically significant.

In the 1840's the proportion was apparently smaller. In Massachusetts and New York, the only states for which we possess anything resembling adequate reports at this early date, the figure was 20 and 22 percent respectively at the end of the decade. In Massachusetts in 1846 and 1840 both, it was a still smaller 17 percent. My suspicion is that proportional expenditure in the 1830's was not far different from this last figure. Although all roads were new, which tended to reduce maintenance outlays, they also were the product of an immature technology, which caused more current expense. By way of meager confirmation the Washington branch of the Baltimore and Ohio experienced an 18 percent allocation of operating expenses, just about equal to the Massachusetts experience.[51]

These ratios provide a base from which to segregate actual renewal expenditures from the routine tasks of maintenance. The latter were by no means insignificant. Track adjustment, cleaning of culverts, repairs of embankment slides, and the like were quite important in the daily operations of railroads. Even after "an uncommonly favorable winter" the Virginia and Tennessee stil found it necessary to expend a third of its road account for removing slides from cuts, opening ditches, raising and widening the embankment, and adjusting the track.[52]

By contrast, renewals of iron were a comparatively minor proportion of the total. In Massachusetts, with the oldest and probably best maintained roads in the country, about 15 percent of maintenance expenses were reported as due to replacement of iron (including laying down) in both 1846 and 1849. This ratio gradually increased to a level in excess of 20 percent in 1860, this latter being a year of especially large replacement. By contrast, the New York proportion remains smaller over the entire period: it starts from 4 percent in 1850, reaches 14 percent in 1856, and

---

[51] *Twelfth Annual Report of the Baltimore and Ohio* (Baltimore, 1839), pp. 15–16. On the older and outdated "main stem," expenses were almost 25 percent.

[52] *Annual Reports of the Railroads of the State of Virginia to Board of Public Works, 1859–1860*, pp. 58, 60, 88.

stays at approximately that level thereafter. This difference is due to the fact that New York railroads were newer. In particular the very small 1850 result can be explained by the extensive rebuilding of the New York roads with T-rail scant years before. In general, the early years of railroad operation saw no need for renewals, and the absence of depreciation accounting meant that no charge was entered. As the chief engineer of the Galena and Chicago explained:

When a road is recently built, and the materials composing the track are new and unworn, the depreciation wear and tear, although going steadily on, is not very noticeable for the first few years, and the current expenses of maintenance of way are small. At length . . . the track begins to fail . . . and expenses . . . increased, until it reaches the maximum, when renewals keep even pace with depreciation.[53]

Although the absolute expenditures for iron renewals increase as a function of the cumulative tonnage carried on the road, and hence with time, the change in the *percentage* of maintenance expenses spent for renewals will be damped since other outlays also expand. In the subsequent calculations, therefore, the assumption of a constant decadal proportion is not so productive of error as might first appear. It may be noted in this connection that some experimentation with both cross-section and time series data in an effort to determine a functional relationship between the percentage of iron renewals and time yielded no evidence of the same.[54]

Generalization of the results in these two states, with a small allowance for the upward tendency of the Massachusetts results, suggests that perhaps 4 percent of total operating expenses during the 1850's were spent for renewals of iron. This is probably nearer the *average* rate than the six to seven percent inferred by the *American Railroad Journal* from the scattered company reports it published.[55] Over a period of years renewals amounted to be-

[53] Annual Report of the Galena and Chicago Railroad for 1859 quoted in *Hillyer's American Railroad Magazine*, III (1860), 98.
[54] Specifically, the correlation between the ratio of iron renewals and age of road for 7 railroads taken from the 1856 New York report was .07. All roads older than 8 years were excluded, to avoid the possibility of recent relaying with new rails. A scatter diagram showed no evidence of nonlinearities.
[55] *American Railroad Journal*, XXXII (1859), 672.

tween 3 and 12 percent of operating expenses on such old and heavily utilized roads as the Boston and Worcester, the Boston and Providence, the Philadelphia and Reading, the Western, and the Erie, with the average on these close to 6 percent. Rather than representing a national standard, such results determine an upper limit, and the 4 percent figure described above is clearly more adequate for our purposes.[56]

Applying this figure to our earlier estimates for operating expenses derived in Appendix A, and interpolating between the benchmark years of 1849, 1855–1856, and 1859 on a percentage basis to obtain the needed summation over the decade, we find about $19.9 million were spent during the 1850's on renewal of rails. A decade before, in spite of the older age structure of the capital stock, a smaller proportional expenditure is indicated for two reasons: the extensive retracking, a large part of which was charged to construction account; and also the lesser traffic carried per mile of road. The former operates here with particular force since the Massachusetts railroads — on whose experience the proportion is almost wholly based — conservatively charged to operating expenses the entire cost of retracking, and so exaggerated replacement outlays during the 1840's. Applying a factor of 2 percent to estimated total operating expenses over the 11-year interval from 1840 to 1850 yields an expenditure of $2.3 million; finally, using a similar charge for the 1830's, the total derived is $0.2 million.

The estimate for the 1850's is particularly susceptible to a commodity flow check. Estimates of total domestic production and imports beginning with 1849 are available in Table 13. Since the requirements for new construction already have been allotted, it is only a matter of their subtraction to get replacement consumption as a residual, if inventories are reasonably similar at the two dates. The mileage added in 1851 and 1861 is almost the same, and since the requirements for *prospective* new construction at the earlier date are balanced by greater future replacement

[56] Virginia results are informative: only 3 railroads provided information indicating renewals of iron in 1858–1859; this is probably indicative of the absence of expenditures on many roads. The 3 roads, 5 years old, reporting such outlays spent 4.2, 1.8, and 0.7 percent of operating expenses. See *Annual Reports of the Railroads of the State of Virginia to Board of Public, 1858–1859.*

requirements at the latter, the assumption of little net change in inventories is a reasonable one. The two total supply estimates (based on two different import series) then yield two replacement estimates for the period 1851–1860: 795,000 and 613,000 gross tons. These quantities next are to be valued by the appropriate decadal average price. More than price fluctuation must be considered in its specification. There is also the scrap value of the replaced rails that must be subtracted from the cost. This is true whether or not the replacement rails were rerolled, as was most often the case. The correct addition to the capital stock is the *incremental* value of the new rails. Accordingly, the decadal price of rails is weighted by annual variation in replacement requirements and then divided by two, on the assumption that scrap rails were worth half their replacements. The resultant two estimates for iron expenditures are $20.5 and $27.9 million, depending upon the iron consumption series used, and after an addition of $400 per mile for the labor costs of replacement.[57] These figures are within a narrow absolute range of the previous estimate of $19.9 million, with the official import series providing the better approximation. This is as it should be. The AISA import series may be a better measure of total iron imports used as rails, but from it should then be subtracted the substantial nonsteam railroad uses. Thus the construction of some 400 miles of city railroads, using heavy rails of more than 100 gross tons, required

[57] The requirements for new construction were annually distributed by the 1880 mileage series, lagged by half a year, and then subtracted from the total consumption data. Thus half the track laid in 1851 and half that in 1852 determine 1851 purchases. The residual is then 1851 replacement. The annual pattern implied is one of relatively heavy replacement in the last 2 years of the decade and seems consistent with other information. The price used is the American rail price, lagged one-half year, owing to the more important position of domestic producers in this market.

On the value of scrap, there are many indications supporting a ratio of one-half the new price. The *American Railroad Journal*, XXXII (1859), 600, assumes that rerolled iron is 100 to 150 percent cheaper than new. Company reports affirm values closer to the former ratio. See, for example, the reports of such disparate roads as the Galena and Chicago, South Carolina, and Philadelphia, Wilmington and Baltimore. *Hillyer's American Railroad Magazine*, III (1860), 98; *American Railroad Journal*, XXXII (1859), 100, 632.

Track laying charges of this magnitude appear in the report on Missouri railroads in the *Missouri Senate Journal*, 1858, appendix, and on the Philadelphia, Wilmington, and Baltimore in *American Railroad Journal*, XXXII (1859), 130.

some 40,000 tons of track, and at least half as much was required in the mining districts.[58] Either series supports replacement of no more than 700,000 tons during the decade.

For the 1840's, unfortunately, the commodity flow technique is less useful. A firm production total is lacking, and the proportion of iron renewals charged to construction account by reason of increased weight is also unknown. Nonetheless, it is possible to set some limits to the likely replacement total. The most optimistic recitals of American production of rails from 1840 to 1848 would lead one to estimate not more than 200,000 gross tons of production over this interval, concentrated in the years 1846–1848. Accept such an estimate provisionally. Then, inclusive of official imports, total consumption over the period 1840–1850 would have come to 733,000 tons, including some accumulation of stock for the imminent boom. Subtraction of the previously determined initial requirements of 550,000 tons yields replacement of 183,000 tons at most. It is doubtful if it reached such heights. Conversion during the decade of all 2,000 miles of strap iron in 1839 indicates a demand for no more than 166,000 tons of iron, and from all accounts there was little need of replacement of edge rails beyond some minor retracking in New England. In light of the rapid flow of imports of rails in the fiscal year 1851 to meet needs of accelerating construction, but partially included in the supply total of the previous decade, the 183,000 maximum is unrealistic as well. An alternative estimate of imports by the American Iron and Steel Association for the calendar year 1850 as reported in Table 13 is 23,000 tons less than an average of the official imports for the two adjacent fiscal years 1850 and 1851; this despite the fact that they are some 7 percent greater in subsequent years. Nor is it improbable that inventory accumulation for track later emplaced must have occurred. In all, therefore, actual replacement during the period was limited to less than 150,000 tons. Using this latter total at a price equal to $\frac{5}{18}$ the average price of imported rails, plus an allowance for labor

[58] The 1854–1855 New York state report (p. 33) indicates an average weight of 109 gross tons per mile for city railroads. The 1860 census tabulated 403 miles during the decade. Daddow and Bannon, *Coal, Iron, and Oil* (p. 729), indicate 780 miles of mining track inside and outside of mines in 1864, some substantial proportion of which must have been either built or replaced in the 1850's.

costs, yields an estimate of $3,300,000, well above the $2,300,000 obtained directly.

The $\frac{5}{18}$ fraction may be at fault here. It was derived by coupling the earlier assumption that scrap iron yielded half the price per ton of newly rolled rails with two others: the iron replaced weighed only one third as much as the replacement rails and only one third of the actual outlays for rails was charged, on average, to operating expenses. It is the last of these two that is difficult to document. The first relationship is guaranteed by the difference in rail weights between the 1830's and 1840's, while the latter depends upon types of accounting procedure used. A still greater frequency of the less conservative practice of allocating the entire charge to capital account would reduce the price at which such replacement rails should be valued and bring the commodity flow estimate more into line with that from the operating accounts. Note, however, that this calculation does suggest that the premise of 200,000 tons of domestic rail production from 1840 to 1848 is quite consistent with total demand during the decade; indeed, the direction of divergence here points to lesser supply.

No similar check is possible for the 1830's, but with estimated renewals so small a proportion of quasi-net expenditure, the absolute error with even substantial misstatement of iron replacement is trifling. We may, therefore, move on to other omissions.

Two further components of capital expenditure included in the maintenance of road account are expenditures for replacement of ties, and also for replacement of structures. The latter is sufficiently small so as to be neglected. Most of the expenditures made by railroads under this head partake more of repairs than replacement, and their contribution is via a lesser rate of capital consumption, not increased gross expenditures.[59] Ties are another matter, however. Although information regarding expenditures actually made for replacement of ties is extremely scanty, a good guess is that they were somewhere between 60 and 100 percent of the costs for renewals of iron. The lower figure derives from the

[59] Repairs of buildings and fences and gates come to perhaps 2 to 3 percent of maintenance costs, although bridges required considerably more. Relative to total operating costs, the total renewals, only a portion of the repairs, are obviously limited. See the Massachusetts and New York reports.

estimates of maintenance of road made by the Philadelphia, Wilmington, and Baltimore in 1859. Something like an 85 percent relationship may be inferred from Poor's comment on maintenance of the Erie Railroad in the same year. And in 1880, when steel rails were still a minority of the total trackage, the ratio was 62 percent, although Wellington notes that renewals of rails were somewhat large in that year, which may indicate a higher "normal" relationship. At the other extreme, Colburn and Holley, contemporary engineers, suggest on the basis of their experience something like equality, and this forms an upper bound.[60]

Fortunately, in this instance, a reasonably satisfactory estimate follows from physical depreciation alone. Unlike rails, whose life was primarily a function of traffic carried, ties were more subject to constant deterioration from weather and age. Again unlike rails, they were not capable of repair; hence when worn out, their actual replacement is more certain, although there was greater variability in this respect before 1860 than after. Suppose an average life of about 7 years for ties, and a pattern of replacement of the following approximate logistic form:[61]

Years subsequent to first operation	1	2	3	4	5	6	7	8	9	10
Cumulative proportion of replacement	0	0	0	$\frac{1}{8}$	$\frac{1}{4}$	$\frac{7}{16}$	$\frac{10}{16}$	$\frac{13}{16}$	$\frac{15}{16}$	1

[60] *American Railroad Journal*, XXXII (1859), 568; *ibid.*, 632; *Tenth Census*, IV, *Transportation*, p. 133; Wellington, *Location*, p. 127; Colburn and Holley, *Permanent Way*, p. 5.

[61] An 8-year average life is indicated by the replies to the census inquiry in 1880. Wellington, *Location*, p. 124, concurs. Since preservation of ties was still not common at that later date, it is relevant to the earlier period as well. Contemporary estimates range from 6 to 10 years. See *American Railroad Journal*, XXXII (1859), 130, 632; *Hillyer's American Railroad Magazine*, III (1860), 98. Kirkland estimates average life at 7 to 8 years in *Men, Cities, and Transportation*, I, 288. The preference for the lower figure is based upon the suspicion that average and maximum were often confused. The results, of course, are not greatly affected by the use of a slightly longer average life.

In addition, the number of replacement cross ties per mile of track varied from 1800 in the 1830's to 2200 in the 1840's to 2400 in the 1850's. The earliest construction, it is true, often used a smaller number of ties, but only because of the substantial subsill structure. A continuous transition to a structure of simple transverse ties without any foundation meant that replacement took the form of the newer style of construction.[62]

From these assumptions it follows that 53.3 million ties were needed for replacement from 1851 to 1860, 14.6 million from 1840 to 1850, and 0.8 million from 1828 to 1839. These physical requirements have been adjusted upward to include sidings and double track by means of a proportional increase in mileage. The prices paid for ties during the three decades is a matter of imperfect knowledge. Scattered information suggests a wide range between 25 and 60 cents per tie.[63] The latter estimate is for the end of the 1830's, but seems high, since lumber was still abundant in the vicinity of rail construction. For the 1850's a figure of 30–35 cents is probably appropriate; for the earlier decades, a somewhat larger 40 cents per tie. The absence of a pronounced trend in lumber prices over the period is consistent with this pattern.[64] Using these valuations, we obtain expenditure totals of $17.3 million, $5.8 million, and $0.3 million for the three periods in inverse temporal order.

These sums include no specific allowance for the labor costs in replacing ties. But some, or all, of such cost is probably already included in the previous estimate of iron renewals. The ratios of replacement expenditures for ties to those for iron do not indicate a need for further adjustment. These are, for the three decades

[62] For indications of the typical quantities required for construction at the various dates, see Ringwalt, *Transport Development*, pp. 84–85; *American Railroad Journal*, XII (1840), 182; *American Railroad Journal*, XX (1847), 28; *Missouri Senate Journal*, 1858, appendix, p. 204; New York and Virginia State Reports in the 1850's (the former gives the information only up to 1856, the latter at the end of the decade).

[63] See the first three references of the preceding note, plus: *Report of the President and Directors of the Ohio and Mississippi Railroad for 1859–60* (Cincinnati, 1860), p. 19; the subcontractor's prices in *Missouri Senate Journal*, 1858, appendix, p. 204; *American Railroad Journal*, XXXII (1859), 489, 632; Colburn and Holley, *Permanent Way*, p. 31. For the range of variation in the valuation of ties in inventory, 21 to 40 cents, among New York railroads in the 1850's see the State reports.

[64] *Historical Statistics*, p. 317.

(again inversely), 0.87, 2.52, and 1.5. Though the last two ratios lie well beyond the range of 0.6 to 1.0 that was suggested earlier, the special circumstances of rail replacement during the early decades have already been explained. If new rails had all been charged to operating expenses in the 1840's, the ratio would have been quite close to unity. The sums involved are inconsequential in any event. A ratio of unity would reduce gross investment by only $3.3 million, far too small to have any effect.

The final adjustment is for replacement of equipment retired and charged to operating accounts by railroads in the nineteenth century. The only railroads with the relevant information are those in Massachusetts. For a variety of years, the proportion such replacements bore to total operating expenses have been calculated from the state reports as follows:

1846	.050
1849	.012
1856	.015
1860	.028

The high 1846 result is the product of chance; excluding the Boston and Lowell and the Western the proportion is reduced to 2.4 percent. Over a number of years, then, replacement of rolling stock averaged something like 2 percent of operating expenses for Massachusetts railroads. In other parts of the country the comparable magnitude was undoubtedly smaller. Massachusetts railroads were among the oldest in the country and, burdened with obsolete equipment, had much greater need for replacement than mileage more recently opened.

This conclusion is affirmed by consideration of the likely retirements during the period. With lives of something like 15–20 years, and still shorter for some of the primitive equipment of the 1830's, only modest amounts of replacement are indicated. Thus, allowance for 50 of the 450 locomotives in service at the end of 1839 to have been scrapped in the 1840's, 600 of the 900 passenger cars, and 1000 of the 3000 freight cars, still yields replacement expenditures of only $1.2 million, or 1.1 percent of operating expenses. The generous treatment of rolling stock other than engines is due to their apparent greater technological immaturity.

Similarly, in the 1850's, if it is assumed that all the equipment from the 1830's was retired and something more than half the 1840–1845 production of cars in addition, we get indicated retirements of 400 locomotives, 400 eight-wheel equivalent passenger cars, 3100 eight-wheel equivalent freight cars, and 1500 coal cars. Renewal outlays of $5.9 million, or 1.2 percent of operating expenses, then result.[65] This retirement model is consistent with the practices of a railroad like the Baltimore and Ohio, and even substantial changes in it, or in the prices used to value the equipment, would lead to small changes in investment. These sums can be used with the confidence that any error is absolutely small.

Table 50 recapitulates the conversion of the decadal quasi-net

TABLE 50. Gross capital formation, by decade (millions of dollars)

Components of gross investment	1828–1839	1840–1850	1851–1860
New construction	96.6	203.6	694.0
Replacement of equipment	0.0	1.2	5.9
Variant I	96.6	204.8	699.9
Replacement of rails and ties	0.5	8.1	37.2
Variant II	97.1	212.9	737.1

Source: See text.

[65] For estimates of numbers of engines and cars see Appendix D. The prices used in the 1840's are $7500 for locomotives, $1000 for passenger cars, and $200 for freight cars, both assumed to be of the 4-wheel variety. In the 1850's, $8000, $2000, $500, and $200 for coal cars were applied. These prices are approximations, but they convey the right magnitudes. Prices for replacement of 4-wheel equivalents in the 1840's are half of the 8-wheel car prices, since any improvements would be charged to capital account. Locomotive prices by year for the equipment of the South Carolina Railroad can be found in Derrick, *Centennial History*, appendix VI; for prices of the equipment of the Philadelphia and Columbia see the *American Railroad Journal*, XXI (1848), 165. There are also single quotations, *ibid.*, XXVI (1853), 487 and 550, in *Railway and Locomotive Historical Society Bulletin*, no. 53 (1940), 64–66, and in Freedley, *Philadelphia and Its Manufactures*, p. 311. For prices of passenger cars much less information is available. There are these however: *American Railroad Journal*, XIV (1842), 380; Chauncey M. Depew, ed., *One Hundred Years of American Commerce* (New York, 1895), I, 115; and Ringwalt, *Transport Development*, p. 103. For prices of freight cars see *Report of the Philadelphia and Reading Railroad, 1856* (Philadelphia, 1857), p. 27; *ibid.*, for 1858 (1859), p. 19; *Thirty-Fourth Annual Report of the Baltimore and Ohio Railroad*, p. 157; and Ringwalt, p. 210.

flows to gross investment. The next step is the annualization of these aggregates.

Annual Gross Investment Estimates

For the period 1828–1839 annual construction expenditures, like the decadal totals, have been obtained by summing over individual railroads.[66] In this, company reports (like those of the Baltimore and Ohio, South Carolina, and Georgia Central) and the reports of different state agencies in Massachusetts, Virginia, Illinois, Michigan, and Pennsylvania, were indispensable. Together these enabled us to derive directly in annual form something more than half of total decadal investment. The residual estimation required varied from less than half for 1838 and 1839, to two thirds and more for some of the earlier years in the decade. This remainder was obtained by allocating the cumulative expenditure of each individual road (secured from Gerstner and the other sources of Table 46) over the construction period plus the first year of operation. The function $Y = .241X + .0236X^2 - .000160X^3$, where Y is the proportion of total expenditure and X the proportion elapsed of the construction period plus one, was used for this purpose. The equation itself was determined from sample data from company and state reports. The cubic form, indicating major expenditures in the center of the gestation period, is also confirmed by other recent research on the time profile of canal construction.[67]

[66] Necessarily the insignificant difference between investment and construction cost (brought about by the failure of land purchases and imputed interest exactly to offset each other) is ignored in these annual estimates. It comes to nothing more than rounding error.

[67] Subsequent research showed that the annual expenditures of two of the Virginia roads used to derive the estimating equation were incorrectly reported by Wicker, "Railroad Investment." Fortunately, the revised equation, $Y = .231X + .024X^2 - .000163X^3$, is almost identical to the function actually used, and recomputation of the results was unnecessary. R^2 was 0.96, but this is slightly misleading since each road included an observation manifesting the identity of completion of expenditure at the end of the gestation period. Only by standardizing to percentages was it possible to incorporate different lengths of periods in a single relationship, but the effect is to increase the proportion of variance explained. Beyond the goodness of fit there are H. Jerome Cranmer's canal estimates indicating a similar profile. Cf. his "Canal Investment, 1815–1860," in *Trends in the American Economy in the Nineteenth Century*, National Bureau of Economic Research, Inc., Studies in Income and Wealth, vol. 24 (Princeton, 1960).

One disadvantage of the method is its confounding of current and constant dollars since the pattern of one part of the decade in current dollars is applied to another part when different prices prevailed. It is unlikely any systematic bias has been introduced thereby, however. On the other hand, the reports on gestation periods are not always explicit, nor for that matter are the decadal totals free from error. Later on, we run a check using a different means of deriving annual expenditures that confirms the validity of these totals. For the moment, Table 51 sets out the data on a state basis.

TABLE 51. Annual construction expense, 1828–1839 (thousands of dollars)

	1828	1829	1830	1831	1832	1833	1834	1835	1836	1837	1838	1839
Me.						0	54	100	100	0	0	0
N.H.										0	20	180
Mass.			0	60	366	1,114	1,334	1,285	1,202	1,203	1,627	2,549
R.I.					0	25	50	312	717	840	456	100
Conn.						0	4	3	265	444	568	1,283
N.Y.		0	97	452	537	454	690	1,821	2,424	1,636	1,189	1,686
N.J.			0	631	798	759	685	454	537	602	844	337
Pa.	83	399	481	634	1,502	1,815	2,517	2,130	3,372	4,105	3,454	2,170
Del.		0	110	184	106	20	10	110	10	0	0	0
Md.	127	570	725	722	770	553	1,151	864	768	805	1,005	993
Va.		0	41	148	241	335	361	899	1,014	787	688	422
N.C.								0	107	800	947	941
S.C.		0	42	284	332	293	334	250	217	315	389	614
Ga.							0	61	487	1,055	1,294	1,869
Fla.							0	48	122	186	258	205
Ala.			0	58	131	69	92	34	82	312	502	230
Miss.							0	166	460	720	1,140	1,009
La.		0	72	140	8	8	8	62	581	598	695	430
Ky.			0	71	126	158	122	68	60	60	40	40
Tenn.									0	62	155	183
Ohio							0	4	54	83	66	108
Ind.									0	377	668	155
Ill.									0	82	898	1,334
Mich.						0	23	124	176	466	565	621
Total	210	969	1,568	3,384	4,917	5,603	7,435	8,795	12,755	15,538	17,468	17,459

Source: See text.

In the later decades such disaggregation is impossible. An alternative technique has therefore been developed. This consists of distributing the decadal construction expenditure of Table 50 by use of an expenditure index. This expenditure index is the product of a quantity index and a cost index and thus measures the relative current dollar outlay in different years of the same decade.[68] Since the decadal flows are in historical cost, this allocation method is perfectly consistent.

The quantity index is a moving average of regionally weighted mileage added, designed to approximate work in process. A three-year average sum was used for 1840, representing a two-year gestation period, tapering off annually to a two-year average for 1850 and thereafter. Such shortening of the gestation period is confirmed by what we know about changing methods of construction and the more amenable terrain of West and South. Appendix C's later comparison of English and American construction employment in the 1850's fully supports the appropriateness of the two-year average for that period. Weights were given to roads built in different regions in rough proportion to their cost per mile. For the 1840's this meant that mileage in the New England and Middle Atlantic states was counted at unity, and that in the South and West at $\frac{1}{2}$; for the 1850's the weights were gradually altered for the West and South to reflect increasing relative cost in those regions.[69] The mileage added data of the 1880 census, somewhat adjusted for the poor portrayal of the period 1837–1843, were used.[70] Such a weighting and averaging scheme not

[68] No attempt is made to separate the annual incidence of adjustments to expenditure like imputation of interest or subtraction of land purchases.

[69] The weights changed as follows: West: 1851, 0.6; 1852, 0.7; 1853, 0.8; 1854, 0.9; 1855 and further, 1.0. South: 1851, 1852, 0.5; 1853, 1854, 0.6; 1855, 1856, 0.7; 1857 and further, 0.8. This is nothing more than a crude approximation to the annual variations that led to the cumulative difference in construction cost observed at the end of the decade.

[70] The adjustments included the transposition of the Housatonic and the Norwich and Worcester from 1840 to 1839; the transposition of the Raleigh and Gaston from 1840 and 1841 to 1839; allocation of the 1842 mileage of the Georgia Central to 1838, 1840–1842; transposition of 25 miles of the Vicksburg and Jackson from 1841 to 1839 and 16 miles of the Northern Cross from 1842 to 1839. The net effects on the regional mileages are as follows (by census groups):

	I	III	IV
1838		+ 50	
1839	+94.75	+122	+16
1840	−94.75	+ 20	
1841		− 57	
1842		+ 15	−16
1843		−150	

only yields an index of mileage *under construction* that differs from
a mileage *added* series, but has the further virtue that it minimizes
the effect of using a particular mileage series rather than another.
This is relevant in view of the inadequacy of such data. Further
evidence on this point is presented below.

With regional variations in costs thus eliminated by weighting,
the final step in deriving the expenditure index is to adjust for
variations in costs over time. There is already one railroad cost
index extending back from 1860 to 1840, but it is of little value.[71]
Ulmer's index is a confused composite of wages and prices compiled by the Aldrich Committee seventy years ago and published
in 1893 as Senate Report No. 1394. The series to represent prices
of metallic materials — which, of course, consisted primarily of
iron rails — contains, among other things, mineral door knobs,
manila rope, quicksilver, lead drop shot and for three years, even
meat cutters. Iron rails make up only one part of the series, and
that beginning with 1847. The wage series is equally inappropriate, consisting for the most part of payments to carpenters,
painters, plasterers, bricklayers, and other crafts used but insig-
nificantly in railroad construction. Unskilled labor is represented
as only two of the many observations. On top of this, Ulmer's
weights are meaningless. They reflect the "relative importance of
the components in the total volume of *maintenance* expenditures
on road (including structures) by Class I roads in 1925, 1935, and
1945, as published in annual reports of the ICC." [72] The weights
appropriate to pre-Civil War construction experience are far different, as one might suspect.

Improvement upon this cost index, therefore, was essential to
the method. A first requirement is a satisfactory index of the
wages of unskilled labor. Here again existing work proved inadequate. Edith Abbott's index from 1840 to 1860, based upon the
wages of unskilled laborers reported by various firms included
in the Aldrich Report, has many weaknesses.[73] Coverage is extremely limited, extending to but a handful of firms and em-

[71] Ulmer, *Capital in Transportation*, pp. 274–275. We ignore the productivity bias
of input rather than price deflation that our own index does not entirely avoid.
[72] Ulmer, p. 277. Italics mine.
[73] Edith Abbott, "The Wages of Unskilled Labor in the United States, 1850–
1900," *Journal of Political Economy*, XIII (1905), 321–367.

ployees in the 1840's and 1850's; at maximum, 1430 workers are included in 1860. Such inadequate coverage means that certain industries, even firms, like two Connecticut quarries, dominate the results. Finally, the index is distorted by the introduction of new firms at different absolute wage levels without any adjustment for continuity: although all firms' wages may have increased in a given year, the introduction of a new firm with a lower average wage may cause the aggregate index to register a decline in wages.

To remedy these defects, an entirely new index of unskilled wages from 1840 to 1860 has been prepared. A link relative method assured that annual changes were taken inclusive of only firms reporting in adjacent years. Second, the more satisfactory — both in number of observations and in geographic coverage — Weeks Report of the Tenth Census was the primary source rather than the Aldrich Report.[74] Lebergott's 1840, 1850, and 1860 estimates of the wage level of unskilled workers served as benchmarks for the series. In this way only the relative accuracy of the annual movements count, not the absolute levels.[75] The resulting index is given in Table 52.

Adjacent to it is an iron rail price index. This has been derived by adding to an import price series an allowance for duty, commission, ocean freight, and domestic transfer costs. This series, used earlier in the commodity flow calculations, has real advantages over the more common AISA index of American rail prices. Whereas the latter starts in 1847, the import series extends back to 1840. Hence annual changes are measured consistently over the

[74] U.S. Bureau of the Census, *Tenth Census*, XX, *Statistics of Wages* (Washington, 1886).

[75] See Stanley Lebergott, "Wage Trends, 1800–1900," in *Trends in the American Economy in the Nineteenth Century*, National Bureau of Economic Research, Inc., Studies in Income and Wealth, vol. 24 (Princeton, 1960), especially pp. 462 and 482–484. The method of adjusting the annual series to benchmark data is described in detail in Frickey, *Production in the United States*, pp. 47–51. Since this index was compiled, Walter B. Smith has published a series of annual modes of wages paid to unskilled labor on the Erie Canal. The absolute levels correspond almost exactly to the Lebergott benchmarks, which confirms the trend in our index. Smith's series, because it is based on the mode rather than the mean shows less annual variation than ours, but even here such intradecadal variations like the low wages of the mid-1840's are corroborated. Cf. "Wage Rates on the Erie Canal, 1828–1881," *Journal of Economic History*, XXIII (1963), 298–311.

TABLE 52. Derivation of annual investment, 1840–1860 (all indexes, 1860 = 100; all outlays millions of current dollars)

Year	Road quantity index	Unskilled labor wage index	Iron rail price index	Lumber & building materials price index	Cost index	Road expenditure index	Current dollar outlay on road	Equipment quantity index	Equipment price index	Equipment expenditure index	Current dollar outlay		Gross capital formation
											on equipment including replacement	on ties & iron	
1840	34.7	81.7	132.7	109.9	99.8	34.6	13.4	7.6	79.3	6.0	0.4	0.3	14.1
1841	29.6	77.9	114.5	111.8	92.3	27.3	10.7	10.1	78.9	8.0	0.5	0.3	11.5
1842	21.1	77.3	109.9	108.7	90.2	19.0	7.4	15.6	76.2	11.9	.8	.4	8.6
1843	12.4	76.4	151.1	105.3	101.7	12.6	5.0	17.7	73.8	13.0	.9	.6	6.5
1844	17.0	81.7	132.1	103.0	99.0	16.8	6.5	19.0	75.5	14.4	1.0	.7	8.2
1845	20.1	80.8	133.4	106.7	99.2	19.9	7.7	28.3	78.2	22.1	1.5	.8	10.0
1846	31.4	79.9	174.6	106.2	110.9	34.8	13.6	37.1	83.3	30.9	2.0	1.0	16.6
1847	55.7	79.0	162.1	108.2	106.9	59.5	23.2	52.6	88.0	46.3	3.1	1.0	27.3
1848	83.8	79.8	136.4	105.2	99.3	83.2	32.4	69.5	86.5	60.1	4.0	1.0	37.4
1849	88.6	85.1	110.7	97.5	94.0	83.3	32.4	58.1	86.0	50.0	3.3	1.0	36.7
1850	92.1	83.6	92.6	102.1	88.2	81.2	31.6	61.0	84.3	51.4	3.4	1.1	36.1
1851	125.7	85.3	91.5	97.2	88.3	111.0	42.5	104.4	85.1	88.8	6.1	2.3	50.9
1852	162.7	86.7	89.6	100.4	89.0	144.8	55.6	133.5	87.1	116.3	8.0	2.8	66.4
1853	213.8	88.1	117.1	103.1	98.3	210.2	80.6	159.6	91.4	145.9	10.0	2.8	93.4
1854	237.7	91.4	139.2	114.0	108.0	256.7	98.7	161.8	96.7	156.5	10.8	1.2	110.7
1855	168.4	91.9	106.8	103.4	97.5	164.2	63.1	118.8	100.0	118.9	8.1	3.0	74.2
1856	150.6	94.8	131.2	102.7	106.5	160.4	61.8	130.0	100.1	133.2	9.0	6.2	77.0
1857	173.6	95.8	136.6	105.0	109.0	189.2	72.5	115.0	103.1	118.5	8.1	3.6	84.2
1858	153.5	93.4	125.1	103.7	104.0	159.6	61.2	41.8	106.3	44.4	3.0	2.9	67.1
1859	128.8	97.9	105.9	98.6	100.4	129.3	50.0	76.0	102.7	78.1	5.4	5.4	60.8
1860	100.0	100.0	100.0	100.0	100.0	100.0	38.7	100.0	100.0	100.0	6.9	7.0	52.6

Source: See text.

entire twenty-one year span. Historical circumstance endorses the appropriateness of an import price series since so much of the initial construction requirements were met from abroad. Likewise, the fiscal year dating of the series acts to lead iron contracts over delivery, again a preferable modification.

Finally, there is the building and materials price index of the Aldrich Report representing lumber, masonry, ballast, and other similar inputs into the construction process. No substitute for this index seemed feasible, although it is admittedly heavily weighted by such irrelevancies as shingles, doors, and flooring. Since it receives relatively little weight in our composite index (but the largest weight in Ulmer's) this does not matter so much. It is weighted one, the iron rail index, three, and the unskilled labor index, six, representing the approximate importance of these components in pre-Civil War railroad construction, as determined from Table 48, to derive the final cost index.

In Table 52, then, there are the quantity index of road construction, the composite cost index and its components, and the expenditure index that is the product of the cost and quantity indexes. It is necessary now to prepare a comparable expenditure index for equipment, built up from quantity and price components in the same way. For the equipment quantity index we use a series of annual changes in locomotive production of the leading American producers, covering about three fourths of total output.[76] This admittedly involves the assumption that purchases of other rolling stock showed the same annual variation. The only alternative, however, is to distribute other equipment expenditure like outlays for construction of road and this is probably less accurate. For a price index to go with the quantity index we use a two-year moving average of prices actually paid for locomotives

[76] These data consist of the annual production of locomotives of the following firms over the following span of years: Baldwin, 1833–1860; Schenectady, 1851–1860; Manchester, 1855–1857; Amoskeag, 1849–1859; Locks and Canals, 1835–1854; Hinkley, 1841–1857; Mason, 1853–1860; Portland, 1848–1860; Taunton, 1847–1860; Rogers, 1837–1860. This information was generously made available from the files of the Railway and Locomotive Historical Society, Baker Library, Harvard University. The data were made comparable for coverage only when observations were missing, but *not* when firms entered or left the industry.

by the South Carolina Railroad over this period.[77] If the latter's acquisition of locomotive power was not untypical in terms of cost and composition of that in the country as a whole, and it does not seem to be, such a price index is a far better indicator of expenditure than such remote proxies as the "average" price of metals and implements.

The proportion of capital expenditure allocated to equipment in the 1840's, when no implicit discount enters, is 9 percent of original accounting cost, following Table 48. In the next decade such a procedure would charge all implicit discounts to construction of road, although it applied to purchases of equipment too. Accordingly, the correct proportion becomes 10 percent of quasi-net *investment*, not outlays. To these sums are added the replacement expenditures in equipment from 1840 to 1860. This works out to a total of $20.9 million from 1840 to 1850 and $75.3 million from 1851 to 1860. The annual outlays on equipment appear in column (11). After subtraction for new equipment purchases, the residual quasi-net flow is allocated to construction of road and distributed by the relevant expenditure index. These annual outlays appear in column (7).

The only expenditures yet to be annualized are those for replacement of ties and rails. For the 1840's both are determined by the annual incidence of the physical requirements generated by the tie replacement scheme described earlier. Although iron rails probably had a slightly longer average life than ties, this does not affect the annual distribution significantly enough to warrant separate computation of this type for the iron component. Adjustment has been made, however, for the divergent weights of iron between the first and second halves of the 1840's; this implies greater outlays for rail replacement in the latter period. The quantities are not weighted by any price index in this instance. The flexibility of replacement within certain limits would tend to generate an inverse correlation between replacement expenditures and the price of materials, and the use of a physical requirements distribution weighted by prices would thus intro-

[77] Compiled from Derrick, *Centennial History*, appendix VI. Interpolation was necessary for 3 of the years.

duce new distortions rather than eliminate price effects. The amounts involved are small in any event and cannot affect the annual pattern of total investment. For the 1850's the preceding method is used for tie replacement, but not for rails. To allocate the latter, the replacement iron series earlier calculated as the annual difference between total consumption and requirements for new construction serves as the quantity index, and the domestic rail price series, lagged by half a year, as the price index. The relative movements of their product determine the annual expenditures for renewal of iron.

The final column of Table 52 contains the gross capital formation series secured as a sum of all outlays.

The Accuracy of the Annual Movements

How much better are such annual investment flows than those implied by the contemporary cost calculations Taylor so effectively took to task? Substantially, I believe. A variety of tests suggests that the data perform rather well. First, we can compare the firm, disaggregated estimates of the 1830's with an alternative annual distribution implied by the expenditure index approach. The fit of the latter is then some indication of its accuracy in other decades.

The results of this experiment are shown in the tabulation.[78] The absolute differences in predicted annual expenditures over the twelve-year period sum to $8.7 million compared with total construction cost of $87.8 million. The average annual error thus

[78] The directly estimated series here excludes expenditure upon those roads that failed and did not appear in the mileage figures. Similarly, the expenditure index was applied not to total decadal investment but to the sum after subtraction for such failures. Because the decade was unique in the large number of failures, and hence exaggerates the limitations of a mileage criterion, such adjustments assure a fairer test. A two-year construction period was assumed to hold throughout the decade, unlike the gradual shortening during the 1840's. The various cost indexes also were slightly altered. The wage index consisted of Lebergott's benchmarks for 1830 and 1840, to which Layer's annual index of wages in New England textile mills was applied. See Layer, *Earnings of Cotton Mill Operatives*, pp. 21, 24. The iron price index was extrapolated back on the English rail prices used for the commodity flow check for the 1830's. The building materials price index was extrapolated on the similar index of Warren and Pearson (*Historical Statistics*, p. 115). Weights of 6 for labor, 2 for iron, and 2 for building materials were used owing to the less iron intensive method of construction.

Railroad investment, 1828–1839
(millions of dollars)

Year	Expenditure index method	Direct estimation	Difference
1828	0.35	0.21	+0.14
1829	1.76	0.97	+0.79
1830	3.07	1.57	+1.50
1831	3.42	3.38	+0.04
1832	4.65	4.92	−0.27
1833	4.39	5.60	−1.21
1834	6.41	7.44	−1.03
1835	7.46	8.77	−1.31
1836	12.03	12.00	+0.03
1837	15.36	14.03	+1.33
1838	13.96	14.54	−0.58
1839	14.84	14.40	+0.44

is roughly 10 percent. The largest specific error (in relative terms) occurs in 1830 and amounts to more than 100 percent of the actual expenditure; the absolute deviation is minor, however, and the error does not lead to invalid conclusions. And although an 1837 turning point in investment is indicated by the expenditure index as it stands, the addition of the failed roads causes the correct 1838–1839 turning point to appear. Even by this rigorous criterion, therefore, the expenditure index emerges unscathed.

Another measure of the accuracy of the method is the correspondence between changes in the expenditure index and changes in the dollar value of construction between the year 1850 and 1851. Because we have imposed the requirement that the sum of the annual expenditures be equal to the decadal totals only within each subperiod, there is no necessary identity between the percentage changes in dollar outlay and in the index for adjacent years overlapping the two different subperiods.[79] Once again the check is encouraging. While the index increases by 37 percent, dollar outlay rises by 35 percent. In absolute dollar terms, the

[79] If 1850 and 1851 agree, all other pairs of years will also correspond, since each decade is internally consistent.

use of the rate of change of the former applied to 1850 investment implies an expenditure of $43.3 million against the actual $42.5 million. The error is thus of the magnitude of only 2 percent. An equivalently small error is indicated by a comparison of the equipment index and equipment outlays; the index goes up by 73 percent, the outlay by 79 percent, and the absolute sum involved is only $0.2 million.

Finally, we may consider the effect of substituting another mileage series for the one actually used. Our over-all preference for the 1880 census series rather than Poor's is based primarily upon their divergence in the 1850's: whereas Poor's series shows a sharp peak in 1856, the census reaches a maximum in 1854. One important reason for Poor's result is his apparent tabulation of the entire mileage of the Illinois Central (more than 700 miles) in 1856. An independent source, namely Paxson, indicates that only 82 miles of the railroad was opened in that year, with 117 miles opened as early as 1853.[80] The census of 1880 duplicates Paxson's allocation almost identically. Moreover, Paxson's mileage added for the West as a whole shows a discernible peak in 1854 just as the 1880 census material does. The series of imports of iron rails, and also rail prices, likewise reach their maximum in 1853–1854. Accordingly, there is good reason to doubt the likelihood of a 50 percent decline in mileage added from 1853 to 1854, followed by a 120 percent increase from 1855 to 1856. Emplacement lags were not that long.

It is still a matter of interest how sensitive the annual data are to a substitution of an alternative mileage index, however, and so another set of estimates has been constructed following Poor's mileage series. This is set off in Chart 2 by dashed lines, while the estimates of Table 52 are in solid form. Not surprisingly, in light of our previous comments, they diverge noticeably in the 1850's, but not so markedly earlier. Both series are at their trough in 1843, and both indicate a vigorous upturn in the latter part of the decade. The one divergence, the lesser rate of growth from 1848 to 1849 of our estimates, seems more consistent with other observations concerning the temporary tightness in the New England capital market in the latter year. In the 1850's,

[80] Paxson, "Railways of the 'Old Northwest,' " pp. 271–272.

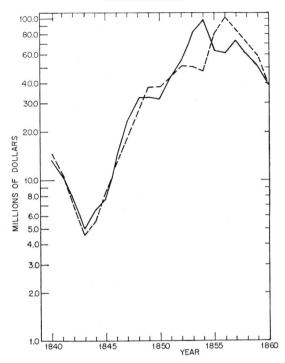

CHART 2. Alternative outlays on road

the investment outlays implied by Poor's mileage series peak sharply in 1856 and show a mild decline in 1854, but this pattern is highly improbable, as we have argued. The choice of a mileage series is thus unimportant for the results in the 1840's, and when it does make a difference, the estimates of Table 52 coincide more closely with other indicators.

Regional Estimates

The preceding estimates have all been framed in national terms, with the exception of those from 1828 to 1839. For many purposes a continuous regional distribution is desirable. In principle, since regional weights have already been used to derive national totals, regional estimates for 1840 to 1860 follow quite readily by application of the same method used to get the total.

The rub is the variety of additional assumptions required. In particular, the transformation of cost into investment was not the same for all regions, nor did prices in each change in exactly the same way. On neither of these points is particularly ample information available. Despite the dubiousness of the procedure, Table 53 sets out such regional estimates.[81] For some purposes the movements are so distinctive that even large margins of error would not matter, and this is the justification for their inclusion. But for some they are not. In particular it is necessary to caution explicitly against comparison of 1839 and 1840. The former year includes expenditures on failed projects while the latter excludes such outlay. Some such expenditure continued in 1840 in Illinois, Tennessee, and Michigan, and perhaps in other states as well. Without any question, the actual outlays in Illinois in 1840 exceed the $200,000 credited in that year to the farther West. Although a similar objection can be levied against the national totals derived in Table 52, its force there is much less than for these regional estimates.

Constant Dollar Totals and Net Investment

All the series thus far developed are in current dollar terms. For the data to serve as evidence of the growth of the real magnitudes, elimination of price variation is necessary. The resulting expenditures, expressed in the prices of a single year, are more useful than a physical index because they allow meaningful comparison with other sectors and national aggregates: the quantity index of mileage in process tells us nothing about the relative importance of real capital formation in railroads. To facilitate exactly such comparisons we have used the 1860 price structure for the conversion, because Gallman's recent constant dollar estimates of pre-Civil War gross national product are expressed in

[81] Note an additional difficulty. Approximate regional weights were used to derive the national total of Table 52 directly since this was the principal objective. Alternatively the decadal investment flows in each region, allocated precisely in proportion to the expenditure flows, might have been distributed annually and then summed. The difference in the two approaches is that in the latter case regional weights are exact. (That the deviations are *small* is testimony to the accuracy of the approximate weights used.)

TABLE 53. Regional distribution of gross investment (millions of current dollars)

Year	New England[a]	Middle Atlantic[b]	Ohio, Indiana, Michigan	Farther West[c]	South[d]	Southwest[e]
1828		0.2				
1829		1.0				
1830		1.4			0.1	0.1
1831	0.1	2.6			.5	.1
1832	.4	3.7			.8	.0
1833	1.1	3.6			.9	.0
1834	1.4	5.1			.9	.0
1835	1.7	5.4	0.1		1.5	.1
1836	2.3	7.1	.2		2.5	.6
1837	2.5	7.2	.9	0.1	4.3	.6
1838	2.7	6.6	1.3	.9	5.5	.7
1839	4.2	5.3	0.9	1.3	5.6	.4
1840	4.3	5.7	.5	0.2	3.3	.2
1841	3.7	4.8	.6	.2	2.0	.2
1842	3.1	3.5	.5	.3	1.0	.2
1843	2.2	1.7	1.7	.0	0.9	.0
1844	3.5	1.7	1.9	.0	1.1	.0
1845	5.4	1.1	1.9	.0	1.6	.0
1846	9.4	3.3	1.7	.0	2.3	.0
1847	15.2	7.4	2.8	.2	1.6	.0
1848	20.4	10.5	3.3	.4	2.8	.0
1849	17.0	12.1	2.4	.4	4.7	.0
1850	8.6	16.7	4.9	.3	5.6	.0
1851	8.6	17.4	15.7	2.6	6.5	.0
1852	9.3	18.3	25.0	5.6	7.8	.4
1853	6.3	21.3	25.3	23.6	16.5	.4
1854	5.9	14.2	23.7	47.4	18.8	.7
1855	3.1	7.6	18.3	33.4[f]	10.7	1.1
1856	2.8	9.8	22.3	22.7[g]	18.8	0.6
1857	2.4	12.3	21.7	24.6	22.5	.8
1858	0.3	11.4	10.9	18.0	25.2	1.2
1859	.2	8.1	5.3	12.3	30.1	4.7
1860	1.6	6.0	2.6	9.9	26.2	6.4

Source: See text.
[a] Me., N.H., Vt., Mass., R.I., Conn.
[b] N.Y., Penn., N.J., Md., Del.
[c] Ill., Iowa, Wisc., Mo., Cal.
[d] Va., W. Va., Ky., Tenn., Miss., Ala., Ga., Fla., N.C., S.C.
[e] La., Texas.
[f] Includes $0.3 million in California.
[g] Includes $0.4 million in California.

prices of the same year.[82] The cost indexes previously used to prepare the expenditure index are appropriate to deflate current dollar outlays without further adjustment. A composite index of construction and equipment prices is used, with the former weighted 9, the latter, 1, except for the 1830's, when only a construction index is available. The relevant outlays and index appear in Table 54.

The final step is the estimation of net investment. Such data are needed to speak of the capital stock, and its contribution to production. This requires the preparation of capital consumption allowances appropriate to the period. For a variety of reasons a 2 percent annual depreciation of the capital stock seems a reasonably accurate portrayal of the combined ravages of obsolescence and physical deterioration. In the first place, there are the physical lives. From what we observe later, a 20-year average for rolling stock is approximately correct, what with the large expenditures for repair of equipment. Similarly, a 7–8-year life for ties and a 20-year span for rails (10 years until renewal, but with 50 percent of the value of the rails salvageable) are of the right magnitude. These rates, weighted by the importance of the various components in the total cost of construction, yield a composite rate of less than 2 percent. Assuming the rest of the road depreciated at $\frac{1}{2}$ percent per annum, not unlikely in light of the greater permanence of embankments, structures, et cetera, the aggregate is then 2.3 percent. Two percent is accurate enough under the circumstances.

Corroborating such a magnitude is the ICC estimated rate for 1917 of 1.54 percent, excluding the renewals of rails and ties.[83] Since this is a composite rate, in which road and equipment appear separately, divergent trends in the components make it relevant to the earlier period as well. Although all investment

---

[82] In a previous version, because Gallman's valued added estimates were in 1879 dollars, that base was used. In light of his shift to 1860 prices, and the advantage of a base close to the period of major outlays to avoid the problem of quality changes over time, investment has been recomputed in 1860 dollars. Should constant dollars of another year be preferred, these can be calculated by converting the component indexes to the new base year. To facilitate such a change here are the 1860 absolute values used for wages, rails, and locomotives: $1.04, $49.98, and $9250.

[83] Found in Ulmer, *Capital in Transportation*, p. 225.

TABLE 54. A summary of the capital formation estimates (millions of dollars, except indexes)

Year	Gross capital formation[a] (current dollars)	Composite cost index (1860 = 100)	Gross capital formation (1860 dollars)	Capital consumption allowance (1860 dollars)	Net capital formation (1860 dollars)	Net capital formation (current dollars)
1828	0.2	99.2	0.2		0.2	0.2
1829	1.0	98.7	1.0		1.0	1.0
1830	1.6	83.0	1.9		1.9	1.6
1831	3.4	84.2	4.0		4.0	3.4
1832	4.9	85.5	5.7	0.1	5.6	4.8
1833	5.6	92.5	6.0	.3	5.7	5.3
1834	7.4	90.6	8.2	.4	7.8	7.1
1835	8.8	88.6	9.9	.5	9.4	8.3
1836	12.8	100.6	12.7	.7	12.0	12.1
1837	15.6	101.9	15.3	1.0	14.3	14.6
1838	17.4	101.8	17.1	1.3	15.8	16.1
1839	17.7	104.3	17.0	1.6	15.4	16.1
1840	14.1	97.8	14.4	2.0	12.4	12.1
1841	11.5	91.0	12.6	2.3	10.3	9.4
1842	8.6	88.8	9.7	2.5	7.2	6.4
1843	6.5	98.9	6.6	2.7	3.9	3.9
1844	8.2	96.6	8.5	2.8	5.7	5.5
1845	10.0	97.1	10.3	3.0	7.3	7.1
1846	16.6	108.1	15.4	3.2	12.2	13.2
1847	27.3	105.0	26.0	3.5	22.5	23.6
1848	37.4	98.0	38.2	4.1	34.1	33.4
1849	36.7	93.2	39.4	4.8	34.6	32.2
1850	36.1	87.8	41.1	5.6	35.5	31.2
1851	50.9	88.0	57.8	6.4	51.4	45.2
1852	66.4	88.8	74.8	7.6	67.2	59.7
1853	93.4	97.6	95.7	9.1	86.6	84.5
1854	110.7	106.9	103.6	11.0	92.6	99.0
1855	74.2	97.8	75.9	13.1	62.8	61.4
1856	77.0	105.9	72.7	14.6	58.1	61.5
1857	84.2	108.4	77.7	16.0	61.7	66.9
1858	67.1	104.2	64.4	17.6	46.8	48.8
1859	60.8	100.6	60.4	18.9	41.5	41.7
1860	52.6	100.0	52.6	20.1	32.5	32.5

Source: See text.

[a] The gross investment figures of Table 51 for the 1830's have had the replacement expenditures added to them.

probably had higher depreciation rates before 1860, equipment, with far the shorter life, received less weight in the early period. Hence the average was not necessarily greater. Ulmer uses this rate for 1870–1916, justifying it by similar logic. Since over the long haul replacement of ties and rails exactly equaled their wearing out, we would add something like $\frac{1}{2}$ percent to this rate in the 1840's and 1850's to compensate for their omission, and thus arrive again at 2 percent.

Finally there is the authority of the New York State Engineer writing in 1855:

> The expense for repairs of iron rails, after allowing for the value of the old material, is equal to the cost of an entire renewal once in fourteen years, that for cross-ties to a renewal once in eight years, for wooden bridges once in ten years, and for wooden stations once in thirty years. This deterioration may be represented in another form, by stating it as equal to from two to four per cent annually on the whole cost of the road. . . . An allowance of one per cent per annum in the whole cost of the roads in this state, would in my opinion, be required to make up the omissions in the reports of the proper allowance for depreciation.[84]

The reason for preferring the lower bound of the 2–4 percent range described above is made clear by the last part of the statement. The Commissioners imply that a 1 percent rate of depreciation plus replacement expenditures is the true rate. Estimated replacement expenditures are less than 1 percent themselves, and hence a total rate of 2 percent for depreciation cannot be far wrong.

Application of the 2 percent rate to accumulated gross investment in constant dollar terms yields constant dollar capital consumption allowances directly. These, subtracted from constant dollar gross investment, give a net investment series that likewise needs no additional deflation. The current dollar net investment series is most easily derived by inflating the constant dollar data. These data appear as the final column of Table 54.

[84] *Annual Report of the Board of Railroad Commissioners of the State of New York for 1855*, pp. 7–8.

Final Note

These estimates, like all synthetic statistics, partake both of observation and conjecture. The relevant issue is not whether assumption should enter — that is inevitable — but whether it is sufficiently limited (and well based) to justify the attempt. Needless to say, I believe this is the case here. The original expenditure flow data are firmly rooted in actual tabulation. Indeed, the reason for developing the techniques used was to take advantage of the discrete evidence on the capital stock as reported by railroads themselves. Adjustments for land purchases and imputed interest depend upon an actual sampling of railroad cost distributions. Greater uncertainty is inherent in the deduction for discount, but even then a wide range of evidence bearing upon the problem was gathered.

The annual series is naturally more suspect, and it would be hazardous to make assertions depending upon small differences in adjacent years. In the 1850's, particularly, the annual incidence of discount may make the 1853–1854 peak more pronounced than it currently appears. Further research upon the actual length of the gestation period in different regions at different times could improve the quantity index also, but experimentation with other variants than the one finally used here indicates that results are not drastically altered: moving averages of roughly similar length inevitably have considerable overlap. So, too, further information on the prices of equipment could strengthen a series based on thin, albeit continuous, observations. Still the pattern of expenditures seems to conform to what other evidence suggests, and these data are undoubtedly a better guide to the relative intensity of investment than the mileage indexes currently in use.

APPENDIX C

The Derivation of Employment Estimates

This appendix presents the details underlying the estimate of pre-Civil War railroad employment, both construction and operating. For the former, there is no official information whatsoever; indeed, little information at all, since construction workers were employed directly by contractors rather than by railroads. For operating employees, the census evidence is positively misleading. In both the Census of Occupations of 1850 and 1860 the category "railroad men" is listed with totals of 4,831 and 35,567 persons, respectively. As other evidence will subsequently suggest, these totals are understated because of a circumscribed definition of "railroad men" that encompassed only those employees who directly operated the trains: engineers, firemen, conductors, et cetera. No wonder that Ringwalt presents the census figures and is perplexed because they fall "far below current estimates." [1]

The method to be followed in deriving the new estimates builds upon the receipts, output, and construction data of Appendixes A and B. From sample data of individual states, usually Massachusetts and New York, it is possible to establish a relationship between operating employment and various measures of output. The national totals of Appendix A are a means of extending these local results to country-wide aggregates. There is less to go on with regard to construction employment. [2] The sources of infor-

[1] Ringwalt, *Transport Development*, p. 140.

[2] The only contemporary estimate of construction employment I have been able to find is indirect. *Hunt's Merchants' Magazine*, XXXVII (1858), 365, cites total railroad employment, operating and construction, as 400,000. Subtracting about 90,000 for operating employees (see below) leaves an estimate of roughly 300,000 men engaged in construction. This turns out to be a rather poor guess, as will be seen presently.

mation that we utilize are the labor content of new construction expenditures and the investment flows of Appendix B. Together with knowledge of the annual wage these yield estimates of construction workers.

Operating Employment

There are three different independent variables that suggest themselves for a regression estimate of aggregate railroad employment: receipts, operating expenses, and the output of passenger- and ton-miles. The most straightforward relationship is that between employment and output; here the crucial assumption is that productivity in the sample states and in the country as a whole is comparable. The use of a linear relationship between employment and operating expenses, on the other hand, assumes that the product of the wage share and the reciprocal of the wage rate are the same for the sample states and the country as a whole. This may be seen by rewriting $E = bO$, in the following form: $E \equiv O \cdot (W/O) \cdot (1/w)$, where E is employment, O, operating expenses, W, the wage bill, and w, the wage rate. The coefficient of operating expenses is then nothing more than $(W/O) \cdot (1/w)$. The final relationship between employment and receipts involves only a slightly different assumption than the preceding. It is now required that the product of the operating ratio, the wage share, and the reciprocal of the wage rate be the same everywhere, since $E \equiv R \cdot (O/R) \cdot (W/O) \cdot (1/w)$.

A priori, one suspects that a physical productivity relationship derived from a single area would serve least well to estimate national employment. In particular, since the sample states in this case were relatively progressive, such an estimate would approximate a lower bound rather than the actual total. With regard to the other two measures, it is impossible to speak so confidently. Because the component parts of the two products may be negatively correlated, the assumption of a single relationship is more reasonable than before. Thus, although the lower the wage rate in a given region the greater the desired ratio of labor to capital, limitations of railroad technology probably lead to a smaller wage share. Then the product of the wage share and the reciprocal of the wage rate is not altered. A similar negative correlation between wage rates and the operating ratio occurred because of the combination of high charges and low wage payments on southern railroads.[3]

These speculations can be tested by the data of the 1880 census. For that year there is information on employment, receipts, ton- and passenger-miles, and operating expenses, all by region.[4] A comparison of actual national employment with that predicted by the three different relationships prevailing in New England alone will therefore indicate the magnitude and direction of the divergences to be expected in our own case. A simple proportion of employees to weighted passenger- and ton-miles yields an estimate of 480,000 employees; the proportion to receipts, 391,000; and that to operating expenses, 347,000. Actual employment was 416,000 in that year. Our expectations are confounded since the method supposed to provide a lower bound yields the highest estimate of all. The reason is, I suspect, that New England preeminence in railroad productivity had faded rather badly by 1880, so that it was no longer in the van; earlier, an extensive passenger traffic and short hauls were typical rather than unusual. Too, the railroad wage rate in the region was kept high — owing to the competing industrial demands — and this contributes to the lowness of the estimates from dollar magnitudes. If we perform the same experiment, using the census Group II Middle Atlantic (and some midwestern) states, the results conform more closely to expectations: the productivity projection yields a total of 346,000 workers, receipts, 430,000, and operating expenses, 422,000. The relative position of Massachusetts and New York railroads to the rest of the country before the Civil War probably conforms more closely to those of Group II in 1880. As will be seen presently, the ranking of the different methods for the earlier period is the same as that for Group II in 1880, and this suggests that the comparison is appropriate.

One important characteristic of the estimating procedure does emerge unequivocally. That is the substantial accuracy involved. At very worst, the error is no more than 17 percent. And these

[3] That is, given the initial variance of wage rates (and labor productivity), positive correlation of W/O with w and O/R with w reduces the relative variance of the products $(W/O) \cdot (1/w)$ and $(W/O) \cdot (O/R) \cdot (1/w)$.

[4] *Tenth Census*, IV, *Transportation*, pp. 133, 226–227, 257.

results were obtained by a simple proportional relationship that takes no account of individual variations among railroads within the region. Since the proportion of total receipts, and so forth, in the New England region in 1880 is much smaller than the coverage of Massachusetts and New York (and Ohio in 1859) in our period, we can also expect to do somewhat better on that count.

For 1849, data from the Massachusetts and New York state reports was used to estimate the three relationships just discussed. Only Massachusetts provided the necessary information on ton- and passenger-miles, however. Since there were no significant differences in the relationships secured in the individual states (as tested by an analysis of covariance), the final functions relating employment to operating expenses and receipts were derived from pooled data. Both of these regressions, as well as the Massachusetts ton- and passenger-mile function, conform to a hypothesis of homogeneity. Because there is no constant in the equations, the only inputs required to estimate total employment are the corresponding national magnitudes of receipts, operating expenses, and ton- and passenger-miles. Had the data rejected the hypothesis of homogeneity, it also would have been necessary to specify the number of railroads.[5] The equations finally used, their coefficients of determination, and the attendant employment estimates are as follows:[6]

C-1 $E = .0173T + .0181P$ $(R^2 = .86)$
$E = 14,640$

C-2 $E = .635R$ $(R^2 = .89)$
$E = 18,547$

C-3 $E = 1.232O$ $(R^2 = .88)$
$E = 18,303$

From these results it seems almost certain that total railroad operating employment in 1849 neither exceeded 20,000 men nor

[5] That is, from the relationship $y = bx$, it follows that $\Sigma y = b\Sigma x$. If $y = a + bx$, $\Sigma y = Na + b\Sigma x$.
[6] E stands for employment, T for ton-miles, P for passenger-miles, R for total receipts, and O for operating expenses. The number of observations is 20 for equation C-1 and 36 for the other two. Hence the association is statistically significant in all cases.

was less than 15,000 men, with the most likely total in the range of 18,000.[7]

Indirectly, the census data on employment bear out the accuracy of these estimates. On the assumption that the census category of "railroad men" in 1850 corresponds rather closely to the "operating employees" classification in the New York state reports, they would constitute about a third of total employees. The two large groups omitted are workers engaged in maintenance of road and repair of equipment whose occupations were presumably recorded as laborers, machinists, carpenters, et cetera. Use of the exact New York relationship scales the census total of 4,381 to roughly 15,000, or within the range just defined.

Lacking any basis upon which to derive an 1839 estimate — since employment data by railroads even in Massachusetts do not become available until later — the 1849 relationships and 1839 aggregates are enlisted to approximate employment data for that year. The three relationships above yield estimates of 2200, 4600, and 5300 men, respectively. The last two are better measures of employment than the first since declining rates prevailed from 1839 to 1849. Use of the later receipts and operating expenses relationships presumes a rate of increase of labor productivity equivalent to the rates of decline in freight and passenger rates. On the contrary, the output relationship transplanted in its 1849 form presumes zero productivity change over the interval, a most unlikely circumstance in view of the substantial fall in rates without large declines in profits. A reasonable guess is a total of 5000 men employed on American railroads in 1839.

The final year for which estimates of operating employment are provided is 1859. Again available are the Massachusetts and New York experiences, but also some additional data for Ohio railroads in 1858.[8] The 1849 technique is thus feasible in 1859 too,

---

[7] Since we are not dealing with a random sample, and also because we are applying the equation to a sum of receipts, operating expenses, etc., it is impossible to specify the confidence interval exactly from the regression equations themselves. That is why standard errors do not appear. If the latter were used, they would indicate that a range of about 10 percent around the estimates would include the true value more than 9 times out of 10.

[8] The New York and Massachusetts data are found in the published state reports for 1856 and 1860, respectively. The Ohio data for 1858 are found in the *Second Annual Report of Ohio Commissioner of Statistics*, pp. 74–75.

but with a broadened sample. All three states report employment, receipts, and operating expense information, but only Massachusetts and New York provide physical output data. The use of a single relationship using the pooled data of all states was impossible except for the employment-output relationship, however. Analysis of covariance indicated enough difference in the functions for the individual states to merit separate equations. Moreover, the problem of a nonzero constant term arises in connection with equation C-6b. The additional accuracy secured by a constant is really spurious, since the errors of observation in counting the number of individual railroads in the country fully offsets it. The concern here is with the quality of the final estimate, not the structural relationship. Our solution, therefore, is to proceed as if the population relationship were homogeneous. (The same situation arises in Appendix D and is treated identically there.) Since the fit is still good in the homogeneous form, no significant distortion is introduced thereby.

Consequently, for 1859, we have the following multiplicity of equations and related estimates:[9]

C-4	$E = .0243T + .0126P$	$(R^2 = .98)$
	$E = 86,508$	
C-5a	$E = .63R$	$(R^2 = .82)$
(Ohio)	$E = 74,897$	
C-5b	$E = .65R$	$(R^2 = .96)$
(Mass.)	$E = 77,650$	
C-5c	$E = .73R$	$(R^2 = .99)$
(N.Y.)	$E = 86,187$	
C-6a	$E = 1.18O$	$(R^2 = .89)$
(Ohio)	$E = 79,528$	
C-6b	$E = 1.23O$	$(R^2 = .96)$
(Mass.)	$E = 82,518$	
C-6c	$E = 1.33O$	$(R^2 = .99)$
(N.Y.)	$E = 89,518$	

[9] Again all relationships are statistically significant. The number of observations ranges from 47 in equation C-4 to 16 in C-5a and C-6a; 17 in C-5c and C-6c; and 30 in equations C-5b and C-6b.

From these results it seems almost certain that operating employment ranged somewhere from 75,000 to 90,000 men in 1859.[10] If the Massachusetts coefficient is applied to total New England receipts, the New York to earnings in the Middle Atlantic states, and also to those in the South — it is not obvious which relationship is the more appropriate for that region — and the Ohio coefficient to western receipts, the national estimate is 82,000; analogously, for operating expenses, it is 85,000. These regionally differentiated estimates are probably best of all.

Contemporary estimates confirm the order of magnitude we find. They range between 80,000 and 100,000, with the *Railroad Record* favoring the former and the New York Chamber of Commerce the latter.[11] These estimates were the result of some rough extrapolation of employment on the leading railroads. Extension of the 1860 census report to compensate for excluded categories, as before with 1850, puts one above the 105,000 mark, and beyond the upper bound indicated here. Use of the later 1880 relationship between the Census of Occupations and railroad employment leaves one too low at 62,000, on the other hand.[12] Neither deviation should be given too much weight, however.

In sum then, railroad operating employment grew from something like 5,000 in 1839 to 18,000 in 1849 to 85,000 in 1859, give or take a 10 percent margin of error, and perhaps more for 1839.[13]

---

[10] Standard errors range from one-fifteenth of the Ohio coefficients to one thirty-fifth of the New York and Massachusetts ones. If we relied solely on a range of plus or minus 2 standard errors to determine the variation in the employment estimate, the limiting bounds would be 64,000 and 95,000. This wider range is narrowed in the text on the basis of considerations discussed earlier.

[11] The estimate of the *Railroad Record* was reprinted in *De Bow's Review*, XXVII (1860), 243, as well as elsewhere. The Chamber of Commerce conjecture can be found in *Hillyer's American Railroad Magazine*, I (1859), 548.

[12] For the 1880 relationship see Daniel Carson, "Changes in the Industrial Composition of Manpower Since the Civil War," National Bureau of Economic Research, Inc., Studies in Income and Wealth, vol. 11 (New York, 1949), 127.

[13] Since these estimates were developed, another, and independent, research effort by Stanley Lebergott has affirmed their magnitude. Using regional relationships between employment and mileage, Lebergott finds employment of 7,000, 21,000, and 82,000 for 1839, 1849, and 1859. While more than 10 percent different in 1839 and 1849, the absolute differences are too small to matter and in 1859 we reach almost identical totals. See his paper "Labor Force and Employment, 1800–1960," *Output, Employment, and Productivity in the United States after 1800*, National Bureau of Economic Research, Inc., Studies in Income and Wealth, vol. 30 (Princeton, 1965).

Employment in Railroad Construction

The most promising approach to an estimate of construction employment builds upon the previous estimates of expenditure on construction of road. By allocating a proportion of that expenditure to wages, and then dividing by an annual wage, an estimate of annual employment is readily obtained. All the information required, with the sole exception of the proportional significance of wage income, has already been calculated in Appendix B.

The approximate size of the wage bill can be derived without too much trouble. From Table 48 we know that grading, masonry, and bridging came to about half of the total expense of construction of road. Almost all of the cost of such work represented labor services under the primitive technology then prevailing. Simple manual exertion without the aid of much more than picks and shovels was all that was used. The following description of railroad construction in the 1850's is not untypical:

> The work of grading had to be done by hand. None of the modern machinery now used for moving dirt was then in existence. The cuts and fills were made by men with wheelbarrows and hand shovels. On the ground where the fills were to be made trestles were placed a few feet apart on which were laid heavy planks, and over these an endless stream of men and wheelbarrows passed, dumping the dirt on either side.[14]

In addition to these costs, engineering expenses consisted largely of labor charges, although admittedly for skilled personnel. Adding in the track laying charges, and the wage payments for construction of buildings and the like, brings the wage share up to something like 60 percent of total expenditure on road.

Table 55 uses this ratio to convert construction outlays to expenditure on wages. This latter must then be divided by an annual wage that is the product of our wage index converted to absolute daily wages and a working year of 210 days. The year is taken so short because construction work was seasonal in character and rarely prosecuted for more than 8 months a year; even

[14] Frank F. Hargrave, *A Pioneer Indiana Railroad* (Indianapolis, 1932), p. 49. A few steam excavators were used in the early 1840's on the Western Railroad of Massachusetts and sold subsequently to the Troy and Schenectady (*American Railroad Journal*, XIV [1842], 177).

TABLE 55.   Construction employment

Year	Average construction outlay[a] (millions of current dollars)	Average wage bill (millions of dollars)	Average annual wage (in dollars)	Average employment[b] (thousands of men)
1830	2.1	1.3	169	8
1835	9.3	5.6	185	30
1840	12.8	7.7	179	43
1845	11.2	6.7	174	39
1850	38.9	23.3	185	126
1855	75.3	45.2	202	224
1859	49.9	29.9	211	142

Source: See text.

[a] Five-year averages centered in given year, except 1859 which is a three-year average.

[b] During a seasonal period of eight months.

in the South the conflicting demands of cotton cultivation limited the supply of labor, and the construction period. The resultant average therefore relates to seasonal employment. It thus appears that railroad employment went as high as 225,000 in the mid-1850's, with an average well above half that for the decade as a whole.

Gallman's most recent estimate of total construction in current dollars in 1859 is $385 million, with a labor force of 520,000 engaged, according to Lebergott.[15] Railroad construction in that same year stands at $38.8 million or roughly 10 percent of this global sum. On a simple proportional basis we might expect employment of 52,000 men in railroad construction; in fact our method indicates average *annual* employment of about 70,000.[16] Given a greater labor content of railroad construction relative to other building, the divergence is both in the right direction and of a reasonable order of magnitude. Both 1839 and 1849 show a similar divergence although the displacements are relatively

[15] See Gallman, "Gross National Product," and Lebergott, "Labor Force."

[16] The 8-month total is converted to a 12-month equivalent for the purposes of this comparison.

smaller in each instance. This may mean either an underestimate in the earlier period or an overestimate later. Wherever the error, if at all, it is not a serious one. A final check is of primary interest for its substantive contribution. British railroads were required by Parliament to report their annual employment, operating and construction, beginning in the 1840's. Since at the same time they presented information both upon mileage under construction and that newly opened, it becomes possible to extrapolate the British experience to the United States. In Britain the stock of mileage under construction was pretty much the sum of the annual flow of that year and the next. Hence by doubling the flow data over a period of years in the United States, and then multiplying by 58, the average number of workers per mile of road under construction during the period 1848–1855, there is basis for yet another estimate of employment.[17] Annual employment on average during the 1850's so calculated ranges around 250,000 with peaks of almost 400,000.

The substantial upward deviation from our data of Table 55 is comforting in this instance. English methods of construction involving double tracking, straighter alignment, elimination of grades, and so on, might be expected to require larger labor inputs per mile than in the United States.[18] Scattered information on construction employment of American roads seems to confirm such anticipations. The Illinois Central, with perhaps 350 miles under construction in 1853, had a labor force of between 6,000 and 10,000, or less than 30 men per mile under way.[19] Even in the extreme rush to push through a connection from Chicago to Calumet, only 50 men per mile were used and that concentration

[17] This information on British railroad employment is conveniently summarized, up to 1855, in Thomas Tooke and William Newmarch, *A History of Prices* (London, 1857), V, 356.

[18] In England in 1856, 71.2 percent of the road was double tracked; the United States ratio was close to 10 percent. Likewise, there were about 70 miles of tunnel in Britain or almost 1 percent of the total length; the United States had little more than 10 miles of tunnel with more than three times as much road. These data (with the exception of the estimate of double tracking) come from Colburn and Holley, *Permanent Way*, pp. 24 ff., where the heavier English earthwork and more favorable alignment is also discussed.

[19] The mileage under construction in 1853 could not have been much less than 350 miles, what with 117 miles opened in that year and 299 in the next. Employment on the Illinois Central from Gates, *Illinois Central*, p. 96.

received comment.[20] On the Louisville and Nashville in 1856 there is a report that 1,120 men were at work on the line, although 134 miles were under contract.[21] If only 30 miles were being actively prosecuted the ratio of employment to the work in progress would still be half that of the English case. On another southern road, the Mississippi and Tennessee, "upon that portion between [milepost] seventy-one and Oakland (a distance of seven and one-fourth miles), they have had a force of from fifty to one hundred hands." [22]

Since the application of the British ratio yields a result too high by a factor of about 100 percent, these indications that the number of men employed per mile was perhaps half as great as that in Britain render the deviation perfectly explicable. Moreover, this explanation also validates the two to one relationship between the stock of mileage under construction and the annual flow of mileage added, a relationship utilized in our quantity index for the 1850's in connection with the capital formation estimates of Appendix B.

[20] Gates, *Illinois Central*, p. 92.
[21] *American Railroad Journal*, XXIX (1856), 531, 731.
[22] *Hillyer's American Railroad Magazine*, II (1859), 123.

APPENDIX D

The Derivation of Equipment Estimates

This appendix describes the various methods used to derive the estimates of railroad rolling stock before 1860. It is convenient first to present the final results, and then to elaborate upon the means of obtaining the various components. Table 56 sets out the

TABLE 56. Railroad rolling stock

Type of equipment	1839	1849	1859
Locomotives	450	1,325	5,400
Average tractive force	2,880 lbs.	4,850 lbs.	7,060 lbs.
Average horsepower	77 hp	129 hp	188 hp
Passenger cars	900	1,500	4,900
8-wheel equivalent	500	1,400	4,900
Freight cars	3,000	17,000	71,000
8-wheel equivalent	1,500	11,000	66,000
Coal cars	a	6,000	22,000
4-wheel equivalent	—	6,250	23,000

Source: See text.
a Included with other freight cars at this date owing to negligible total.

estimates of the number of locomotives, passenger, and freight cars for the terminal dates of each of the pre-1860 railroad decades. In addition, average tractive force of the locomotives is given as well as a homogeneous equivalent for the number of passenger and freight cars. These further refinements are necessary for more meaningful interpretation of the data. We now take up the specific entries in turn.

Locomotives

The number of locomotives in 1839 is a rounded approximation to Gerstner's tabulation at the end of 1839. He totaled 463 engines, but subsequent research indicates that some of the locomotives were only on order and had not yet been delivered.[1] This 450 total is substantially greater than the 350 listed by the 1838 Report on Steam Engines.[2] The divergence is not due to the rapid increase of production within a single year, but rather to the considerable undercount of the 1838 report.

For 1849 no equivalent census of locomotives was available. A sampling procedure was therefore used. Two states, New York and Massachusetts, requested enumeration of equipment in the reports filed by railroads. A linear and homogeneous regression of locomotives upon receipts derived from this sample permits an estimate of the total number of locomotives solely from aggregate receipts; and these latter have already been prepared in Appendix A. Both the hypothesis of homogeneity and that of a single equation were confirmed by the data. The function used, therefore, was $L = .045R$, where L, locomotives, is expressed in single units and R, receipts, in thousands of dollars. The fit was good, 86 percent of the variance in locomotives being explained by the variation in receipts, and this suggests a relatively small margin of error.[3] The exact error of the estimate depends upon the distribution of individual receipts data, as well as the aptness of the assumption that the Massachusetts and New York relationship is appropriate for the country as a whole.

With regard to this latter point, we know that rates were higher in other parts of the country than in those two states, which implies fewer train-miles elsewhere per dollar of receipts, and hence fewer locomotives; the more regular and frequent scheduling of trains in the northern states would also tend to require more

---

[1] Gerstner's estimate can be found in the *American Railroad Journal*, XII (1840), 187. For evidence concerning his slight overcount see *Railway and Locomotive Historical Society Bulletin*, no. 62 (1943), 44–62 and no. 101 (1959), *passim*.

[2] *Report on Steam Engines*, House Document No. 21, 25th Congress, 3rd Session (Washington, 1839).

[3] The number of observations is 36, so there is no question of significance. Two standard errors of the coefficient define a range of ±13 percent about the estimate of Table 56.

engines. On the other hand, these two states alone represent about 40 percent of total receipts in 1849, and any error is therefore considerably circumscribed. With smaller roads in the West and South in need of a minimum number of locomotives, moreover, the Massachusetts and New York relationship may not over-estimate requirements.

Production data are consistent with our total. Known output of eight locomotive firms up to the end of 1850 totaled 1372 engines. Included are the leading producers in the country: Baldwin, Norris, Rogers, and so forth.[4] Adding to this 34 engines produced for the Baltimore and Ohio by Ross Winans and others, plus imports of 119 engines from Britain, and subtracting exports of approximately the same magnitude, we get an estimate of total American consumption of about 1400 engines.[5] Since some of the production in the 1830's was retired by the later date, as well as the fact that the data extend to 1850, this compares favorably with our estimate of 1325 as the stock at the end of 1849.

A ratio estimate was used to derive the 1859 stock. The *American Railroad Journal* share list began to publish information on the quantity of equipment on railroads at the end of 1859. Thus by the time that the reports for 1859 began to appear, the weekly share list tabulated the rolling stock for individual railroads. The number of locomotives and corresponding receipts for individual railroads were totaled by state, and then the total number of locomotives per state estimated by applying the ratio of locomotives per dollar of receipts to the receipts data, by state, of Appendix A. The final estimate was obtained by summing over all states. Locomotives corresponding to more than 80 percent of

[4] The eight producers are Baldwin, Locks and Canals, Rogers, Norris, Amoskeag, Hinkley, Portland, and Taunton. The data come from *Railway and Locomotive Historical Society Bulletin*, no. 58 (1942), 68, and from the files of that society at Baker Library, Harvard University.

[5] The Winans data are from the *Twenty-Fifth Annual Report of the Baltimore and Ohio Railroad* (Baltimore, 1851), Table G, opposite p. 50; the import data are found in *Railway and Locomotive Historical Society Bulletin*, no. 20 (1929), 36–43. Estimated exports are only approximate but still close to the mark. We know that Norris exported 97 locomotives up to 1844 and Baldwin at least 2. Again, we know that total exports of the Norris firm to 1855 were only 117. Baldwin was not very active in the export market in the 1840's. Hence to assume total exports equaled imports at 119 is quite justified. (*Railway and Locomotive Historical Society Bulletin*, no. 79 [1950], 44, 49; no. 8 [1924], 12.)

total 1859 receipts were tabulated directly, although the proportion naturally varied from state to state. Where state information was too scanty, as when only a single railroad in a state reported the necessary information, the ratio of a similar state was substituted.[6]

The error associated with such a technique depends upon the correlation between receipts and locomotives. When this is strong, as we know it is, ratio estimates considerably increase the precision of estimates.[7] Although the specific sampling error here depends upon the errors in the individual states, we may gain some idea of its likely magnitude indirectly. The rel-variance of a total estimated through simple random sampling can be approximately expressed as follows:

$$V_X^2 = (1 - f)\left[\frac{V_x^2 + V_y^2 - 2\rho V_x V_y}{n}\right]$$

where the population values can be estimated from the corresponding sample values. Then, substituting the already computed 1849 Massachusetts results for V_x^2, V_y^2 and $2\rho V_x V_y$, and using the aggregate sampling fraction and sample size of 1859, we reconstruct a situation in which we assume each state in the 1859 sample to be as homogeneous as the 1849 Massachusetts case. A constant sampling fraction for each state is also required. The standard error of the total estimate of locomotives, as thus computed, is of the order of 34. This implies, in turn, despite the simplifications, that a range of plus or minus 100 locomotives around the estimate of 5400 almost certainly contains the true value.

Again we can avail ourselves of a check from the production side. The total output of 12 locomotive producers until the end of 1860 amounts to 4083.[8] This excludes a considerable proportion

[6] This was necessary in only 4 instances involving less than 100 locomotives in total.

[7] On all this, see the relevant sections in vol. I of Morris H. Hansen, William N. Hurwitz, and William G. Madow, *Sample Survey Methods and Theory* (New York: J. Wiley and Sons, 1953), 2 vols. There is no danger of bias due to the use of a stratified ratio estimate, it should be added. The linear and homogeneous relationship between locomotives and receipts makes it a trivial problem.

[8] The producers are the 8 of 1849, plus Schenectady, Manchester, Mason, and Cook.

of the industry from 1850 to 1860, however. In the mid-1850's an enumeration of locomotive producers then in operation indicated a total greater than 40.[9] On the other hand, it is quite doubtful that much more than 30 percent of the total could have arisen from such other sources during the decade. Hence our 5400 is not a considerable underestimate, taking into account retirements and a slight positive export balance. This assurance is comforting since 2 contemporary estimates suggest much larger quantities. Ringwalt, for example, speaks of 9000 engines at this time, and another writer, in De Bow's Review, comes up with 6000. On the other side, the American Railway Review is undoubtedly too low with its figure of 4000.[10]

The power of a locomotive is commonly expressed in tractive force: the maximum number of pounds it is capable of pulling, given its adhesion on the rails. Horsepower adds the additional elements of distance and time that are lacking from this measure, and so depends upon the speed that can be continuously maintained with the given load. One can substitute one measure for the other through the following formula, which is a valid transformation for the specified speed of ten miles per hour:[11]

$$H.P. = \frac{T.F. \times 5,280 \times 10}{33,000 \times 60}.$$

Since one of the considerations in Chapter III is the relative position of locomotive power in the total energy developed in the pre-Civil War economy, the horsepower magnitude is necessary for comparative purposes.

The information on tractive power comes from a discussion of the American, or 4-4-0, engine in one of the bulletins of the Railway and Locomotive Historical Society.[12] The typical characteristics of these most popular of American pre-Civil War locomo-

[9] Railway and Locomotive Historical Society Bulletin, no. 8 (1924), 24–31. The original source of much of the list appears to be American Railroad Journal, XXVI (1853), 443.

[10] Ringwalt, Transport Development, p. 161; De Bow's Review, XXVII (1860), 243, reprinted from the Railroad Record; American Railway Review, March 26, 1859.

[11] John C. Trautwine, Civil Engineering Pocket Book, 20th ed. (Wallingford, Pa.: Trautwine Co., 1922), p. 1047.

[12] Railway and Locomotive Historical Society Bulletin, no. 35 (1934), 10–37.

tives are given there for various dates. Around 1840, engines of
15 tons were being produced with tractive force of 4329 pounds;
in 1850 the weight had increased to 24 tons and tractive force
correspondingly to 6400 pounds; finally, in 1860, the relevant
dimensions are 31 tons and 9200 pounds. (The increase in weight
was, of course, accompanied by increases in steam pressure, heat-
ing surface, and cylinder area, that enabled the heavier engine to
develop more tractive force.) These weights and tractive forces
are marginal rather than average characteristics, it must be emphasized; they describe the locomotives built at a particular time
rather than the average component of the existing locomotive
stock. Relatively few engines of the 5400 in existence in 1859
were as powerful as the 1860 American engine just described.
For example, only 3 of the 34 engines used on the eastern division
of the Pennsylvania Railroad in 1859 met such a standard; the
average was not far from an average of the 1850 and 1860 tractive
forces.[13]

Thus some adjustment for the composition of the stock is necessary to secure average representations. Probably two thirds of
the 1840 tractive force is a reasonable average for the 450 engines
in 1839, since 10 tons is often cited as the weight of a typical
engine at that date. For 1849, with a residual 400 engines from the
1830's, say, some 925 must have been built in the 1840's; applying
the 1840 tractive force plus two thirds of the difference between
the 1840 and 1850 tractive force to these (since their production
was probably skewed to the latter part of the decade), we get an
average of 4850 pounds. The 1859 average is derived in the same
way. This time we assume that only 50 of the original 450 engines
survive,[14] and that 1275 of the 1325 engines of 1849 survive. The
typical engine produced in the decade is considered to have a
tractive force equal to the average of the 1850 and 1860 forces.

[13] *Thirteenth Annual Report of the Pennsylvania Railroad Company* (Philadelphia,
1860), p. 80. The engines on the mountain division of the road, most modern, and
also requiring the most power, had a higher tractive force than the American type
because they used 6 and 8 driving wheels. Such engines were not common though-
out the country, however.

[14] Such a large survival is surprising but probably correct. The Baltimore and
Ohio Railroad itself had 22 engines of vintage 1839 and earlier in its locomotive
roster in 1860. *Thirty-Fourth Annual Report of the Baltimore and Ohio Railroad
Company*, p. 168.

From these conditions it follows that the average tractive force of the 1859 locomotive stock was 7060 pounds.

By application of the above formula, the average horsepowers are derived from these average tractive forces.

Passenger Cars

The physical characteristics of the early passenger car have been summarized in a recent volume by August Mencken.[15] While we thus know what the cars looked like, we do not know how many there were. The present estimates of the passenger car stock utilize techniques similar to those described for the estimation of locomotives in 1849 and 1859; unfortunately Gerstner's interests did not extend specifically to passenger cars and it is necessary to extend the 1849 estimates back a decade to get an 1839 total.

For 1849 a linear and homogeneous regression of passenger cars upon passenger receipts was derived for New York and Massachusetts railroads. Then, using the passenger receipts of Table 43, an aggregate estimate was secured. In this instance, as before, the data allow pooling. But the hypothesis of homogeneity is rejected. We proceed with a homogeneous function, nonetheless, for the estimation advantages it provides. Since the fit of the homogeneous function, $P = .103R_p$ (in thousands of dollars), was quite satisfactory, R^2 being .83, it is doubtful whether there is any great loss in such a procedure.[16]

This 1849 estimate is, so far as was possible, net of baggage and express cars sometimes included as passenger cars. The relationship also is expressed in terms of an eight-wheel equivalent. There were some older four-wheel coaches still in use in 1849, the Boston and Worcester apparently having quite a few, and for this reason the *total* number of passenger cars is listed as 1500, although the estimating equation indicates only 1400. In this adjustment we have assumed that four-wheeled cars made up less

---

[15] *The Railroad Passenger Car* (Baltimore, 1957).

[16] P stands for passenger cars, R_p for passenger receipts. There is no question of statistical significance since 28 observations were available. The potential error imbedded in the estimate is indicated to be in the range of ±10 percent by the regression equation; although it does not apply strictly in this case, the standard error gives some indication of the reliability to be attached to the final estimate.

than one seventh of the total rolling stock in 1849; i.e., there were 1300 eight-wheel types and 200 of the older sort.[17]

For 1839 a variety of approximations is possible. An upper bound probably results by use of the 1849 functional form directly, since passenger receipts at the later date represented a substantially larger number of passenger-miles than at the earlier. On this basis an 1839 estimate of 753 eight-wheel equivalent cars is obtained. Similarly, a lower bound is approximated by applying the 1839 to 1849 ratio of passenger-miles to the 1849 estimates. This presumes an equivalent state of organization and efficiency in the earlier period, as well as perfect proportionality between equipment and service. Neither of these conditions is appropriate, and their violation leads to an underestimate: extrapolation yields a total of only 270 eight-wheel equivalent units in 1839. These results suggest that the correct eight-wheel equivalent is probably somewhere near the 500 unit mark, and that is the sum entered in Table 56. To get the total number of cars at that date we have assumed that there were then in existence 800 four-wheel cars and 100 of the newer eight-wheel variety.

For 1859, we again used a ratio estimate, with passenger cars and total receipts the two variables. Passenger receipts would have been preferable, but the information was not readily available. The use of a stratified ratio estimate does tend to compensate, however. The error in the estimate of 4900 cars can again be crudely approximated from the formula presented earlier, partially using the Massachusetts relationships of 1849. It is of the order of the magnitude of 100; even if it understates the true error, as it does, the bounds of accuracy are still quite respectable. By way of confirmation, there is a contemporary estimate of 5000 passenger cars at the end of the 1850's. This is from the same source that was within 10 percent of our previous locomotive estimate.[18]

By 1859 almost all passenger cars had 8 wheels. The few remaining older vehicles were probably more than matched by the

---

[17] "Four-wheel cars were in general use until 1838, and a few were still running in 1850, but they were rapidly replaced after that time by the double-truck, eight-wheel car with a center aisle . . ." Mencken, *Passenger Car*, p. 12.

[18] *De Bow's Review*, XXVII (1860), 243.

occasional 12-wheel cars employed on such roads as the Michigan Central.[19] Hence we have presented the 8-wheel equivalent as equal to the total number of cars in this year.

Freight Cars

The method of estimating the number of freight cars is exactly that used for passenger cars. Our total for 1849 is derived by a regression estimate, that for 1839 by extrapolation, and that for 1859 by a ratio estimate.

The 1849 estimate in this instance is a generalization only of the Massachusetts experience. Most Massachusetts railroads reported their rolling stock either directly in 4-wheel equivalent terms, or provided sufficient additional information to permit such a conversion. In New York, one suspects, but does not really know, that many roads were reporting 8-wheel equivalents. The coefficients secured in the two states are far different for this reason. Massachusetts railroads show more than half again as many freight cars per dollar of freight receipts as New York ones. Since there were no significant differences between the two states for the other components of rolling stock, it seems reasonable to infer that variation in reporting is the cause of the divergence in this instance. Accordingly, it seemed wise to use the state where the type of rolling stock was explicitly specified.

The function used, therefore, was $F = 1.752R_f$ (in thousands of dollars). As before, the hypothesis of homogeneity is rejected by the data, but again the form is used due to its computational advantage. Since $R^2 = .87$, the loss of accuracy in the fit is small.[20] This estimating relationship is applied to total 1849 freight receipts, less those of the Reading Railroad, and yields an aggregate of about 22,000 four-wheel equivalent freight cars. These are then converted to 11,000 eight-wheel equivalents, and

[19] The Michigan Central in 1859 had 68 12-wheel cars and only 43 8-wheel cars. *Annual Report of the Michigan Central Railroad for 1859* (Boston, 1859), p. 35. From Mencken's descriptions we may infer that such rolling stock was an exception. It may be noted that the Michigan Central built all of its cars itself.

[20] F stands for freight cars, R_f for freight receipts. Even with the smaller number of observations dictated by the use of a single state, 17, the association is statistically significant. A range of 2 standard errors defines bounds of ± 12 percent around the 22,000 estimate.

this is the entry in Table 56. The Reading is excluded from the previous calculations since it was the principal rail coal carrier at this date and information on its cars, principally coal cars, could be obtained directly. At the end of 1849 the Reading possessed approximately 4,600 coal cars.[21] An additional 1,400 cars are added to include the rolling stock of other operators like the Beaver Meadow Railroad, et cetera, in Pennsylvania, and elsewhere.

The conversion from eight-wheel equivalent freight cars to actual number of cars involves the assumption that something less than a third of the cars were actually of the eight-wheel type; specifically it means that there were 12,000 four-wheel cars and 5,000 eight-wheel cars in operation in 1849. The mix on the Massachusetts roads — the only ones for which such information is available — suggests a slightly higher ratio of the smaller to the larger cars. But this is to be expected of an area with many older roads. Moreover, since baggage and mail cars are included in this category at this date, and these were generally of the double truck sort, this is additional reason to retain the estimate unchanged. In any event, it is not very sensitive to the range of admissible alternative assumptions. In similar fashion the 6,000 coal car unit total has been transposed into a four-wheel equivalent through the assumption that only about 5 percent of the cars were eight-wheeled: there was but a single eight-wheel coal car on the Reading in 1846 and fewer than 10 percent in 1859.

The application to 1839 of the regression relationship of 1849 indicates a 4-wheel equivalent stock of less than 3700 cars. Extrapolation by the ratio of 1839 to 1849 ton-miles (excluding the Reading) gives a lower bound of almost half as much, namely 2340 units. The estimate of 3000 cars, all assumed to be 4-wheel, entered in Table 56 cannot be too far off in absolute number.

The total number of freight cars in 1859, 89,000, is obtained by a ratio estimate from total receipts. Both ordinary and coal cars are included in this total, however, and it is necessary to segregate the two components as well as to estimate standardized

---

[21] The road possessed 4559 coal cars in 1846 according to the report published in the *American Railroad Journal*, XX (1847), 103, and 4567 in 1850 from the report published, *ibid.*, XXIV (1851), 37.

equivalents. The number of coal cars on all Pennsylvania railroads in 1859 was reported at 20,411.[22] Some of these may have belonged to private shippers or were primarily used by companies within their mines. At any rate, aggregation over the Pennsylvania railroads reported in Poor's *Railroads and Canals* reveals only 18,000 coal cars, including 4,000 cars of the Pennsylvania Coal Company and the Delaware and Hudson Company.[23] With some allowance for coal cars in other states — the Baltimore and Ohio had almost 1,300, and Ohio railroads at least the equivalent — the 22,000 estimate is a good approximation.

In any case it is clear that the 89,000 aggregate is appropriate. It compares favorably with the contemporary estimate of 80,000 made by the astute editor of the *Railroad Record*.[24] Moreover, the approximated standard error is equal to only 1,113 cars.

The final step is the derivation of standardized equivalents. We have assumed that something like 15 percent of the freight cars in 1859 were of the single truck variety. Since the freight car tabulation includes such vehicles as hand cars, gravel cars, and so forth, all of which were four-wheeled, the approximation seems tolerable enough.[25] The adjustment for coal cars involves the assumption that only 1000 cars were of the eight-wheel type in 1859; this approximation is readily confirmed: the Reading and the Delaware, Lackawanna and Western, together accounting for almost half the coal cars in the country had between them only 700 eight-wheel cars in 1859.[26] These being the most progressive of the coal roads, it is doubtful whether the national total much exceeded a thousand.

[22] *Hunt's Merchants' Magazine*, XLII (1860), 503. This is a reprint of the Auditor General's Report on railroads for 1859.

[23] Poor, *Railroads and Canals*.

[24] *De Bow's Review*, XXVII (1860), 243.

[25] Thus the Michigan Central in 1859 had 1568 cars and an 8-wheel equivalent of 1415 for a ratio of 0.9; the Pennsylvania Railroad a total of 2559 and an 8-wheel equivalent of 2343, again for a 0.9 ratio; the Fitchburg, 689 cars and an 8-wheel equivalent of 527 for a ratio of 0.77. (*Annual Report of the Michigan Central Railroad for 1859*, p. 39; *Thirteenth Annual Report of the Pennsylvania Railroad*, p. 31; *Report of the Fitchburg Railroad Corporation for 1860* [Boston, 1860], p. 6.)

[26] Poor, *Railroads and Canals*, pp. 435, 482.

Selected Bibliography

A. *Periodicals and other Serials*

American Iron and Steel Association. *Annual Statistical Report*. Philadelphia, 1872 — .

American Railroad Journal. New York, 1832 — . Weekly.

American Railway Times. Boston, 1859–1861. Weekly.

Boston Board of Trade. *Annual Report*. Boston, 1855 — .

Chicago Board of Trade. *Annual Report*. Chicago, 1858 — .

Chicago Democratic Press. *Annual Review of Commerce, Railroads and Manufactures*. Chicago, 1855–1860.

De Bow's Commercial Review. New Orleans, 1846–1870. Monthly.

Hazard's Register of Pennsylvania. Philadelphia, 1828–1835. Weekly.

Hazard's United States Statistical and Commercial Register. Philadelphia, 1839–1842. Weekly.

Hillyer's American Railroad Magazine. New York, 1859–1861. Monthly.

Hunt's Merchants' Magazine and Commercial Review. New York, 1839–1870. Monthly.

Journal of the Franklin Institute. Philadelphia, 1826 — . Monthly.

Nile's Weekly Register. Baltimore, 1811–1849. Weekly.

Poor's Manual of the Railroads of the United States. New York, 1868 — . Annual.

Railway and Locomotive Historical Society. *Bulletin*. Boston, 1922 — .

B. *Railroad Reports*

State

The reports of the following states were issued continuously over a large portion of the period:

Massachusetts Committee [of the General Court] on Railways and Canals. *Annual Reports of the Railroad Corporations of Massachusetts*, 1836–1856. (For later years, reports are issued by the Secretary of the Commonwealth.)

New York State Engineer and Surveyor. *Annual Report on the Railroads of the State of New York*, 1847 —. (Title varies.)

Virginia Board of Public Works. *Annual Reports of the Railroads of the State of Virginia*, 1853–1854 — . (Earlier reports are contained in the Annual Report of the Board of Public Works.)

Individual Railroads

A variety of reports for individual railroads were consulted from the abundant collection at Baker Library, Harvard University, Cambridge, Massachusetts. Among those most useful (and with issues available for more than one or two years) were the following:

Baltimore and Ohio Railroad. Baltimore, 1827 — .

Illinois Central Railroad. Chicago, 1855 — .

Michigan Central Railroad. Boston, 1847 — .

Pennsylvania Railroad. Philadelphia, 1847 — .

Philadelphia and Reading Railroad. Philadelphia, 1845 — .

Pittsburgh, Fort Wayne, and Chicago Railroad. Pittsburgh, 1858 — .

C. *Government Documents*
State

In addition to the occasional references to the legislative journals and documents of Michigan, Mississippi, Missouri, New York, Ohio, Pennsylvania, and Virginia, the following specific publications are worthy of special mention:

Iowa

Secretary of State. *Census for 1880*. Des Moines, 1883.

Massachusetts

Secretary of the Commonwealth. *Statistical Tables: Exhibiting the Condition and Products of Certain Branches of Industry in Massachusetts, for the Year Ending April 1, 1837*. Boston, 1838.

——— *Statistics of the Condition and Products of Certain Branches of Industry in Massachusetts, for the Year Ending April 1, 1845*. Boston, 1846.

——— *Statistical Information Relating to Certain Branches of Industry in Massachusetts, for the Year Ending June 1, 1855*. Boston, 1856.

New York

Secretary of State. *Census of the State of New York* for the Years 1845 and 1855. Albany, 1846 and 1856.

Ohio

Commissioner of Statistics. *Annual Report,* 1857 — . Columbus, 1858 — .

Federal

United States Bureau of the Census. *Compendium of the Seventh Census, 1850.* Washington, D.C., 1854.
—— *Preliminary Report on the Eighth Census.* Washington, D.C., 1862.
—— *Eighth Census of the United States, 1860, Population.* Washington, D.C., 1864.
—— *Eighth Census of the United States, 1860, Agriculture.* Washington, D.C., 1864.
—— *Eighth Census of the United States, 1860, Manufactures.* Washington, D.C., 1865.
—— *Compendium of the Ninth Census.* Washington, D.C., 1872.
—— *Ninth Census of the United States, 1870, III, Statistics of Wealth and Industry.* Washington, D.C., 1872.
—— *Compendium of the Tenth Census,* Washington, D.C., 1883.
—— *Tenth Census of the United States, 1880, IV, Transportation.* Washington, D.C., 1883.
—— *Tenth Census of the United States, 1880, XX, Statistics of Wages.* Washington, D.C., 1886.
—— *Eleventh Census of the United States, 1890, I, Population.* Washington, D.C., 1895.
—— *Eleventh Census of the United States, 1890, VI, Manufactures.* Washington, D.C., 1895.
—— *Eleventh Census of the United States, 1890, XIV, Transportation.* Washington, D.C., 1895.
—— *Historical Statistics of the United States.* Washington, D.C., 1960.
United States Congress, House. *Report on Steam Engines.* Executive Document No. 21, 25th Congress, 3rd Session, 1839.
—— Executive Document No. 172, 26th Congress, 1st Session, 1840.
—— *Trade and Commerce of the British North American Colonies.* Executive Document No. 136, 32nd Congress, 1st Session, 1853.
United States Congress, Joint Economic Committee. Hearings on Employment, Growth, and Price Levels, pt. 2, *Historical and Comparative Rates of Production, Productivity, and Prices.* 86th Congress, 1st Session. 1959.

United States Congress, Senate. Miscellaneous Document No. 192, 20th Congress, 1st Session, 1828.

―――― *Report on Finances, 1855–56.* Executive Document No. 2, 34th Congress, 2nd Session. 1856.

―――― Executive Document No. 55, 34th Congress, 3rd Session. 1857.

―――― *Transportation Routes to the Seaboard.* Report No. 307, 43rd Congress, 1st Session. 1874.

―――― *Wholesale Prices, Wages, and Transportation.* Report No. 1394, 52nd Congress, 2nd Session. 1893.

―――― *Preliminary Report of the Inland Waterways Commission.* Executive Document No. 325, 60th Congress, 1st Session. 1908.

United States Patent Office. *Annual Reports of the Commissioner,* 1848–1861.

United States Treasury Department, Bureau of Statistics. *Annual Report on the Internal Commerce of the United States,* 1876 — .

D. *Secondary Sources*

Abbott, Edith. "The Wages of Unskilled Labor in the United States, 1850–1900," *Journal of Political Economy,* XIII (1905), 321–367.

Adams, Charles F., Jr. *Railroads: Their Origin and Problems.* Rev. ed. New York, 1878.

Albion, Robert G. *Square Riggers on Schedule.* Princeton: Princeton University Press, 1938.

Ambler, Charles H. *A History of Transportation in the Ohio Valley.* Glendale, Calif.: Arthur H. Clark Co., 1932.

Baker, George P. *The Formation of the New England Railroad Systems: A Study of Railroad Combination in the Nineteenth Century.* Cambridge, Mass.: Harvard University Press, 1937.

Beard, Earl S. "Local Aid to Railroads in Iowa," *Iowa Journal of History,* L (1952), 1–34.

Benton, Elbert Jay. "The Wabash Trade Route in the Development of the Old Northwest," *Johns Hopkins University Studies in Historical and Political Science,* XXI, nos. 1–2 (1903).

Berry, Thomas S. *Western Prices before 1861.* Cambridge, Mass.: Harvard University Press, 1943.

Bezanson, Anne, *et al. Wholesale Prices in Philadelphia, 1784–1861.* 2 vols. Philadelphia: University of Pennsylvania Press, 1937.

Bidwell, Percy W., and John I. Falconer. *History of Agriculture in the Northern United States, 1620–1860.* Washington, D.C.: Carnegie Institution, 1925.

Bishop, James L. *A History of American Manufactures from 1608 to 1860.* 2 vols. 3rd ed. Philadelphia, 1866.

Black, Robert C., III. *The Railroads of the Confederacy.* Chapel Hill: University of North Carolina Press, 1952.

Black, Robert L. *The Little Miami Railroad.* Cincinnati: The Author, 1939.

Bliss, George. *Historical Memoirs of the Western Railroad.* Springfield, Mass., 1863.

Board of Lake Underwriters. *Report of the Fourth Annual Meeting.* Buffalo, 1858.

Bogart, E. L. *Internal Improvements in Ohio.* New York: Longmans, Green, & Co., 1924.

Bogen, Jules I. *The Anthracite Railroads.* New York: Ronald Press, 1927.

Bogue, Allan G., and Margaret B. Bogue. " 'Profits' and the Frontier Land Speculator," *Journal of Economic History*, XVII (1957), 1–24.

Brady's Bend Iron Company: Its Real Estate, Materials, Works, and Manufactures. Boston, 1858.

Broome, George W. *The Amoskeag Manufacturing Company.* Manchester, N.H.: Amoskeag Co., 1915.

Burgess, George H., and Miles C. Kennedy. *Centennial History of the Pennsylvania Railroad Company.* Philadelphia: Pennsylvania Railroad Company, 1949.

Burgess, Josiah J. *Railway Directory for 1861.* New York, 1861.

Burgy, J. Herbert. *The New England Textile Industry.* Baltimore, 1932.

Callender, Guy Stevens. "The Early Transportation and Banking Enterprises of the States in Relation to the Growth of Corporations." *Quarterly Journal of Economics*, XVII (1902), 111–162.

——— *Selections from the Economic History of the United States, 1765–1860.* New York: Ginn and Co., 1909.

Carter, Charles F. *When Railroads Were New.* New York: Simmons-Boardman, 1926.

Chandler, Alfred D., Jr. *Henry Varnum Poor.* Cambridge, Mass.: Harvard University Press, 1956.

——— "Patterns of American Railroad Finance, 1830–1850." *Business History Review*, XXVIII (1954), 248–263.

Chevalier, Michel. *Histoire et Description des Voies des Communications aux Etats-Unis.* Paris, 1840–1841.

——— *Society, Manners, and Politics in the United States.* Garden City, N.Y.: Doubleday Anchor Books, 1961. Edited and with an introduction by John William Ward.

Clark, Thomas D. *The Beginning of the L & N; The Development of the*

Louisville and Nashville Railroad and Its Memphis Branches from 1836 to 1860. Louisville, Ky.: Standard Printing Co., 1933.

———— *A Pioneer Southern Railroad.* Chapel Hill: University of North Carolina Press, 1936.

Clark, Victor S. *History of Manufactures in the United States.* 2 vols. Washington, D.C.: Carnegie Institution, 1916.

Cleveland, Frederick A., and Fred W. Powell. *Railroad Promotion and Capitalization in the United States.* New York: Longmans, Green, & Co., 1909.

———— *Railroad Finance.* New York: Appleton-Century, 1912.

Cochran, Thomas C. *Railroad Leaders, 1845–1890: The Business Mind in Action.* Cambridge, Mass.: Harvard University Press, 1953.

Colburn, Zerah and Alexander Holley. *The Permanent Way.* New York, 1858.

Cole, Arthur H. *The American Wool Manufacture.* 2 vols. Cambridge, Mass.: Harvard University Press, 1926.

Conference in Income and Wealth. *Trends in the American Economy in the Nineteenth Century,* Studies in Income and Wealth, vol. 24. Princeton: Princeton University Press for the National Bureau of Economic Research, 1960.

———— *Output, Employment, and Productivity in the United States after 1800,* Studies in Income and Wealth, vol. 30. New York: Columbia University Press for the National Bureau of Economic Research, 1965.

Conrad, Alfred H., and John R. Meyer. "Economics of Slavery in the Ante-Bellum South," *Journal of Political Economy,* LXVI (1958), 95–130.

Cootner, Paul H. "Social Overhead Capital and Economic Growth," in Walt W. Rostow, ed. *The Economics of Take-Off into Sustained Growth.* London: Macmillan Co., 1963.

———— "Transport Innovation and Economic Development: The Case of the U.S. Steam Railroads." Unpub. diss., Massachusetts Institute of Technology, 1953.

Copeland, Melvin T. *The Cotton Manufacturing Industry of the United States.* Cambridge, Mass.: Harvard University Press, 1917.

Corliss, Carlton J. *Mainline of Mid-America: The Story of the Illinois Central.* New York: Creative Age Press, 1950.

Cotterill, R. S. "Southern Railroads and Western Trade, 1840–1850," *Mississippi Valley Historical Review,* III (1917), 427–441.

———— "The Beginnings of Railroads in the Southwest," *Mississippi Valley Historical Review,* VIII (1922), 318–326.

—— "Southern Railroads, 1850–1860," *Mississippi Valley Historical Review*, X (1924), 398–405.

Crescent Iron Manufacturing Company. Boston, 1855.

Curti, Merle. *The Making of an American Community*. Stanford: Stanford University Press, 1959.

Daddow, Samuel H., and Benjamin Bannon. *Coal, Iron, and Oil*. Pottsville, 1866.

Danhof, Clarence H. "Farm-Making Costs and the 'Safety Valve': 1850–1860," *Journal of Political Economy*, XLIX (1941), 317–359.

—— "The Fencing Problem in the Eighteen-Fifties," *Agricultural History*, XVIII (1944), 168–186.

Daniels, Wylie J., "The Village at the End of the Road: A Chapter in Early Indiana Railroad History," *Indiana Historical Society Publications*, XIII, no. 1 (1938).

Daugherty, C. D. "An Index of the Installation of Machinery in the United States since 1850," *Harvard Business Review*, VI (1927–28), 278–292.

Davis, Lance E. "Sources of Industrial Finance: The American Textile Industry, a Case Study," *Explorations in Entrepreneurial History*, IX (1957), 189–203.

De Bow, J. D. B. *Industrial Resources of the Western and Southern States*. 3 vols. New Orleans, 1853.

—— *Encyclopedia of the Trade and Commerce of the United States*. 2nd ed. London, 1854.

DePew, Chauncy, ed. *One Hundred Years of American Commerce*. 2 vols. New York, 1895.

Derrick, Samuel Melanchthon. *Centennial History of the South Carolina Railroad*. Columbia, S.C.: The State Company, 1930.

Dorsey, Edward B. *English and American Railroads Compared*. 2nd ed. New York, 1887

Dozier, Howard D. *A History of the Atlantic Coast Line Railroad*. Boston: Houghton Mifflin, 1920.

Duesenberry, James S. "Some Aspects of the Theory of Economic Development," *Explorations in Entrepreneurial History*, III (1950), 63–102.

Dunbar, Seymour. *A History of Travel in America*. 4 vols. Indianapolis: Bobbs-Merrill, 1915.

Easterlin, Richard A. "Influences in European Overseas Emigration before World War I," *Economic Development and Cultural Change*, IX (1961), 331–351.

Eavenson, Howard N. *The First Century and a Quarter of American Coal Industry.* Privately printed, Pittsburgh, 1942.

Eckstein, Otto. *Water Resource Development: The Economics of Project Evaluation.* Cambridge, Mass.: Harvard University Press, 1958.

Eighty Years' Progress of the United States. Hartford, 1868.

Ellis, Howard S., ed. *Economic Development for Latin America.* New York: St. Martin's Press, 1961.

Esarey, Logan. "Internal Improvements in Early Indiana," *Indiana Historical Society Publications,* V, no. 2 (1912).

Ferguson, William. *America by River and Rail.* London, 1856.

Fishlow, Albert. "Antebellum Interregional Trade Reconsidered," *American Economic Review,* LIV (1964), 352–364.

―――― "Productivity and Technological Change in the Railroad Sector, 1840–1910," *Output, Employment, and Productivity in the United States after 1800.* National Bureau of Economic Research, Inc., Studies in Income and Wealth, vol. 30. New York: Columbia University Press, 1965.

Fite, Emerson D. *Social and Industrial Conditions in the North during the Civil War.* New York: Macmillan Co., 1910.

Flint, Henry M. *The Railroads of the United States; Their History and Statistics.* Philadelphia, 1868.

Fogel, Robert W. *Railroads and American Economic Growth: Essays in Econometric History.* Baltimore: Johns Hopkins Press, 1964.

―――― "A Quantitative Approach to the Study of Railroads in American Economic Growth: A Report of Some Preliminary Findings," *Journal of Economic History,* XXII (1962), 163–197.

Folmsbee, Stanley J. *Sectionalism and Internal Improvements in Tennessee, 1796–1845.* Philadelphia: University of Pennsylvania Press, 1939.

Forney, M. N. *Locomotives and Locomotive Building.* New York, 1886.

Freedley, Edwin T. *Philadelphia and Its Manufactures.* Philadelphia, 1859.

Frickey, Edwin. *Production in the United States, 1860–1914.* Cambridge, Mass.: Harvard University Press, 1947.

French, Benjamin. *History of the Iron Trade of the United States.* New York, 1858.

Gallman, Robert. "Commodity Output, 1839–1899," *Trends in the American Economy in the Nineteenth Century.* National Bureau of Economic Research, Inc., Studies in Income and Wealth, vol. 24. Princeton: Princeton University Press, 1960.

———— "Gross National Product in the United States, 1834–1909," *Output, Employment, and Productivity in the United States after 1800.* National Bureau of Economic Research, Inc., Studies in Income and Wealth, vol. 30. New York: Columbia University Press, 1965.

Galton, Douglass. *Report to the Lords of the Committee of Privy Council for Trade and Foreign Plantations on the Railways of the United States.* London: Board of Trade, 1857.

Gates, Paul W. *The Illinois Central and Its Colonization Work.* Cambridge, Mass.: Harvard University Press, 1934.

———— *The Farmers Age: Agriculture 1815–1860.* New York: Holt, Rinehart and Winston, 1961.

Geographical, Geological, and Statistical Relations of the Ohio and Mississippi Railroad. No publisher, no date.

Gephart, William F. "Transportation and Industrial Development in the Middle West," *Columbia University Studies in History, Economics, and Public Law,* XXXIV, no. 1 (1909).

Gerstner, Franz Anton Ritter von. *Die Innern Communicationen der Vereinigten Staaten von Nord Amerika.* 2 vols. Vienna, 1842–1843.

Gibb, George S. *The Saco-Lowell Shops.* Cambridge, Mass.: Harvard University Press, 1950.

Goodrich, Carter, *et al. Canals and American Economic Development.* New York: Columbia University Press, 1961.

Goodrich, Carter. *Government Promotion of American Canals and Railroads.* New York: Columbia University Press, 1960.

———— and Harvey H. Segal. "Baltimore's Aid to Railroads: A Study in the Municipal Planning of Internal Improvements," *Journal of Economic History,* XIII (1953), 2–35.

Gray, Lewis C. *History of Agriculture in the Southern United States to 1860.* 2 vols. Washington, D.C.: Carnegie Institution, 1933.

Green, Constance M. *Holyoke, Massachusetts.* New Haven: Yale University Press, 1939.

Grosvenor, William M. *Does Protection Protect?* New York, 1871.

Habakkuk, H. J. *British and American Technology in the Nineteenth Century.* Cambridge, Eng.: University Press, 1962.

Hadley, Arthur T. *Railroad Transportation: Its History and Laws.* New York, 1903.

Hammond, Matthew B. *The Cotton Industry.* New York, 1897.

Haney, Lewis H. *A Congressional History of Railways in the United States to 1850.* Madison, Wisconsin: Democrat Printing Co., 1908.

——— *A Congressional History of Railways in the United States from 1850 to 1887*. Madison, Wisconsin: Democrat Printing Co., 1910.

Hargrave, Frank F. *A Pioneer Indiana Railroad*. Indianapolis: The Author, 1932.

Harlow, Alvin F. *The Road of the Century*. New York: Creative Age Press, 1947.

Harrison, Joseph, Jr. *The Locomotive Engine*. Philadelphia, 1872.

Hazard, Blanche E. *Organization of the Boot and Shoe Industry in Massachusetts before 1875*. Cambridge, Mass.: Harvard University Press, 1921.

Heath, Milton S. *Constructive Liberalism: The Role of the State in Economic Development in Georgia to 1860*. Cambridge, Mass.: Harvard University Press, 1954.

——— "Public Cooperation in Railroad Construction in the Southern United States to 1861." Unpub. diss. Harvard University, 1937.

——— "Public Railroad Construction and the Development of Private Enterprise in the South before 1861," *Journal of Economic History*, X (1950), 40–53.

Henlein, Paul C. *The Cattle Kingdom of the Ohio Valley*. Lexington: University of Kentucky Press, 1959.

Hibbard, Benjamin H. "The History of Agriculture in Dane County, Wisconsin," *Bulletin of the University of Wisconsin*, Economics and Political Science Series, I, no. 2 (1904).

Hidy, Ralph W. *The House of Baring in American Trade and Finance: English Merchant Bankers at Work, 1763–1861*. Cambridge, Mass.: Harvard University Press, 1949.

Hill, Forest G. *Roads, Rails and Waterways: The Army Engineers and Early Transportation*. Norman: University of Oklahoma Press, 1957.

Hirschman, Albert O. *The Strategy of Economic Development*. New Haven: Yale University Press, 1958.

History of the Baldwin Locomotive Works, 1831–1923. No publisher, no date.

Holbrook, Stewart H. *The Story of American Railroads*. New York: Crown Publishers, 1947.

Holmstrom, J. Edwin. *Railways and Roads in Pioneer Development Overseas*. London: P. S. King and Son, 1934.

Hulbert, Archer B. *The Paths of Inland Commerce*. Chronicles of America Series, vol. 21. New Haven: Yale University Press, 1920.

Hungerford, Edward. *The Story of the Baltimore and Ohio Railroad*. 2 vols. New York: G. P. Putnam's Sons, 1928.

Hunt, Robert S. *Law and Locomotives*. Madison: State Historical Society of Wisconsin, 1958.

Hunter, Louis C. *Steamboats on the Western Rivers: An Economic and Technological History*. Cambridge, Mass.: Harvard University Press, 1949.

―― "Influence of the Market upon Technique in the Iron Industry in Western Pennsylvania up to 1860," *Journal of Economic and Business History*, I (1929), 241–281.

―― "Studies in the Economic History of the Ohio Valley," *Smith College Studies in History*, XIX, no. 1–2 (1933–1934).

Isard, Walter. "A Neglected Cycle: The Transport Building Cycle," *Review of Economic Statistics*, XXIV (1942), 149–158.

―― "Transport Development and Building Cycles," *Quarterly Journal of Economics*, LVII (November 1942), 90–112.

―― "Some Locational Factors in the Iron and Steel Industry in the Early Nineteenth Century," *Journal of Political Economy*, LVI (1948), 203–217.

Jenks, Leland Hamilton. *The Migration of British Capital to 1875*. New York: Alfred A. Knopf, 1927.

―― "Railroads as an Economic Force in American Development," *Journal of Economic History*, IV (1944), 1–20.

Jervis, John B. *Railway Property*. New York, 1861.

Johnson, Emory R., *et al. History of Domestic and Foreign Commerce of the United States*. 2 vols. Washington, D.C.: Carnegie Institution, 1915.

Jones, Chester L. "The Economic History of the Anthracite-Tidewater Canals," University of Pennsylvania Series in Political Economy and Public Law, no. 22 (1908).

Jones, Fred M. "Middlemen in the Domestic Trade in the United States, 1800–1860," *Illinois Studies in the Social Sciences*, XXI, no. 3 (1937).

Kemmerer, Donald L. "The Pre-Civil War South's Leading Crop, Corn," *Agricultural History*, XXIII (1949), 236–239.

Kettell, Thomas P. *Southern Wealth and Northern Profits*. New York, 1860.

King, Willford I. *The Wealth and Income of the People of the United States*. New York: Macmillan Co., 1915.

Kirkland, Edward C. *Men, Cities, and Transportation: A Study in New England History, 1820–1900*. 2 vols. Cambridge, Mass.: Harvard University Press, 1948.

Kistler, Thelma M. "The Rise of Railroads in the Connecticut River

Valley," *Smith College Studies in History*, XXIII, nos. 1–4 (1937–1938).

Knowlton, Evelyn H. *Pepperell's Progress: History of a Cotton Textile Company, 1844–1945*. Cambridge, Mass.: Harvard University Press, 1948.

Kohlmeier, A. L. *The Old Northwest as the Keystone of the Arch of the American Federal Union*. Bloomington, Ind.: The Principia Press, 1938.

Krenkel, John H. *Illinois Internal Improvements, 1818–1848*. Cedar Rapids, Iowa: The Torch Press, 1958.

Kuznets, Simon. *Capital in the American Economy*. Princeton: Princeton University Press, 1961.

Lardner, Dionysius. *Railway Economy*. London, 1850.

Larson, Laurence M. "A Financial and Administrative History of Milwaukee," *Bulletin of the University of Wisconsin*, Economic and Political Science Series, IV, no. 2 (1908).

Layer, Robert G. *Earnings of Cotton Mill Operatives, 1825–1914*. Cambridge, Mass.: Harvard University Press, 1955.

Lebergott, Stanley. "Labor Force and Employment, 1800–1960." *Output, Employment, and Productivity in the United States after 1800*. National Bureau of Economic Research, Inc., Studies in Income and Wealth, vol. 30. New York: Columbia University Press, 1965.

Leland, Cyrus P. "The Ohio Railroad: That Famous Structure Built on Stilts," *Magazine of Western History*, XIII (1891), 742–756.

Lesley, J. P. *The Iron Manufacturers' Guide to the Furnaces, Forges and Rolling Mills of the United States*. New York, 1859.

Lippincott, Isaac. "Internal Trade of the United States, 1700–1860," *Washington University Studies*, IV, pt. II, no. I, (1916).

Lively, Robert A. "The American System: A Review Article," *Business History Review*, XXIX (1955), 81–96.

Livingood, James Weston. *The Philadelphia-Baltimore Trade Rivalry, 1780–1860*. Harrisburg: Pennsylvania Historical and Museum Commission, 1947.

MacGregor, John. *Commercial Statistics of America*. London, 1849.

Martin, Joseph G. *A Century of Finance*. Boston, 1898.

Matthews, R. C. O. *A Study in Trade-Cycle History*. Cambridge, Eng.: University Press, 1954.

McClelland, C. P., and C. C. Huntington. *History of the Ohio Canals*. Columbus: Ohio State Archaeological Society, 1905.

McGill, Caroline E., *et al*. *History of Transportation in the United States before 1860*. Washington, D.C.: Carnegie Institution, 1917.

McGowan, Joseph A. "Freighting to the Mines in California, 1849–1859." Unpub. diss. University of California, Berkeley, 1949.

McGrane, Reginald C. *The Panic of 1837*. Chicago: University of Chicago Press, 1924.

—— *Foreign Bondholders and American State Debts*. New York: Macmillan Co., 1935.

McNall, Neil A. *An Agricultural History of the Genesee Valley, 1790–1860*. Philadelphia: University of Pennsylvania Press, 1952.

Mencken, August. *The Railroad Passenger Car*. Baltimore: Johns Hopkins Press, 1957.

Merk, Frederick. *Economic History of Wisconsin during the Civil War Decade*. Madison: State Historical Society of Wisconsin, 1916.

Middleton, P. Harvey. *Railways and Public Opinion*. Chicago: Railway Business Association, 1941.

Million, John W. *State Aid to Railways in Missouri*. Chicago: University of Chicago Press, 1896.

Mills, Georgia. *West of the River*. Cedar Rapids, Iowa: The Torch Press, 1958.

Moody, John. *The Railroad Builders*. Chronicles of America Series, vol. 38. New Haven: Yale University Press, 1919.

Moore, John H. *Agriculture in Ante-Bellum Mississippi*. New York: Bookman Associates, 1958.

Morrell, Daniel J. *The Manufacture of Railroad Iron*. Washington: U.S. Treasury Department Revenue Commission, 1866.

Mott, Edward H. *Between the Ocean and the Lakes*. New York, 1899.

Moulton, Harold G. *Waterways Versus Railways*. Boston: Houghton Mifflin, 1926.

Nevins, Allan. *Abram S. Hewitt, with Some Account of Peter Cooper*. New York: Harper, 1935.

North, Douglass C. *The Economic Growth of the United States, 1790–1860*. Englewood Cliffs, N.J.: Prentice Hall, 1961.

Nurkse, Ragnar. "International Investment Today in the Light of Nincteenth-Century Experience," *Economic Journal*, LXIV (1954), 744–758.

Overton, Richard C. *Burlington West*. Cambridge, Mass.: Harvard University Press, 1941.

Parker, William N., and Judith L. V. Klein. "Productivity Growth in Grain Production in the United States, 1840–60 and 1900–10," in *Output, Employment, and Productivity in the United States after 1800*. National Bureau of Economic Research, Inc., Studies in Income and Wealth, vol. 30. New York: Columbia University Press, 1965.

Paxson, Frederic L. "The Railroads of the 'Old Northwest' before the Civil War," *Transactions of the Wisconsin Academy of Sciences, Arts, and Letters*, XVII, pt. I, no. 4 (1914).

Peto, Morton. *The Resources and Prospects of America*. London, 1866.

Phillips, Ulrich Bonnell. *A History of Transportation in the Eastern Cotton Belt to 1860*. New York: Columbia University Press, 1908.

Pierce, Bessie L. *History of Chicago*. 2 vols. New York: Alfred A. Knopf, 1937–1940.

Pierce, Harry H. *Railroads of New York: A Study of Government Aid, 1826–1875*. Cambridge, Mass.: Harvard University Press, 1953.

Poor, Henry Varnum. *History of the Railroads and Canals of the United States of America*. New York, 1860.

Poussin, Guillaume Tell. *Chemins de Fer Américains*. Paris, 1836.

Primack, Martin L. "Land Clearing under Nineteenth-Century Techniques: Some Preliminary Calculations," *Journal of Economic History*, XXII (1962), 484–497.

Primm, James Neal. *Economic Policy in the Development of a Western State: Missouri, 1820–1860*. Cambridge, Mass.: Harvard University Press, 1954.

Proceedings of the National Ship-Canal Convention. Chicago, 1863.

Putnam, James William. *The Illinois and Michigan Canal: A Study in Economic History*. Chicago: University of Chicago Press, 1918.

Reizenstein, Milton. "The Economic History of the Baltimore and Ohio Railroad, 1827–1853," *Johns Hopkins University Studies in Historical and Political Science*, XV, nos. 7–8 (1897).

Riegel, Robert Edgar. *The Story of the Western Railroads*. New York: Macmillan Co., 1926.

Ringwalt, John L. *Development of Transportation Systems in the United States*. Philadelphia, 1888.

Ritchie, James S. *Wisconsin and its Resources*. Philadelphia, 1857.

Roberts, Christopher. *The Middlesex Canal*. Cambridge, Mass.: Harvard University Press, 1938.

Rostow, Walt W. *The Stages of Economic Growth*. Cambridge, Eng.: University Press, 1960.

—— "Leading Sectors and the Take-off," in Walt W. Rostow, ed. *The Economics of Take-off into Sustained Growth*. London: Macmillan and Co., 1963.

Rubin, Julius. "Canal or Railroad?" *Transactions of the American Philosophical Society*, n.s., vol. 51, pt. 7 (1961).

Sadove, Abraham H. "Transport Improvement and the Appalachian Barrier: A Case Study in Economic Innovation." Unpub. diss. Harvard University, 1950.

Sale, Randall D., and Edwin D. Karn. *American Expansion: A Book of Maps.* Homewood, Ill.: Dorsey Press, 1962.

Sanderlin, Walter S. "The Great National Project: A History of the Chesapeake and Ohio Canal Company," *Johns Hopkins University Studies in Historical and Political Science,* LXIV, no. 1 (1946).

Schmidt, Louis B. "The Internal Grain Trade of the United States, 1850–1860," *Iowa Journal of History and Politics,* XVIII (1920), 94–124.

———— "Internal Commerce and the Development of a National Economy before 1860," *Journal of Political Economy,* XLVII (1939), 798–822.

Schumpeter, Joseph A. *Business Cycles.* 2 vols. New York: McGraw-Hill, 1939.

Schurr, Sam H., Bruce C. Netschert, *et al. Energy in the American Economy.* Baltimore: Johns Hopkins Press, 1960.

Scitovsky, Tibor. "Two Concepts of External Economies," *Journal of Political Economy,* LXII (1954), 143–151.

Shlakman, Vera. "Economic History of a Factory Town," *Smith College Studies in History,* XX, nos. 1–4 (1934–1935).

Sinclair, Angus. *Development of the Locomotive Engine.* New York: A. Sinclair Publishing Co., 1907.

Smith, Alfred G., Jr. *Economic Readjustment of an Old Cotton State: South Carolina, 1820–1860.* Columbia: South Carolina Press, 1958.

Smith, Walter B. "Wage Rates on the Erie Canal, 1828–1881," *Journal of Economic History,* XXIII (1963), 298–311.

Smith, Walter B., and Arthur H. Cole. *Fluctuations in American Business, 1790–1860.* Cambridge, Mass.: Harvard University Press, 1935.

Smith, William P. *The Book of the Great Railway Celebrations of 1857.* New York, 1858.

Stevens, Frank W. *The Beginnings of the New York Central Railroad.* New York: G. P. Putnam's Sons, 1926.

Stevenson, David. *Sketch of the Civil Engineering of North America.* London, 1838; 2nd ed., London, 1859.

Stover, John F. *American Railroads.* Chicago: University of Chicago Press, 1961.

Stow, Frederick H. *Capitalist's Guide and Railway Annual.* New York, 1859.

Strickland, William. *Reports on Canals, Railways and Other Subjects.* Philadelphia, 1826.

Swain, Henry H. "Economic Aspects of Railroad Receiverships,"

American Economic Association Economic Studies, III, no. 2 (1898).

Swank, James M. *History of the Manufacture of Iron in All Ages.* Philadelphia, 1892.

Tanner, Henry S. *A Description of the Canals and Railroads of the United States.* New York, 1840.

Taylor, George Rogers. *The Transportation Revolution, 1815–1860.* New York: Rinehart, 1951.

Taylor, George Rogers, and Irene D. Neu. *The American Railroad Network, 1861–1890.* Cambridge, Mass.: Harvard University Press, 1956.

Thomas, Brinley. *Migration and Economic Growth.* Cambridge, Eng.: University Press, 1954.

Thompson, John G. "The Rise and Decline of the Wheat Growing Industry in Wisconsin," *Bulletin of the University of Wisconsin,* Economics and Political Science Series, V, no. 3 (1909).

Thorp, Willard. *Business Annals.* New York: National Bureau of Economic Research, 1926.

Tooke, Thomas and William Newmarch. *A History of Prices.* 6 vols. London, 1838–1857.

Tredgold, Thomas. *A Treatise on Railroads and Carriages.* 2nd ed. London, 1835.

Tucker, George. *Progress of the United States.* New York, 1843.

Turner, Charles W. "The Virginia Railroads, 1828–1860." Unpub. diss. University of Minnesota, 1946.

Ulmer, Melville. *Trends and Cycles in Capital Formation by United States Railroads, 1870–1950.* Occasional Paper 43. New York: National Bureau of Economic Research, 1954.

———— *Capital in Transportation, Communication, and Public Utilities.* Princeton: Princeton University Press, 1960.

Van Oss, S. F. *American Railroads as Investments.* New York, 1893.

Van Vleck, George W. *The Panic of 1857.* New York: Columbia University Press, 1943.

Vernon, Edward, ed. *American Railroad Manual.* Philadelphia, 1873.

Ware, Caroline F. *The Early New England Cotton Manufacture.* Boston: Houghton Mifflin, 1931.

Weaver, Herbert. *Mississippi Farmers, 1850–1860.* Nashville: Vanderbilt University Press, 1945.

Webb, Walter L. *The Economics of Railroad Construction.* 2nd ed. New York: J. Wiley and Sons, 1912.

Weber, Thomas. *The Northern Railroads in the Civil War, 1861–1865.* New York: Columbia University Press, 1952.

Weld, Charles Richard. *A Vacation Tour in the United States and Canada*. London, 1855.

Wellington, Arthur M. *The Economic Theory of the Location of Railways*. 6th ed. New York, 1887.

Wells, David A. *Recent Economic Changes*. New York, 1890.

Whitford, Noble E. *History of the Canal System of the State of New York*. 2 vols. Albany: Brandown Printing Company, 1906.

Whiton, James M. *Railroads and Their Management*. Concord, N.H., 1856.

Whitworth, Joseph and George Wallis. *The Industry of the United States in Machinery, Manufactures, and Useful and Ornamental Arts*. London, 1854.

Williamson, Harold F., ed. *The Growth of the American Economy*. Rev. ed. New York: Prentice Hall, 1951.

Wilson, Harold F. *The Hill Country of New England*. New York: Columbia University Press, 1936.

Wilson, William H. *History of the Pennsylvania Railroad*. 2 vols. Philadelphia, 1899.

Wood, Nicholas. *A Practical Treatise on Railroads*. First American from Second English Edition. Philadelphia, 1832.

Wright, Chester W. *Wool-Growing and the Tariff*. Boston: Houghton Mifflin, 1910.

Index

(Numbers in italics refer to tables or charts.)

328, 330–33, 337, 338; subsidies, 190, 192

Industrialization: and agricultural development, 206–07; eastern, 237–38; and processing, 228; and railroad demands, 99–100, 130–31, 132, 155–56, 158; and railroad expansion, 239–40, 250–56, 260–61, 297–98, 303; and sectoral demand, 16, 302, 306; and southern demand, 275; and transport innovation, 12–15; and urbanization, 231–33, 235

Interest: calculation of, 360–62; and calculation of local aid, 192–93; and capital accounting, 351–52; as construction cost, *119, 350, 351*, 353

Interstate Commerce Commission: 11; on depreciation, 398; on discount, 354; on interest, 353; statistics of, 316

Investment: *101, 104, 110*; and business cycles,105–07, 110–12; and capital availability, 108–09, 244; and construction ahead of demand, 166–69; foreign, 113, 117, 238, 302, 305; and interior development, 212; and local aid, 193–95; and manufacturing profits, 244–46; and mileage data, 109, 201; in New England, 241, *245*; in Panic of 1857, 116, 186–87; private, and social return, *53*, 307–09; and rate of return, 53–54, 56, 61–62, 182–83, 301; regional variations, 103–05; and theory of social overhead, 23–28, 310–11; and total capital formation, 100–04

Investment estimates: *358*, 401; and construction expenditures, 351; gross annual, 384–95, *388*; gross regional, 395–96, *397*; and mileage data, 359–60, 394–95; net, constant dollar, 397–400; quasi-net, 341, 357, *358*, 401

Iowa: grain production, *46*, 207, 211, 218, 225; land value increase, 199; migration to, 114; population densities in, 175–76, *176*; processing industry in, 229

Iowa railroads: earnings estimates, *178*; mileage, 163, 171, *172*; output estimates, *337, 338*; subsidies, 191, 192; success, 178, 183

Irish famine, 112, 197, 238, 303

Iron consumption: in bridge construction, 120; British, 121–22; and coal demand, 156–57; in rolling stock, 121

Iron consumption estimates: prices, 365–66, 368, 371; as proportion of superstructure cost, 366–67, 369, 371; renewals, 375–76, 377

Iron imports: 260; nonrail, 144; as proportion of total production, 133

Iron production: 134–36, 160, 302–03; and British iron, 137–38; coal consumed in, 157; growth of, 139–40; and rail demands, 145, 149; transport requirements, 243–44. *See also* Pig iron production; Rails

Isard, Walter, 156, 164, 230, 231–32, 235

Jenks, Leland H., 14n, 108n, 165n, 205

Kettel, Thomas P., 271–73, 275
Kirkland, Edward C., 88, 240n, 241, 242n, 271
Kistler, Thelma, 244–45
Klein, Judith L. V., 217, 218–19, 220
Klein, Ludwig, 346
Kohlmeier, A. L.: 79n, 81n, 185n, 267; on West-South trade, 286, 289n, 290, 291, 292, 296, 296n
Krenkel, John H., 190

Labor costs: in land improvement, 41–42; in rail replacement, 377; in railroad construction, 119–20, 121; in tie replacement, 381

Labor productivity: and calculation of direct benefits, 29–30; and grain production, 217–18; and land improvement, 40n; in milling, 227; and regional redistribution, 220, 222, 305; and skills, and transport industry demands, 123–24, 131–32, 152, 155, 160

Lake transport: *266*; from Boston, 241; capacity, and corn production, 293; direct benefits, 48; insurance costs, 80–81; proposed rail links, 6; steam driven tonnage on, 151; and trade flow shift, 291, 295; and western exports, 64–65, 263

Land: cost of, in railroad investment, *119, 350*, 351, *351, 358*; preparation cost variations, 41–42, 206, 216–17,

232; sales, and business cycles, 111,
114; sales, and railroad entry, 175
Land value increase: and anticipatory
settlement, 198–99; causes, 40–41, 43;
end of, 238; and interior development,
213; and price increases, 43–44
Latrobe, Benjamin, 164, 366n
Lebergott, Stanley, 388, 408n, 410
Lippincott, Isaac, 276n
Livestock: alternative transport methods, 68–69, *266*; direct benefits, 44,
47, 79–80; and eastbound through
freight, 78, 265; southern production,
276–77; through ton-mileage, 69n,
79–80, *80*; and trade flow shift, 292–
93; as way freight, 76
Local aid, *see* Subsidy
Locomotive power: 8; estimation of,
413, 417–19; as fraction of total
horsepower, 150–52
Locomotives: 5, 7, 10; export of, 154n;
fuel use, 128–29; imports of, 149; pig
iron demands, *142*; prices, 383n; production estimate, 149, 152–54, 414–
17; repairs, 131; replacement, 382–83.
See also Rolling stock
Lumber: and building inputs, 232–33;
cost in ties, 381; and railroad operating requirements, 129–30, 131, 132,
158, *159*; and rolling-stock cost, 121

McGill, Caroline E., 14n
MacGrane, Reginald C., 109, 110
Maintenance: and industrial demand,
130–31, 154–56; iron consumption,
139, 141; and labor skills, 123–24; as
proportion of operating expenditure,
124, 373–74. *See also* Operating expenditures
Mansfield, Edwin, 39, 356, 362
Massachusetts railroads: 4, 7, 240; accounting, 320; and boot and shoe
manufacture, 258–59; construction
expenditure estimates, *348*, *385*;
earnings, 246n; equipment replacement costs, 382; freight receipts, 249–
50; investment in, *246*; maintenance
of way, 374; output estimates, *250*,
322, *326*, *328*, *330–33*, *337*; rate estimates, *334*; securities in Panic of
1837, 107; and textile manufactures

location, 252, 256; trackage, 367, 368,
370; and urbanization, 256–57
Michigan: overland deliveries in, 82;
population, 170; state railroad subsidies, 190; transportation growth,
238; wheat production, *46*, 218
Michigan Central Railroad: 178; cars
on, 421n, 423n; rate of return, *183*;
sale of, 238, 245; shops, 155; through
freight receipts, 77–78; water competition, 81
Michigan Southern Railroad: 178; decline, 147; rate of return, *183*; through
freight receipts, 77–78; water competition, 81
Migration: 114, 197; agricultural nature
of, 230; and building, 234; decrease
in, 202–03, 238; and European immigration, 200–02; and grain production, 219–20; in Illinois, 174–75; and
land value, 198; and processing shift,
226; and railroad investment, 111,
200
Milling, *see* Processing industry

Neu, Irene P., 8n, 10, 208n, 286
New England railroads: earnings, 246n;
fuel use, 127; gross investment, *397*;
and industrial concentrations, 251–
59; investment in, 104, 187; investors,
244–46; mileage, extent, 7, 237, 248;
mileage, nature of, 240–42; output
estimates, *322*, *326*, *328*, *330–33*, 335,
337, 339; rates, 250; rates, estimated,
334. *See also* individual railroads and
states
New Orleans: 286, 287, 290; as port of
entry, 295; receipts of cotton, *278*;
receipts of western produce, 215, 277–
79, *284*, 288–89, 291; retention of imports, 279–85, *280*; and trade flow
shifts, 292–94
New York: investment in western railroads, 245; as port of entry, 295;
southerly trade, 271; textile manufacture in, 255, 256–57; wheat production costs, *46*, 218
New York and Erie, *see* Erie Railroad
New York Central Railroad: 10, 22,
101n; grain carriage, 263–65, *264*;
immigrant traffic on, 201n; midwest-

mestic manufacture of, 144; estimation of, 413–21, *413*; imports, 149; pig iron demands, *141*; prices, 383n; as proportion of equipment cost, 121; repairs, 131; replacement of, 382–83, 390–91

Rostow, Walt W.: 143; on industrialization, 150–51, 303, 304; on railroad construction, 308; on "take off," 13, 16, 16n, 100

Rubin, Julius, 4n, 11n, 132–33

Schmidt, Louis B., 263n, 276

Schumpeter, Joseph: 13; on construction ahead of demand, 164–65, 167, 168n; statistics of, 317

Schuyler, Robert, 113

Schuylkill Navigation Canal, *21*, 89n; and coal mines, 242; competition with Philadelphia and Reading Railroad, 18–19, 243

Scitowsky, Tibor, 309

Securities: 13; and construction, 354–56; and direct benefits, 39; discount of, 352–54, 363; and foreign capital, 117; and iron imports, 138–39; and state aid, calculation of, 192–93; of western railroads, 179, 187–88. *See also* Discount; Interest

Segal, Harvey, 20, 22, 55–56, 109, 110–11

Shlakman, Vera, 245, 246n

Sidings, *see* Double tracking

Smith, Walter B., 105, 111n, 114, 186–87, 388n

South Carolina Railroad: 287, 365, 383n; rates, 321, 323; repairs, 155; water competition, 85, 86

Southern railroads: 9; construction, 5, 365; construction cost estimates, *348, 385*; and cotton production, 248; direct benefits, 84–86; financing, 9, 273, 362; fuel use, 128; gross investment estimate, *397*; and industrialization, 306; intraregional, 286; investment, 105, 107, 187; locomotive production and repair, 153, 155; operating expenditures, 124n; output estimates, *322, 326, 328, 330–33*, 335, *337, 338*, 339; rate estimates, *334*; water competition, 33, 84-86

Southern states: agricultural self-sufficiency, 276, 283–85, 297; consumption of western products, 279–82, *281*; corn production, *219*; crops, labor productivity in, 222; Depression of 1839–43, 7, 108; export potential, *274*; exports to North, 287; imports to interior, 285–86; interregional trade, 271–75, 288–97; intraregional trade, 277, 282; land value rise, 44; in Panic of 1857, 115; rivers, 35, 84, 85–86

Stagecoaches, *see* Overland transport

State aid, *see* Subsidy

Steamboats: 56, 151–52; advantages, 35; and industrialization, 156; rates 49, 86, 90

Stevenson, David, 308, 365

Stow, Frederick H., 35

Subsidy: 8, 189–95, *194*; calculation of, 192–93; and construction ahead of demand, 167, 191, 195; and Depression of 1839, 6–7, 107–08; effects of, 310; land grants as, 174, 175; municipal, 185; and social overhead investment, 307; state, 9, 117, 190; in West, 191

Swank, James M., 134, 137, 144n, 145n

Swine, *see* Livestock

Tariffs: and iron prices, 366n, 368n, 371n; and iron production, 133–34, 136; on textiles, 260

Taylor, George Rogers, 43n, 55, 114n, 208n, 285, 318n, 345; on contemporary cost calculations, 342, 392; on integration, 8n, 10; on railroad resource requirements, 118; on rates, 49n, 73n, 74n, 91; on shift to rail freight, 70; on state debt, 107

Technological development: 15, 302; and interior development, 213; in iron production, 136, 145; of locomotives, 125–26; and processing, 228–29; of railroads, 5, 7–8, 13, 56; in textile industry, 251, 260

Textile manufacture: coal consumption, 157; and home manufacture, 255, 256–57; industrial requirements, 156; locational aspects of, 249, 251–53, *252*, 256; and locomotive production, 152–53; railroad contribution, 248;

and railroad financing, 244–45; and tariffs, 260; transport requirements, 249, 253–55, 256, 270

Thomas, Brinley, 200, 201

Through freight: 64–65; in coastal trade, 87; direct benefits, 69–70, 72, *78*; and livestock shipment on, 68; and local aid, 193

Ties: depreciation, 398; lumber consumption, *159*; replacement, 129–30, 373; replacement cost, 379–82, *383*

Trollope, Anthony, 197, 198

Trunk lines: 9, 33–34, 36–37, 77–82; direct benefits, *37*, *78*, *93*; immigrant traffic, 201; in interregional trade, 185, 263–65, 288; and intraregional feeders, 268; receipts, *34*; through freight, 270; and trade flow shift, 293–94

Turner, Frederick Jackson, 197–98, 232

Ulmer, Melville: on construction costs, 387, 390; on depreciation, 398, 400; on investment, 102, 116n, 372, 373n

Van Oss, S. F., 165

Van Vleck, 55, 114n, 115

von Gerstner, Franz Anton Ritter, *see* Gerstner, Franz Anton

Wabash and Erie Canal: 19, *21*; and grain trade shift, 35, 293

Water transport: 19; of coal, 261; coastal, 87–88; cost, 66–67; of cotton, 270; and direct benefits, 58–59, 63; of flour and provisions, 65–66; of livestock, 68; in Midwest, 81; of passengers, 90–91; in South, 85–86, 288; and way freight, 72. *See also* Canals; Lake transport; River traffic

Way freight: 79n; and coasting trade, 87–88; composition of, 72; and direct benefits, 72–77, *78*; in Midwest, 81

Weeks Report, 388

Wellington, Arthur M., 125n, 127n, 131

Wells, David A., 56–57

West-South trade, 280–82, *281*, 283, *284*, 285, 286–87; traditional view, 275–76

Western railroads: 6, 8, 115, 238; bond discounts, 363; capacity, 265n; failures, 187–88; feeders, 268; fuel use, 127–28; gross investment estimate, *397*; and imports, 295–96; and interior development, 207–15; investment in, 105, 107, 112, 245, 247; output estimates, *322*, *326*, *328*, *330–33*, 335, *337*, *338*, 339; overexpansion, 184; passenger traffic, 202–03; and processing industry, 228–29; rate estimates, *334*; rate of return, 177–78, *178*, 182–86, *182*, 188, 189; repair shops, 155; subsidies, 191, 193; and wool manufacture, 256

Western states: building demands, 229–31, 232–35; canals in, 83; capital availability, 269; corn production, *219*; exports, 215, 277–79, 288–89; exports and trade flow shift, 291, 293–97; imports, 296; population densities, 172, 174–76; rivers, 151; urban growth, 230. *See also* individual states

Wheat: 59n, 214; crop value changes, 45–47; regional price changes, *46*; shipment of, 58–59; southern imports of, 285

Wheat production: concentration of, 173–74, *210*, *211*; interior, and railroad entry, 163, *173*, 207, 209–14; and regional redistribution, 220; regional variations in, *46*, 217–18; southern, 285; and trade flow shift, 289–90; water access, 208–09, *209*

Wicker, E. R., 109n, 318n, 347n, 384n

Wisconsin: immigrant settlement, 201; land grants, 191; population densities, 172; processing in, 229; wheat production, *46*, 218

Wisconsin railroads: 89n; construction cost estimates, 345; early returns, *178*, 183; local aid in, 192–93, *194*; mileage, 171, *172*; mileage concentration, 173–74, *173*; output estimates, *322*, *326*, *328*, *330–33*, *337*, *338*

Wool manufacture, *see* Textile manufacture

Date Due